Cooking Adventures for Kids

Sharon Cadwallader

Cooking Adventures for Kids

ILLUSTRATED BY DIANE DEVINE

A San Francisco Book Company / Houghton Mifflin Book

HOUGHTON MIFFLIN COMPANY   BOSTON

Library of Congress Cataloging in Publication Data

Cadwallader, Sharon.
  Cooking adventures for kids.

  SUMMARY: Basic hints on kitchen procedures and herbs
accompany recipes for a variety of dishes for every meal
numbered according to degree of simplicity.
  "A San Francisco Book Company/Houghton Mifflin book."
  1. Cookery — Juvenile literature. [1. Cookery]
I. Devine, Diane, illus. II. Title.
TX652.5.C28   641.5'02'405   74-9544
ISBN 0-395-19976-X
ISBN 0-395-19980-9 (pbk.)   ISBN 0–913374–10–5
                                 ISBN 0–913374–11–3 (pbk.)

A 10 9 8 7 6 5 4 3

This SAN FRANCISCO BOOK
COMPANY/HOUGHTON MIFFLIN
BOOK originated in San Francisco
and was produced and published
jointly. Distribution is by Houghton
Mifflin Company, 2 Park Street,
Boston, Massachusetts 02107.

Book design by Anita Walker Scott

For PAM, PAULA, *and* MEGHAN, *who willingly tested,*
   and for
JULIE, LEE, CORI, JOSH, GABBY, *and* LAURA,
   who obediently tasted.

All of the recipes in this
book are numbered according
to the following key:
(1)—a snap
(2)—easy
(3)—pretty easy

Contents

Contents • viii

Introduction

COOKING ADVENTURES FOR KIDS is written for and dedicated to school-age children everywhere—in public schools, private schools, alternative schools, and home schools. It is a combination of easy recipes and simple cooking instructions for all the potential cooks in today's world.

The emphasis is on learning to prepare tasty and nourishing dishes, rather than becoming dependent on processed, prepared foods that rob our health and stifle our creativity. The recipes are numbered according to degree of simplicity (see page vi), but none of them are too complicated for an ambitious beginner. Although some of the ingredients may be new to the everyday diet, they all can be found in most supermarkets.

Don't feel threatened by the restrictions of a recipe; once you learn a few basic cooking techniques, you can become a real adventurer in the kitchen and create your own original and amazing dishes. Try to think of the kitchen as an artist's studio and combine foods as you would colors, words, or musical notes.

Please read the next few pages, then go to it, kids—just remember to clean up after yourselves.

Things Every Good Cook Should Know

Kitchen Manners and Safety

Some of you may have mothers, fathers, and older sisters or brothers who will roll their eyes and raise their eyebrows when you announce that you are going to teach yourself to cook. Simply disregard these standard reactions to children in the kitchen, smile patiently, and proceed when you won't be in anyone's way. *First*, however, think about the following advice.

A good cook washes his or her hands before doing anything in the kitchen. Your hands, nails, hair, and clothes should be clean while you are working with food, and it is a good idea to wear an apron or tie a towel around your waist to protect your clothing from spatters and batter. Keep your work area from getting cluttered with used pots, dishes, and utensils. Rinse each item after you use it and set it neatly aside. You will thank yourself when it comes time to wash the dishes.

In this time of long hair, boys and girls alike may feel that it is safer and more hygienic to tie back their hair while working in the kitchen. It hurts to get it caught in the electric mixer, and peanut butter in your hair and hair in your peanut butter are two of life's real unpleasantries.

Remind yourself of the dangers of hot grease, open flames, and sharp knives. You should not wear loose garments, especially big sleeves, while working around the stove. Use pot holders to handle anything that has been on the burner or in the oven, and turn off the burner before removing a pot or pan. Concentrate while slicing and chopping. Even if someone says something funny, it is unwise to laugh while working with knives. If you spill something, clean it up immediately, or you may end up lying in it.

Kitchen Conservation

As you enter the kitchen with determination, you might hear, "Now be careful you don't waste anything." Again, smile warmly while you show them all a thing or two about conservation in the kitchen. In your grandmother's time, very little was wasted in the kitchen. True, there are techniques that you may not be able to use now, like sweeping the carpet with the old tea leaves or saving the water from boiling potatoes to use when making bread. But I think that today we are so accustomed to throwing away wrappers and containers without a thought that we also discard many usable food items without a thought. Here are a few suggestions for making your kitchen experience both economical and ecological.

Save vegetable cooking or steaming water to use in soups or stews. It can be kept for many days in the refrigerator and for many weeks in the freezer. If you or a neighbor has a garden and keeps a compost heap, save all your parings and scraps for it. Or, if you have house plants, you can put the vegetable and fruit remains into a blender with a little warm water and make a nice meal for them.

Save all unused bread and cracker scraps until they get stale and hard (exposing them to the air speeds up the process), then put them through a meat grinder or in an electric blender, or simply roll them out into crumbs with a rolling pin. They will make wonderful extenders for meatloaf or meatballs, or you can use them for breading or for toppings on casseroles. Rolling out the bread crumbs was my first kitchen job as a child, and I still have the habit. Keep the crumbs in a tightly covered container.

When a recipe calls for egg yolks only, save the whites and use them for leavening when you are baking, or add them to puddings for extra lightness.

See how creative you can become with leftovers. Just as leftover grains and stale bread can be the bases for some delicious puddings (see page 62), you can also add them to yeast and quick breads, casseroles, and even cakes and cookies. Let these creative liberties be the beginning of your reputation as a great cook. Leftover vegetables can be put into quesadillas (page 13), omelets, scrambled eggs, or casseroles. Leftover meat can be used in practically anything. Invent your own refrigerator stew. Who knows, you may make culinary history.

Be sparing when using aluminum foil, plastic bags, and aluminum and plastic containers from the market. Use and reuse everything until it is worn.

A Word About Herbs

Herbs and spices make the cook! Learn to use them first in "tried and true" combinations of food and seasoning, then begin to experiment as you cook. You may come up with a special dish and make yourself famous. Basil in your scrambled eggs? Nutmeg in your pancakes?

There are many different herbs and spices in the world. The following are only the more common ones used in our country. Don't overseason, and be sure to use half the amount of dried herbs that you would use fresh.

Here is a list of herbs and the foods that taste especially good with them.

BASIL—tomato dishes, egg dishes, cheese dishes, salads, vegetables

BAY LEAF—soups, meats, fish, stews

CARAWAY—stews, salads, baked goods, apple dishes, cheese dishes

CHERVIL—soups, salads, vegetables, omelets

CHILI POWDER—stews, Mexican dishes

CHIVES—where any delicate onion flavor is desired

CINNAMON—baked goods, Mexican and Greek dishes

CLOVES
    whole—ham, fruit dishes
    powdered—baked goods

CUMIN—stews, beans, Mexican and Middle Eastern dishes

CURRY—salads, egg dishes, cheese dishes, East Indian dishes, meats, fish, fowl

DILL

    weed—salads, egg dishes, cheese dishes, sauces

    seed—slaw-type salads, pickles

GARLIC—in anything nonsweet (garlic is a matter of preference, but important in Mexican, Italian, and Oriental foods)

GINGER (may be powdered or grated from the root)—meats, fish, Oriental dishes, baked goods, puddings

MACE (outer covering of nutmeg)—use where you would nutmeg or cinnamon, as it tastes slightly like a combination of the two spices

MARJORAM—meats, fowl, fish, salads, vegetables

NUTMEG—meats, sauces, soups, baked goods

OREGANO—tomato dishes, egg dishes, cheese dishes, beans, meats, fish, fowl, salads, Mexican and Italian foods

PAPRIKA—stews, chicken, fish, potatoes, rice

PARSLEY—in any dish that is not sweet, or all by itself—it's healthful

PEPPER

black—nearly everything nonsweet, or bread

cayenne—in anything that needs a hot taste (it's made from hot chilis)

ROSEMARY—fowl, meats, fish, vegetables, salads

TARRAGON—fish especially; also salads, fowl, sauces

THYME—same foods in which you use oregano

NOTE: Some herbs, such as oregano and thyme, come in both dried leaves and powder. Use less when you are using powder.

Now, after you select a recipe you want to try, read it carefully. If you have any questions about the ingredients or directions, turn to the back of the book, where there are explanations of cooking terms and nutritional items and information about weights and measures, including a table of Metric System measurements.

 Breakfast

Quick Dry Cereal   (1)

Mix well beforehand and store covered in the refrigerator:

      2 cups quick oats
      1 cup toasted wheat germ
      1 cup rolled wheat
      ½ cup unsweetened coconut
      ½ cup shelled sunflower seeds
      1 cup raisins, or other dried fruit, chopped in
         small pieces
      1 cup chopped nuts (optional)

Serve with milk and honey or raw sugar. Fresh fruits such as bananas, strawberries, or berries can be added when served.

      Serves 5-6

Old-Fashioned Oatmeal   (1)

      1¼ cups water
      1   cup rolled oats (not quick)
      dash of salt

Bring water to boil in a covered saucepan. Add oats and salt, stir, and reduce heat to simmer. Cook uncovered for 3-4 minutes, or until all water is absorbed.

This makes a nonmushy oatmeal. If you prefer a mush-type cereal, add more water and cook it longer.

Serve oatmeal with milk and honey or raw sugar. Top with 1 tablespoon of raw or toasted wheat germ for variety and extra nutrition. Or throw a few raisins into the boiling water and cook with the oats.

Serves 2

Cottage Cheese Crêpes (Pancakes) (2)

1   cup cottage cheese
4   eggs
½   cup unbleached flour
1   teaspoon honey or natural sugar
¼   teaspoon salt

Put all ingredients in an electric blender and blend well. If you do not have a blender, use an electric or a hand beater and beat until the batter is smooth. Pour by spoonfuls into a hot, greased frying pan. Keep the flame under the pan or griddle at a high medium and be sure the pan is hot before pouring the batter. Turn when air bubbles form on the top, or tip up the edge and watch it brown.

These are not as thin as French crêpes, but they are equally delicate and light. If you make them large, you can spread them with butter, honey, or jam and roll them into a tube.

Makes 7–8 3-inch pancakes

Scrambled Egg with Sunflower Seeds (1)

1   egg
1   tablespoon shelled sunflower seeds
1   teaspoon salad oil
salt and pepper

Scramble the egg with a fork in a small bowl. Put the oil in a small frying pan over a medium heat and get the pan good and hot. If the pan is hot, the egg will not stick. Pour in the egg and the sunflower seeds and stir together until the egg is cooked. The sunflower seeds will soften slightly while cooking. Salt and pepper to taste. A little basil or oregano is also nice in this egg. Serve with toasted Whole-Wheat Bread (page 51).

Makes 1 serving

These are speedy but healthful breakfast ideas, especially nice for summer.

The Great Yogurt Bowl (1)

In a cereal bowl put:

    1   cup plain yogurt

    1   tablespoon raw or toasted wheat germ

    $\frac{2}{3}$ cup cut-up fruit, fresh, fresh frozen (thawed), or canned

Top with:

    2   tablespoons honey, or

    1   tablespoon honey mixed with 2 tablespoons fruit juice

Serve with Grandma's Bran Muffins (page 55).

    Makes 1 serving

Super Egg and Fruit Drink (1)

In a blender put:

$2\frac{1}{2}$ cups orange juice, or any natural fruit juice
  you like

$\frac{1}{2}$ cup plain yogurt

$\frac{1}{4}$ cup powdered milk

$\frac{1}{2}$ cup whole or nonfat milk

2 raw egg yolks (separate eggs and save whites
  for baking or for adding to scrambled eggs)

1 banana, peeled

1 apple, peeled and cut into pieces

1 orange, peeled and divided into segments

1 tablespoon honey (optional)

1-2 tablespoons nutritional yeast (optional)

Blend all ingredients well. Serve in mugs or tall glasses.

Serves 2-3

 Lunch

Fresh Vegetable Soup (2)

For stock:

> 3   quarts water
> leaves and tops of 1 bunch celery, or 4 large stalks
>   celery, cut into 3-inch pieces
> 1   large onion, peeled and sliced thin
> 1   large clove garlic, peeled and mashed

Put celery, onion, and garlic in a soup pot and add the 3 quarts water. Bring to a boil, reduce heat to simmer, cover the pot, and cook for 45 minutes. Then remove vegetables with a strainer or slotted spoon and discard or put into garden compost. The remaining broth is the soup stock. It can be made the day before and refrigerated.

To boiling stock add:

> $\frac{1}{2}$ cup barley (unhulled, if possible)
> 2   cups finely sliced carrots

Reduce heat to simmer and cook for 25 minutes. Meanwhile, with a blender or beater, mix:

> 1   12-ounce can V-8 juice
> 1   tablespoon dried basil
> 1   teaspoon garlic powder
> 3   tablespoons olive oil, or any good salad oil
> $\frac{3}{4}$ cup grated Parmesan cheese
> 2   teaspoons salt

Blend well and add to soup along with:

>   1   cup turnips, peeled and cut into ½-inch pieces
>   1   cup zucchini squash, cut into ½-inch slices
>   (fresh or canned corn and green beans can be
>   added or substituted, if the cook prefers)

Simmer all the ingredients another 20 minutes and add salt to taste. Serve with Whole-Wheat Bread (page 51) or Country Kitchen Egg Bread (page 53).

>   This serves 6–8, depending on appetites.
>   Leftover soup can be frozen.

California Quesadillas   (1)

(KĀ-SÄ-DĒ-YÄS)

This is a variation of a grilled cheese sandwich, only a tortilla— a common Mexican food—is used instead of bread.

>   corn or flour tortilla
>   ⅓   cup Jack or Cheddar cheese, sliced or grated
>   oil (1 teaspoon to 1 quesadilla)

Heat oil in a frying pan and set in 1 tortilla. Let the tortilla soften in the oil for a minute or so, then turn it over. Cover ½ the tortilla with cheese. Fold the remaining ½ over the cheese and fry on both sides until the cheese is melted.

Set the quesadilla on a paper towel to absorb any excess oil and carefully spread open the tortilla. Add to the melted cheese any of the following suggestions:

> alfalfa sprouts
> chopped parsley or lettuce
> sliced onions
> sliced tomatoes
> hot sauce
> mashed avocado
> mustard
> mayonnaise
> catsup
> shelled sunflower seeds
> any chopped leftover raw or cooked vegetables
> any chopped leftover meat or fowl

Or you can just eat the quesadilla as it is!

Grated Cheese and Sprout Sandwich   (1)

Alfalfa sprouts are the extra nutrient in this sandwich, but you can substitute fresh grated zucchini squash or finely shredded lettuce.

Mix together:

    1½   cups grated cheese, Jack, Cheddar, or Swiss

    1   cup alfalfa sprouts

    dash of onion powder

    dash of salt

Add mayonnaise and/or catsup to give enough moisture to the spread. Just add a little at a time and mix. Serve on Whole-Wheat Bread (page 51).

Makes 3–4 sandwiches

Grilled Cheese and Tomato Sandwich   (1)

Preheat broiler.

On a piece of Whole-Wheat Bread (page 51), spread slices of any cheese you like. Sprinkle a little dill weed, salt, and onion powder on the cheese. Place slices of tomato on top of the cheese and cover with another piece of bread.

Put sandwich in the broiler, 2–3 inches from the flames or coil. Watch carefully and toast until bread turns golden brown and cheese begins to melt. Turn sandwich over and repeat process.

Tuna and Sunflower Seed Sandwich (1)

Drain: 1 6½-ounce can tuna, put into a bowl, and flake.

Add:

> ½ cup shelled sunflower seeds
> ¼ cup finely chopped red onion (red onion tastes the sweetest in this sandwich, but you can use any type of onion)

Mix tuna, seeds, and onion together and add enough mayonnaise to get the texture you like. Add salt to taste and spread on Whole-Wheat Bread (page 51) or Country Kitchen Egg Bread (page 53). Add lettuce or sprouts to this sandwich, if you wish. Or try the spread on crackers.

For a heartier lunch, serve these sandwiches with Summer Fruit Salad (page 42).

Makes 4 sandwiches

 Dinner

Corn Country Casserole   (3)

Filling:

    1   pound ground beef
    1   2¼-ounce can sliced olives
    ½   cup chopped green pepper
    1   cup stewed tomatoes
    1   teaspoon dried oregano
    1   teaspoon dried basil
    1   teaspoon chili powder
    1   teaspoon salt

In frying pan, brown meat and green pepper. Blend tomatoes with beater or electric blender and add to ground meat, along with olives, oregano, basil, chili powder, and salt. Simmer together for 5 minutes and pour into an 8-inch square baking pan.

Cornmeal batter:

    1   cup stone-ground cornmeal
    ½   cup powdered milk
    1   teaspoon baking powder
    1   cup cold milk
    ½   teaspoon salt
    1½ cups water

Mix together cornmeal, powdered milk, baking powder, salt, and milk in a bowl. Bring water to boil in a saucepan and slowly add cornmeal mixture. Reduce heat and stir constantly until thickened (as if you were making pudding).

Spoon cornmeal batter evenly over meat mixture. Bake in 350° oven until batter is set (about 30 minutes). Batter is set when it is firm and lightly browned. Meat mixture will bubble up around the edges. Serve with cheese and a vegetable or green salad (page 38).

Serves 4-5

Meat and Sunflower Seed Loaf (1)

1   slice fresh bread
1   pound ground beef
1   egg
1   cup shelled sunflower seeds
$\frac{1}{4}$ cup finely chopped onion
$\frac{1}{4}$ cup catsup
$\frac{1}{2}$ teaspoon salt
$\frac{1}{4}$ teaspoon pepper
$\frac{1}{4}$ teaspoon ground nutmeg

Beat egg in a small bowl. Break bread into little pieces and let it soak in the egg while you mix other ingredients. In a larger bowl, mix meat, seeds, onion, catsup, and spices. Add egg and bread and mix everything together. Shape into a loaf with your hands and place in bread pan or oven baking dish. Bake in 350° oven for 50 minutes. Serve with Bulgur Wheat (page 76), Buckwheat Groats (page 77), or Brown Rice (page 76), with salad and/or vegetables.

Serves 4 well, and leftover makes good sandwiches

Tunaburgers (2)

1   12½-ounce can tuna, drained
½   cup finely chopped onion
⅓   cup finely chopped parsley
1   egg, well beaten
½   teaspoon garlic powder
1   teaspoon dried oregano
½   teaspoon salt
1½   cups raw wheat germ
1   cup grated cheese, Jack, Cheddar, or Swiss
4   tablespoons salad oil

Mix together all ingredients except cheese and oil. Form into 3-inch patties with your hands. In large frying pan, heat oil over medium heat and brown tunaburgers on 1 side for 3–4 minutes.

Turn over with a spatula and sprinkle cheese on top of browned side. Cook another 3–4 minutes, or until cheese is melted. If you put a cover over the pan, the cheese will melt faster. Serve with Brown Rice (page 76), or with steamed vegetables (page 43) and Cabbage and Carrot Slaw (page 41).

Makes 7–8 burgers

Yankee Fish Fillets   (2)

1   pound sole fillets, or any white fish, cut into thin fillets
½   cup stale bread crumbs
⅓   cup raw wheat germ
2   eggs, well beaten
⅓   cup oil
½   teaspoon salt
dash of pepper

Beat eggs in one bowl, then mix bread crumbs, wheat germ, salt, and pepper in a separate, shallow bowl. Heat oil for several minutes in a large, heavy-bottomed frying pan over low-medium heat.

Dip fish first in egg, then in crumb-and-wheat-germ mixture. Fry on 1 side for 3–5 minutes and turn over to repeat process. The thicker the fillets, the longer cooking time the fish requires. An adequately cooked piece of fish should be flaky, with no transparency. Do not overcook fish, or it will become dry. If you keep the flame at a low medium, the coating will not burn before the fish is cooked.

Serve immediately with tartar sauce, baked potatoes (page 73), and a green salad (page 38).

Serves 4

Tartar Sauce (1)

$\frac{3}{4}$ cup plain yogurt
$\frac{1}{2}$ cup finely chopped dill or sweet pickles
$\frac{1}{3}$ cup finely chopped onion
$\frac{1}{2}$ teaspoon dill weed
$\frac{1}{2}$ teaspoon garlic powder
$\frac{1}{2}$ teaspoon horseradish powder
dash of salt
dash of cayenne pepper

Mix all ingredients together and refrigerate until fish is ready.

These are good recipes for creative cooks. They are very basic, and you can add to them any number of things that appeal to your taste, such as cooked sausage, canned tuna, leftover fish or fowl, onions, or mushrooms. With the quiche, the important thing to remember is that any addition must be well drained, as too much liquid will prevent the dish from setting.

Your Creative Quiche   (2)

(KĒSH)

    1   pound summer squash, green or yellow
    4   eggs
    2   cups grated Jack or Swiss cheese
    1½ teaspoons of any of the following herbs or
        spices: oregano, basil, dill weed, curry powder,
        or caraway seeds. Caraway seeds are especially
        nice with sausage.
    1   teaspoon salt

Cut squash into pieces and steam or cook briefly (6–10 minutes) in a small amount of water. Drain well, mash with a potato masher, then drain again to remove any excess liquid.

In a mixing bowl, beat eggs well and add squash, cheese, salt, and herbs or spices. Add 1½-2 cups of optional ingredients at this time, if desired (any meat must be cooked, and mushrooms or onions should be lightly steamed first). Pour everything into an 8-inch square baking dish or casserole. Bake at 325° for 30–40 minutes, or until quiche is firm in the middle and lightly browned on the edges. Serve with a green salad (page 38) and Whole-Wheat Bread (page 51) or Country Kitchen Egg Bread (page 53).

Serves 4-5

Family Macaroni and Cheese (1)

1½ quarts water
1   teaspoon salt
2   cups soy and wheat macaroni (available at natural food stores)
2   cups Cheddar or Jack cheese, cubed or grated
½   cup whole milk
½   teaspoon paprika
2   tablespoons wheat germ
salt and pepper

Bring water to a boil and add salt and macaroni. Reduce heat to simmer and cook uncovered for 12–15 minutes, or until macaroni is tender. Drain well.

Add cheese, milk, and optional ingredients, if desired. Salt and pepper very lightly.

Pour into a medium-sized, buttered casserole dish and top with wheat germ and paprika. Bake at 325° for 20–25 minutes. Serve with steamed vegetables (page 43) and salad.

Serves 4–5

Paprika-Garlic Roast Chicken   (2)

1   medium whole frying chicken ($2\frac{1}{2}$–$2\frac{3}{4}$ pounds)
$1\frac{1}{2}$ teaspoons garlic powder
$1\frac{1}{2}$ teaspoons paprika
3   tablespoons salad oil
salt and pepper

Preheat oven to 325°.

Remove giblets from inside chicken and save for chicken stew or soup. Wash and dry chicken inside and outside. (Don't use soap!)

Rub chicken inside and out with garlic powder. Using a pastry brush or paper towel, coat chicken with oil and sprinkle with paprika to give it a nice red tint. Salt and pepper lightly.

Place chicken in a deep oven pan, breast down, and cover tightly with aluminum foil. The juices will seep into the breast and keep the chicken moist.

Roast in oven for 40 minutes. At the end of this time, turn chicken breast up and cover again with foil. Return to oven for another 30 minutes. Then remove foil and continue roasting for 20–30 minutes more, or until chicken is fork tender and golden brown. Serve with Brown Rice (page 76) or Bulgur Wheat (page 76).

Serves 4–5

Country Chicken Stew (2)

1   medium frying chicken, cut up
1   large onion, peeled and sliced thin
3   large carrots, cut into 3-inch pieces
2   cups zucchini squash, cut into 2-inch pieces
1   large tomato, quartered
1   13$\frac{3}{4}$-ounce can chicken broth or stock
4   tablespoons vegetable oil
$\frac{1}{2}$ teaspoon garlic powder
$\frac{1}{2}$ teaspoon dried oregano
$\frac{1}{2}$ teaspoon dried rosemary
$\frac{1}{2}$ teaspoon dried thyme
1   teaspoon salt
dash of pepper

Wash and dry chicken pieces.

Heat oil in heavy-bottomed stew pan. Lightly brown all chicken pieces, including giblets. Reduce heat to simmer and add broth, onion, spices, salt, and pepper. Cover pan tightly and simmer for 40 minutes. Add carrots and tomato and simmer another 30 minutes. Then add squash and cook 10–15 minutes, or until chicken is very tender.

Serve over Brown Rice (page 76) and sprinkle with Parmesan cheese, or scoop into soup bowls and serve simply as stew.

Serves 5–6

Beans

Beans have been a source of food for man since the dawn of civilization. They are part of the wider family of legumes, and either dried or fresh, they are very nutritious.

Dried beans are high in protein, especially the soybean. Although it has been used in the Orient for 3000 years (think of soy sauce), the soybean was not brought to Europe until the end of the 17th century. Even then it was not well known until the end of the 19th century. Up until the last few years, the soybean was used only as animal feed in the United States, although large fields are cultivated in the midwestern states.

Now, with the price of meat rising steadily and the warnings of future food shortages, we must all learn to eat more foods that yield the highest protein in relation to the amount of land they require for growing. This means that beans, as well as grains and nuts, are important foods for the future.

There are many varieties of soybeans, but I think the smaller type has the best flavor. The following recipe is extremely simple and tasty for the beginning cook and soybean eater. Remember, once dried beans are cooked to tenderness, you can do anything you want with them. They are wonderful for the creative cook.

South Country Soybeans   (2)

Wash and drain 2 cups of soybeans, then soak them overnight in 6 cups of water. You should begin to cook these beans at least 3–4 hours in advance of your meal, to make certain they are tender, and use the same water for cooking as you do for soaking so you will not lose the vitamins and minerals.

Bring the beans to a boil, reduce the heat to simmer, and let them cook until they are tender. Sometimes they need to have water added, so check the pot periodically. Burned beans are no good to anyone, and the pot is terrible to clean. When the beans are tender, drain off the remaining water and prepare in the following way.

4   cups cooked soybeans (approximately)
1   small onion, chopped
½   cup green pepper, diced
1   12-ounce can V-8 juice*
3   garlic cloves, mashed, or 1 teaspoon garlic powder
1½   teaspoons chili powder
½   teaspoon cinnamon
½   teaspoon powdered cumin
salt and pepper to taste
¼   cup chopped raw bacon (about 2 strips)

Sauté bacon in frying pan over a medium heat. When it is cooking well, add the onion and green pepper and sauté until they are slightly tender. Add to bean pot with all other ingredients and simmer covered for 20 minutes (use very low heat). Serve with California Quesadillas (page 12) and a green salad (page 38).

Serves 3-4

NOTE: In cooking dried beans, it is best to add all other ingredients after the beans are tender. Salt and fats, especially, toughen beans in the early cooking stage.

*Canned enchilada sauce can be used in place of the V 8 juice if you like a spicier flavor.

Lima Bean Special (1)

2 cups dried baby limas
1 quart water
2 tablespoons butter or margarine
½ cup onion, chopped
¾ teaspoon oregano
¼ cup parsley (without stems), chopped
2 garlic cloves, mashed
1 small carton (½ pint) sour cream
1 teaspoon Dijon mustard
salt and pepper to taste

Bring water to boil and add beans. Reduce heat to simmer and cook covered for 2 hours, or until tender. Be sure to watch the water and add more when necessary. When the beans are tender, drain off any excess water and prepare in the following manner.

Sauté onions in butter or margarine until they are clear. Add garlic, parsley, and oregano and sauté a few more minutes. Add these ingredients to the beans, then add sour cream, mustard, and salt and pepper. Beans should be fairly hot (not steaming) when you add the sour cream. If necessary, reheat the beans over a low fire before serving, but be careful not to curdle the sour cream.

Serve with a green salad (page 38) and Western Cornbread (page 54).

Serves 3–4

Salads and Vegetables

Salad Dressing (1)

Most all of you probably like some kind of dressing on your salad, either an oil and vinegar or one of the cream varieties. If you are a salad eater, you would do well to learn to make a zesty little dressing. It is a very simple process, and there is no reason why you need to pay for prepared dressings in the market. Really, no specific measurements are necessary for salad dressing. Just proceed carefully, one step at a time, tasting as you go. It is fun to watch an experienced chef dress a salad.

Oil and Vinegar or Lemon Dressing

When you have combined all the ingredients of your salad, toss it well to mix. Dribble a little oil over the entire salad, 2-3 tablespoons, depending on the size of the salad. It should be lightly coated, as too much oil makes the salad heavy.

Toss and add salt, pepper, and seasonings. Some nice suggestions are oregano, basil, dill (basil and dill are my favorites), marjoram, tarragon, curry, fresh garlic, or garlic powder.

Toss once again and add 2-3 tablespoons of wine vinegar or lemon or lime juice, again depending on the size of the salad. Toss again and taste.

FRENCH DRESSING—add a little mustard and a dash of sugar to the lemon or vinegar.

ITALIC DRESSING—use vinegar and add tomato sauce or catsup to it.

SLAW DRESSINGS—try apple-cider vinegar and add a little sugar or honey and dill or caraway seeds. You can add a little yogurt or mayonnaise if you like your dressing creamy.

Cream Dressings

If you like blue cheese or Roquefort cheese dressings, simply crumble some of the cheese (how strong do you like it?) into mayonnaise and/or sour cream. Add garlic and pepper.

If you prefer a Thousand Island-style dressing, mix mayonnaise and catsup until you get the taste you like. Add a little garlic and onion powder. A touch of horseradish is nice too.

For those who like yogurt, a simple dressing can be made by combining equal parts yogurt and mayonnaise. Add some chopped olives, salt and pepper, garlic, and perhaps some onion powder. This is especially nice on a spinach salad.

Salads

The following salads are only a few suggestions in a multitude of possibilities. Use them as guides and have fun inventing your own. Use any raw vegetable that interests you (except winter squash and artichokes). Some of the tougher greens, like kale, collard greens, and mustard greens, should be cut into very thin pieces, or else used when they are young, tender leaves. Root vegetables and summer squashes can be grated or sliced thin.

Use your own sense with any vegetable you meet. Nuts, seeds, sliced apples or oranges, grated hard cheeses, and raisins are all nice additions to vegetable salads.

Of course you can combine any fruits for separate fruit salads, but do try putting fruits and vegetables together in salads. How about chopped lettuce, sliced bananas, and peanuts with a yogurt dressing? Why not combine shredded cabbage, drained, chopped pineapple, and walnuts with a slaw-type dressing (leave out the sugar in the dressing, as the pineapple is sweet). Become a salad artist!

Cheese and Fresh Greens   (1)

1   bunch fresh spinach or young Swiss chard, washed
    well and chopped (remove end stems)
2   cups any leaf lettuce, broken into pieces
1   cup fresh parsley (without stems), chopped
1   cup grated cheese, Swiss or Jack
salt and pepper
seasonings (curry and garlic powder are nice in
    this salad)

Mix all ingredients together and dress lightly. Always taste your salad as you dress and season it. Be careful not to oversalt.

Serves 4–5

Spinach Lover's Salad   (1)

1 bunch spinach
½   cup chopped parsley
½   small red (Bermuda) onion

Wash spinach well (spinach is nearly always dirty) and break off heavier stems (for soup stock or the compost). Tear into fairly large pieces. Slice the onion *very* thin, add parsley, and toss with a yogurt- or lemon-and-oil-type dressing.

Other nice additions to this salad are sliced hard-boiled eggs, grated Swiss cheese, or a couple of crumpled, cooked pieces of bacon. If you use these ingredients, use the lighter, oil-based dressing.

Serves 4

Winter Carrot-Raisin Salad   (1)

4-5   medium carrots
1   cup raisins

Scrub carrots and grate them with a coarse grater (unless you prefer a fine shred). Add raisins and dress with a slaw-type dressing or Blender Mayonnaise (page 71).

Serves 4-5

Cabbage and Carrot Slaw   (2)

$\frac{1}{2}$ small head each red and green cabbage, finely shredded
2   large carrots, coarsely grated
1   cup green onion (scallion), finely chopped
salt and pepper
seasonings (dill seed is best in this salad)

Mix all ingredients together and dress lightly.

Serves 4-5

This salad can accompany a green salad at dinner, or be a main dish for lunch with plain yogurt or cottage cheese. It makes a wonderful dessert alone, or served over ice cream. This gives you a chance to be very creative in combining your favorite summer fruits.

Summer Fruit Salad (1)

2   oranges, peeled and sliced horizontally
2   cups fresh strawberries or berries, washed and stems removed, cut up or left whole
2   cups seedless grapes, or, if the grapes contain seeds, they should be cut in half and seeded
3   bananas, peeled and sliced
½   cantaloupe, peeled and cut into 1-inch pieces
1   cup unsweetened coconut
1   teaspoon cinnamon
½   cup honey mixed in a cup with 2 tablespoons lemon juice

Mix together carefully and serve.

Any other available fruit can be added or substituted. Try pineapple, peaches, pears, apricots, nectarines, tangerines, other melons, etc. If you increase the ingredients, you must also increase the coconut, cinnamon, honey, and lemon.

Makes 6 good servings

Vegetable Preparation

A beginning cook should learn to prepare vegetables carefully and tastefully to insure maximum nutrition and flavor. Vegetables may be the food with which you can be the most creative, but if you overcook them and forget to season, they will be very ordinary.

We all know that vegetables and fruit should be washed carefully, but do you know that vegetables should never be soaked? The water will leach out the important vitamins and minerals, as will overcooking.

All vegetables can be steamed; this helps prevent the loss of nutrients because the vegetables sit above the water instead of in the water. There are many kinds of vegetable steamers sold today, but one of the most practical is the collapsible stainless-steel variety that fits into any size pan. It is sold in kitchenware, hardware, and import stores.

Winter squashes (did you know that pumpkin is a squash?) are often baked or boiled and mashed with butter, salt and pepper, and sometimes a little honey. Root vegetables, or vegetables that grow deep in the ground, like carrots, turnips, beets, and parsnips, take longer to steam and may be simmered in a little water over a low heat for quicker cooking than steaming, although if you are a real purist you can steam *all* vegetables. Here is a chart of ideas on how you can prepare certain vegetables, but feel free to vary it as you wish.

STEAMED	BAKED	BOILED	SAUTÉED
artichokes	broccoli	any of the	all vegetables
asparagus	cauliflower	first two	except winter
beet tops	(especially	columns,	squash
broccoli	in sauces)	although the	
cabbage	eggplant	green leafy	
cauliflower	(stuffed)	vegetables	
collard greens	root vegetables	are much	
corn	winter squash	better if	
kale	acorn	they are	
mustard greens	Golden Delicious	steamed	
okra	Hubbard		
peas	pumpkin		
root vegetables	turban		
spinach			
string beans			
summer squash			
Swiss chard			
turnip tops			

Salads and Vegetables • 44

Seasonings for Vegetables

ROOT VEGETABLES and winter squashes taste best with butter or margarine and seasonings such as parsley, dill, caraway, onion, curry, or a little honey, if you prefer sweetness.

STEAMED VEGETABLES really need no oil or butter, but you can add either if you wish. Lemon or a little wine vinegar enhances the flavor of steamed vegetables, and seasonings like oregano, basil, thyme, tarragon, chives, parsley, rosemary, garlic, onion (fresh or powdered), curry, or even crushed, dried, hot chili peppers (just a little) add a special touch.

SAUTÉED VEGETABLES can be cooked in butter, margarine, or oil, although I think it is tastier and more nutritious to use oil. Sautéed vegetables should be served slightly crisp, and onions and garlic do add to the flavor of sautéed vegetables. Use any of the seasonings suggested for steamed vegetables.

SPECIAL HINTS: Try adding a few sunflower, pumpkin, or sesame seeds (raw or toasted) to your vegetables. How about chopped or slivered nuts? Try baking root vegetables and squashes with pears or apples (with a little butter and honey).

French Vegetable Stew   (2)

1 small eggplant
2 large tomatoes
1 large onion
1 8-ounce can corn, or kernels from 2 ears
1 bunch spinach
½ pound fresh string beans
3 garlic cloves, peeled and mashed
½ cup chopped parsley
¼ cup vegetable oil
salt, pepper, thyme, chervil, or basil and oregano

Snip ends from beans. Steam them alone for 5 minutes. Meanwhile cut unskinned eggplant into 2-inch pieces. Slice and quarter tomatoes. Chop onion coarsely and wash spinach and break into large pieces.

Pour the oil into a large, heavy-bottomed frying pan or stew pot. Using a medium heat, sauté onions first. Wait 3–4 minutes, then add string beans and eggplant. Add garlic cloves and cook together for 8–10 minutes. Add tomatoes, corn, and spinach, turn the heat down to simmer, cover the pan, and cook all ingredients 10–15 minutes, or until the tomatoes make a nice juice and things are cooked to your taste. Add seasonings to taste.

This can be served in bowls with grated Parmesan or Romano cheese and French bread for a lunch dish. It can also be used as the vegetable dish at dinner, or you can add more tomatoes to make more sauce and serve it over rice as the main dish. Add some pitted green olives and garnish with lemon or lime wedges for an extra touch.

This amount feeds quite a few, depending on how you serve it and the size of the servings.

Baked Zucchini Parmesan   (1)

4   medium zucchini squashes
butter
salt, pepper
Parmesan cheese
paprika
garlic powder

Cut zucchini in half, lengthwise. Steam for 5–6 minutes, or until the squash is slightly tender. Remove from steamer and place in a flat oven dish or cookie sheet with the inside of the squash facing up. Spread lightly with butter or margarine first, and sprinkle with a little garlic powder, salt, and pepper. Cover amply with Parmesan cheese, and sprinkle well with paprika. Place under the broiler and watch. When cheese is melted and beginning to brown, zucchini is ready to serve.

Serves 4

 Yeast Breads and Quick Breads

Whole-Wheat Bread (3)

2 packages dry yeast
$\frac{1}{4}$ cup lukewarm water
1 cup unbleached flour
4 cups whole-wheat flour
$1\frac{3}{4}$ cups lukewarm water
5 tablespoons honey
1 teaspoon salt
$\frac{1}{3}$ cup vegetable oil
$\frac{2}{3}$ cup flour for kneading

In a small bowl, dissolve 2 packages of dry yeast in $\frac{1}{4}$ cup luke-warm water. Stir and let soften for 5 minutes, or until it becomes pasty.

Mix honey with the $1\frac{3}{4}$ cups of lukewarm water in a large mix-ing bowl. Add 1 cup unbleached flour and 1 cup whole-wheat flour.

Add yeast to this after it has softened and beat well with an egg beater. The texture will be like pancake batter. Cover the bowl with a thin cloth and set it in a warm place for 1 hour, or until it rises nearly double in size. The batter will be bubbly. This part of bread making is called a "sponge." The purpose of this first rising with only 2 cups of flour is to make the bread lighter.

Next add oil, salt, and the remaining 3 cups of whole-wheat flour. Mix the dough well after each cup of flour. Dough will be stiff but sticky.

Sprinkle a cutting board or counter with flour and transfer the dough to the counter. When you work with the dough, keep your hands well floured, using the extra $\frac{2}{3}$ cup of flour for kneading, so the dough will be easy to handle. Flatten the dough and begin kneading by folding $\frac{1}{2}$ the dough over toward you and punching it down with the heels of your hands. Keep up this motion in a circular pattern, as if you were working with a large pancake.

Do this for 4 or 5 minutes, making the dough very elastic. Remember to keep the counter and your hands well floured so it is easy to work with the dough. Place dough in a clean, oiled bowl and cover with cloth. Leave in a warm place until it rises double in size, about $\frac{3}{4}$–$1\frac{1}{2}$ hours.

When it has risen, punch the dough down, divide it into 2 equal parts, and shape into loaves. Put in 2 standard ($4\frac{1}{2}$ × $8\frac{1}{2}$ inches), well-oiled bread pans, allowing each end of the dough to touch the pan. Cover and let rise for $\frac{1}{2}$ hour more.

Preheat oven to 375°. Bake the loaves until they are golden brown, or for approximately 1 hour. Remove from oven, place pans on their sides, and let the bread cool for 10 minutes. Then carefully remove bread from pans with a spatula and cool them on a wire rack.

NOTE: Rising time will depend on the warmth of your kitchen and the season of the year. Baking time depends on your oven setting. You must use your own judgement.

Country Kitchen Egg Bread (3)

2 packages dry yeast
$\frac{1}{4}$ cup lukewarm water
1$\frac{1}{2}$ cups powdered milk
1$\frac{1}{3}$ cups water
3 medium eggs
4 tablespoons brown sugar
$\frac{1}{3}$ cup oil
1$\frac{1}{2}$ teaspoons salt
6 cups unbleached flour
$\frac{2}{3}$ cup unbleached flour for kneading

Dissolve yeast in $\frac{1}{4}$ cup lukewarm water. Let sit for 5 minutes.

With an egg beater, mix powdered milk and 1$\frac{1}{3}$ cups water. Add eggs, oil, sugar, and salt and continue to beat well. Add yeast mixture and flour, 1 cup at a time. When you can no longer beat dough with an egg beater, use a spoon. Dough will be light and wiggly. Transfer dough to a well-floured counter or cutting board and knead as explained in the Whole-Wheat Bread recipe (page 52). Use the extra $\frac{2}{3}$ cup of flour for this procedure.

Place dough in a clean, well-oiled bowl, cover with a cloth, and let rise in a warm place until double in size, about 1 hour. The eggs in this recipe not only help the bread to rise faster, but also give the baked bread a cakelike texture.

When the dough has risen, divide it into 2 equal parts. Shape into loaves and place in 2 well-oiled bread pans. As with the

Whole-Wheat Bread, allow the dough to touch both ends of the loaf pans, as this helps support the bread while it is rising and baking. Cover the pans with a cloth and let dough rise another $\frac{1}{2}$ hour.

Preheat oven to 375° and bake bread for 45–50 minutes, or until it is golden brown. Remove loaves from oven, cool, and remove from pans as instructed in the Whole-Wheat Bread recipe.

Western Cornbread (2)

$1\frac{1}{2}$ cups stone-ground cornmeal
1   cup unbleached flour
$\frac{1}{2}$ cup powdered milk
3   teaspoons baking powder
1   teaspoon salt
$\frac{1}{3}$ cup brown or natural sugar
2   eggs
$\frac{1}{3}$ cup oil
$1\frac{1}{2}$ cups milk

Mix together all dry ingredients. In a separate bowl, beat eggs well and mix with oil and milk. Add liquid to dry ingredients and blend well.

Preheat oven to 400° and pour batter into a well-oiled 8-inch square baking pan. Bake for 20–25 minutes. Test by inserting a toothpick into the center of the cornbread. If it comes out clean, the bread is done. Serve with butter and honey.

Grandma's Bran Muffins (1)

1½ cups whole-wheat flour
½ cup powdered milk
3 teaspoons baking powder
1 teaspoon cinnamon
1 teaspoon salt
2 eggs
1 cup milk
⅓ cup oil
1½ cups bran flakes (not bran cereal)
3 tablespoons honey

Mix together all dry ingredients except bran flakes. In a separate bowl, beat eggs well and mix with milk, oil, and honey. Blend liquid with dry ingredients and add bran flakes. Do not stir more than necessary to mix.

Preheat oven to 375°. Fill well-oiled muffin cups ¾ full with batter. Bake for 20–25 minutes. Remove from oven and slide a knife around each muffin to extract from pan. Serve with butter and/or honey.

Makes 12 muffins

Sweet Zucchini Bread   (2)

2   eggs
1   cup oil
1   cup honey, or 1½ cups brown sugar, firmly
    packed
2   cups flour, unbleached
¾   cup wheat germ
3   teaspoons baking powder
1   teaspoon salt
1   teaspoon vanilla
1   teaspoon cinnamon
2½   cups grated zucchini squash
1   cup chopped nuts (optional)

Beat together eggs, oil, and honey or sugar. Add the next 6 ingredients and mix well. Fold in zucchini and nuts. Spoon into 2
standard, greased bread pans and bake in a 300° oven for about
1 hour, or until nicely browned.

Oatmeal-Sunflower Seed Muffins   (1)

1 cup unbleached flour
3 teaspoons baking powder
$\frac{1}{2}$ teaspoon salt
$\frac{1}{4}$ cup sugar
1 cup milk
$\frac{1}{4}$ cup vegetable oil
1 egg
1 cup oatmeal
$\frac{1}{3}$ cup shelled sunflower seeds

Mix together all dry ingredients but oatmeal. Beat egg and mix well with milk and oil. Combine the 2 mixtures and stir until blended. Add oatmeal and seeds and stir again. Don't overstir. Divide batter equally among 12 well-greased muffin cups and bake in a preheated 425° oven for 15–20 minutes, or until browned.

 Desserts and Goodies

Carob Brownies (2)

3 eggs
½ cup oil
1 cup brown sugar, firmly packed
1 teaspoon vanilla
1 cup carob powder
1 cup unbleached flour, sifted
2 teaspoons baking powder
½ teaspoon salt
½ cup hot water
1 medium carrot, grated
1 cup chopped nuts

Beat together eggs, oil, sugar, and vanilla. Add carob powder, flour, baking powder, salt, and hot water. Beat all ingredients well (use an electric beater, if you have one). Stir in nuts and carrot.

Preheat oven to 325°. Pour batter into oiled 8-inch square pan (spread evenly) and bake for 30–35 minutes, or until toothpick comes out clean. Cool briefly and cut into bars.

*Artist's Bread Pudding   (1)

6   cups ($\frac{1}{2}$ loaf) stale bread, broken into 1-inch
    pieces
1$\frac{1}{2}$ cups raisins
1   cup unsweetened coconut
1$\frac{1}{2}$ cups milk
4   eggs
$\frac{2}{3}$ cup honey
1   teaspoon vanilla
$\frac{1}{4}$ teaspoon salt

Mix together bread, raisins, and coconut. Beat together well eggs, milk, honey, vanilla, and salt. Then mix all ingredients together and pour into an 8-inch square baking dish. Bake at 350° for 20–25 minutes, or until eggs and milk are set. This should be a moist, puddinglike cake. If you like it more moist, just add more milk and eggs.

*Because you can add anything you like to the basic pudding.
    Try: grated lemon or orange rind
            chopped nuts
            chopped dried apricots
            grated apple
            chopped dates
            drained canned pineapple

    What else?

Apple Upside-Down Cake   (2)

Cake:

       1   cup whole-wheat flour, sifted
       1   cup unbleached flour, sifted
       3   teaspoons baking powder
       ½   teaspoon salt
       1   teaspoon allspice
       3   eggs
       ½   cup honey
       ⅓   cup oil
       1   cup hot water

Sift together dry ingredients. Separate eggs and beat the yolks with honey, oil, and hot water. Beat the whites until stiff and set aside. Slowly add liquid to dry ingredients, beating well (use an electric beater, if you have one). Carefully fold in egg whites and set the batter aside.

Bottom topping:

       ⅓   cup butter (amounts are marked on cube
            wrapper)
       ½   cup brown sugar, firmly packed
       1   teaspoon cinnamon
       1½ cups grated apple (1 large apple)
       1   cup raisins
       1   cup chopped nuts

In a 9 × 12-inch baking pan, melt the butter with the sugar and cinnamon directly over a low heat. Spread this syrup evenly over the bottom of the pan. Spread grated apple, nuts, and raisins evenly on the syrup. Remove from heat.

Preheat oven to 350°. Spread the batter gently over the topping in the pan and bake for 45–50 minutes, or until cake looks firm and golden.

You can cut this cake and serve directly from the pan, or you can take a large platter that covers the entire pan, place the platter on top of the pan, and quickly invert the pan and platter. It is nice to see the bottom as the frosting. That's how the cake gets its name.

Norwegian Fruit Soup (1)

My grandmother, Ingeborg, made this fruit soup for family gatherings. It is delicious.

$\frac{3}{4}$	pound pitted prunes
$\frac{1}{2}$	pound dried apricots, cut up
1	cup raisins
1	cup grape juice
1	cup water
$\frac{1}{2}$	cup brown sugar
1	can cherries and juice (any sweet variety)

1   orange, peeled and sliced
1   apple, cored and sliced
1   lemon, sliced (not peeled)
2   tablespoons instant tapioca
1   stick cinnamon

In 1 cup water, steam or simmer apricots, prunes, and raisins until they are soft. Then add all other ingredients and cook until the mixture thickens, about 15–20 minutes. The cooking time will depend on how cold the fruit was first. Stir while it is thickening. Serve hot or cold in small soup bowls as an appetizer or a dessert, or serve in large bowls as a lunch soup. Add a glob of yogurt, sour cream, or whipped cream, if you like.

Serves 5–6

Banana Tapioca Pudding   (1)

$1\frac{1}{2}$ cups powdered milk
6   tablespoons instant tapioca
$3\frac{1}{2}$ cups water
$\frac{1}{4}$ teaspoon salt
1   teaspoon cinnamon
2   eggs, separated

$\frac{1}{2}$ cup honey
1 teaspoon vanilla
1 banana, peeled and sliced

In a saucepan, mix powdered milk, tapioca, water, salt, cinnamon, and egg yolks. Beat well and set aside for 5 minutes. Meanwhile, beat egg whites until stiff and slice banana.

Bring powdered-milk mixture to a boil over medium heat, stirring constantly so that it doesn't burn as it thickens. Remove from heat and quickly add honey, vanilla, and banana. Fold in egg whites. Pour into dessert bowls, cool, then chill. This is nice topped with coconut or chopped nuts.

Serves 5–6

 Extras / Necessities

Blender Mayonnaise (1)

2 egg yolks (save the whites for tapioca pudding)
$\frac{1}{2}$ teaspoon salt
2 tablespoons white-wine vinegar
2 tablespoons lemon juice
$\frac{1}{4}$ teaspoon dry mustard
$1\frac{1}{2}$–2 cups salad oil

Mix in an electric blender all ingredients except oil. Then pour the oil very slowly into the mixture in the blender *as it is blending*. The success of the thickening depends on a very slow and steady pour. As it thickens you may have to stop and stir it with a spatula. This is a very easy recipe.

Alfalfa Sprouts (1)

1 Mason jar, quart size
1 ring-top canning lid with a piece of wire mesh
   cut to fit into the ring top

2   tablespoons alfalfa seeds (get them at natural
     food stores)
    water

Put the seeds in the jar at night. Cover them with water and let them soak overnight. Drain water through the wire mesh the next morning, shaking *all* the water out. Lay the jar aside on its side. Rinse the seeds and repeat the draining process a couple of times a day for 3–4 days as the seeds sprout. Usually on the fourth day the sprouts will be finished. Let them sit in a sunny window for several hours until the chlorophyll appears, giving the sprouts a nice green color.

Use any seed or legume you wish for sprouting. Alfalfa sprouts are generally the most delicate in taste.

Potatoes Potatoes Potatoes

Potatoes are a good source of vitamins and minerals and should be included in our basic diet. Unfortunately, the preparation of potatoes has been taken away from the cook by the canning and frozen food industries. Since all food is the most nutritious the less it is processed, and because potatoes are so simple to fix, it is wise for young cooks to learn to prepare them in their natural form. Here are three simple ways of fixing potatoes.

The Big Baked Potato   (1)

Use a thick-skinned potato recommended for baking, such as a russet. Wash it well and scrub any dirt or spots with a brush.

Preheat oven to 425° and prick the potato with a fork so it will not build up internal pressure as it heats and explode in the oven (a mess to clean up). Rub the skin with oil and bake for 45–50 minutes, or until you can put a fork easily into the center of the potato. Baking time depends on the size of the potato.

Split the potato lengthwise and serve with butter, sour cream, or yogurt. Eat the skin too. It is good, and good for you, because much of the vitamin and mineral content of a vegetable is in the skin. Because of the use of chemical sprays in agriculture, however, you must wash the skin very well. *Never* peel an organically grown potato.

The Old Boiled Potato   (1)

Select thinner-skinned potatoes for boiling. You can tell the difference in the skins by looking at them; thinner skins are lighter colored. Wash them well, cut in half, and quarter. Put them in a saucepan and add about $\frac{1}{2}$ as much water as you have potatoes. Bring the water to a boil, reduce to simmer, and cook until the potatoes are fork tender.

Serve them alone with butter, or with fresh peas or string beans. The skins are great, but you can let the individual eaters peel their own at the table, if they want to.

The Mountain Fried Potato   (2)

Wash and peel potatoes (unless organically grown). Cut potatoes lengthwise, then slice the pieces $\frac{1}{8}$ inch thick. Put a few tablespoons of salad oil in a frying pan and fry the potatoes over a medium heat until they are golden brown. You may have to add more oil as you are frying them.

Serve with salt and pepper. If you have any leftover meat or meatloaf, you can cut it up and add it to the frying potatoes and make a quick hash. Serve with poached eggs and/or catsup—ranch style.

NOTE: If you like fried potatoes to have a soft center and crisp outside, bake the whole potato first and then cut and fry.

Grains Grains Grains

Learning to fix grains is a satisfaction for the young cook, since most everyone likes them and they are so simple to prepare. Certainly they are a nutritious part of our diet, and as meat prices continue to rise, more and more people are using grains as an intermittent staple.

I have included here basic methods for cooking rice, bulgur wheat, and buckwheat groats. Be creative in your variations of these grains. All are fine served simply with butter or soy sauce to accompany meat, fish, or fowl, and all three make good bases over which stews and sauces can be served. They can be steamed with water, or with vegetable or meat stocks; they can be sautéed with vegetables and/or leftover meat or fowl; or they can be added to stews and soups for thickening and flavor.

Leftover rice and bulgur wheat are wonderful for a pudding base, and you can use the recipe in this book for bread pudding (page 62) as a guide. Bulgur wheat cooked with raisins and served with honey and milk makes a good cereal for breakfast. I once knew a young man in college who literally lived on bulgur wheat. He was very poor and it was a good source of cheap nutrition. He had it as a cereal for breakfast and refried with a few vegetables for lunch and dinner. He even ate it as a dessert, with cream, sugar, and cinnamon. I wonder if he still eats it.

Brown Rice (1)

4 cups water
2 cups brown rice
1 teaspoon salt

Bring water to a boil. Add rice and salt and stir once. Reduce to a very low simmer, cover, and steam until rice is tender, about 1 hour.

Serves 5-6

Bulgur Wheat (Ala) (1)

1 cup bulgur wheat
1 teaspoon oil
2 cups hot water
$\frac{1}{2}$ teaspoon salt

Sauté bulgur wheat in oil in a small frying pan. It will be quite dry. Reduce heat to simmer and add the hot water and salt. Cover and steam about 15 minutes, or until all liquid is absorbed.

Serves 3-4

Buckwheat Groats (Kasha)   (2)

1   cup buckwheat groats
1   egg, beaten
2   cups boiling water
$\frac{1}{2}$ teaspoon salt

Put groats and egg in a small frying pan over a high heat. Stir constantly until the grains are dry and separated. Reduce heat to simmer and add salt and boiling water. Cover and steam for 25–30 minutes.

Serves 3–4

Glossary of Cooking Terms

Here is a list of terms commonly used in cooking, some of which may not be familiar to you.

BASTE—To periodically pour sauce or drippings over a food as it cooks.

BATTER—A thick, beaten mixture of liquid ingredients to be cooked or baked.

BEAT—A repeated overhand motion used to combine ingredients and provide lightness to the dish. This can be done by hand with a spoon, or with a hand or an electric beater.

BEAT EGG WHITES UNTIL STIFF —To beat egg whites well until they are frothy and light, increase in volume, and become almost stiff. Adding beaten egg whites to foods insures lightness.

BLEND—To combine all ingredients gently.

BOIL—When cooking mixture begins to bubble.

BREAD—To coat with bread or cracker crumbs before cooking.

BROWN—To fry something until it turns brown on the outside. Instructions for preparing meat and fowl often say "brown it first."

CHOP—To cut into pieces. The desired size may or may not be specified in the recipe.

CLOVE GARLIC—A section of the whole garlic bulb.

CULL—In kitchen terms, to remove ends and stems.

DASH—A very small amount—less than $\frac{1}{8}$ teaspoon.

DOUGH—A thick, sticky mixture of flour or meal, liquids, and various dry ingredients, baked as bread or pastry.

DRAIN—To remove the water from food.

FILLET—A thin piece of meat, fish, or fowl that has been boned.

FLAKE—To separate into flakes (small shreds).

FOLD—To add an ingredient gently to a batter. Because beaten egg whites are delicate, we are instructed to fold them into the mixture instead of stirring them in quickly.

FORK TENDER—When a fork can penetrate the food easily.

GIBLETS—The liver, heart, and gizzard of a fowl. Usually wrapped separately and stuffed inside the bird. Sometimes includes the neck.

GRATE—To cut into pieces using a standard kitchen utensil called a grater. It comes in various sizes; thus, the instructions "grate coarsely" or "grate finely."

GREASE OR OIL—To cover the inside of a bowl or baking dish, or the bottom of a frying pan, with oil or grease so that the food will not stick.

GRIDDLE—A pan with no sides used especially for frying.

KNEAD—A repeated flattening movement made with the heels of the hands. Explained more thoroughly in the directions for bread making (page 52).

LEACH—To lose or remove part of a food's nutritional value by soaking it in a liquid.

LEAVENING—A substance that aids the rising or lightness of baked goods. Yeast, eggs, and baking powder are leavenings.

LUKEWARM—Comfortably warm to the touch.

MIX—To combine all ingredients together.

PALATE—In cooking or eating refers to our sense of taste, or lack of it.

PARINGS—The pieces or skins removed from fruits and vegetables.

PASTRY BRUSH—A small brush used to baste fowl and meat as it cooks or to brush butter or egg whites on the tops of baked goods.

POACH—To cook gently in simmering water or liquid.

PREHEAT—To turn on the oven or the fire under a pan before putting the food in.

QUARTER—To cut something into quarters.

SALT TO TASTE—To put a little salt in the food, taste it, and add more if it needs it.

SAUCEPAN—A high-sided pan for the top of the stove. It comes in different sizes.

SAUTÉ—To cook lightly in a shallow pan using oil, butter, or margarine.

SCRAMBLE- To mix up. Commonly used to explain how to mix eggs before cooking them in butter or oil.

SEAR—To cook quickly an item such as meat over a high heat in order to prevent the juices from leaking out.

SEPARATE EGGS—To separate the yolk from the white part of the egg by cracking the egg, then juggling the yolk back and forth in the broken shell and allowing the white to fall into a bowl.

SHRED—To slice into sliverlike pieces with a knife, a grater, or a special shredding instrument.

SIFT—To put flour through a utensil with a wire mesh in order to remove or separate the rough shaft and refine the flour.

SIMMER—To cook over a very low flame with little movement in the liquid.

SLICE—To cut into slices. The thickness may or may not be specified in the recipe.

SPATULA—A utensil with a wide, flat end used for lifting and turning foods in a frying pan or griddle.

STAPLE—Basic ingredients commonly used in cooking.

STEAM—To cook above a liquid in a covered pan with a steaming section inside so that the steam penetrates and cooks the food.

STEW PAN—A deep, heavy-bottomed pan for browning and cooking.

STRAINER—A scooped utensil, sometimes made of wire mesh, used for straining and draining.

Glossary of Nutritional Terms and Natural Food Items

Here are some common words used in discussing foods. Anyone of any age who is interested in cooking should be familiar with these terms.

CARBOHYDRATES—Foods containing a lot of starch and sugar. These should be eaten lightly.

FATS—Foods containing solid and semisolid compounds of fatty acids that are necessary in moderation for body growth. Some food sources that contain fats are absorbed in the body better than others, and these are referred to as "unsaturated fats."

MINERALS—Natural substances found in basic foods and necessary to build healthy bodies.

NUTRIENTS—The substances in food that contain the elements necessary for healthy body growth.

ORGANIC—The natural, nonchemical method of growing foods and raising animals that preserves the vitamins and minerals.

PROTEIN—The substance in foods that is responsible for body growth and repair. Protein is most commonly found in meat, fish and fowl, and dairy products. Legumes, nuts, seeds, and grains also contain protein in varying degrees.

VITAMINS—Natural substances found in plants and animals and needed to build healthy bodies. Vitamins can be made synthetically, too, as in vitamin pills.

The following list contains some of the most common food items used in natural, healthful cooking today. Most are found on supermarket shelves now.

BARLEY—A ricelike grain commonly used in soups and stews. The type found in the markets has been hulled and polished, a process that removes many of the nutrients. If possible, buy the unhulled variety found in natural food stores and special sections of some supermarkets.

BRAN FLAKES—The outer layers of the whole-wheat kernel, which are removed in the milling process to make white flour. They are very nice in muffins and cookies.

BROWN RICE—Unhulled, unpolished rice. It is more nutritious than white rice and has a nutlike flavor.

BUCKWHEAT GROATS—The cracked kernels of the buckwheat plant (not actually part of the wheat family) and very common to Eastern European cooking. They are sold under the trade name of "kasha" in supermarkets and as "buckwheat," or "groats," in natural food stores.

BULGUR—A cracked, roasted whole wheat, originally used in Near Eastern foods. Bulgur cooks very quickly and is sold under the trade name of "ala" in supermarkets and as "bulgur wheat" in natural food stores.

CAROB—The pod of the carob plant, also known as St. John's bread. Low in fats and carbohydrates and rich in protein, it is a common substitute for chocolate. It is made into powder or syrup for cooking and baking.

COCONUT—The fruit of the coconut palm, an important tropical plant. It is sold in shreds for baking and garnishing. It is best to buy the unsweetened variety, which has no preservatives added and whose flavor is more like the natural fruit.

CORNMEAL—The ground product of the dried corn kernel. It is best to buy stone-ground cornmeal, which contains the germ of the kernel and has much more taste than the refined variety.

FLOUR—The following are the most common flours used in natural baking today. All of them contain some gluten, which is the protein substance that combined with water, yeast, or baking powder makes baked goods rise. Many other grains and legumes are also ground into flour, but they do not contain gluten. Therefore, it is important to use them in combination with flours containing gluten to insure some lightness in your baked goods. Add the nongluten flours last in baking.

GLUTEN FLOUR—A special product of washing the gluten out of wheat flour and spray-drying it to make a special flour. Always use it when baking with nongluten flours, such as rice, oat, or corn flour.

GRAHAM FLOUR—Whole-wheat flour with part of the outer bran removed.

RYE FLOUR—Flour made from the rye kernel, a very healthful, nutritious grain commonly used in Central and Northern Europe.

UNBLEACHED FLOUR—Wheat flour without the bran (the outer shell of the wheat kernel) or the germ (the center of the wheat kernel). It does not contain much nutrition, but it is better than the refined white flours, which are processed with chemical bleaches.

WHOLE-WHEAT FLOUR—Flour made from the whole-wheat kernel.

HONEY—A natural, sweet substance from bees. When economically possible, it should be used in place of sugar, especially refined sugar. Unfortunately, many commercial honeys have been filtered and cooked, processes that destroy many of the natural enzymes (proteinlike substances that help digestion of other nutrients). Also, many bees are fed sugar water and not allowed to get their nourishment from blossoms. Try to find natural, uncooked honeys, if possible. But remember, the real issue confronting us today is not so much the *type* of sweetening we consume, but how *much* we consume.

LEGUMES—All beans and peas, and peanuts. The common legumes dried and used for soups and stews are: split peas, lentils, navy, lima, white, pinto, and soybeans. Dried legumes are a good, inexpensive source of protein, but, except for soybeans, they also contain a good amount of starch. Soybeans are unusually rich in protein and low in starch. They are still rather foreign to the American, however, as humans have only recently used them as food.

POWDERED MILK—Milk that has been dried into powder by a spray or heat-roller process. Instant milk carried by the supermarkets dissolves more rapidly than the noninstant variety found in health food stores.

RAW SUGAR—Sugar that has undergone less refinement than white sugar but still has little nutritional value. Brown sugar is white sugar that has been coated with molasses.

SEEDS—Increasingly common ingredients in today's cooking and baking, especially sunflower, pumpkin, and sesame seeds. They are rich in nutrition and add flavor to modern cooking. Sunflower and pumpkin seeds are great snacks.

SOYBEANS—An excellent source of protein. Occasionally they can be found fresh, but most often they are dried and/or ground into flour for baking, or into grits for breading and baking.

SPROUTS—Any seed or legume that has been cultivated for several days to a sprout form. Sprouts contain more vitamins than the seed and are tasty in salads and sandwiches. Directions for sprouting are on page 71.

TAPIOCA—The starchy root from the cassava plant, a tropical American plant. It is used for thickening and in puddings and is very good for you.

VEGETABLE OIL—Safflower, corn, olive, peanut, sesame, sunflower, and soybean are common varieties in today's natural cooking. An oil is a liquid at room temperature, in contrast to a fat, which is solid at room temperature. Oil is a good source of unsaturated fats and for this reason should be used in both cooking and baking. Look for oil that does not have chemicals added and keep the tin or bottle closed and refrigerated, as it can become rancid like any fat.

WHEAT GERM—The center of the wheat kernel and considered a rich source of B vitamins. It is extracted and sold separately for baking and breading. Because it contains oil, it should be refrigerated.

YEAST—In the baker's form gives lightness to baked goods. Nutritional yeast, obtainable in powder, flakes, and pills, is a powerful source of vitamins and minerals. Because of its unusual taste, it should be disguised in drinks and baked goods until you acquire a liking for it.

YOGURT—A cultured-milk product, originally from the Middle East. It has become a common food item in the last few years. It is very pleasant to eat and a good source of digestive bacteria.

Weights and Measures

The standard kitchen equipment for measuring cooking ingredients in our country consists of:

1. A set of measuring spoons that includes a tablespoon, a teaspoon, and the fractions of a teaspoon, $\frac{1}{4}$, $\frac{1}{2}$, and $\frac{3}{4}$

2. A 1-to-4-cup measuring receptacle with the fractions of the cup marked on the side. Often a cup will mark the fluid ounces on the side too.

Cooking directions in the United States are given in these measurements, and the common way to use them is to measure the ingredient level to the fraction or ounce line on the cup, or level to the edge of the spoon. Occasionally a recipe will call for a heaping cup, which means to be generous with the ingredient and not to be concerned about keeping a level measure. Often a recipe will specify a cup plus 1 or 2 tablespoons, to keep your generosity under control.

Sometimes ingredients are listed in pounds or fractions of a pound. The weight of meat and produce is usually marked on the package, but if not, you can use the scales in the market to weigh them. Nowadays many dry ingredients, such as rice, pasta, sugar, and dairy products, also carry the weight on the package. You may have to estimate the fractions of a pound, but more often than not, your recipe will call for volume.

Cooking really requires only simple arithmetic and, in the interest of creativity, should not be considered a project demanding scientific accuracy. At first, however, the need to measure in a reasonably correct manner is important. With time and experience, you will be able to measure your flour for bread making by the handful, baking powder in your palm, and water for the soup pot with your eye. Of course it is important to recognize when and with what ingredients you can be more casual. You wouldn't, for instance, be able to add an extra teaspoon of hot pepper to your stew without detecting a difference in the taste. On the other hand, an extra tablespoon of raisins in a cookie recipe is incidental to the taste or consistency. As time goes by, you will learn, partly by trial and error, when you can estimate.

You will need a little math sense when you are cutting in half or doubling a recipe. And, incidentally, if you are cutting in half a recipe that calls for 1 egg, don't bother to divide the egg—use it all.

The measuring part of cooking is very easy. It will become even easier in the next few years, as we make the conversions from out present system of weights and measures, called the U.S. Customary System, to the Metric System. Most of the major countries in the world today already use the Metric System, as does the entire scientific world. Naturally it is to our advantage to share the most common system of weights and measures, especially for economic communication and exchange.

You will begin investigating the Metric System in your school studies first, and later it will be fundamental in dealing with weight (mass or density) and volume (capacity) in science, math, home economics, and shop classes. Because cooking is not as exacting as other activities (like sewing or carpentry), it is a good place for you to start making conversions. For that reason I have included here a table of conversions for the basic weights and measurements used in cooking. You will see in the table of U.S. Customary measurements how much multiplying must be done to change a teaspoon to a tablespoon to a cup, etc. But to change one metric value to a larger metric value, you simply move the decimal point one place to the left, as metric units are measured in ten. The relationships within the Metric System are easy to see and understand.

It is important for you to realize that the conversion factor used in these tables to convert customary units to metric units is not exact, and that the metric value has been rounded off to

make it more convenient to work with and remember. For instance, 1 cup is given as 2.40 deciliters rather than 2.365835 deciliters. You may have learned in your school math that any measure includes a tolerance which is a fraction of that unit of measure. In an engineering project the tolerance would naturally have to be small so that the crucial parts would fit. In cooking there is much less need for critical measure. By starting with the conversion of 1 teaspoon to .05 deciliters (that is such a small number that the correct fraction is unimportant in cooking), you are able to figure out a cup conversion by yourself. Just multiply .05 by 48 (the number of teaspoons in a cup) and you get 2.40 deciliters. See? Look at the other conversions and play with the computation. You will see where figures have been rounded off.

Someday we will have measuring utensils to conform to metric units. Perhaps we will even have gram scales as a part of our kitchen equipment. Then, when everything is weighed and measured in metric units, a liter will no longer be a little larger than a quart to you, or a kilogram a little more than 2 pounds. They will be just a liter and a kilo in your eyes and in your hands.

Have fun thinking . . .

Metric Unit Definitions

In the Metric System the *meter* is the fundamental unit of length, the *liter* is the fundamental unit of capacity, and the *kilogram* is the fundamental unit of weight. The following prefixes, when combined with the basic unit names, provide the multiples and submultiples in the Metric System.

mili—one-thousandth (.001)
centi—one-hundredth (.01)
deci—one-tenth (.1)
deca—ten (10)
hecto—one hundred (100)
kilo—one thousand (1,000)

WEIGHT CONVERSION (MASS)

U.S. Customary Units		Metric Equivalents	
Ounces (oz.)	Pounds (lb.)	Grams (g.)	Kilograms (kg.)
$\frac{1}{2}$	$\frac{1}{32}$	14.175	.014
1	$\frac{1}{16}$	28.35	.028
4	$\frac{1}{4}$	113.40	.113
8	$\frac{1}{2}$	226.80	.227
12	$\frac{3}{4}$	340.20	.340
16	1	453.60	.454

1 kilogram (1,000 grams) equals about 2.2 pounds

VOLUME CONVERSIONS (CAPACITY)

Teaspoons (tsp.)	Tablespoons (tbsp.)	Fluid Ounces (fl.oz.)	Cups (c.)	Pints (pt.)	Quarts (qt.)	Deciliters (dl.)	Liters (l.)
1	$\frac{1}{3}$	$\frac{1}{6}$	$\frac{1}{48}$			.05	.005
3	1	$\frac{1}{2}$	$\frac{1}{16}$			.15	.015
6	2	1	$\frac{1}{8}$	$\frac{1}{16}$		.30	.030
12	4	2	$\frac{1}{4}$	$\frac{1}{8}$		.60	.060
24	8	4	$\frac{1}{2}$	$\frac{1}{4}$	$\frac{1}{8}$	1.20	.120
36	12	6	$\frac{3}{4}$	$\frac{3}{8}$	$\frac{3}{16}$	1.80	.180
48	16	8	1	$\frac{1}{2}$	$\frac{1}{4}$	2.40	.240
				1	$\frac{1}{2}$	4.80	.480
				2	1	9.60	.960

(Columns under **U.S. Customary Units**: Teaspoons through Quarts. Columns under **Metric Equivalents**: Deciliters and Liters.)

Fractions of a cup in thirds are not shown in this table. See if you can make those conversions yourself!

NOTE: Do not confuse the present British System with the Metric System. British countries use the same system of weights we do, but their cooking utensils (cups and spoons) are slightly larger than those used in the United States and Canada. British countries, too, are converting to the Metric System now.

To give you an example of how easily the ingredients for recipes in this book can be converted into their metric equivalents, I have made that conversion here for the Western Cornbread recipe (page 54).

1½ cups stone-ground cornmeal	(.360 liter, or a little more than ⅓ liter)
1 cup unbleached flour	(.240 liter, or a little less than ¼ liter)
½ cup powdered milk	(.120 liter, or a little less than ⅛ liter)
3 teaspoons baking powder	(.15 deciliter)
1 teaspoon salt	(.05 deciliter)
⅓ cup brown or natural sugar	(.080 liter)
2 eggs	2 eggs
⅓ cup oil	(.080 liter)
1½ cups milk	(.360 liter)

Try converting one of the recipes yourself!

Miscellaneous Equivalents

In the United States we measure certain dry ingredients in spoons and cups instead of ounces and pounds. The following are conversion approximations of some of the more common items in our everyday diet.

	U.S. Customary Unit	Metric Equivalent
Baking Powder	1 teaspoon	4.3 grams
Bread Crumbs		
dry	1 cup	90 grams
fresh	1 cup	45 grams
Butter	1 tablespoon	15 grams
$\frac{1}{4}$ pound or	$\frac{1}{2}$ cup	125 grams
Cheese		
$\frac{1}{4}$ pound or	1 cup	125 grams
grated, dry	1 cup	100 grams
Dried Fruit	1 cup	200 grams
Flour		
whole-wheat or		
unbleached	1 cup	140 grams
Rice	1 cup	240 grams
Salt	1 tablespoon	15 grams
Brown or Natural Sugar	1 tablespoon	10 grams

As you can see, cups and spoons of certain foods weigh more or less than cups and spoons of other foods. This is because they have different densities. It also explains why it is sometimes difficult to convert weight into volume. Notice how food increases in volume after it is cooked. Consequently many recipes ask specifically for cooked or uncooked foods. For instance: 1 cup uncooked rice, grains, or pasta = 2 cups cooked.

Now here are a few U.S. equivalents you should know:

5 large eggs = 1 cup
8 egg whites = 1 cup
12–15 egg yolks = 1 cup
$\frac{1}{2}$ pound dried fruit = $1\frac{1}{4}$ cups
5 ounces chopped nuts = 1 cup

Temperature Conversions

Fahrenheit and Celsius (often known as Centigrade) temperatures may be converted into each other by use of the following simple equations:

$$\text{Fahrenheit} = \tfrac{9}{5}\,\text{Celsius} + 32°$$

or

$$\text{Celsius} = \tfrac{5}{9}\,(\text{Fahrenheit} - 32°)$$

Fahrenheit	Celsius	Fahrenheit	Celsius	Fahrenheit	Celsius
−40	−40	149	65	329	165
−31	−35	150	65.5	338	170
−22	−30	158	70	347	175
−13	−25	167	75	350	176.6
− 4	−20	176	80	356	180
0	−17.7	185	85	365	185
5	−15	194	90	374	190
14	−10	200	93.3	383	195
23	− 5	203	95	392	200
*32	*0	212	100	400	204.4
41	5	221	105	401	205
50	10	230	110	410	210
59	15	239	115	419	215
68	20	248	120	428	220
72	22.2	250	121.1	437	225
77	25	257	125	446	230
86	30	266	130	450	231.1
95	35	275	135	455	235
100	37.7	284	140	464	240
104	40	293	145	473	245
113	45	300	148.9	482	250
122	50	302	150	491	255
131	55	311	155	500	260
140	60	320	160	600	315.5

As you may have noticed, our oven gauges (Fahrenheit Scale) begin at 150° (or warm) and increase by 25° to 550° or 600° (or broil). Celsius gauges will probably be numbered from 65° to 315°.

*water freezes at these temperatures.

Index

Ala
  see Bulgur wheat
Alfalfa sprouts
  see Sprouts
Apples
  in cake, 64–65
Beans, dried
  as nonmeat protein, 29
  nutritional value of, 29
  recipes for
    lima beans, 31–32
    soybeans, 30–31
Beef, ground
  recipes with, 19–20, 20–21
Bread
  in pudding, 62
  recipes for
    corn, 54
    egg, 53–54
    whole-wheat, 50–52
    zucchini, 56
  uses of leftover, xiv–xv
Brownies
  recipe for, 61
Buckwheat groats
  description of, 84

  how to prepare, 77
  variations of, 75
Bulgur wheat
  description of, 84
  how to prepare, 76
  uses of, 75
  variations of, 75
Cabbage
  in salad, 41–42
Cake
  apple, 64–65
Carob
  description of, 84
  recipe with, 61
Carrots
  in salad, 41–42
  recipe with, 61
Cereal
  dry, 3
  oatmeal, 3–4
Cheese
  in salad, 39
  recipes with, 4, 11, 12, 13, 14,
    25, 26, 47
Chicken
  recipes for, 27, 28

ASPEN PUBLISHERS

Understanding, Creating, and Implementing Contracts

◆ ◆ ◆

An Activities-Based Approach

Laurel A. Vietzen

Elgin Community College

Wolters Kluwer
Law & Business

AUSTIN   BOSTON   CHICAGO   NEW YORK   THE NETHERLANDS

Aspen Publishers
Attn: Permissions Department
76 Ninth Avenue, 7th Floor
New York, NY 10011-5201

To contact Customer Care, e-mail customer.care@aspenpublishers.com, call
1-800-234-1660, fax 1-800-901-9075, or mail correspondence to:

Aspen Publishers
Attn: Order Department
PO Box 990
Frederick, MD 21705

Printed in the United States of America.

1 2 3 4 5 6 7 8 9 0

ISBN 978-0-7355-6536-4

Library of Congress Cataloging-in-Publication Data

Vietzen, Laurel A.
    Understanding, creating, and implementing contracts : an activities-based
    approach / Laurel A. Vietzen.
        p. cm.
    Includes index.
    ISBN 978-0-7355-6536-4
    1. Contracts—United States.   2. Legal assistants—United States—
    Handbooks, manuals, etc.   I. Title.
KF801.Z9V54 2008
346.7302—dc22

                                                              2007025966

About Wolters Kluwer Law & Business

Wolters Kluwer Law & Business is a leading provider of research information and workflow solutions in key specialty areas. The strengths of the individual brands of Aspen Publishers, CCH, Kluwer Law International and Loislaw are aligned within Wolters Kluwer Law & Business to provide comprehensive, in-depth solutions and expert-authored content for the legal, professional and education markets.

CCH was founded in 1913 and has served more than four generations of business professionals and their clients. The CCH products in the Wolters Kluwer Law & Business group are highly regarded electronic and print resources for legal, securities, antitrust and trade regulation, government contracting, banking, pension, payroll, employment and labor, and healthcare reimbursement and compliance professionals.

Aspen Publishers is a leading information provider for attorneys, business professionals and law students. Written by preeminent authorities, Aspen products offer analytical and practical information in a range of specialty practice areas from securities law and intellectual property to mergers and acquisitions and pension/benefits. Aspen's trusted legal education resources provide professors and students with high-quality, up-to-date and effective resources for successful instruction and study in all areas of the law.

Kluwer Law International supplies the global business community with comprehensive English-language international legal information. Legal practitioners, corporate counsel and business executives around the world rely on the Kluwer Law International journals, loose-leafs, books and electronic products for authoritative information in many areas of international legal practice.

Loislaw is a premier provider of digitized legal content to small law firm practitioners of various specializations. Loislaw provides attorneys with the ability to quickly and efficiently find the necessary legal information they need, when and where they need it, by facilitating access to primary law as well as state-specific law, records, forms and treatises.

Wolters Kluwer Law & Business, a unit of Wolters Kluwer, is headquartered in New York and Riverwoods, Illinois. Wolters Kluwer is a leading multinational publisher and information services company.

Summary of Contents

Table of Contents

Introduction to Law and Preparation for Self-Guided Learning

1

◆ ◆ ◆

What Is Contract Law?

2

◆ ◆ ◆

Sources of Contract Law: Common Law and Uniform Commercial Code

3

◆ ◆ ◆

Agreement

4

◆ ◆ ◆

Invalid Assent

5

◆ ◆ ◆

Consideration

6

◆ ◆ ◆

Legality

7

◆ ◆ ◆

Capacity

8

◆ ◆ ◆

Statute of Frauds

9

◆ ◆ ◆

Third Parties/Secured Transactions

10

◆ ◆ ◆

Performance: Required or Excused?

11

◆ ◆ ◆

Remedies

12

◆ ◆ ◆

Contract Interpretation

13

◆ ◆ ◆

Working with Contracts

List of Contracts and Clauses

Preface

Since 1989 I have been a full-time teacher in, and coordinator of, an ABA-approved paralegal program. Before that, I was a transactional lawyer in private practice and worked with many excellent paralegals. My experiences in practice, combined with countless surveys of graduates and employers and working to obtain initial and re-approval by the ABA, have taught me the importance of:

- Teaching students to be independent learners so that they can arrive on the job as self-starters;
- Integrating ethics into every topic;
- Integrating the use of research and communications skills into every topic;
- Ensuring that students have adequate computer skills;
- Encouraging students to engage with the material, so that they retain what they learn; and
- Teaching state-specific law and procedures.

It is not easy to achieve these goals with a traditional textbook. Many such books tend to speak in generalities. Many paralegal teachers are adjuncts and may not have the time or resources to create challenging, practical, state-specific assignments to supplement the texts. They may want to develop alternatives to lecture format or they may be trying to offer the class alternative formats: online, hybrid, or even independent study.

This book is intended to go beyond such limitations, to:

- Engage students by making them responsible for finding local law.
- Require students to use computer skills to complete assignments.
- Include enough hands-on assignments (and guidance for doing those assignments) to ensure that a course offered in an alternative format will be the equivalent of a traditional class.
- Include assignments requiring student-led discussion of cases as an alternative to lecture in a classroom setting or to stimulate interaction in an online setting.
- Ensure hands-on experience doing legal research, summarizing cases, and finding their own answers so that students can hit the ground running in a law office.

- Make students aware of job opportunities and the skills required for those opportunities.
- Be adaptable to schools that schedule in semesters, trimesters, or quarters and to schools that integrate contract law into a course that includes other topics.

The sample cases are not cases that were highly controversial or that were landmarks in the development of law. Paralegals must understand legal theory, but they are not responsible for developing strategy or arguing cases. The cases were chosen to provide short, easy-to-read vignettes of the real-life practice of law. Many involve lawyers and paralegals as parties. They are intended to give students insights that will help ease the transition from school to the law office.

Laurel A. Vietzen

June 2007

Acknowledgments

The author gratefully acknowledges permission from the following sources to use excerpts from their works:

The Illinois State Bar Association, 424 South Second Street, Springfield, IL 62701-1779, 800-252-8908, www.isba.org. ISBA Advisory Opinions on Professional Conduct are prepared as an educational service to members of the ISBA. While the opinions express the ISBA interpretation of the Illinois Rules of Professional Conduct and other relevant materials in response to a specific hypothesized fact situation, they do not have the weight of law and should not be relied upon as a substitute for individual legal advice.

The Chicago Daily Law Bulletin,® 415 North State Street, Chicago, IL 60610, 312.644.7800.

Opinion 218 of the D.C. Bar's Legal Ethics Committee (issued June 18, 1991)(Washington, D.C., The District of Columbia Bar). Copyright 2006 by the District of Columbia Bar. Reprinted by permission of the Publisher.

Ethics Committee of the Colorado Bar Association, http://www.cobar.org, 1900 Grant Street, Suite 900, Denver, Colorado, 80203, 301-860-1115.

The Alaska Court System, 820 W. 4th Ave., Anchorage, AK 99501.

Introduction to Law and Preparation for Self-Guided Learning

This text requires that the student do a substantial amount of independent research to find the law applicable in the student's jurisdiction. This chapter provides an overview or refresher course on the concepts necessary to find and analyze law: sources of primary law, use of secondary sources, formulating a search query, reading and analyzing legal authority, and the consequences of bad research.

A. Sources of Legal Authority

Criminal Law
Prosecuted by a governmental body involving a matter of concern to society as a whole

Civil Law
Pursued by an individual or group of people, a business, or a governmental body acting in a private capacity; result may be damages or court order

Municipal Law
Local law (as opposed to federal or state law)

Constitution
One of five sources of legal authority

Legislation
Supreme source of legal authority; also called code or statute; enacted by an elected body (*e.g.*, Congress)

Code
Legislation; also called statute

Statute
Legislation; also called code

Judicial Decisions
Source of legal authority; also called common law or precedent

Common Law
Judicial decisions; also called precedent

Case Law
Judicial decisions

Precedent
Judicial decisions; also called common law; past decisions used to justify current decisions

Some students will have taken an introduction to law or a legal research class before using this book. For them, the special features of this book will provide an unusual and very valuable opportunity to practice their research and writing skills. Students who have not taken those classes can learn enough about the basics of research to do well in this class just by reading this chapter. Those students will still have much to learn when they study legal research, but they will become comfortable with simple online research.

Let's start with some basics:

1. Success in law is not about enjoying a good argument; it is about having legal authority to support your arguments.

2. There are two types of law: civil and criminal. A **criminal law** matter is prosecuted by a governmental body, such as the district attorney, and involves a matter of concern to society as a whole, such as burglary or murder. The result may be prison time, probation, even the death penalty, if the defendant is found guilty. A **civil law** matter is pursued by an individual or group of private people, a business entity, or a governmental body acting in a "private" capacity. Breach of contract is an example of a civil matter and, if the defendant is found liable (don't use the word *guilty*!) the result is an award of damages (money) or a court order requiring or prohibiting specific actions.

3. Legal authority comes from five sources. These sources exist in federal and state law, and most exist even in local (**municipal**) **law**.

   a. **Constitution** (even municipalities have a charter or other governing document);
   b. **Legislation** enacted by an elected body such as Congress, a state legislature, a county board, or city council (also called **code** or **statute**);
   c. **Judicial decisions**, also called **common law**, **case law**, or **precedent**;
   d. **Administrative agency regulations and rulings**, such as the "rules and regs" of the Internal Revenue Service, Federal Trade Commission, your state environmental protection department, or a local planning board. An administrative agency is established to administer a particular law or program (*e.g.*, the National Labor Relations Board was created to administer the National Labor Relations Act), and;
   e. **Executive actions**, which are executive orders signed by the President or governor (or even the mayor) and treaties signed by the President and approved by the Senate.

4. Legal problems presented by clients are often unique. Lawyers and paralegals can memorize the basics of an area of law, such as contract law, but often don't know "the answer" to the problem presented. To find that answer they must research those sources of law to find authority to support their theories.

5. When you find authority, you must be able to understand, analyze, and write about it, and also **cite**[1] it so that those who read your work can find your sources.

---

[1]To cite authority is to give its citation, the address at which it can be found in law books or online.

B.   Steps in Preparing to Research a Legal Issue

Before you start to research a legal problem you will ask yourself several questions:

1. *Is this a matter of state law or federal law?* By the time you finish your paralegal education, you will usually be able to answer this question without help. Most law relevant to contracts comes from state case law or state statutes. This book will guide you through the law of your own state.

2. *What is the desired work product and how much time should be spent on the research?* These are important questions on the job and in other classes. Paralegals often prepare **interoffice memos** (also called **objective memos**) that cite authority to analyze the client's situation without arguing a position; paralegals also work on **adversarial** memos and briefs that argue the client's position. This book will give you clear instructions on the work product.

3. *Does this project require primary authority or secondary authority?* When you are researching a question of law, you will generally be looking for **primary authority**—one of the five sources previously listed. **Secondary authority** is not, itself, the law; it includes textbooks and scholarly articles that help you understand primary law as well as form books, procedure manuals, and "practice" handbooks that help you accomplish a specific task. Many times a legal problem involves finding the right form or procedure, rather than finding the actual law. Secondary authority also includes material to help you find primary authority when you are using books; these "finding tools," such as digests and encyclopedias, are not necessary when you look for primary law online.

4. *Which of the five sources of law is likely to govern?* Most contract law comes from code (statutes) and case law; there is some relevant administrative law, as discussed in the next chapter. When a statute governs, it is often written in broad terms (*e.g.,* "seller shall have a reasonable time . . ."); you will need to find cases that provide insight on how courts interpret terms such as "reasonable" in specific fact situations. **Statutory interpretation (statutory construction)** is a major function of the courts and a major purpose of legal research.

5. *Where will I do this research?* At some point in your paralegal career you will learn to use books for legal research, but in this class you will probably complete your assignments using a subscription computer-assisted legal research (**CALR**) system. Your school may provide you with access to WestLaw, Lexis, Loislaw, or some other system. If you do not have access to a subscription CALR system, you can create an account at http://www.lexisone.com that will allow you to search for judicial decisions from all 50 states and the federal system, going back five years, without paying a fee. You can find statutes on a government-sponsored site, without paying a fee.

6. *How should I describe the problem?* As explained below, you must describe your problem in a few words that can be used in an index or to create a query to use in an online search engine.

Many people use the traditional questions of journalism, who, what, when, where, why, and how, to arrive at their search terms. Choosing terms is difficult because they have to be broad enough that they are likely to appear in most relevant cases and narrow enough that you won't have to read 5,000 cases. Your choice of search terms will depend on whether you are using books or CALR.

Administrative Agency
Source of legal authority; administers a particular law or program

Regulations
Established by administrative agencies

Executive Actions
Source of legal authority; including orders signed by the President or governor

Cite
Verb form of citation (*i.e.,* to cite)

Interoffice Memo
Also called objective memo, analyzes fact situation with citations to sources of law

Objective Memo
Also called interoffice memo, analyzes fact situation with citations to legal authority

Adversarial
Argues a position

Primary Authority
One of the five sources of law

Secondary Authority
Material such as textbooks and articles that help locate (finding tools) and understand primary law; form books, handbooks, encyclopedias, digests, etc.; not actual law

Statutory Interpretation
Interpretation of statute's terms; also called statutory construction

CALR
Computer-assisted legal research system

CALR works well with narrow, specific terms, but if you are using a printed index, you need to think in broader terms

---

Example

If you were researching whether prescribing the drug Allegra has ever resulted in a malpractice case, you would find the term "Allegra" too narrow and unlikely to appear in a print index. However, using the word "Allegra" in a computerized search would probably get you to the most relevant material quickly. On the other hand, the term "prescription" would work well in a printed index, but would probably result in a list with hundreds of cases if used in a computerized search.

Another challenge in brainstorming a problem is the unique language of the law. As you take classes and read cases, this will become second nature to you, but it may seem foreign at first. For example, a problem involving marital property might be classified under "husband and wife" in a legal index; a problem involving a 17-year-old might fall into the category "infants."

Here is a sample of how you might "brainstorm" a problem and develop a list of words and phrases that describe the problem:

Example

Several years ago, Dan Developer knew that he would want to build 50 houses on his vacant property. He wanted to "lock in" the costs, so he approached the local school district and asked whether he could pre-pay the school impact fees. School impact fees are paid by a developer to help the school district pay the cost of educating students who will enter the local schools because their families have moved into a new development. The district agreed and the parties entered into a contract, under which Dan paid $65,000. Three years later, when Dan applied for permits to begin construction, he was told that the district had enacted a new fee. According to the district, the fee Dan had paid was for school buildings, and the new fee is for equipment and staff. Dan thought he had protected himself against all school fees and asks your firm to research the issue.

Who	School district, developer
What	Impact fees
Where	Subdivision
When	Pre-payment
Why	Vested rights*
How	Contract

An example of a term that may be unfamiliar, "vested rights" refers to rights that have become definite entitlements at a point in time.

Identifying synonyms and similar terms is an essential part of the process. For example, in the chart, you might insert "builder" next to "developer" and "government agency" next to "school district."

C. Formulating a Query

If you are going to conduct your search using a computer, you will connect several of your search terms to create a **search query**. The **connectors** describe the relationship between your search terms. All of the major CALR services include some common connectors. Some examples of how they work:

- You decide to use "developer" and "impact fee" as search terms and enter the query [developer & "impact fee"]. You get a list of hundreds of cases because the "&" connector only requires that each term appear at some spot in the case.
- To narrow the search, use a "proximity" or "near" connector. Most CALR systems have connectors to require that terms be in the same paragraph [/p], the same sentence [/s], or within a specified number of words of each other [search term/# search term,]. You might search [developer/25 "impact fee"] to find cases in which the word developer appears within 25 words of "impact fee."
- The term "impact fee" is in quotes because some CALR systems require quotes to identify a phrase; failure to include quotes would cause the system to read the search as [developer within 25 words of impact **"or"** fee].
- Still have too many results? Add terms: [developer/25 "impact fee"/25 subdivision].
- If you aren't getting enough results, broaden your search to look for [developer or builder/25 "impact fee"]. The "or" connector is often used to search for synonyms.
- Suppose that your search pulls up several cases in which a developer challenged the existence of impact fees, claiming they were unconstitutional. To eliminate these cases, use the "not" connector [%], [developer/25 "impact fee" % unconstitutional].
- Use **"root expanders"** [!] to pick up variations such as subdivision or subdivide [subdivi!]. To find woman or women you might use a **"wildcard"** [wom*n].

If you are not familiar with the connectors and wildcards for your CALR system, you can likely find its use guide when you sign on, usually by using the HELP tab. Many of the CALR providers have online tutorials you can use even before you sign on. Your instructor will show you how to sign on.[2] In addition, the next chapter specifically describes the steps taken to research particular problems.

Search Query
Terms and connectors or natural language used in CALR search

Connector
Symbol describing relationship between CALR search terms

Root Expander
Symbol used to pick up word variations in a CALR search

Wildcard
Symbol used to pick up word variations in a CALR search

---

[2]The examples are "terms and connectors" searches; it is also possible to search using "natural language" on some systems, by entering a question without connectors. A "field search," with which you search or limit the search by names of parties, judges, or lawyers; by citation; or by dates is also possible, but beyond the scope of this book.

Assignment I-1

Brainstorm the following problems and write a CALR search query for each. Remember, you are not trying to find an answer to the problem at this point, but are only practicing formulating queries.

◆ Jim has leased a building in a strip mall to operate a Francesca's Pizza restaurant. The contract provides that the landlord will not lease space to a "competing business" in the same shopping center, but it does not define that term or give examples. The landlord is planning to lease the space next to Francesca's to a take-out sandwich shop and claims that such a business would not compete with Jim's business. Jim disagrees.

◆ Dan Developer signed contracts to sell houses in his new subdivision. The contracts provided that each house would have King brand, double-pane, vinyl, double-hung windows. Before construction began, King raised its prices substantially. Dan substituted Della brand, double-pane, vinyl, double-hung windows and feels that they are substantially the same product. Some of the buyers are claiming that this violated their rights — they want a reduction of the purchase price.

◆ Dr. Hirsch is a successful psychiatrist (M.D.) and wants to expand her practice by hiring a psychologist (Ph.D.) to do counseling. She is concerned that the psychologist might work for her just long enough to become popular with her patients, open his own office, and that she could lose patients. She wonders whether a court would enforce a clause, in the employment contract, prohibiting her employee from opening his own counseling business within 50 miles of her office, for two years after leaving Dr. Hirsch's employ.

D. Primary Authority

The following is an overview of the primary authority you will find when you use CALR. In later chapters, you will use secondary sources:

1. Statutes

Topic
Generally, statutes are organized by topic; breaking the code into titles, acts, chapters, or sections

Titles
See Topic

Statutes (also called *legislation* or *code*) are enacted by a legislative body (Congress or a state legislature) and are generally organized by **topics**, which are divided into subtopics and sub-subtopics. You should be familiar with the major topics, often called **titles** or chapters, of the statutes for your jurisdiction. Knowing the major topics gives you a starting point for statutory research, even if the most recent amendments may not have been **"codified"** (*i.e.*, put into the topical system). To find your state statutes and look at those topics, start at www. ncsl.org/public/leglinks.cfm. Select your state and "statutes" in the boxes.

Citations to statutes do not use page numbers because the topics can expand or contract. Using references to titles, chapters, acts, sections, or paragraphs eliminates the need to change all references when a law is amended or repealed. For example, Section 17 might be one-half page long or it might grow to eight pages long, but it can still be cited as Section (§) 17. If section 17 grows to 13 pages, Section 18 will begin on a later page, but it can still be called §18. A citation to a statute generally consists of the name of the law, an abbreviation indicating the source (*e.g.*, U.S.C. indicates that the statute was found in U.S. Code; ILCS indicates Illinois Compiled Statutes), and numbers indicating the title, chapter, act, and/or section.

If you examine an **annotated statute**, the text of the law as enacted by the legislature appears first, followed by references to cases, administrative regulations, law review articles, and other materials that explain and interpret the law. Statutes found on government sites on the Internet are not annotated.

Reading and comprehending statutes takes a lot of practice. Statutes often include non-specific language, so that courts have discretion to interpret and apply the law. This is necessary because legislation is intended to govern large groups of people or situations; being too specific would create loopholes. Unlike judicial decisions, which deal with specific situations after they have occurred, statutes often govern conduct in advance. Think about the speed limit that applies in bad weather. It is not a specific number; in most states it is represented by the phrase "safe for conditions" or a similar description. Stating a specific speed would not govern all possible weather situations that could arise in the future on all possible roads. Statutes may also contain long, confusing sentences. A few tips for reading statutes:

1. *Look at the index for the whole chapter or act* (often located at the beginning of the chapter or act) to get a feel for the law as a whole;
2. *Check whether the act has a "definitions" section* that defines the terms used in the various sections;
3. *Read the sections immediately before and after the section applicable to your research*; they may shed light on the statutory scheme;
4. *Write out the statute and break long sentences into "outline" form* so that you can sort out the "ands" from the "ors."

Codify
To enter a statute into a topical system

Annotated Statute
Statue with references to articles, cases, and other materials that explain and interpret the law

---

EXHIBIT I-1
Example of State Statutes Organized by Topic

From www.ilga.gov/legislation. Illinois statutes are organized into 9 major topics, each of which is divided into chapters. The chapters are divided into Acts, which are further divided into sections. This is a typical scheme of organization for state statutes.

Illinois Compiled Statutes
Information maintained by the Legislative Reference Bureau
Updating the database of the Illinois Compiled Statutes (ILCS) is an ongoing process. Recent laws may not yet be included in the ILCS database, but they are found on this site as Public Acts soon after they become law. For information concerning the relationship between statutes and Public Acts, refer to the Guide.

GOVERNMENT

- CHAPTER 5 GENERAL PROVISIONS
- CHAPTER 10 ELECTIONS
- CHAPTER 15 EXECUTIVE OFFICERS
- CHAPTER 20 EXECUTIVE BRANCH
- CHAPTER 25 LEGISLATURE
- CHAPTER 30 FINANCE
- CHAPTER 35 REVENUE
- CHAPTER 40 PENSIONS
- CHAPTER 45 INTERSTATE COMPACTS
- CHAPTER 50 LOCAL GOVERNMENT
- CHAPTER 55 COUNTIES
- CHAPTER 60 TOWNSHIPS
- CHAPTER 65 MUNICIPALITIES
- CHAPTER 70 SPECIAL DISTRICTS
- CHAPTER 75 LIBRARIES

EDUCATION

- CHAPTER 105 SCHOOLS
- CHAPTER 110 HIGHER EDUCATION
- CHAPTER 115 EDUCATIONAL LABOR RELATIONS

REGULATION

- CHAPTER 205 FINANCIAL REGULATION
- CHAPTER 210 HEALTH FACILITIES
- CHAPTER 215 INSURANCE
- CHAPTER 220 UTILITIES
- CHAPTER 225 PROFESSIONS AND OCCUPATIONS
- CHAPTER 230 GAMING
- CHAPTER 235 LIQUOR
- CHAPTER 240 WAREHOUSES

HUMAN NEEDS

- CHAPTER 305 PUBLIC AID
- CHAPTER 310 HOUSING
- CHAPTER 315 URBAN PROBLEMS
- CHAPTER 320 AGING
- CHAPTER 325 CHILDREN
- CHAPTER 330 VETERANS

**EXHIBIT I-1
(continued)**

HEALTH AND SAFETY

CHAPTER 405 MENTAL HEALTH
CHAPTER 410 PUBLIC HEALTH
CHAPTER 415 ENVIRONMENTAL
    SAFETY
CHAPTER 420 NUCLEAR SAFETY
◆ CHAPTER 425 FIRE SAFETY
CHAPTER 430 PUBLIC SAFETY

HUSBANDRY

CHAPTER 505 AGRICULTURE
CHAPTER 510 ANIMALS
CHAPTER 515 FISH
◆ CHAPTER 520 WILDLIFE
◆ CHAPTER 525 CONSERVATION

TRANSPORTATION

CHAPTER 605 ROADS AND BRIDGES
CHAPTER 610 RAILROADS
◆ CHAPTER 615 WATERWAYS
CHAPTER 620 AIR TRANSPORTATION
CHAPTER 625 VEHICLES

RIGHTS AND REMEDIES

◆ CHAPTER 705 COURTS
◆ CHAPTER 710 ALTERNATIVE DISPUTE
        RESOLUTION
◆ CHAPTER 715 NOTICES
◆ CHAPTER 720 CRIMINAL OFFENSES
◆ CHAPTER 725 CRIMINAL PROCEDURE
◆ CHAPTER 730 CORRECTIONS
◆ CHAPTER 735 CIVIL PROCEDURE
◆ CHAPTER 740 CIVIL LIABILITIES
◆ CHAPTER 745 CIVIL IMMUNITIES
◆ CHAPTER 750 FAMILIES
◆ CHAPTER 755 ESTATES
◆ CHAPTER 760 TRUSTS AND
        FIDUCIARIES
◆ CHAPTER 765 PROPERTY
◆ CHAPTER 770 LIENS
◆ CHAPTER 775 HUMAN RIGHTS

BUSINESS

◆ CHAPTER 805 BUSINESS
        ORGANIZATIONS
◆ CHAPTER 810 COMMERCIAL CODE
◆ CHAPTER 815 BUSINESS
        TRANSACTIONS

---

2. Judicial Decisions

With a few exceptions, print volumes containing judicial decisions (called **reporters**) are not organized by topic and you must use an encyclopedia, digest, or other index to find relevant cases. To avoid this two-step process, CALR is an efficient way of locating judicial decisions. Once you find cases, reading and understanding what you've found requires a solid understanding of court systems.

Reporters
Print volumes that contain judicial decisions

a. Trial Courts vs. Appellate Courts

Trial Court
Court in which most cases start, generally concerned with deciding issues of fact

Issues of Fact
Trial courts use testimony and evidence to decide facts (i.e. what happened)

Legal Issues
Determining appropriate consequences of the facts or whether a trial court handled a case properly

Affirm
Appellate or higher court's decision to support or uphold the decision of the lower court

Reverse
Appellate or higher court's decision to invalidate the decision of the lower court

Remand
Appellate or higher court's decision to send the case back to the lower court

Modify
Appellate or higher court's decision to change the decision of the lower court

Dissenting Opinion
Opinion written by a judge who disagrees with the majority; not law but provides interesting facts and opinions about case

Majority Decision
That which governs the outcome of cases; also called decision of the court

Decision of the Court
Majority decision, governs outcome of the case

Concurring Opinion
Written by a judge who agrees with majority decision but for different reasons

Most cases enter the legal system in a **trial court**. A trial court is most concerned with **issues of fact**. An issue of fact concerns what happened: Did he shoot the gun? Did she run the red light? Trial courts examine evidence and take testimony to make factual decisions. Factual determinations often resolve the case without any need for legal research. For example, in most situations, if she ran the red light, she is responsible for the collision. Because factual decisions do not make or interpret the law, most states do not report (publish) trial court decisions; therefore, when you find a reported state court case, it is often a case from an appeals court or the highest court in the system. These courts are concerned with **legal issues**: the appropriate consequences of the facts or how the lower court handled the case. Some federal trial decisions are reported.

When you read a decision from an appeals court or the highest court, remember that the court is not hearing a "new" case, but reviewing a decision made by a lower court. The appeals court can **affirm**, **reverse**, **remand**, or **modify** (or some combination thereof) the lower court's decision. For example, an appellate court could affirm the trial court's decision that a defendant was responsible for a collision, but find the award of damages unreasonable and reverse and remand on the determination of appropriate damages. If an appellate court determines that a trial court made an error in admitting evidence or making a calculation, the appellate court will generally remand — send the case back the lower court — because it will not accept evidence or make determinations of fact.

Appeals courts use panels of judges. The decision of the majority governs the outcome of the case (whether to affirm, reverse, or remand), but the other (non-majority) judges may write their own opinions. A **dissenting opinion** is written by a judge who disagrees with the **majority decision**; the majority decision is also called the **decision of the court**. A dissenting opinion is not the law, but often provides interesting facts and opinions about the case. A **concurring opinion** is written by a judge who agrees with the majority's decision, but for different reasons.

b. Reading Cases

The physical layout of cases can be confusing. Depending on your source, publishers' enhancements such as a **synopsis** (summary of the case) and **headnotes** (summaries of individual points made in the case) may or may not be included. If headnotes are included, they may include references to supplemental materials and serve as an outline of the case. As you read a case, keep a legal dictionary and a piece of paper close by. You will probably have to look up at least a couple of new legal terms with each case you read. You may also want to draw a timeline on a piece of paper so that you can visualize the events before and during the litigation. Judges usually do not give facts in the order in which they occurred (*i.e.*, chronological order), which can be confusing. Often the first paragraph in the opinion recites **procedural history**, the court decisions that brought the case to its current position (*e.g.*, "Plaintiff-appellant sought review of summary judgment entered by the Circuit Court of Kendall County. The appellate court, second district, reversed. We granted certiorari . . .”). To a beginner, this usually makes no sense until the underlying facts are clear. Skip this paragraph, read the underlying facts and do a **timeline**, then go back to the procedural history and add it to the timeline (at the end of the underlying facts, of course).

If there are multiple parties, particularly if the judges refer to those parties as **“appellant”** and **“appellee”** jot down a quick way of identifying the parties (*e.g.,* you might note that appellant = employer; appellee = employee). The appellant is the party bringing the appeal; in other words, this party lost in the lower court. The appellee won in the lower court. Because appellate courts frequently make different rulings on different issues, it is not uncommon for both sides to appeal. For example, the defendant might appeal, arguing that the trial court **“erred”** (made an error) in finding her responsible (**liable**) for a collision. At the same time, the plaintiff might appeal, arguing that the award of $50,000 in damages was insufficient because of the extent of his injuries. Reading an opinion is particularly confusing when the court refers to “plaintiff, cross-appellee,” etc.

One of the most difficult things about reading a judicial decision is that the opinion will contain discussions of several other decisions made by other courts. The primary function of an appeals court is to review the decisions of lower courts with respect to the case under consideration (also called the **case at hand**). An opinion may contain an extensive discussion of what the court below it did and why that was correct or incorrect.

In addition, the appellate-level court may discuss other cases decided in the past (**precedent**) in depth and either **analogize** or **distinguish** those cases—find them similar or different, respectively, than the case being decided. The court may also discuss the meaning of a statute. It’s easy to get lost; it can be helpful to either take notes or physically mark your copy of the case.

When you find a case online, the body of the case may include numbers spaced at intervals to indicate where the page number would change if you were looking at print material. Sometimes you will want to know the exact page number on which a fact or quote appears in a case (**jump cite**). Online citations to precedent may include links, so that you can click on the citation and see the case being discussed. The first sample case in the next chapter identifies some of these features.

c. Briefing Cases

The best way to practice reading and truly understanding cases is to write short case summaries, called **briefs**. Although case briefs are not part of the everyday practice of law, they are time-honored teaching tools. Law students must brief several cases for each class they attend daily. You can expect to brief many cases while you are in school.

You will find that each instructor has a preferred format for case briefs. Most instructors will want you to put a heading on the brief, including the name, **citation** (its official “address” within law books), and year of the case. You should also include a section for “facts,” a statement of the legal issue(s) on appeal, the holding, and a summary of the reasoning. Some instructors also want separate sections reciting the procedural history and the contentions (arguments) of the

---

Synopsis
Summary of case, often provided in publishers’ enhancements

Headnotes
Summaries of individual points made in the case

Procedural History
The history of the court decisions that have moved the case to its current position

Timeline
A schedule of the times at which certain events took place

Appellant
Party bringing an appeal; lost in the lower court

Appellee
The party that won in the lower court

Err
To make an error

Liable
Found responsible

Case at Hand
The case under consideration

Analogize
To compare cases and find them similar

Distinguish
To compare cases and find them to be different

Jump Cite
The exact page number on which a fact or quote appears in a case

Brief
Short case summary

Citation
Address at which authority is found in law books or on line

parties. Be sure that you understand which sections your instructor wants included and your instructor's preferences regarding headings, spacing, etc.

Facts   Because a brief should be brief, one page if possible, it is not usually a good idea to copy the facts as stated by the court. Edit out all insignificant facts. To determine whether a fact is significant, ask yourself: "If this fact were changed, would it change the outcome?" For example, assume the case states that the plaintiff was driving her 2005 Ford Mustang to school, on Maple Street, when the defendant ran a red light and caused a collision. Ask yourself: would the result be different if the plaintiff had been driving her 2006 Chevy Aveo to the store on Elm Street when the defendant ran a red light and caused a collision?

Recite the facts in chronological order, as they happened, and in past tense (because the facts are not continuing to occur). Your instructor may want you to include procedural history in the facts; others may prefer a separate section. In either case, the procedural history is important and should be included.

Find an easy way to refer to the parties. Using either plaintiff-defendant or the names of the parties (Smith-Jones) can be confusing, particularly if there are several parties. It is often possible to identify the parties by their roles (*e.g.,* landlord-tenant, husband-wife-child, employer-secretary, or buyer-seller).

Issue and Holding   The issue on appeal is never a factual issue such as "whether the light was red." That may have been the issue at trial, but the trial court made a decision. On appeal, something about how the lower court made that decision is in question. Try to identify the ruling or rulings in question and the arguments made by the parties and you will be able to spot the issue.

Holding
Answer to the legal issue in a judicial decision

The **holding** is the answer to the question posed by the issue. It generally includes this court's disposition of the case (affirm, reverse, etc.) and a short summary of the court's conclusion. For example, if the issue is "whether the trial court erred in refusing to permit testimony of a blind witness," the holding might be "Reversed; a witness may not be considered incompetent to testify based on physical disability alone." Do not accidentally state the holding of a lower court.

Reasoning
Summary of the court's explanation of its decision

Reasoning   The **reasoning** is a summary of the court's explanation of its decision — the "why" behind the holding. Most instructors prefer that you explain reasoning in your own words. It is almost never sufficient to simply state that the court based its decision on precedent. It is also not helpful to refer to cited cases unless a reader would know what the reference means. Try to explain how the unique facts of this case add to or clarify the law.

Instructors differ on whether dissenting or concurring opinions should be included in a brief. Read these opinions. If they make the facts or the legal arguments more understandable, write a short summary.

E.   Practical and Ethical Issues

Contract law presents unique ethical and practical issues for legal professionals. This book includes material on these issues at the end of every chapter. This chapter, however, focused on the legal system and legal research, rather than contract law. The *Massey* case at the end of this chapter provides insight into ethical and practical problems presented by legal research.

The practice of law is regulated on a state-by-state basis, so ethical rules may be slightly different in different states. You can find your state's Rules of Professional Conduct by using the American Bar Association (ABA) Center for Professional Responsibility, http://www.abanet.org/cpr/links.html. The ABA promulgates "Model Rules," which can be found on the site, but has no enforcement authority, so it is important that you become familiar with the rules enforced in your state.

Assignment I-2

Find and print your state's Rules of Professional Conduct, relating to Competence and Candor toward the Tribunal for use with the discussion questions that follow.

Read the case at the end of this chapter and prepare a case brief. The case involves a contract between a lawyer and a client that is ambiguous and not in compliance with ethical rules. It is intended to show the need for good research and show how precedent is used in deciding cases. While most of the cases presented as samples in this book have been heavily edited, this case has only been slightly edited, so that you can see how cases look when you find them online.

1. Read the case twice before you write anything.
2. Make a timeline showing the chronology: the accident, the signing of the contingency agreement, the change in the rules, the bankruptcy filing etc. You will notice that the court does not present the facts in the order in which they occurred, which can be confusing.
3. Consider the following discussion questions:
   a. Because the original contingency fee agreement made no reference to expenses, it appears that the issue would not have come up if the Morans had not filed a bankruptcy petition. Did the trustee attempt to add a new term to the contract existing between the Morans and Coghlan? Why would that happen? Do you think the trustee was sloppy or deceitful? Should the trustee have been sanctioned?
   b. What is your opinion about why the lawyers did not initially disclose the changes?
   c. Although the decision refers to ethical rules, this is not a disciplinary proceeding under those rules. Do you think that the failure of the attorneys to discover or disclose the change in the rules could be a basis for discipline under your state's ethical rules?
   d. Do you think that failure to discover the changes could be considered malpractice if the Coghlan firm had been representing an outside client, rather than itself? Is there any possibility of the Morans suing the

firm for malpractice? Did you notice that the Morans were acting without representation by a lawyer in this proceeding?

e. Do you think the sanction was adequate?

Review Questions

1. Identify the three main sources of contract law.
2. Is contract law primarily state or federal law?
3. Acme Builders realizes it under-priced its contract to build Jilly's Bakery and will lose money if it builds at the contract price. Acme intentionally breaches the contract by refusing to begin construction; this will cause substantial delay in Jilly's opening. Is this a civil or criminal matter?
4. While researching a legal question, you are lucky enough to find an article written by a prominent Harvard professor. The article discusses your precise issue in depth. Is the article primary or secondary authority?
5. When you find a statute that addresses your issue, you still might have to look for case law. Why?
6. Identify three types of connectors that can be used in a terms and connectors search and describe the functions of wildcards and root expanders.
7. Page numbers are not used in referring to a particular part of a statute. Why?
8. The relevant statute describes "DUI" as being in control of a "vehicle" while intoxicated. Your client was arrested for riding a horse while intoxicated. Describe strategies you would use to determine whether the horse should be considered a "vehicle."
9. Your DUI client is also claiming that he was not intoxicated while riding the horse, but was suffering a reaction to a prescription drug. What type of issue does this present, and would legal research be appropriate?

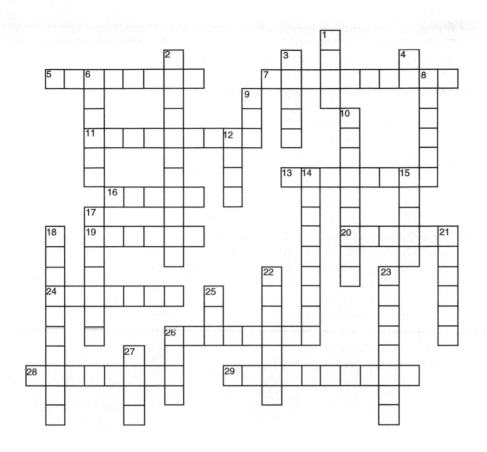

ACROSS

5. * is the root _____

7. _____ history, court decisions that led to case's current position

11. party who lost in lower court

13. another term for decision of the court

16. _____ lawsuit generally results in award of money

19. to send a case back to lower court

20. uphold lower court decision

24. another word for legislation

26. for a statute to have been entered into topical system

28. * is the _____, used to find variations such as woman/women

29. _____ opinion, agrees with decision but may state different reasons

DOWN

1. issues of _____ dealt with in trial court
2. type of law made by agencies
3. _____ court decisions are often not published
4. connector useful for finding synonyms
6. quotation marks are used for _____ searching
8. IRS is an administrative _____
9. % is the _____ connector
10. _____ authority explains or helps locate the law, but is not actually law
12. / is the _____ or proximity connector
14. _____ statute has references to cases, articles, etc.
15. statutes are organized by _____
17. _____ law comes from one of five sources
18. _____ opinion, by a judge who disagrees
21. change a decision
22. Loislaw automatically retrieves most _____ forms
23. _____ prosecution can result in prison sentence
25. connector that will find terms in case regardless of proximity
26. another word for legislation
27. initials, Loislaw is this type of research

In re: TODD B. MORAN and MARY MORAN, Debtors.
No. 96 B 06133, Chapter 7

The court's internal docket number.

UNITED STATES BANKRUPTCY COURT FOR THE NORTHERN DISTRICT OF ILLINOIS, EASTERN DIVISION

231 B.R. 290
December 1, 1998, Filed

The citation: the case is found in volume 231 of the Bankruptcy Reporter on page 290.

Attorney for Movant: Andrew J. Maxwell, Trustee. Attorney for Respondent: Moran, Pro Se.

SUSAN PIERSON SONDERBY, United States Bankruptcy Judge.
[*291]

Note the inclusion of reporter page numbers for jump cites

This matter came before the Court on the Trustee's Application to Approve Compromise of Lawsuit, for Authorization for Pay Special Counsel, for Authorization to Make Interim Distribution to Debtor and for Other Relief. A hearing was held and an order was entered by this Court approving the subject settlement. Left for resolution was the issue of whether costs expended in the debtors' personal injury lawsuit are to be paid out of the attorneys' share of the settlement proceeds, out of the gross settlement prior to paying the attorneys' contingency fee or are to be paid directly out of the debtors' share of the settlement. n1

This case commenced by Moran's filing a petition in 1996 for relief under the Bankruptcy Code. A trustee was appointed and qualified. The first meeting of creditors was held.

The above paragraph is procedural history. The U.S. District Court is a trial court.

[*292] Trustee identified as an asset of the estate the debtors' interest in a lawsuit pending in the Cook County for damages from personal injuries, encaptioned Moran v. Illinois Sports Facilities Authority, Near North Insurance Agency, Inc., Chicago White Sox (the "Lawsuit").

The Lawsuit arose from an accident. Mr. Moran suffered a serious injury in 1991. Moran hired James A. Coghlan Ltd. ("Coghlan") to represent him. The Trustee applied to this Court in 1996 to employ Coghlan as special counsel to liquidate the Morans' rights in the Lawsuit.

Keep a dictionary close! Did you look up creditor, trustee, pro se, or liquidate? In this part of the opinion, the court is stating facts.

The order authorizing Coghlan's retention states in pertinent part as follows:

> Compensation for special counsel is approved pursuant to terms set forth in contingent fee agreement between Debtor and special counsel, a copy of which is made part of the Declaration attached to the Application. In addition to fees, special counsel shall be entitled to reimbursement for costs, to the extent there is recovery from the lawsuit. Payment of compensation and expenses to Trustee's special counsel shall be subject to further application and approval of this Court.

The contingent fee agreement makes no mention of the payment of expenses. Neither Mr. Coghlan's declaration submitted with the Trustee's application nor the application itself mentions expenses. Mr. Moran testified that the issue of expenses did not come up at the signing. Mrs. Moran testified that the issue of expenses was not mentioned until the first settlement offer was made in 1998.

In 1998 the Lawsuit settled subject to Court approval. The Trustee is to receive $540,000 in proceeds. Out of that money, Trustee requested permission to pay $150,000 to Liberty Mutual Insurance in satisfaction of its worker's compensation lien, $179,982 to Coghlan in satisfaction of attorneys' fees — 33% of the gross settlement and $11,969.31 to Coghlan in costs expended. The balance to pay claims scheduled in the bankruptcy case and the surplus to the debtors.

The Trustee put on his case for settlement. The Morans, not represented, had the opportunity to question witnesses and to make sworn statements. The Morans expressed deep disappointment with the settlement. They explained that the attorneys told them that the case was worth $3.2 million. Morans' testimony regarding what they were told about the reimbursement of expenses was unclear. The Court surmises that expenses were not a significant issue at the time that they were anticipating a multi-million dollar recovery.

An associate of Coghlan testified about problems with the case, including changes in law that worked to the Morans' detriment. He testified that the Court's release of certain defendants seriously and adversely affected the case and that his firm vigorously but unsuccessfully prosecuted an appeal. The Morans reluctantly agreed to the settlement. However, they argued that the expenses of the litigation [*293] should not be borne by them and the Court took the issue under advisement.

Here the court begins reasoning & cites authority in support of its decision.

Coghlan argues that Illinois law prevents an attorney from assuming ultimate responsibility for costs and expenses of litigation. It cites *Partee v. Compton, 273 Ill. App. 3d 721, 653 N.E.2d 454 (5th Dist. 1995)* and *Schlosser v. Jursich, 87 Ill. App. 3d 824, 410 N.E.2d 257 (2nd Dist. 1980)*. In *Schlosser,* the Court considered whether an attorney can be ordered to pay costs in a personal injury suit when the fee contract made no provision for the payment of expenses. The Court opined that "it has long been the rule in Illinois that a contingency fee contract requiring the attorney to assume ultimate responsibility for costs and expenses of litigation is champertous and void as against public policy. This view has been reiterated in the [then] newly adopted Code of Professional Responsibility (Supreme Court Rule 5-103(b)) . . ." *Id. at 825-826, 410 N.E.2d at 258.*

The Rule on which the Schlosser Court relied provided as follows:

(b) While representing a client in . . . litigation, a lawyer shall not advance or guarantee financial assistance . . . except that a lawyer may advance or guarantee expenses of litigation, including court costs, expenses of investigation, expenses of medical examination, and costs of obtaining and presenting evidence, provided the client remains ultimately liable for such expenses. Code of Professional Responsibility, Canon 5, Rule 5-103(b)(effective 1980).

Partee, also cited by Coghlan, is inapposite to this case. The fee agreement at issue contained no language regarding expenses. The clients argued that the agreement was void because it did not comply with the Code and that the attorney was not entitled to his fee. The Court refused to allow the clients to reap the benefits of a contract and then render it void. There has been no such argument in this case and the Morans have not raised the issue of not paying Coghlan at all. The Partee Court relied on the 1980 version of the Code even though it is a 1995 opinion because the agreement in that case was executed when the Code was still in effect.

In 1990 the Code was repealed and current Rules of Professional Responsibility ("RPC") became effective, before the agreement in this case was executed. The RPC provides:

> (d) While representing a client in connection with contemplated or pending litigation, a lawyer shall not advance or guarantee financial assistance to the client, except that a lawyer may advance or guarantee the expenses of litigation, including, but not limited to, court costs, expenses of investigation, expenses of medical examination, and costs of obtaining and presenting evidence, if:
>
> (1) the client remains ultimately liable for such expenses; or
> (2) the repayment is contingent on the outcome of the matter; or
> (3) the client is indigent.

Coghlan never brought this to the Court's attention nor did it mention that cases it relied upon were predicated on a repealed version of the Code. The amendment adds conditions under which an attorney can pay costs. The repayment may be contingent on outcome of the case or the client may be excused from repayment if indigent. Clearly this evidences a shift in the [*294] Supreme Court's view. This Court's review of the case law in this area did not uncover any precise authority under the new RPC.

What the Court did find was Rule 1.5 of the RPC which provides in pertinent part as follows:

> (c) A fee may be contingent on the outcome of the matter for which the service is rendered . . . A contingent fee agreement shall be in writing and shall state the method by which the fee is to be determined, . . . litigation and other expenses to be deducted from the recovery, and whether such expenses are to be deducted before or after the contingent fee is calculated. . . . Illinois Rules of Professional Conduct, Art. VIII, Rule 1.5(c).

This Court cannot rely on the conclusion of the Schlosser Court insofar as it predicated its ruling on the repealed Code. Nonetheless, the Court was correct that "the relationship between attorney and client is a fiduciary one requiring good faith, fairness and full disclosure. . . . attorneys are under a particularly sensitive obligation to explain carefully and completely the allocation of expenses associated with legal representation." *Schlosser, 87 Ill. App. 3d at 826.*

This was not done in this case. The fee agreement in this case was on a form prepared by Coghlan and contains no provision regarding payment of expenses. The Morans testified that the issue of expenses was not raised until early this year. The fee agreement violated the RPC. The order retaining Coghlan was prepared by the Trustee. It provides for repayment of expenses but contradicts the fee agreement and the application itself. While the Court was impressed with the lengths to which Coghlan went to obtain a good result, failure to comply with the RPC is a serious breach of its ethical obligations.

Furthermore, Coghlan failed to comply with Rule 3.3(a)(3) of the RPC which provides that "in appearing . . . before a tribunal, a lawyer shall not: . . . fail to disclose . . . legal authority in the controlling jurisdiction known to the lawyer to be directly adverse to the position of the client and not disclosed by opposing counsel; . . ." Coghlan never brought to this Court's attention the fact that the cases it relied upon were predicated on a repealed version of the Code.

The Court grants the application to pay James A. Coghlan, Ltd. $179,982 in fees and to pay Moran $100,000 as an interim distribution of surplus proceeds. Coghlan is sanctioned in the amount of the expenses of $11,969.31. In satisfaction of the sanction, the application is denied [*295] to reimburse to James A. Coghlan, Ltd. the sum of $11,969.31.

1

◆ ◆ ◆

What Is Contract Law?

◆ ◆ ◆

This chapter explores the types of contract recognized by law: express, implied, unilateral, bilateral, formal, informal, enforceable, unenforceable, void, and voidable. The role of paralegals in contract law is introduced, along with some of the ethical problems unique to contract law. Students will learn to recognize situations that are similar to contracts, but are treated differently: gifts, promissory estoppel, and quasi-contract.

Two cases and an ethical opinion concerning issues discussed in this chapter are reproduced at the end of the chapter. The first of the sample cases includes an explanation of how the case was found, using computer-assisted legal research (CALR) techniques, and a sample brief of the case. Students who are not yet confident in their ability to find, read, and summarize cases may want to review the sample before attempting the assignments in this unit.

Introduction
A. What Is a Contract?
  1. Types of Contract: Express or Implied
  2. Types of Contract: Unilateral or Bilateral
  3. Other Classifications of Contracts
B. Alternatives to Contracts
  1. Gifts
  2. Promissory Estoppel
  3. Quasi-Contract
C. Practical and Ethical Issues

Introduction

What is contract law? The short answer is that all of law is related to contract law. That is why almost all law schools require that first-year students take a course in contract law. **Contracts** are, themselves, the subject of much litigation; contracts can be used to resolve matters involving crimes (plea agreements), property, **torts** (injuries to people or property), estates and inheritance, divorce and parenting, and businesses. Is it "dry" or boring? Only if psychology is boring; a real grasp of contract law requires a solid understanding of motives, patterns of behavior, communication, negotiation and the balance of power among parties, and probabilities.

Contract
Set of legally enforceable promises

Torts
Law applicable to injuries to people or property

Example

Understanding motivation is the key to understanding contract law. Consider: Client is entering a contract with Builder for construction of an office building and wonders how to set the price. A flat price for materials and labor would give Client peace of mind, knowing what the ultimate price will be. Client has limited funds available and wants certainty. But, will Builder be tempted to use the cheapest (perhaps low-quality) materials to maximize profit? Builder is also concerned about the bottom line. If the price of materials goes up as it did, for example, after Hurricane Katrina, he may be working for almost nothing. If the contract is structured so that Client will pay the cost of materials plus XX%, might Builder be motivated to use the most expensive materials? If Client wants to pay the cost of materials plus a set amount for labor, Client is assuming all of the risk with respect to the cost of materials. If Client decides to acquire materials independently, will the price be as good as the price Builder could negotiate? What is the value of Client's time? Can you think of a solution?

Every lawyer must have a good understanding of contract law, and paralegals need to understand the theory and much more. Paralegals play important roles in negotiating, drafting, and implementing contracts and, when a contract is litigated, are often called upon to conduct factual and legal research and assist with trial preparation. To be an effective paralegal, you need to understand contract theory, be familiar with the vocabulary, be able to identify and research legal issues, and have the practical skills for drafting and implementing contracts.

The most important thing you can learn is to work independently. You could try to memorize every word in this book, including every reference to a case or statute, but that would not be of much benefit in the workplace. Many fact situations you encounter on the job will not have been addressed in this book; your state may have unusual contract precedents, or your local courts may have practices not addressed in this book. Most importantly, the law will continue to evolve after this book is finished. This book will give you the language and skills you will need to handle those issues. It's a do-it-yourself approach that should help you retain what you learn well past the final exam. You will be instructed to use the Internet and CALR to research certain issues and find your own answers.

EXHIBIT 1-1
Is this important? Only if you want a career in law: examine the following and note the references to working with contracts, conducting research, and using computers.

U.S. Department of Labor
Bureau of Labor Statistics
Occupational Outlook Handbook

Paralegals and Legal Assistants

◆ Nature of the Work
◆ Working Conditions
◆ Training, Other Qualifications, and Advancement
◆ Employment
◆ Job Outlook
◆ Earnings
◆ Related Occupations
◆ Sources of Additional Information

SIGNIFICANT POINTS

About 7 out of 10 work for law firms; others work for corporate legal departments and government agencies.

Most entrants have an associate's degree in paralegal studies, or a bachelor's degree coupled with a certificate in paralegal studies.

Employment is projected to grow much faster than average, as employers try to reduce costs by hiring paralegals to perform tasks formerly carried out by lawyers.

Competition for jobs should continue; experienced, formally trained paralegals should have the best employment opportunities.

NATURE OF THE WORK

While lawyers assume ultimate responsibility for legal work, they often delegate many of their tasks to paralegals. In fact, paralegals—also called legal assistants—are continuing to assume a growing range of tasks in legal offices and perform many of the same tasks as lawyers. Nevertheless, they are explicitly prohibited from carrying out duties that are considered to be the practice of law, such as setting legal fees, giving legal advice, and presenting cases in court.

One of a paralegal's most important tasks is helping lawyers prepare for closings, hearings, trials, and corporate meetings. Paralegals investigate the facts of cases and ensure that all relevant information is considered. They also identify

EXHIBIT 1-1
(continued)

appropriate laws, judicial decisions, legal articles, and other materials that are relevant to assigned cases. After they analyze and organize the information, paralegals may prepare written reports that attorneys use in determining how cases should be handled. Should attorneys decide to file lawsuits on behalf of clients, paralegals may help prepare the legal arguments, draft pleadings and motions to be filed with the court, obtain affidavits, and assist attorneys during trials. Paralegals also organize and track files of all important case documents and make them available and easily accessible to attorneys.

In addition to this preparatory work, paralegals perform a number of other vital functions. For example, they help **draft contracts**, mortgages, separation agreements, and instruments of trust. They also may assist in preparing tax returns and planning estates. Some paralegals coordinate the activities of other law office employees and maintain financial office records. Various additional tasks may differ, depending on the employer.

Paralegals are found in all types of organizations, but most are employed by law firms, corporate legal departments, and various government offices. In these organizations, they can work in many different areas of the law, including litigation, personal injury, corporate law, criminal law, employee benefits, intellectual property, labor law, bankruptcy, immigration, family law, and real estate. As the law has become more complex, paralegals have responded by becoming more specialized. Within specialties, functions often are broken down further so that paralegals may deal with a specific area. For example, paralegals specializing in labor law may concentrate exclusively on employee benefits.

The duties of paralegals also differ widely with the type of organization in which they are employed. Paralegals who work for corporations often assist attorneys with **employee contracts**, shareholder agreements, stock-option plans, and employee benefit plans. They also may help prepare and file annual financial reports, maintain corporate minutes, record resolutions, and prepare forms to secure loans for the corporation. Paralegals often monitor and review government regulations to ensure that the corporation is aware of new requirements and is operating within the law. Increasingly, experienced paralegals are assuming additional supervisory responsibilities such as overseeing team projects and serving as a communications link between the team and the corporation.

The duties of paralegals in the public sector usually vary within each agency. In general, paralegals analyze legal material for internal use, maintain reference files, conduct research for attorneys, and collect and analyze evidence for agency hearings. They may prepare informative or explanatory material on laws, agency regulations, and agency policy for general use by the agency and the public. Paralegals employed in community legal-service projects help the poor, the aged, and others in need of legal assistance. They file forms, conduct research, prepare

EXHIBIT 1-1 **(continued)**	

documents, and, when authorized by law, may represent clients at administrative hearings.

Paralegals in small and medium-size law firms usually perform a variety of duties that require a general knowledge of the law. They may research judicial decisions on improper police arrests or help prepare a mortgage contract. Paralegals employed by large law firms, government agencies, and corporations, however, are more likely to specialize in one aspect of the law.

Familiarity with computers use and technical knowledge have become essential to paralegal work. Computer software packages and the Internet are used to search legal literature stored in computer databases and on CD-ROM. In litigation involving many supporting documents, paralegals usually use computer databases to retrieve, organize, and index various materials. Imaging software allows paralegals to scan documents directly into a database, while billing programs help them to track hours billed to clients. Computer software packages also are used to perform tax computations and explore the consequences of various tax strategies for clients.

Bureau of Labor Statistics, U.S. Department of Labor, *Occupational Outlook Handbook, 2006-07 Edition*, Paralegals and Legal Assistants, on the Internet at http://www.bls.gov/oco/ocos114. htm (visited May 15, 2007).

Dealing with a contract in any context involves: determining whether a contract has formed or will form; knowing how to interpret and implement the agreement; and determining the consequences when something goes wrong. This book is organized according to those concerns. The first chapters deal with the elements of formation; the middle concerns implementation and interpretation; and the final chapters concern rights and remedies

A. What Is a Contract?

When you think of a "contract," do you picture the five pages of mind-numbing, tiny print you signed when you took a car loan? Do you picture yourself going through the cafeteria at work or school with a cup of coffee and toast on your tray, saying nothing, but handing the cashier a five-dollar bill? You should picture both. *A contract is a set of legally enforceable promises, entered into by two or more parties, to make their dealings predictable and to allocate risk.* The law of contracts will make more sense to you if you remember that people enter into contracts to keep their dealings predictable. Very few people could enter into any relationship, whether buying toast and coffee or building a mansion, without having some way to predict the outcome.

Not all promises are contracts. To be enforceable, a contract must meet certain requirements: **agreement** (also called **manifestation of mutual assent), consideration, capacity,** and **legality**. Those requirements are discussed in depth in later chapters. A promise that is not a contract might be enforceable under another theory such as completed gift, quasi-contract, or promissory estoppel; these theories are explained later in this chapter.

1. Types of Contract: Express or Implied

Contracts can be classified in many ways. An **express** contract has its important terms explicitly stated, either orally or in writing. The enforceability of oral contracts is discussed later. A contract can also be **implied** from the words and actions of the parties, even if they never expressed an agreement.

Example

Contract law does not favor the "gotcha" approach to doing business and includes a theory for most situations. Terry, a certified public accountant, has prepared Lee's tax returns every March for the last six years. This year, Terry came back from lunch on March 2 and found an envelope, containing all of Lee's receipts and tax forms, under the office door. Terry completed Lee's returns and mailed them, along with a bill, to Lee. Can Lee refuse to pay on the grounds that they never entered into an agreement this year? Probably not; there was an implied contract.

---

2. Types of Contract: Unilateral or Bilateral

Most contracts are **bilateral**, meaning that both parties made *promises*. It may be that nothing has been done yet; it may be some time before anything is done, but a contract has formed. Sam orally promises to paint Taylor's building next month; Taylor agrees to pay $3,000, but neither has taken any action beyond making promises. A binding contract exists between them. It is an **executory** contract because there are obligations that have not yet been fulfilled. When Sam paints the building and Taylor pays Sam, it will be a fully **executed** contract.

Agreement
"Meeting of the minds"

Manifestation of Mutual Assent
Appearance that an agreement has been reached

Consideration
The give and take that distinguishes a contract from a gift

Capacity
Ability, as determined by age and mental competence, to enter into a contract

Legality
An element of an enforceable contract

Express
Contract with significant terms stated orally or in writing

Implied
Contract formed without express statement of terms, by words and actions

Bilateral
Contract in which both parties make promises

Executory
Contract in which obligations have not been fulfilled

Executed
Contract in which all obligations have been fulfilled

A **unilateral** contract does not form until one party *acts* in response to the other's promise. A typical example is an offer of a reward. I may offer $100 for the return of my missing cat, but there is no point in your promising me that you will find the cat. The contract forms when you find the cat.

Unilateral
Contract formed when one party acts in response to other party's promise

---

Examples

Why does this distinction matter? Sometimes it is essential to know exactly when a contract forms.
   Bilateral Contract: Sam orally promised to paint Taylor's building next month; Taylor agreed to pay $3,000. Two days later Taylor decided to cancel; it would be more economical to install vinyl siding. Taylor is in breach of contract and Sam may sue for damages.
   Unilateral: On the other hand, assume that Taylor said: "You know that old garage behind my house on Main Street? It needs painting, but I don't want to get involved in any big contract deal. If you have any time next month, get over there and paint it. I've got all the paint and stuff in the basement. When you finish I'll pay you $3,000." Sam just smiled and nodded, but planned to do the job. Two days later, Taylor called Sam and revoked the offer. Taylor has not breached a contract, because no contract had formed. A unilateral contract forms when there is an act in response to a promise and Sam had not yet acted.

Assignment 1-1

In Exhibit 1-2 you will find samples of a "Consignment Contract" and an "Option Contract." Don't worry too much about the component parts of the contract, some of which are labeled. Those are discussed thoroughly in a later chapter. Read the contracts and determine the following:

1. Is the Option Contract a unilateral or bilateral contract?
2. Is anything obvious missing from the Consignment agreement?
3. Robin's jewelry may be very ugly and overpriced; Betty may be unable to sell a single piece. If she never sells a piece, she never has to pay Robin anything. Does that mean that this is a unilateral contract, which will be accepted only when Merchandise is sold?

EXHIBIT 1-2

OPTION CONTRACT

OPTION AGREEMENT by and between Jan West ("Owner") and Rene Miller ("Buyer").

Identification and defined terms

Buyer hereby pays to the Owner the sum of $10.00 in consideration for this option, which option payment shall be credited to the purchase price if the option is exercised.

Buyer has the option and right to buy the vacant and undeveloped property commonly known as 140 S. Wood Road, more fully described on the survey attached to and made part of this Agreement, within the option period for the full price of $70,000 (Seventy Thousand Dollars).

This option shall remain in effect until August 31, 2007, and thereupon expire unless this option is sooner exercised. To exercise this option, Buyer must notify Owner of same by certified mail within the option period. All notices shall be sent to the owner at 325 River Ave., Dundee, IN.

Time is of the essence in this agreement. Should the Buyer exercise the option, the Owner and the Buyer agree to promptly execute any and all documents necessary to consummate the sale on these terms.

The Buyer may extend this agreement, for a period of six months, by sending certified funds in the amount of $100.00, by certified mail, to the Owner at the aforementioned address, within the option period.

This option agreement shall be binding upon and inure to the benefit of the parties, their successors, assigns, and personal representatives. Signed this _____ day of May, 2007.

Owner _____   Buyer _____

CONSIGNMENT CONTRACT

Agreement between Elizabeth Jones, owner of Betty's Boutique, "Consignee" and Robin Smith, "Consignor," made August 2, 2007.

WHEREAS:

Consignee and Consignor are defined terms

Consignor designs and creates unique jewelry pieces "the Merchandise" and wishes to sell the Merchandise to the public, and

This section is called Recitals

Consignee is the owner of a boutique store at 123 High Street, Geneva, "the Boutique" and wishes to be the exclusive area seller of the Merchandise,

Consignor and Consignee agree as follows:

1. **OBLIGATIONS OF CONSIGNOR**

a. Consignor shall deliver to the Boutique, on the first Monday morning of each calendar month, a quantity of Merchandise so that the total marked prices of

---

EXHIBIT 1-2
(continued)

---

all Consignor's Merchandise on display at the Boutique shall be in the range of $1,000 to $1,200 at all times.

b. Consignor shall attach to each piece of Merchandise a tag on which Consignor has marked the price at which the piece may be sold.

2. OBLIGATIONS OF CONSIGNEE

a. Consignee shall at all times display all Merchandise in Consignee's possession in the glass display counter on which the cash register is located.

b. Consignee may display and sell other jewelry, but may not display other jewelry in the same display case as the Merchandise.

c. Whenever Consignee engages in print advertising, such advertising shall contain the statement, "Exclusive Kane County seller of Robin's Eggs jewelry."

d. Consignee shall use best efforts to sell the Merchandise at the marked price and shall not discount the Merchandise. Consignee shall display a sign and enforce a policy that no returns of the Merchandise will be allowed unless the Merchandise is defective. Any Merchandise returned as defective shall be returned to Consignor at the time of the next delivery of Merchandise and shall not be included in the accounting described below. Consignee may sell the Merchandise for cash, check, or credit, but Consignor shall not be responsible for any costs associated with selling on credit or any losses due to fraudulent use of credit or checks.

e. Consignee shall, on the first Monday of each calendar month, prepare an accounting of Merchandise sold during the previous calendar month, and deliver that account statement to Consignor along with a check representing sixty percent (60%) of the total amount paid for Merchandise (exclusive of sales tax) during the previous month.

3. RELATIONSHIP

a. Neither party is an employee of the other; neither has any interest in the business operation of the other except as described in this agreement. Consignee is Consignor's agent solely for the purpose of selling Merchandise.

b. Consignor shall retain title to Merchandise until sold to a customer and shall insure against loss by theft or casualty.

c. This agreement may not be assigned.

d. Consignor shall not sell or allow sale of Merchandise in King County except at Boutique.

_____   _____

_____   _____

Signatures   Date

Formal
A contract required to be in a particular form

Informal
Contract for which no particular form is required

3. Other Classifications of Contracts

Some contracts must be in a particular form, for example, a **letter of credit**. These are **formal** contracts. All contracts for which no particular form is mandatory are **informal**.

EXHIBIT 1-3

Letter of Credit
An irrevocable promise by a buyer's bank to pay the seller when conditions are met

A **letter of credit** is an irrevocable promise by a buyer's bank to pay the seller (generally through the seller's bank) when certain conditions are met. Letters of credit are used, almost exclusively, in international business, to manage unique risks, such as unexpected governmental interference or control of export/import, as well as problems stemming from buyers and sellers dealing in different currencies. The formalities for a letter of credit are generally dictated by the Uniform Customs and Practices for Documentary Credits established by the International Chamber of Commerce (for more information, visit http://www.iccwbo.org/policy/banking/iccffjj/index.html).

Here is how it works. Suppose that Big Box imports computers manufactured by Shanghai Sal (Sal). Sal banks with the Beijing Business Bank (BBB). Big Box banks at Elgin Federal (EF) in Texas and wants to buy $800,000 worth of computers from Sal. Understandably, Big Box does not want to pay in advance. Sal is willing to ship the computers and give Big Box 60 days to pay if Big Box provides a 90-day letter of credit for the full amount.

1. Big Box goes to EF and requests an $800,000 letter of credit with Sal as beneficiary.
2. EF will issue the letter after Big Box either deposits $800,000 plus fees or is approved for a loan in that amount.
3. EF sends the letter to BBB, which notifies Sal that payment is ready.
4. Sal can ship the computers to Big Box with full assurance of payment.
5. On presentation of documents and compliance with terms listed in the letter EF must transfer the $800,000 to BBB, which credits Sal's account. If the documents are presented and the terms of the letter are met, the issuing bank is obligated to pay, even if the underlying transaction is not fulfilled (*i.e., the computers are never actually received or are defective*). The bank is not required to pay if the documents are not presented or the terms are not met, even if the underlying transaction was fulfilled.

Bill of Lading
Documentation of the receipt of goods for shipment, issued by a party in the business of transporting goods

The documents and conditions normally include a **bill of lading**, which is documentation of the receipt of goods for shipment, issued by a party in the business of transporting goods; proof of insurance; a certificate showing clearance by customs officials; and a commercial invoice.

EXHIBIT 1-3
(continued)

TO SEE A SAMPLE LETTER OF CREDIT:
http://contracts.onecle.com/interwoven/wellsfargo.credit.2004.06.01.shtml

TO SEE A SAMPLE BILL OF LADING:
http://www.unzco.com/basicguide/figure3.html

An agreement that has no legal effect is referred to as **void**. If a person enters into a contract to perform an illegal act, for example, the contract is void. Neither party can enforce the contract. On the other hand, a contract's enforceability may be in the hands of one of the parties. For example, if an adult and a minor enter into a contract, that contract is **voidable** at the option of the minor. If the minor does not void the contract, it remains in force.

    Finally, a contract might be valid, but **unenforceable**. For example, an otherwise valid contract might be unenforceable because the **limitations period** (time limit on bringing a lawsuit) has passed.

Void
An agreement with no legal effect

Voidable
One party has power to invalidate contract

Unenforceable
A contract, otherwise valid, that cannot be enforced in court

Limitations Period
Time limit on bringing lawsuit, based on statute of limitations

---

Assignment 1-2

Describe a situation other than an offer of a reward that fits the definition of unilateral contract. Describe a situation, other than the example given in this chapter, that fits the definition of an implied contract. You may find it difficult to identify examples, yet you enter into such contracts regularly. It is important that you start to recognize these situations. Use CALR to find a case, decided in your state, involving an "implied contract" and a case involving a "unilateral contract" (your instructor will assign your topic). Describe the cases to your class in a few sentences.

B. Alternatives to Contract

Sometimes people develop expectations based on facts that do not establish an enforceable contract. When those expectations are not met, they may try to obtain a remedy in court based on another theory.

1. Gifts

Gift
Completed transfer of property without consideration

As described in a later chapter, a contract requires consideration (in very simple terms, mutual give-and-take). When consideration is lacking, the situation may be a gift. A gift becomes irrevocable when:

Donor
Person making a gift

Donee
Person receiving a gift

- a **donor** (person making the gift), with capacity (adult, sound mind, etc.)
- has voluntarily made a transfer
- that has been accepted by the **donee** (person receiving the gift).

A promise to make a gift is not a gift until transfer and acceptance are completed; if it is not supported by consideration, it is not a contract either. The only possibility for enforcement of an incomplete gift is promissory estoppel, discussed below.

Example

When looking at the elements of a legal claim, consider it an "all or nothing" proposition. When Lou finished his sophomore year at State U with a 4.0 grade point average, Dad was so pleased that he gave Lou a new notebook computer. During his junior year, Lou's grades took a slide. Dad now says that he has the right to reclaim the computer. He is likely wrong—the computer was a completed gift—all of the elements were satisfied. If, on the other hand, Dad had promised a computer and never delivered, Lou is out of luck.

---

2. Promissory Estoppel

Alternate Example

At the end of sophomore year Lou told Dad that going to school on a shoestring budget was just too hard. Lou planned to take a year off to save money for "necessities" like a computer. Concerned that Lou would never return to school, Dad wrote a note, promising to give Lou a computer if Lou enrolled in and started classes for junior year. Lou took classes, rather than work, in reliance on Dad's promise, but after the start of the semester, Dad died. Dad's will leaves everything to Lou's stepmother. Lou may be able to make a successful claim against the estate.

Promissory estoppel is a legal theory for enforcing a promise if:

- The defendant knew the plaintiff would rely on the promise;
- The plaintiff did rely on the promise; and
- Enforcement is necessary to avoid injustice.

In promissory estoppel cases, no contract ever formed because there was no consideration; the defendant's promise was essentially an incomplete gift. The difference between promissory estoppel and an incomplete gift is reliance on the promise.

Promissory Estoppel
Theory under which a promise can be enforced, despite lack of consideration, because of reliance on that promise and knowledge of that reliance

---

Assignment 1-3

Medical Office called Insurance Co. to determine whether Pat Patient had insurance to cover removal of a cyst. A new clerk mistakenly stated that Pat had coverage; in fact, Pat's coverage had expired. Medical performed the procedure and billed Insurance for $900. Insurance is refusing to pay and Pat, unemployed for several months, cannot pay. There is no contractual relationship between Medical and Insurance. Medical has not given Insurance any benefit, payment, or other consideration, that would obligate Insurance to pay Pat's bill, but only acted in reliance.

1.   In the previous example, Lou's dad "put it in writing." Does it make any difference that the "promise" in this situation was oral rather than written? Would you have a different opinion of the situation if Insurance had faxed its response? If you are like most people, you may feel, instinctively, that written promises should be enforceable simply because they are written and that oral promises are not enforceable simply because they were not written. Stop thinking like that! The **statute of frauds** (discussed later) dictates whether a contract must be in writing. Many oral agreements (including dad's promise, had it been oral, and Insurance Company's promise) are enforceable, but people are (rightfully) concerned with how to prove that the promise was made.

Statute of Frauds
Dictates types of contracts that must be written

2.   On the subject of getting past emotional triggers: would your reaction to the examples change if Lou were suing his still-living father or if the Medical Office scenario involved a charity rather than an insurance company? Because estoppel is an **equitable** theory, based on fairness and individual circumstances rather than strict application of legal elements, the parties may matter.

Equitable
Based on fairness and individual circumstances

3.   There is no question that the "contract" in this situation is between Pat and Medical Office. Should Insurance be "punished" for Pat's inability to pay, coupled with its employee's mistake?

4.   Courts have good reason to protect the definition of a contract and avoid applying the estoppel doctrine freely. Suppose Dad always told Jill that he would pay her college tuition. In reliance, Jill worked only occasionally while in high school and spent all earnings on entertainment.

Dad, having been laid off, now tells Jill that she will have to find a way to pay her own tuition. Do you think a court would enforce the promise?

5. Now, check your theories. Use CALR to find a case from a court in your state, in which the court either accepted or rejected a claim of estoppel. Write a summary (**case brief**) to share with the class, focusing on how the court described the "fairness" aspect of the situation. Pay particular attention to the identities of the parties and their relationship, who was at "fault," and any "bad behavior." You can find a sample case brief at the end of the chapter.

Case Brief
Short summary of facts, issues, holding, and reasoning of a judicial decision

3. Quasi-Contract

Example

Quasi-contract is another theory for avoiding the "gotcha" approach. An infestation of pine moth has left many dead trees in the neighborhood. Pat, who lives at 123 N. Diane Lane, was told by Trees-R-Us that it would cost $800 to remove a dead tree and decided not to have it done. Chris, who lives at 123 S. Diane Lane, entered into a contract with Trees-R-Us for removal of a dead tree at a cost of $600 (smaller tree). Both Pat and Chris have "123" on their mailboxes and no other identification. One morning, Pat woke to the sound of saws in the yard, looked out, and saw Trees-R-Us employees taking down the dead tree. Thrilled at the $800 "gift," Pat called in sick and stayed in bed until the workers finished. When the company tries to bill Pat, what result?

Quasi-Contract
Theory for avoiding unjust enrichment in situations in which a contract did not actually form

Quasi-contract is a legal theory, based in equity, for compensating a plaintiff if:

- Plaintiff gave some benefit to the defendant;
- Plaintiff expected to be paid;
- Defendant had knowledge of plaintiff's actions and expectations; and
- Defendant would be unjustly enriched if not required to pay.

In the Trees-R-Us situation a contract can be **implied from the facts**. In other situations, a contract might be **implied by law**.

Example

What if defendant's conduct reveals nothing about defendant's knowledge? In some cases the law will create a contract to prevent injustice. Pat falls to the floor, unconscious, while grocery shopping. The store manager calls 911 and Pat is taken to a hospital. When Pat wakes up, the doctors discover that Pat has been on a starvation diet and had not eaten in almost 24 hours. Pat does not have insurance and does not want to pay the $800 bill for emergency room treatment. Pat would never have agreed to be taken to the hospital or treated had he been conscious, and there is no evidence of behavior on Pat's part from which agreement can be implied.[1]

---

[1] See *Cotman v. Wisdom*, 104 S.W. 164 (Ark. 1907).

Discussion Questions/Assignment 1-4

◆ Should Trees-R-Us receive $600 or $800? Would some other amount, to compensate for the hourly cost of the workers and equipment, be fair?
◆ Would it make a difference if Pat's mailbox clearly stated "123 North," along with Pat's last name?
◆ How can Trees-R-Us establish that Pat knew of the benefit being conferred?
◆ Should the result change if Pat had been at work when the tree was removed?

Test your theories:
Use CALR to find a case, from your state, that contains the term "quasi contract" or "unjust enrichment" or "quantum meruit." Write a short summary to share with the class. Focus on how the court determined correct compensation and how the knowledge element was established. The *Cruz* case, at the end of this chapter, is a quasi contract case. Instructions on how the case was found and a sample case brief are also included.

C. Practical and Ethical Issues

You've just studied two equitable concepts, estoppel and quasi-contract, developed from concepts of "fairness," but working in our legal system is not based in fairness. Our system is an adversarial system; the parties to a legal dispute are not neutral and are not seeking the "fairest" result. A lawyer's obligation, as an advocate, is to zealously assert the client's interests within the bounds of the law. But, in a contract situation, too much advocacy may be contrary to the client's interests. It is generally in the client's best interest that a contract be performed as agreed; arriving at an agreement that is too favorable to one side may motivate the other side to not honor its obligations.

Another ethical issue in contract law, relating to advocacy, is **conflict of interest**. A lawyer cannot be a zealous advocate if the lawyer has conflicting interests. Conflicts are discussed in ABA Model Rules 1.7-1.11. Using your state's online ethical rules, find and print rules relating to conflicts of interests with current clients, conflicts of interests with past clients, and imputed conflicts of interest.

A lawyer who is uncertain about the application of an ethics rule to a particular situation may seek an opinion from a bar association. The ABA website that provided a link to your state's Rules of Professional Conduct also contains links to state ethical opinions. A sample opinion concerning contract law and a sample case concerning a conflict of interests are reproduced at the end of this chapter. Read the Colorado Bar Association opinion and the *Spear* case and

Conflict of Interest
Ethical issue: legal professional's loyalties divided

identify the two types of situations that most commonly result in a conflict in a contract matter.

Assignment 1-5

Identify the rule of professional conduct that would apply to each of the following situations and discuss potential problems and possible solutions:

◆ John wants to buy land from his Aunt Lill, in order to build a house. They have agreed to all of the terms and do not want to pay two lawyers. Frank Fuller has been the "family lawyer" for many years and has handled matters for Lill when her parents died (she inherited the land she is now selling to John) and for John when he was involved in an auto accident. John and Lill ask Fuller to prepare all of the documents needed to complete the transaction.

◆ If Fuller is not willing to act as attorney for both John and Lill, can he act on behalf of one of them? Would it make a difference whether he represents John or Lill?

◆ Would Fuller be able to represent John if John were buying the land from a church that Fuller attends?

◆ Fuller has a partner in his law firm, Gail Grady. Could Gail represent either the church or Lill if Fuller were representing John? Could Gail represent John if Fuller were representing the church or Lill?

Read the cases and ethical opinion at the end of this chapter and discuss the following:

◆ Would the result in *Cruz* be the same if the case did not involve a licensed professional? Suppose that Benny Bigbux asked Sammy Student to help him locate a rare 1959 Mercedes Benz, in mint condition, in time for Benny's annual open house in May. Benny likes to show off his collection of rare cars at this party and agreed to pay Sammy 1% of the ultimate purchase price. Sammy spent hours online and driving to auction houses and finally located the perfect car at the end of April. Unfortunately, Benny and the car's owner are both very eccentric and hot-tempered. They were unable to agree to terms before the open house. Should Sammy be able to recover anything for the time and effort invested in the search?

◆ If you have reached the conclusion that courts often do consider a party's particular knowledge and sophistication, you are correct. Contracts involving lawyers, who are generally more knowledgeable and sophisticated than their clients, are particularly subject to scrutiny.

   ◆ Read the ethical opinion following the *Cruz* case. How does the situation described involve two parties with particular knowledge and sophistication? Might the court take a different view if the situation did not involve referrals from a bank?

◆ What were the unique, aggravating facts in the *Spear* case? Would the court have taken a different view if the property purchased by the client was not sold by the lawyer himself? Is the lawyer's training as a CPA important? Did the back-dating of documents have any particular significance?

Review Questions

1. What is the difference between promissory estoppel and quasi-contract?
2. Describe an implied contract to which you have recently been a party.
3. Identify three ways in which a conflict of interest may arise and ways in which the law firm might deal with the conflict, based on the Model Rules.
4. Explain how a letter of credit works.
5. Identify the issues presented by the following facts:

Jay, newly graduated paralegal, interviewed for a job in the legal department at Acme Co. During the interview, Jay was given an employee handbook. Among other things, the book described vacation benefits; during the first year of employment employees were to have three weeks paid vacation. Jay ultimately had job offers from Acme and from a major law firm. The firm offered slightly better pay than Acme, but Jay wanted the long vacations. Jay never spoke to anyone at Acme about vacation time and did not receive an employment contract when he accepted the job. After working for a few months, Jay asked his supervisor about taking the first week of his vacation time. The supervisor replied that Jay was entitled to only one week in the first year.

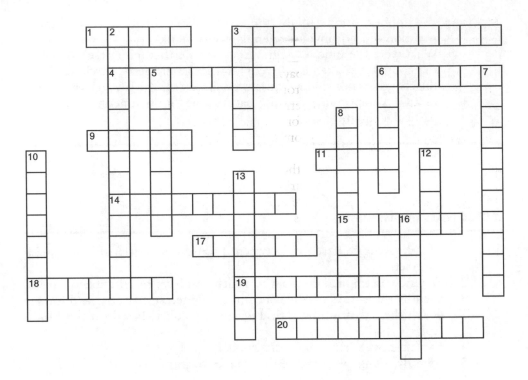

ACROSS

1. _____-contract, based on unjust enrichment
3. the mutual give-and-take necessary for a contract
4. contract with all duties fulfilled
6. contract that must be in a particular form
9. person who makes a gift
11. of no legal effect
14. contract with duties unfulfilled
15. based on fairness
17. bill of _____, documentation of receipt of goods for shipment
18. contract with terms written or spoken
19. contract formed by mutual promises
20. one party performs an act in response to a promise

DOWN

2. a valid contract might be _____ if the limitations period has passed
3. letter of credit, guarantees payment in international sales
5. promissory _____, promisor knew other would rely
6. statute of _____ determines whether contract must be written
7. _____ period, time for bringing lawsuit
8. both quasi-contract and promissory estoppel require certain _____ on the part of defendant
10. a gift is not complete until there has been a _____ of property
12. area of law dealing with injuries to people or property
13. one party has power to make agreement unenforceable
16. a contract that is not express

Sample Cases: Finding and Briefing Cases for Assignments

CALR providers are very similar. If you use your school's subscription, follow the instructions for that provider. The following is the process that was used to find a case on the Loislaw system for one of the assignments in this chapter:

1. Sign onto http://www.Loislawschool.com, using name and password
2. Choose database. For this case, CASE LAW within PRIMARY LAW
3. Check the court(s) of your state (in this case, Illinois)
4. On the "Search Multiple Case Law" screen, enter your search terms and connectors. The following entry found this case:

Search Entire Document:
Quantum meruit & Quasi Contract

One of the results was:

CARMEN CRUZ, Plaintiff and Counterdefendant-Appellee, v. EDWARD STAPLETON III, Indiv. and d/b/a Sedaer Buyer's Broker, Defendant and Counterplaintiff-Appellant. Appellate Court of Illinois, Second District.

Opinion filed November 2, 1993.

Note: The page numbers in bold appear in cases retrieved from CALR and show where the page breaks would occur if the reader were looking at hard copy. This enables the reader to cite to an exact page, for example, for a quote.

Page 834

Appeal from the Circuit Court of De Kalb County.
Edward Stapleton III, of Chicago Heights, appellant *pro se*.
Donald Henderson, Jr., of De Kalb, for appellee.

JUSTICE BOWMAN delivered the opinion:

Plaintiff, Cruz, sought to purchase a home in the De Kalb area. She and defendant, Stapleton, entered into an oral agreement under which defendant would act as buyer's broker to help her find suitable property. Plaintiff was unable to close on a purchase within the time she desired, and she terminated the agreement.

Plaintiff sued defendant for return of an escrow account of $500 that she paid to facilitate bids on properties. Defendant denied liability and filed a counterclaim for $1,263.50, which he alleged plaintiff owed him for the 35 hours of service. The trial court awarded plaintiff $500 plus costs and attorney fees and denied the counterclaim. Defendant timely appealed.

Defendant's *pro se* brief in essence argues that the trial court erred in denying him recovery under a theory of *quantum meruit*. We disagree and affirm.

Plaintiff alleged that in December 1991, the parties agreed orally that defendant would act as plaintiff's broker to find a residence to purchase. Under the agreement, defendant's sole remuneration would be commission that defendant would receive if plaintiff purchased a home. The agreement specified no time

---

Sidebar notes:

Here you may find numbered paragraphs, with topic names & numbers, such as **CONTRACTS §236**. The **headnotes** are enhancements, added by the publisher or court, to categorize the case by areas of law addressed. They summarize main points of the case and can lead to additional material, but are not written by judges, and should not be not quoted.

Published opinions are usually from appellate level courts, which have panels of judges. A trial court, where a case usually begins, has one judge & resolves factual disputes, rather than legal issues. Panel members may not agree with majority & can write separate opinions, which appear at the end of the case.

The above paragraph is **procedural history**, an explanation of what happened in the court(s) below the court writing this opinion. Below, notice the search term, highlighted.

limit. Defendant told plaintiff that her opportunity to bid on a home would improve if he had $500 at his disposal to use as earnest money. Plaintiff tendered a check for $500. **Page 835**

Despite best efforts, plaintiff was unable to purchase any property. Plaintiff sought to terminate the oral contract and asked defendant to return the $500. Defendant refused and demanded an additional $795 for services.

Plaintiff alleged that defendant owed her $500 and that he procured this money by fraud . . . sought the return of the $500, punitive damages, costs, and attorney fees. Defendant filed a counterclaim alleging that plaintiff owed him $763.50, the balance of $1,263.50 for services at his normal rate of $35 per hour minus a credit for the $500 payment.

The trial court found no fraud by defendant, but awarded plaintiff $500 plus attorney fees and costs. The court held that defendant had not proved his counterclaim. The court made findings that the $500 was intended for use toward purchase and not payment for services; the parties agreed that defendant would be paid not by the hour, but out of money available when plaintiff closed a purchase. The parties never agreed that defendant would receive $35 per hour whether or not he succeeded in finding a house. Plaintiff would not have agreed to such an arrangement, as it could have cost her greatly even if defendant's efforts were in vain. As brokers customarily work on commission, and nothing here suggested the parties agreed **Page 837** to deviate from custom, defendant was entitled only to a commission at the time of a closing.

On appeal, defendant argues that the trial court's decision is contrary to case law under which a broker may be compensated in *quantum meruit* for services he rendered before his client unilaterally terminated the client-broker relationship. Defendant does not directly challenge the finding that, under his oral contract, he was to be compensated by a commission at the time of a closing rather than by an hourly fee. Rather, he argues that, even where a broker's payment is contingent upon a condition that goes unfulfilled, *quantum meruit* allows recovery when the client unilaterally terminates the contract and thus prevents the contingency from occurring. We disagree with defendant's interpretation of the case law of *quantum meruit*.

Recovery in *quantum meruit,* or quasi-contract, is a substitute for recovery on an express contract. Where there is no contract in fact, a party may recover in *quantum meruit* where the other party has received benefit for which justice requires payment. Recovery in quasi-contract requires a reasonable expectation that the other party would pay for the services rendered . . . is not a vehicle by which a party who has made a bad agreement may ask a court to change the terms . . . *quantum meruit* has no application to this case. The parties agreed that defendant would be compensated by commission. There was no reason to expect that defendant would be compensated for time he expended in negotiations. Defendant, a licensed professional, assumed the risk that he would not be compensated if efforts failed.

Directly on point is *Argiris & Co. v. F M C Corp.* (1986), 144 Ill. App.3d 750, a case neither party cited. In *Argiris,* a broker sought to recover the value of preliminary services it rendered to defendant, a seller that later selected another broker as its agent. Although defendant eventually sold the property, evidence showed that the second broker, not plaintiff, procured the sale. The plaintiff made efforts on defendant's behalf, but these efforts did not lead to finding a buyer.

> Courts often do not present facts in chronological order. When reading a complex case, draw a timeline to keep track of the order of events.

In holding that the plaintiff could not recover in *quantum meruit*, the appellate court noted that, customarily, brokers are compensated only when they present buyers; preliminary activities such as showing properties and making calls are not a separate benefit for which clients are liable if the broker never procures a buyer. The court concluded, in reasoning equally applicable here, that "[w]here preliminary services are rendered to gain a business advantage with the expectation of obtaining a contract, without any reasonable anticipation that reimbursement will directly result, quasi-contractual relief is unwarranted." *Argiris*, 144 Ill. App.3d at 755. **Page 839** Affirmed. GEIGER and COLWELL, JJ., concur.

BRIEF OF *Cruz v. Stapleton*, 251 Ill. App.3d 83, 622 N.E.2d 1253 (1993)

FACTS: Client sought to buy a house and orally agreed that Broker would assist her. Client gave Broker $500 to facilitate bidding. Client agreed to pay Broker $2000 if he succeeded at securing a contract to buy a house. Two offers failed to result in a purchase. Those offers included statements that Broker's fee would be paid at closing. Client told Broker that she no longer needed his services and requested return of the $500. Broker refused.

Tips:

1. Put the facts in chronological order and relate them in past tense.
2. For brevity, eliminate unnecessary facts. How can you tell whether a fact is necessary? Ask yourself whether changing the fact would change the result.
3. Do not make assumptions about the facts.
4. To keep track of the parties, create labels, such as "employer/worker" or "driver/passenger."
5. Do not include law or reasoning in the facts section.
6. You may want to write the procedural history first to remind you of where the case is in THIS court. Don't become confused between what the lower court(s) did and what is being done in this opinion.

PROCEDURAL HISTORY: Client sued Broker for return of the $500 escrow; Broker counterclaimed, seeking $1,264 ($500 escrow plus $763) for his services. The trial court ruled in favor of Client. The appeals court affirmed.

ISSUE/ANSWER: Was Broker entitled to an hourly fee for his work on Client's behalf, under a theory of quasi-contract or quantum meruit?

No, Broker had no reasonable expectation of payment if he did not succeed in obtaining a contract for a house.

---

1. Find the legal issue; do not concern yourself with **factual issues**, such as whether Broker ever actually mentioned an hourly fee. For better or for worse, factual determinations have already been made by the trial court.
2. Keep in mind that you are summarizing the important points for someone who has not read the case. Any references to cases cited in the decision will probably be meaningless to that person. Avoid quotes, put it in your own words.

Factual Issues
Trial courts use testimony and evidence to decide facts (*i.e.*, what happened)

ARGUMENTS/HOLDING: Broker claimed that if he was not entitled to compensation under the oral contract, because that contract called for payment only upon closing of a purchase, he was still entitled to the reasonable value of his services. Broker claimed that Client's termination of the oral contract before he had a reasonable time to find a house made him unable to earn his fee. Rejecting the argument, the court stated that quasi-contract applies when there was no actual contract, but one party had a reasonable expectation of payment. It is not a vehicle for a party who made a bad agreement to ask a court to change that agreement. Broker, a license professional, had no reasonable expectation of being paid for his work if Client did not purchase a house.

SAMPLE ETHICAL OPINION FROM www.cobar.org/group/display.cfm?GenID=1748

Ethics Opinion 29: Representation of Seller, Buyer or Borrower by Lawyer for Financial Institution, 01/18/64 reprinted with permission of the Colorado Bar Assoc.

The following Formal Opinion was written by the Ethics Committee of the Colorado Bar Association

---

[Formal Ethics Opinions are issued for advisory purposes only and are not in any way binding on the Colorado Supreme Court, the Presiding Disciplinary Judge, the Attorney Regulation Committee, or the Office of Attorney Regulation Counsel and do not provide protection against disciplinary actions.]

29   REPRESENTATION OF SELLER, BUYER OR BORROWER BY LAWYER FOR FINANCIAL INSTITUTION
Adopted January 18, 1964. Addendum issued 1995.

Syllabus

A lawyer who represents a financial institution may not permit his client systematically to refer its customers to him for legal services the customers may require personally in connection with loans in which the financial institution is involved. Furthermore, the lawyer may not represent, in addition to the financial institution, the seller, buyer, or borrower, unless he has the express consent of such parties given after a full disclosure of the facts.

Facts

A lawyer represents a financial institution engaged in making residential loans. Home owners and purchasers who apply for loans are directed by the financial institution to its lawyer, who then prepares the contract of sale between the parties. Later, for the closing, this lawyer prepares the deed, the note and deed of trust, and any second mortgage papers. He also examines the abstract and performs necessary title remedial work. The seller is charged by the lawyer for the deed, the remedial work, and one-half of the fee for the contract and the closing. The buyer is charged for the abstract examination, the note and deed of trust to the lending institution, any second mortgage papers, and one-half of the fee for the contract and closing.

Is the lawyer in violation of the Canons of Professional Ethics? In the opinion of the Committee, the lawyer may be in violation of Canon 27 (solicitation of professional employment), Canon 35 (intervention of lay intermediary), and Canon 6 (representation of conflicting interests). The lawyer is in violation of Canon 27 if the financial institution, with his knowledge and consent, systematically refers its customers to him for such legal services as the customers may require personally in connection with loans in which the financial institution is involved. The lender is utilizing the services of its own lawyer in the preparation of the loan statement and the note and deed of trust to which it is a party. The other documents, while necessary to the loan, are instruments to which the lender is not a party and which should be drawn by the parties' own attorneys. The lender's lawyer, in systematically accepting this employment and charging the parties therefor, is guilty of the solicitation of professional employment through touters in violation of Canon 27. The lawyer should request his client not to refer customers to him unless they have no attorney of their own and unless they ask the lender to recommend counsel. Even in these circumstances, the customers should be apprised by the lender of the other local counsel available for such services, in addition to the lender's lawyer.

If the lawyer permits the systematic referral to him of the lender's customers, he is also in violation of Canon 35, because of the intervention of the lay intermediary between himself and the parties to the transaction. It is obvious that if the parties do not freely select the lawyer, but instead are routinely referred to him, he has allowed his lay client to intervene between himself and the parties whose rights and liabilities are affected by the performance of his services. The lawyer's relation to these parties becomes impersonal and his responsibility, rather than being direct to them, is to the lender to whom he owes his primary allegiance.

Finally, the lawyer violates Canon 6 unless he obtains the express consent of all parties whom he represents after a full disclosure of the facts. The interests of the lender may conflict with the interests of the buyer and seller and the interests of the buyer and seller may conflict with each other. If the lender's lawyer also represents either the buyer or seller or both, he must have their consent to do so. The lawyer is "representing" these parties if he prepares documents affecting their rights and liabilities for a fee as in the instant case. The above conclusions apply whether the loan involved is a residential loan or other type of real estate loan. The Committee has relied in part upon its prior Opinion No. 12, adopted March 12, 1960, Opinion No. 17, adopted January 20, 1961, and Opinion No. 24, adopted July 20, 1962.

***

This case, discussing a lawyer's ethical obligations in entering a contract with a client, was found by a search for [attorney or lawyer / "conflict of interest" / contract]

In the Matter of a Member of State Bar of Arizona Donald B. SPEAR, Jr., Respondent, Supreme Court of Arizona 160 Ariz. 545; 774 P.2d 1335; 34 Ariz. Adv. Rep. 17, May 16, 1989

Material omitted, concerning procedural history & standard of review

Respondent, a Tucson attorney, began representing Canterman, in approximately 1982. Canterman is a Tucson entrepreneur with interests in video rental and music stores. He has no special tax or real estate training. . . . Canterman's accountant suggested he utilize respondent's services as a tax attorney and a certified public accountant (CPA). In late 1983, Canterman approached respondent for advice on how to reduce tax consequences of a cash bonus Canterman would receive. Respondent informed Canterman that Spear Investment Co., of which he was a partner, was interested in selling duplexes. Respondent explained that tax benefits from the purchase of the duplexes (depreciation and book loss) would minimize tax consequences from receiving a large cash bonus. Respondent never informed Canterman that previously he had unsuccessfully listed the duplexes with a Realtor. Canterman could not close the purchase before the end of 1983, but signed two land sale contracts, supposedly securing tax benefits for the 1983 tax year.

Two contracts memorialize the November 1983 land deal. The first is the mortgage company's form "Deposit Receipt & Agreement," accurately showing a signature date and payment of earnest money on November 1, 1983. The second is a "Land Contract," drafted by respondent and dated "the 31st day of March, 1983." This contract recites that Canterman paid earnest money on March 31. It provides for a January 14, 1984 closing date, although Canterman was to receive all rents and accept responsibility for mortgage payments and other liabilities as of November 1, 1983. Respondent testified that he dated it "March 31" to establish the date from which Canterman would be entitled to claim depreciation. This backdated contract is the gravamen of these disciplinary proceedings.

Based on the contract, respondent completed Canterman's tax returns, claiming depreciation for April through December 1983. Canterman questioned the legality of the backdated contract, but respondent assured him it was legal. . . . Canterman filed a civil action against respondent. Canterman sought independent advice. A CPA told Canterman the depreciation allowances were inappropriate. Canterman filed amended returns, paying $10,034 in back taxes, interest, and penalties.

The Committee and Commission found respondent violated DR 1-102(A)(4) . . . [which] prohibits an attorney from "engag[ing] in conduct involving dishonesty, fraud, deceit, or misrepresentation." [R]espondent does not deny he intentionally backdated the contract. Elementary tax law teaches that a taxpayer may not claim depreciation until he assumes some of the benefits and burdens attributable to the asset. . . . Canterman assumed no benefits or burdens until at least November, 1983 . . . respondent backdated the contract to mislead the revenue agencies.

[T]he Commission found respondent violated DR 4-101(B)(3), which prohibits an attorney from misusing a client's confidences or secrets, and DR 5-104(A), which forbids an attorney from entering into a business relationship with a client who has differing interests, expects the attorney to protect his interests and has not consented after full disclosure. . . .

DR 4-101(B)(3). . . . provides that a lawyer shall not knowingly (3) Use a confidence or secret of his client for the advantage of himself or of a third person, unless the client consents after full disclosure.

Respondent does not deny that he gained access to Canterman's income and tax information through the attorney-client relationship . . . respondent contends that he met the burden of full disclosure because he revealed his interest in the duplexes, told Canterman he was representing the sellers in this transaction, and gave him an opportunity to consult other attorneys.

[T]o satisfy the burden of "full disclosure" under DR 5-104(A), an attorney must not only advise his client about the need to seek independent legal advice, but also [must give] "a detailed explanation of the risks and disadvantages." . . . even when not acting as counsel in the precise transaction in question, an attorney owes his client a fiduciary duty to explain fully all documents affecting the client. This is particularly true where the lawyer is transacting business with his client. . . . In tax matters, an attorney has the responsibility to *avoid* involving his client in murky areas of the law . . . Respondent met none of these duties here. . . .

(1) Respondent failed to disclose to Canterman, the risk of entering into the agreement and taking the position taken on the tax returns, all to the personal benefit of the respondent. (2) Respondent inadequately disclosed to client that the IRS might take a different view of the transaction. (3) Respondent failed to advise Canterman, to seek outside counsel.

Respondent received confidential information from Canterman. Respondent used that information to structure the land deal. Respondent's motive, of course, was not just to help the client. His interest in disposing of the property was advanced only if Canterman found it advantageous to buy. Respondent and his partners would benefit by selling property they could not sell earlier. Canterman was jeopardized by agreeing to an apparently illegal attempted transfer of tax depreciation allowances.

[R]espondent violated DR 5-104(A): (A) A lawyer shall not enter into a business transaction with a client if they have differing interests therein and if the client expects the lawyer to exercise his professional judgment therein for the protection of the client, unless the client has consented after full disclosure. . . . requires that if a lawyer and his client have "differing interests," the lawyer must fully disclose those differences and obtain client consent before proceeding with the transaction. Canterman relied on respondent's statements regarding the backdated contract's supposed tax advantages. . . . Respondent, however, points out he told Canterman he was not representing him in the land deal and was acting on behalf of himself and his partnership as sellers . . . we focus on the client's perceptions. Only on respondent's advice did Canterman purchase the duplexes. Canterman is the quintessential client DR 5-104(A) seeks to protect. . . . Respondent's actions fell far short of the full disclosure requirement of DR 5-104(A).

The better rule may be to prohibit entirely lawyer-client business dealings . . . The difficulties with an absolute bar, however, prevents its enactment. . . . to minimize ethical problems, no lawyer should allow a client to invest or participate in the lawyer's business ventures unless the client obtains independent legal advice. We suspend respondent from the practice of law for five years . . . order respondent to make full restitution to Canterman . . . order that respondent pay the State Bar $1,516.50 in costs and expenses.

2

Sources of Contract Law: Common Law and Uniform Commercial Code

This chapter explains the distinction between contracts governed by common law and those governed by the Uniform Commercial Code (UCC). It introduces the contents of the Code as a whole and with Article II, in particular, and explains how and why the Code differs from common law. In addition, students will learn to take a "holistic" approach and be aware that many other sources of law may govern the contracts of the clients they serve.

A. Common Law
B. Uniform Commercial Code
   1. Coverage
   2. Departures from Common Law
C. Other Statutes
D. International Law
E. Administrative Law
F. Practical and Ethical Issues

You are familiar with the five sources of law: the Constitution, the courts, legislative bodies, the executive branch, and administrative agencies. Three of these sources are particularly important in working with contracts: the courts, legislative bodies, and administrative agencies.

A.   Common Law

Common law
Law from judicial decisions;
governs contract disputes
involving real property,
intangible property, and
services

Real Estate
Also called real property or
realty, consists of land and
buildings

Intangible Property
Has no physical existence,
such as debt

Intellectual Property
Includes patents,
trademarks, copyrights,
trade secrets

Restatement of Contracts
Summary of judicial
doctrines on contract law

Contract law evolved in the courts, over the course of hundreds of years. **Common law** (from judicial decisions) still governs many contract disputes, particularly those involving **real estate** (land and buildings), **intangible property** (not having a physical existence, *e.g.,* the debt your brother owes because he borrowed $500 from you), **intellectual property** (patents, copyrights, trade marks, and trade secrets), and **services** (such as employment contracts and insurance). In some respects common law reflects the assumptions and practices of another age. In addition, the common law evolved differently in different jurisdictions.

In an effort to clarify and simplify the common law, the American Law Institute (ALI; http://www.ali.org/) drafted the **Restatement of Contracts** in 1932 and has revised it over the years. A Restatement is essentially a summary of judge-made doctrines that have developed over time; it is persuasive because it is formulated over several years with extensive input from law professors, practicing attorneys, and judges. At its best, the Restatement reflects the consensus of the legal community as to what the law is (and in some areas, what it should become).

Because ALI is a private group, the Restatement is not "the law," but it is well respected. Part of the Restatement becomes the law of a jurisdiction when a court relies on it in making a decision. Courts often do rely on the Restatement because its sections accurately state established law in the jurisdiction, or, on issues of first impression (issues not previously considered by the court), are persuasive to show the trend that other jurisdictions are following.

Assignment 2-1

Services
Actions, not items

Have the courts of your state used the Restatement as authority on contract law? Use your computer-assisted legal research (CALR) account to find a case in which a court in your state referred to the Restatement of Contracts.

B.   Uniform Commercial Code

1.   Coverage

**Uniform Commercial
Code (UCC)**
A uniform law, enacted as
statutory law in all 50 states,
in an attempt to harmonize
the law of sales and other
commercial transactions

The need for a more modern, uniform body of law gave rise to the **Uniform Commercial Code (UCC)**. The UCC was initially developed by a private group that lacked authority to make law, but all 50 states eventually enacted some version of the Code. Because uniformity is most needed when a transaction involves different states, the UCC was drafted to cover transactions that often have roots in different states, including the sale (and, in some states, lease) of moveable items (also called **personal property**, **chattel**, or **goods**). The UCC also covers transactions involving the following:

Personal Property
Also called "goods" or "chattel," consists of tangible, moveable items

- **negotiable instruments** (*a signed, unconditional promise or order to pay a certain sum, e.g., checks, notes, certificates of deposit*);
- banking;
- documents of title;
- investment securities;
- **bulk sales** (*transfer of a major part of inventory, outside the normal course of business*); and
- **letters of credit** (*written documents, usually issued by a bank, promising to honor drafts or other payment instruments issued by its customer or another person*).

Assignment 2-2

Visit the website for your state legislature and find the online site for your state's code (statutes). A simple way to find the site: http://www.ncsl.org/ public/leglinks.cfm; select your state and "statutes." When you get to the page for your state code, bookmark it! Scan the topics until you find your state's version of the UCC. If the list of topics does not contain "Uniform Commercial Code," look at all topics containing the word "commercial."

1. Find the section of the UCC titled "sales," and make a list of the "parts" and major subtopics. You will have to refer to many of these topics in later chapters because they deal with formation and interpretation of contracts and remedies, when something goes wrong. For example, you should find provisions concerning contract formalities and implied warranties.
2. Not all states have enacted all sections of the UCC. Are leases of goods covered by your state's enactment of the Code?

The Articles of the Code are listed on the next page. This book will focus on Article II, concerning sales of goods, so understanding the term "goods" is essential. Goods include items with a physical existence that are moveable at the time of identification to the contract. A crop of corn growing in the field is not currently moveable, but when it is harvested and set aside to fulfill a purchase contract, it will be moveable — so the crop is covered by the Code. The money used to pay the price of a contract does not come within the definition of "goods," but a collection of coins being sold would come within the definition. Investment securities are not covered by Article II.

Out-of-Date?

Some say that the UCC focus on goods reflects the economy of a bygone era, when commerce was driven by tractors and tires. Today's economy is more dependent on information and communication. For that reason, many people believe that the Code should apply to advertising claims and technology products. While recent amendments to Article II show movement in that direction, no state has adopted the amendments as of this writing. In addition, some courts apply UCC rules to problems that would not fit within the definition of goods.

While Article II creates a body of contract law governing a huge number of contracts, some kinds of contracts implicate other Articles. For example, a contract to have a barn painted is not covered by the UCC, but if the owner writes a check to pay for the service, Article III, relating to negotiable instruments, governs liability under and handling of the check.

This text focuses on the UCC as it governs contracts for the sale of goods, but there is much more to it. Much of the law governing banking comes from the Code; see http://www.law.syr.edu/Pdfs/0BankingLaw.pdf

---

Commercial
Between or pertaining to businesses

Consumer
Party to the contract who is not engaged in business, but has entered the contract for personal or family reasons

Merchants
Deal in goods of the kind involved in transaction or, by their occupations, hold themselves out as having knowledge or skills relating to the goods or practice

If a contract is mixed (*i.e.,* concerns goods and services), the relevant law depends on the dominant category. For example, payment for installation of custom shelving might be one-third for material and two-thirds for labor. If the contract separates the two, *e.g.,* $900 for purchase of materials at LumberLand and $1,800 for carpentry, the UCC may apply to the purchase of materials, while common law applies to the contract for work.

The name "Uniform Commercial Code" is not entirely accurate. Because the UCC has been revised, and different revisions have been adopted by different states at different times, it is not truly "uniform" across the states. Similarly, the Code is not limited to **commercial** transactions (between businesses), but also covers some **consumer** transactions between people not engaged in business. The UCC does contain some provisions applicable only to **merchants**: defined as those who deal in goods of the kind involved in the transaction or who, by their occupations, hold themselves out as having knowledge or skills relating to the goods or practices involved in the transaction, or to whom such knowledge or skills may be attributed.

EXHIBIT 2-1
Coverage of the UCC

ARTICLE I:

Purposes of the law; rules of construction; definitions; general principles
(e.g., obligation of good faith.)

ARTICLE II:

Contacts for the sale of goods

ARTICLE IIA:

Leases of goods (not adopted in every state)

ARTICLE III:

Negotiable instruments

ARTICLE IV:

Bank deposits and collections

ARTICLE IVA:

Funds transfers (banking)

ARTICLE V:

Letters of credit

ARTICLE VI:

Bulk transfers (repealed in many states)

ARTICLE VII:

Warehouse receipts, bills of lading and other documents of title
(proof of ownership of goods being stored or transported)

ARTICLE VIII:

Investment securities (stock and other ownership interests)

ARTICLE IX:

Secured transactions (a security interest is an interest in personal
property to secure performance of an obligation, *e.g., a loan to buy a car
is generally secured by the right to take possession of the car*)

*For overviews of the UCC, see http://www.law.cornell.edu/ucc/2/overview.html
and www.law.cornell.edu/ucc/9/overview.html*

Assignment 2-3

The meaning of "goods" is sometimes an issue. Use your CALR subscription and search all states for cases (as assigned by your instructor) discussing whether:

◆ Sale of electricity falls within the definition;
◆ Sale of computer software falls within the definition.

Summarize the case(s) for class discussion.

The UCC was drafted by a private group, with no power to enact laws, and became law only when the individual state legislatures enacted its provisions, so it is important to work with your state's enactment. As with most statutory law, judicial decisions remain an important source of interpretation of the Code. For example, the UCC makes several references to a "reasonable" period of time. What does that mean? Does it mean the same thing when applied to a shipment of lettuce as when applied to a shipment of drinking glasses? To find out, you would have to research cases **decided under the UCC**, involving shipment of produce and cases involving shipment of house wares.

2. Departures from Common Law

The philosophy behind the UCC is to make it easier for people to make contracts that meet their needs, but at the same time to fill in missing provisions, when people fail to cover every possibility. The UCC is intended to promote commerce, reflects modern business practices, and is not as rigid as common law, but the basic framework of contract law remains the same. This book is, therefore, organized according to that basic framework. The differences between the UCC and the common law are discussed in depth in the relevant chapters.

THE UCC

Good Faith
UCC definition: as applied to a merchant, means honesty in fact and the observance of reasonable commercial standards of fair dealing in the trade

- *Encourages fair play*
  - *Requires that "Every contract or duty within this Act imposes an obligation of **good faith** in its performance or enforcement."*
  - *Imposes greater responsibility on merchants.*
  - *Defines unconscionability as a contract that is fundamentally unfair.*
  - *Upholds certain modifications without new consideration.*
- *Encourages resolution of disputes without resort to litigation*
  - *Establishes presumptions concerning passing of title (ownership), risk of loss, and transportation.*
  - *Establishes presumptions concerning warranties.*

- *Establishes rights and obligations concerning performance, breach, and remedies.*
- *Acknowledges the way businesses really operate*
  - *Allows enforcement of an agreement despite open terms and, in some cases, despite addition of or contradiction of, terms.*
  - *Allows formation in any manner that shows agreement.*
  - *Is less rigid with respect to contracts that must be in writing.*
  - *Repeatedly refers to "reasonable" performance, industry practices, and past dealings between the parties.*

C. Other Statutes

Clients in some industries must be made aware of laws, other than contract law, that govern aspects of contracts they enter. While this book cannot cover every statute that has an impact on some types of contracts, you should be aware of the major categories. Note that many of these laws involve disclosure and many are intended to protect consumers, those who enter into a contract for personal or family reasons.

As a working paralegal, you should make it a habit to look for these laws. Surprisingly, clients are often unaware of the many laws affecting their business dealings. Learn to search websites of local governing bodies, state legislation, and regulatory agencies to find these laws and you will be a valuable part of the legal team.

- **Real estate transactions** are heavily regulated. For example, federal law includes (among others) the Fair Housing Act, the Interstate Land Full Disclosure Act, the Real Estate Settlement Procedures Act, various environmental laws, and many laws relating to mortgages. Many states have laws requiring disclosures concerning the condition of the property and laws protecting tenants in residential leases. Local law generally includes zoning restrictions and rules regarding the recording of leases, options, and other agreements in the public records of title.
- Contracts involving **lending**, especially consumer loans, may be governed by (among others) the Federal Consumer Credit Protection Act, the Equal Credit Opportunity Act, the Truth-in-Lending Act, the Fair Credit and Charge Card Disclosure Act, the Fair Credit Billing Act, the Fair Credit Reporting Act, or the Fair Debt Collection Practices Act. Most states also have laws.
- A contract that may **restrain competition**, for example, by limiting a party's ability to do business with others, may be subject to federal or state anti-trust laws.
- Most states have laws concerning the sale of **vehicles**; dealerships are also regulated by the Federal Trade Commission (FTC) (discussed later in this chapter).
- Any business with high **potential for fraud** or an industry history of abusing consumers, such as sale of pre-need funeral packages, or sale of dance lessons or health club memberships, may be subject to special state or local laws.

- Many businesses must be **licensed** by federal, state, or local authorities. For example, it might surprise a client to learn that in some states only a licensed cosmetologist can braid hair for customers.
- Any contract involving a **governmental body or a public official** may be subject to laws concerning bidding, accounting, or conflicts of interests.
- **Employment** contracts may implicate labor and anti-discrimination laws.
- Finally, if a contract involves **countries other than the U.S.,** the parties must comply with export and/or tariff laws

D. International Law

Although international law is beyond the scope of this book, you should be aware of the existence of treaties and protocols governing international contracts. The previous chapter discussed the International Chamber of Commerce publications dealing with letters of credit. In addition, the United States has ratified the United Nations Convention on Contracts for the International Sales of Goods, which is like an international version of the UCC. The United Nations has a website on which you can see some of those treaties: http://untreaty.un.org; the World Trade Organization's site is http://www.wto.org.

Contracts within Europe find guidance from the European Union (EU), which has adopted directives aimed at eliminating obstacles to contracting between member countries, particularly with respect to electronic commerce, insurance and banking, intellectual and industrial property, and consumer protection. The EU does not possess general regulatory power in areas such as contract law but can only intervene in cases that require a solution at EU level. For more information, visit: http://ec.europa.eu/internal_market/contractlaw/index_en.htm.

E. Administrative Law

Legislation, including many of the statutes listed above, is often enforced by federal, state, or local administrative agencies. These agencies enact regulations that govern specific aspects of contracts or govern contracts involving a particular type of transaction or a regulated industry.

Example

Consider the administrative agencies that might be involved in the contracts necessary for building and opening a small restaurant, even assuming that the land has already been purchased:

- Contracts for the location and construction of the building might be subject to the requirements of the U.S. Environmental Protection Agency, a state department of environmental protection, the highway department, local zoning and planning commissions, and the local department of building inspection;
- Contracts with employees may require consideration of agency regulations concerning worker safety (OSHA), compensation for workers injured on the

job, unemployment compensation, tax and social security withholding, wages and hours, even immigration status;

- Contracts with customers may implicate department of health or U.S. Food and Drug Administration regulations;
- Contracts with suppliers may implicate anti-trust regulations, regulations concerning truck deliveries . . .

It is no wonder that many clients regard agencies as the "bureaucracy" that creates the "red tape" that hinders American business. In fact, dealing with agencies can be complicated and frustrating, but there are many good things about administrative agencies:

- Agencies are increasingly user-friendly. It is now possible to access their regulations and forms, complete required filings, and ask questions through websites.
- Agencies create and enforce regulations that protect our quality of life.
- Agencies often provide assistance with problems faced by consumers who are not able to retain private lawyers.
- Agencies employ many paralegals. Among federal agencies, the Department of Justice is the largest employer, followed by the Social Security Administration and the Department of the Treasury (source: http:// www.bls.gov/oco/content/ocos114.stm).
- Expertise in dealing with agencies enables paralegals to find high-level jobs with law firms and corporations.
- Many agencies allow paralegals and other non-lawyers to represent clients in ways that would not be allowed in a court. For more information, visit the website of the National Federation of Paralegal Associations (http://www.paralegals.org); click PROFESSIONAL DEVELOPMENT, then click Agencies That Allow Nonlawyer Practice.

EXHIBIT 2-2
From the FTC Website

Paralegal Positions

The FTC accepts applications for Paralegal Specialist at grades GS-5 and GS-7 primarily from January through March. Appointments are competitive and include the Outstanding Scholar Program. For that program, applicants must have received a Bachelor's degree and maintained a grade point average of 3.45 or better on a 4.0 scale for all undergraduate course work, or have graduated in the upper 10% of their graduating class. Applicants should apply directly to a vacancy announcement posted at http://www.usajobs.opm.gov/a9ftci.htm (*see* "How to Find Out About Vacancies").

Assignment 2-4

1. The FTC is the federal agency most concerned with consumer contracts. Visit http://www.ftc.gov; navigate through the pages "for business" to "products and services" to find pages explaining the Magnuson-Moss Warranty Act. The Act was intended to improve on the warranty provisions of the UCC. Does the Act apply to oral warranties? Does it require that sellers provide a written warranty? What are the requirements for a full warranty?
2. Navigate through the FTC "legal" tab; list the statutes enforced by the FTC as part of its consumer protection mission.
3. From your state's official homepage, find the list of state agencies, boards, and departments. Identify agencies that govern particular types of businesses. Next, find the page for your state's attorney general (most likely to regulate consumer contracts). Is there a division or department for consumer protection? Identify any consumer protection rules that might be relevant to contracts. Does your state have a "lemon law" applicable to automobile sales? Does it have a 3-day right of recission (cancellation) for certain contracts?

Example

Why regulate specific contract provisions rather than leaving it to the market place? After all, every person is free to accept or reject contract terms depending on the particular situation, right? Exhibit 2-3 is an example of a limited warranty. Would the average buyer read it? Could that buyer understand it? Could the buyer obtain the product without agreeing to this term? Presumably this warranty complied with applicable statutes and regulations; how might this term be different (worse for the buyer) if those statutes and regulations did not exist?

EXHIBIT 2-3

This Software is subject to a limited warranty. Licensor warrants to Licensee that physical medium on which Software is distributed is free from defects in materials and workmanship. Under normal use, Software will perform according to its printed documentation. To the best of Licensor's knowledge Licensee's use of this Software according to the printed documentation is not an infringement of any

EXHIBIT 2-3
(continued)

third party's intellectual property rights. This limited warranty lasts for a period of 90 days after delivery. To the extent permitted by law, THE ABOVE-STATED LIMITED WARRANTY REPLACES ALL OTHER WARRANTIES, EXPRESS OR IMPLIED, AND LICENSOR DISCLAIMS ALL IMPLIED WARRANTIES INCLUDING ANY IMPLIED WARRANTY OF TITLE, MERCHANTABILITY, NONINFRINGEMENT, OR OF FITNESS FOR A PARTICULAR PURPOSE. No agent of Licensor is authorized to make any other warranties or to modify this limited warranty. Any action for breach of this limited warranty must be commenced within one year of the expiration of the warranty. Because some jurisdictions do not allow any limit on the length of an implied warranty, the above limitation may not apply to this Licensee. If the law does not allow disclaimer of implied warranties, then any implied warranty is limited to 90 days after delivery of the Software to Licensee. Licensee has specific legal rights pursuant to this warranty and, depending on Licensee's jurisdiction, may have additional rights. In case of a breach of the Limited Warranty, Licensee's exclusive remedy is as follows: Licensee will return all copies of the Software to Licensor, at Licensee's cost, along with proof of purchase. At Licensor's option, Licensor will either send Licensee a replacement copy of the Software, at Licensor's expense, or issue a full refund. Notwithstanding the foregoing, LICENSOR IS NOT LIABLE TO LICENSEE FOR ANY DAMAGES, INCLUDING COMPENSATORY, SPECIAL, INCIDENTAL, EXEMPLARY, PUNITIVE, OR CONSEQUENTIAL DAMAGES, CONNECTED WITH OR RESULTING FROM THIS LICENSE AGREEMENT OR LICENSEE'S USE OF THIS SOFTWARE.

Keep in mind that most contract law, from any of these sources, is back-up law. The UCC or common law may dictate whether a set of promises is a contract and may require certain formalities, but the parties are generally free to negotiate the substantive provisions. Much of contract law applies only if the parties have not addressed the topic in their contract.

Do the laws from various sources ever conflict? Yes, for example some states have specific statutes concerning blood for transfusions. Those laws may conflict with the UCC's general provisions, which include blood within the general category of "goods." Normally the more specific law (the specific "blood" statute) prevails.

F. Practical and Ethical Issues

If you work for a law firm, you will regularly encounter or implement the terms of a contract: the contract between the firm and the client. Every state has an agency that regulates lawyers and is, therefore, relevant to that contract. That agency likely is the source of ethical opinions and investigates violations of the Rules of Professional Conduct used in previous chapters.

To find the agency for your state, visit http://www.abanet.org/cpr/regulation/scpd/disciplinary.html. To what extent does the agency involve itself in the attorney-client contract? Does it have a fee arbitration board or a grievance procedure? Does it have a "lawyer search" feature that gives a lawyer's address, disciplinary status, or other information?

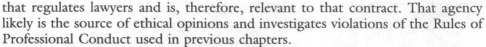

EXHIBIT 2-4
Dealing With Changes in the Law

CAUTION! THIS BOOK COULD BE WRONG!

Something may have changed while this book was being printed or shipped to your bookstore. As you know, the common law has the potential to change with every case decided. Even statutes are amended regularly. As Professor Larry Garvin wrote in 1999, in the Florida State University Law Review, "The Uniform Commercial Code of today is not the Uniform Commercial Code of our youth. . . . Since 1990, most of the Code has been revised or written anew, including those parts now under change. State legislatures have been busy keeping up with the onslaught of revised articles, new articles, and conforming amendments; law professors have come out with many profitable new editions of casebooks; practitioners have attended countless slumbrous CLE sessions in which the new rules were more or less explained. If only through revision, commercial law is a growth industry."

As recently as 2003, the National Conference of Commissioners on Uniform State Laws and the American Law Institute approved amendments to Article 2 of the UCC. Individual states have NOT rushed to adopt the changes and many groups oppose revisions. You may some day work with a client with valid reasons for opposing changes. To see an example of an industry group's (National Association of Manufacturers) opposition to the Article 2 revisions, visit http://www.nam.org/s_nam/sec.asp?CID=107&DID=105. To find out whether your state is moving toward enacting the amendments, visit http://www.nccusl.org/Update/DesktopDefault.aspx?tabindex=2&tabid=60.

How do legal professionals keep up with these changes? As noted by professor Garvin, they sometimes attend continuing legal education sessions (CLE), but very often they do not have time to attend those sessions. Sometimes governmental agencies amend their forms and information to

EXHIBIT 2-4
(continued)

make practitioners aware of changes. The following language appeared on the website for the Illinois Secretary of State:

The administration of the UCC has an important impact on the economy and upon the rights of the public, in this state & in the United States. The volume of international, interstate & multistate transactions pursuant to the UCC requires that the administration of the UCC be conducted in a manner that promotes both local & multi-jurisdictional commerce by striving for uniformity in policies and procedures among the various states.

Article 9 of the Uniform Commercial Code was amended effective July 1, 2001 as a part of a nationwide effort by the National Conference of Commissioners on Uniform State Laws. The amendments made sweeping changes to the law in Illinois and other states with the purpose of bringing greater certainty to financing transactions. Section 5 of Article 9 charges the Secretary of State's office with the duty of accepting financing statements for filing and maintaining a record keeping system to allow quick and accurate searches by lenders and others.

EFFECTIVE OCTOBER 1, 2001
DUE TO NEW POLICIES IN THE UCC DIVISION ALL FORMS MUST BE TYPEWRITTEN, INCLUDING SEARCHES. THIS MEANS THAT WE WILL START REJECTING ALL HANDWRITTEN IN-FORMATION, SUCH AS TYPE OF ORGANIZATION, JURISDIC-TION AND ORGANIZATION ID NUMBER. ALSO PLEASE KEEP IN MIND THAT THE DEBTOR AND SECURED PARTY INFORMA-TION MUST BE IN ALL CAPS AND 12 POINT TIMES NEW ROMAN FONT.

There is not always an agency to provide notice, however, so a diligent paralegal always checks the current status of the law in the relevant juris-diction before taking action or making a recommendation. Your ability to check the current status of the law and your inclination to do so will make you a valuable asset to your firm and ensure your success!

Review: Research for Drafting, Interpreting, or Litigating a Contract Issue

1. Determine whether the contract is governed by the UCC or by common law. The UCC governs any contract that primarily involves the sale of **goods**. Other sections of the UCC govern negotiable instruments, such as checks. Common law governs contracts involving **real property** or **intellectual property** and contracts involving services.
2. Determine the relevant state. If you are dealing with an existing contract, it probably includes a "choice of governing law" provision, in which the parties have agreed that the law of a particular state will govern.[1] If you are helping to negotiate or draft a contract, you may include such a provision. If you are dealing with a contract that has ties to two or more states and that does not include a choice of law, you may have to research choice of law precedents.
3. Familiarize yourself with the relevant provisions of the UCC, as adopted by the relevant state, or the relevant common law of that state.
4. Determine whether the subject of the contract (*e.g.*, consumer financing) or the business involved in the contract (*e.g.*, a lender) is regulated by a state or federal administrative agency that may have rules governing contracts.

Review Questions

1. Which of the following contracts would be covered by Article II of the UCC? Explain your reasoning.
   a. A California corporation is buying the Sears Tower (Chicago).
   b. Ian Investor is selling 10,000 shares of stock in McDonald's Corp.
   c. Giacomo, winner of the 2005 Kentucky Derby, is being sold to a horse breeder in Michigan.
   d. Farmer Brown, planning to quit farming and develop the land, sells his entire crop of apples, to be harvested in three months, as well as the trees themselves, to be cut and processed into mulch immediately after harvest.
   e. Jamie takes a job on an assembly line, manufacturing automobiles, and signs an employment contract.
   f. Farmer Brown hires an exterminator to apply pesticides to his 50-acre farm.
2. What is the Restatement?
3. Why is the UCC not really uniform?

---

[1] A "choice of law" provision requiring application of the law of a jurisdiction with no relationship to the contract or parties may be unconstitutional or violate public policy.

4. In what ways does the UCC acknowledge the informal ways in which modern businesses often operate?
5. In what ways does the UCC encourage fair play?
6. In what ways does the UCC discourage litigation?
7. Identify types of contracts still covered by common law.
8. Other than sale of goods, name the major activities/transactions covered by the UCC.
9. Name the state and federal agencies most concerned with regulating consumer contracts.
10. Identify particular types of contracts likely to be subject to particular statutes or regulations.

ACROSS

1. property without a physical existence
5. _____ instrument, an unconditional, signed, promise or order to pay a certain sum
10. UCC often refers to _____ practices
11. one who is in the business of selling the goods
13. Cases are still relevant to _____ of UCC terms
14. UCC imposes a duty of good _____
16. UCC includes an article dealing with _____ transactions, in which goods serve as security for payment
17. initials, federal agency responsible for consumer protection
18. another term for personal property
19. _____ of goods is covered by UCC in some states
20. a term frequently used in UCC to describe time, etc.
21. _____ dealings between parties, often relevant under UCC

DOWN

1. UCC includes an article dealing with stock and other _____ securities
2. UCC contains _____ regarding risk of loss, transportation, etc.
3. UCC does not cover contracts for _____
4. _____ property=goods
6. _____ sale of large amount of inventory, not in the regular course of business
7. transactions between businesses
8. _____ property transactions are not covered by UCC
9. _____ property: patents, trademarks
12. a transaction for personal or family use
15. letter of _____, bank promises to honor checks of customer

3

Agreement

The most common question in contract law is whether the parties reached an agreement and, if so, when it was reached. This chapter focuses on the critical distinction between negotiation and agreement and on the factors relevant to that distinction.

A contract begins with an agreement. Legal scholars sometimes refer to a "meeting of the minds," but in practice an agreement is the "manifestation" (indication) of mutual assent by the parties. The "manifestation" is important because we cannot read each others' minds and must rely on an

Objective Standard
Used to determine whether parties had "meeting of the minds," looks to what a reasonable person would believe, based on circumstances

objective standard: what reasonably appears to be true, based on the surrounding circumstances. Those circumstances include the previous relationship of the parties, the context (in a bar vs. in a business meeting), the words used by the parties, and what motivated the "offer."

Example

The objective standard is another way in which contract law eschews the "gotcha." Lynn knows that her co-worker, Mary, loves an antique bracelet that Lynn often wears. Mary has, in the past, offered to buy the bracelet. While waiting for Mary to return from lunch, Lynn is talking to Donna, another co-worker. Lynn tells Donna that Mary is very gullible and that she intends to play a joke on Mary, by falsely promising to sell her the bracelet. Mary walks in and Lynn says: "I am kind of tired of this bracelet and I'd sell it to you for $300 if you could give me cash by the end of the day." Mary happens to have $300 cash in her purse and pulls it out. While it is true that Lynn can "prove" that she was joking, her actions and words objectively indicated intent to enter a contract. On the other hand, if Lynn had said "I'd sell it to you for a dollar," would an objective, reasonable observer believe that it was a joke?

But wait! What if, before Mary can respond at all, Lynn says: "Oh Mary, I'm only joking! You are so naïve." It might make a difference because every agreement has two parts: an offer and an acceptance.

A. Offer

Offer
An indication of current willingness to enter into a contract, communicated by the person making the offer

Offeror
Party making an offer

Offeree
Party receiving an offer

An **offer** is an indication of current willingness to enter into a contract, communicated by the person making the offer (the **offeror**) to an **offeree**. To indicate a current willingness to enter into a contract, an offer must be sufficiently definite in its terms. Why do we care whether the terms are definite enough to constitute an offer? If they are not definite enough, there is no response by the offeree that will create a contract. Of course we care whether a contract formed. Without a contract, it was "just talk" and there is no basis for going to court.

1. Definite Terms in an Offer

Consideration
Something promised, given, refrained-from, or done that has the effect of making an agreement a legally enforceable contract

If, in the above example, Lynn said to Mary, "I'll sell you this bracelet someday, when I am tired of it," could Mary respond "I'll buy it," and create a binding contract? No, she could not; Lynn's "offer" leaves too many details (*e.g.,* price, timing) unresolved. The parties may not think of every detail and, in some cases, a court will fill in a missing detail with a requirement of "reasonableness," but generally the agreement itself, or the surrounding circumstances, must indicate the subject of the contract (my bracelet vs. "a piece of my jewelry"); the **consideration** (price); the parties (not just "I am going to sell my bracelet"; more on this below); and the time. These factors do not necessarily have to be written or spoken, but they must be ascertainable; a court will not create a contract for people who have failed to do so. On the other hand, courts don't appreciate trickery. If, after weeks of talking about the antique ivory bracelet, Lynn said, "I'll sell you my bracelet tomorrow; bring in $300," and the next day brought in a *different* bracelet, a court would not likely allow her to claim there was no contract.

Do modern businesses always operate with this level of specificity? Consider the following example:

Example

Jerry arrives to open Jer's restaurant for breakfast and discovers that during the night, the container of coffee spilled on the floor. Horrified at the prospect of breakfast customers with no coffee, Jerry calls the supplier. Luckily, the supervisor is in. Jerry says "Lee, I'm in deep trouble here, can you get me some coffee by 7:00?" Lee responds, "You're in luck, I have a truck going in that direction and I'll have him stop before 7:00 and drop off coffee."

Do they have a contract? Jerry thinks so and is counting on it. If there were no contract, Jerry would either run to the store or call another supplier. Lee thinks so too, otherwise she wouldn't send the delivery — she expects to be paid. But, under the common law, would the offer be too indefinite? While Jerry was specific about time, place, and subject matter, there was no discussion of price, quantity, or method of payment

---

2. Essential Terms

Common law does not govern this situation, however, because this is a transaction between **merchants** for the sale of goods. The UCC defines a merchant as any person who regularly deals in the kind of goods covered by the contract or who, by occupation, holds himself out as having knowledge or skills peculiar to dealing with the goods in question. The UCC includes specific rules for dealing with **open terms**.

Open Terms
Also called "gap-filling" provisions; under the UCC a contract may form despite failure to specify certain terms

---

Assignment 3-1

---

1. Return to the website you bookmarked last chapter and examine your state's version of the UCC:

    ◆ Find a section, perhaps titled, "Formation in General," that allows for open terms. Under what circumstances can a contract exist despite open terms?
    ◆ Find and list provisions relating to specific open terms, such as price. What seems to be most important in resolving open terms in general? Particularly look for provisions relating to "course of performance."

2. Use computer-assisted legal research (CALR) to find a case, decided in your state, in which the court dealt with resolving an open term under

the UCC. Summarize the case for class discussion, focusing on the factors the court looked at in "filling the gap."

3. Communication of an Offer

The offeror must communicate the offer to the offeree. If Pat Paralegal tells Lou Lawyer that he is willing to do freelance work for $40 per hour, and Lou tells Alex Attorney that Pat is available for $40 per hour, Pat has not made an offer to Alex. If you overhear me, angry at my laptop computer, muttering "I'd sell this *! *!*! thing for fifty cents," I have not made an offer at all.

On the other hand, there can be multiple offerees. General advertising is usually not considered an offer because it is not sufficiently definite, but an ad with specifics could be construed as an offer. Some scholars think of this as a "legal fiction" to protect businesses from mistakes in ads.

Example

> Lou runs an ad in the local paper: "Leaving the state, must sell by Saturday, 1-yr old 27" Sony plasma TV model X-187, $900 to first cash buyer." J.R. is first to arrive with cash, and says he wants the television, but Lou has disliked J.R. since grade school. Lou says he has changed his mind. J.R. can likely take Lou to small claims court and win.

> BigBuy runs an ad in the Sunday paper: "27" Sony plasmas — $100." It's a typo! It should have said $1,100. J.R. walks into BigBuy, ready to buy and, ultimately, sues in small claims court. In this situation, BigBuy likely wins. The court will say that the ad was an invitation to make offers, not an offer, because it did not contain sufficient detail: how many, terms of payment, etc.

4. Lifespan of an Offer

Once an offer is accepted, a contract forms. A lawsuit may follow if a party refuses to honor that contract (as with J.R. and Lou in the previous example), so it is essential to know whether there was an offer to be accepted. Although an offer with adequate detail may have been communicated, various factors may "kill" that offer before it is accepted.

a. Revocation

The most common way that an offer ceases to exist is by revocation. At common law, an offer that is not, in itself, a contract, can be revoked at any time before acceptance (unless promissory estoppel applies).

Example

The difference between an unaccepted offer and a contract can have a huge impact on the parties. On a Friday afternoon, two weeks before spring break, Pat Professor mentions to one of her students, Sam, that she would like to have her garage painted over spring break. She has all of the materials ready and is willing to pay $1,000. Sam does not immediately accept, wanting to check on family plans before making a commitment. Pat says that Sam can consider the offer over the weekend and give an answer on Monday. Sam decides to accept and, on Monday morning, arrives at Pat's office early. Before Sam can speak, Pat says that she has changed her mind and is going to have vinyl siding installed. Sam is extremely upset, having imagined spending the money, and wants to go to small claims court. Sam will lose. Pat's statement that Sam could take until Monday to decide was an unenforceable gift; Pat got nothing in return (consideration).

With the addition of consideration, an offer can be made into a separate contract, called an **option** contract.

Option
An offer, supported by consideration, may not be revoked at will

---

Example

The parties can protect themselves. Dale Developer is considering a piece of property for construction of an apartment building. The location is ideal; the price is right. Unfortunately, the property is zoned for single-family housing only. Dale is sure that rezoning is possible, but will take several months. If Dale waits and pursues the zoning issue before purchasing the property, another developer may buy it, even if the owner has promised to hold it for Dale. On the other hand, Dale cannot risk completing the purchase immediately and then being unable to obtain rezoning. Dale could enter into an option contract by paying the owner, perhaps $500, to "hold" the property for six months at the current price. Dale may, or may not, ultimately purchase the property; a decision to actually purchase the property would create a second contract, but the option is a contract in its own right.

---

b. UCC Firm Offer

Does the Pat/Sam example seem wrong to you? If so, you are not alone. Again, the UCC is more in line with modern expectations the common law. Under the **"firm offer"** rule, a signed offer, between merchants, to keep an offer open, is binding for a stated time, or, if no time is stated, for a "reasonable" time, not to exceed three months.

Firm Offer
UCC rule, no consideration required to hold offer open between merchants

---

Assignment 3-2

Find the firm offer rule in your state's version of the UCC and get the section number.

If the offer proposed a unilateral contract (promise/act), the ability to revoke is limited, once the offeree has begun substantial performance. For example, if Pat said, "paint my garage over spring break and I will pay you $1,000" and Sam had begun painting, Pat may not revoke the offer before Sam has had a reasonable chance to complete performance. Similarly, in an **auction without reserve**, the seller has agreed to sell to the highest bidder and not to revoke the offer to sell, even if bids are disappointingly low.

> **Auction without Reserve**
> A seller agrees to sell to the highest bidder and cannot revoke the offer to sell, even if bids are disappointingly low

Auctions have never been more popular. From online auctions to auctions of hard-to-sell houses, buyers are looking for great deals. But, sellers don't always want to give great deals. Whether a seller is making an offer or just inviting offers when an item is put up for bid depends on whether the auction is with reserve or without reserve.

c. Rejection/Counter-Offer

An offer can also "die" as the result of actions by the offeree. If an offeree rejects an offer, the **rejection** terminates that offer and any subsequent attempt to accept is an offer. For example, Pat Professor asks Sam to paint her garage for $1,000; Sam says, "no, I can't do it, I'm going to Cancun." About an hour later, Sam gets a call and learns that the plans for Cancun have fallen through. Sam goes to Pat's office and says, "I've decided to paint your garage." This is an offer and Pat is free to accept or reject. This makes sense if you consider that Pat may have hired someone else during the hour that has passed.

> **Rejection**
> Offeree terminates offer

> **Counter-offer**
> Offeree responds to offer with an offer

A **counter-offer** is less clear cut. Suppose that Sam said, "I can't do the job for $1,000; I'd need at least $1,500." Pat just shrugs and walks away. An hour later, Sam returns and says, "OK, you win, $1,000." Sam is now making an offer and Pat is free to accept or reject. Sam's counter-offer "killed" Pat's original offer. Again, Pat may have hired someone else during the hour. On the other hand, parties can negotiate without terminating an offer. Sam might say, "How 'bout $1,200?" and, when Pat starts to walk away, yells "OK, $1,000!" without having terminated the offer. Whether the exchange constituted a counter-offer or just negotiation depends on all of the surrounding circumstances, including the amount of time that has passed and the language used.

Assignment 3-3

Some experts say that in the modern business world, contracts are not often formed by discrete offer and acceptance, but "result from a gradual flow of information between the parties followed by a series of compromises and tentative agreements on major points which are finally refined into contract terms." The reality of this ongoing process sometimes makes it hard to distinguish a counter-offer from a negotiation. The parties may have invested substantial time and resources to the negotiation process and may feel that they have an "investment" in keeping the process alive. The parties may even sign a "letter of intent" or an "agreement in principle" in which they indicate an intention to form a contract. In such cases, a party might challenge the assertion that a communication constituted a counter-offer or may assert that the parties have an agreement or a duty to continue negotiations.

Discuss:

What outcome would you expect from these facts:

Klein was looking for a used corporate jet; he contacted Janas, President of Universal Jet Services, who provided information about several aircraft including the PepsiCo aircraft. The jet was flown to Arkansas for inspection. Klein gave Janas $200,000 as a deposit, and told Janas to offer $4.4 million. Janas telexed the $4.4 million offer, subject to a satisfactory inspection, and preparation of a definitive contract. PepsiCo counter offered $4.6 million. Janas accepted the offer by telex, planning to sell the jet to Klein for $4.75 million, and sent out copies of the Klein/UJS agreement and the UJS-PepsiCo agreement to all the parties. Janas sent a bill of sale to PepsiCo, which sent the bill of sale to the escrow agent handling the deal. PepsiCo's lawyer spoke with Janas about the standard contract sent by Janas and noted only that the delivery date should be changed.

The aircraft was flown to Georgia for inspection. There were cracks in the blades of an engine and on the turbine blades. The cost of repair would be about $28,000. PepsiCo apparently agreed to pay for the repair, but then decided to withdraw the plane from the market. Klein telexed UJS demanding delivery and expressing satisfaction with the inspection. The jet was one of only three comparable planes on the market. PepsiCo responded with a telex saying that it refused to negotiate further because discussions had not reached the point of agreement, arguing that the parties did not intend to be bound until a complete contract was written in final form. The telexes explicitly stated that no contract would exist until a written agreement was executed. PepsiCo also argued that no contract formed because the condition of inspection had not been met. PepsiCo urged that neither UJS nor Klein were willing to accept the aircraft "as is."

Using CALR, find and summarize, for class discussion, a case from your jurisdiction, in which the court dealt with one of the following issues (as assigned by your instructor):

◆ whether an offer was rejected or terminated by a proposal from the other party (focus on how the court characterizes the disputed communication, as a "proposal," a "counter-offer," or a "negotiation"); or

◆ whether the power to accept an offer terminated because of the passage of time (focus on how the subject matter of the contract governed what was "reasonable").

Operation of Law
Events, including death, insanity, destruction of subject matter, and illegality, may terminate an offer

d. Termination by Operation of Law

Illegality   An offer can also be terminated by intervening illegality: Pete offers to enter into a contract with Stan, for construction of a shed. Pete requests an answer by Monday. Before Stan can begin work, the city amends its zoning ordinance to prohibit outbuildings, such as sheds, in the area. Stan cannot "pull a fast one" by accepting the offer and requiring Pete to pay for a building that cannot be built.

Passage of Time   The passage of time can terminate an offer. The time may be stated or may be implied. In the previous example, if Stan had not responded by Monday, but had come in on Wednesday and told Pete, "I've decided that I will build your shed over spring break," Stan is making an offer that Pete is free to accept or reject. The original offer ended on Monday. If no time is stated, the law implies a reasonable time. What is reasonable? That is up to a court, which is why every offer should state a time at which it expires.

Even a stated time may be unclear: At noon on Saturday, Billie Buyer signs an offer to purchase a house, including a statement that "Seller may accept this offer within two days, after which this offer shall be void." Suppose that Seller attempts to accept at 1:00 pm on Monday, but Buyer has now found another house and likes it better?

Death/Insanity   The death or insanity of the offeror or the destruction of the subject matter will also terminate an offer. If Pete died or if the land was ruined by mudslide over the weekend, while Stan was still considering the offer, the offer would automatically terminate.

B.   Acceptance

If there is a "live" offer to accept, how can it be accepted? Remember, in a bilateral contract situation, the acceptance is by promise; acceptance of a unilateral contract is by act. Some offers dictate a means of **acceptance**. For example, the offer might state: "to accept these terms, return a signed copy to Contractor's office no later than Friday, October 23. . . ." In other cases, the offer does not include specifics about acceptance and, by default, a number of rules apply. Some of these rules may seem unreasonable or impractical, so an offeror should control the situation by communicating an offer that is not ambiguous.

Acceptance
Compliance or agreement by one party with the terms and of another's offer so that a contract forms

1.   Implied Acceptance

Normally "pure" silence does not operate as acceptance.

Example

Read the fine print; you may not be as "silent" as you think. A package containing five music CDs arrived in your mail today, with a note indicating you should send them back within 10 days if you do not want them. You have had no previous contact with the company, but the note states that if you do not return them, you will have agreed to buy the CDs and must pay immediately. Your "silence," in the form of not responding, does not create a contract. On the other hand, if you order five CDs for $1 without reading the fine print, you might find that you have specifically (not impliedly) agreed that you will either return or pay for the CDs mailed to your home every month for the next year.

Acceptance can be implied based on behavior, partial performance, or past dealings.

Examples

Behavior, or lack thereof, can establish acceptance, especially when the parties have a continuing relationship. At the end of July, Community College mails all of its part-time instructors offers to teach. Toni Torteacher, a six-year veteran teacher, receives an offer to teach a paralegal class that meets on Thursday nights, beginning on August 24. Toni forgets to sign and return the contract and the college administration does not notice. Toni arrives on August 24 and teaches the class. Acceptance is implied.

The auctioneer yells: "Do I hear 75?" Peggy stretches her arm far above her head, numbered paddle in hand, and the auctioneer yells: "Sold to Bidder 17 at $75."

2. Mailbox Rule

At common law an acceptance is considered effective when "properly dispatched," even if it is not actually received until much later (or, perhaps not received at all). The **mailbox rule** made sense in times when business communication was done in person or by regular mail, but can result in bizarre situations today.

Mailbox Rule
Common law rule, acceptance occurs when dispatched by appropriate means

---

Example

Barry visits Sela's open house and wants to buy, but says, "I can't sign an offer until I talk to my dad because he is helping me with the down payment; he won't be available until late this evening." Sela suggests that Barry return the next day, but Barry is leaving on a business trip in the morning. Afraid that Barry's enthusiasm will die down if too much time passes, Sela writes up terms (price, possession date, property included, etc.), signs it, and hands it to Barry. She tells Barry, "Talk to your dad tonight, then you can sign this, drop it in the mail, and we'll be all set." Barry is so excited about the house that he drives straight to his dad's office, rather than waiting for evening. After talking it over with dad, Barry signs the contract, sticks it in an envelope addressed to Sela, and walks with his dad to a mailbox. (NOTE: Barry's dad has witnessed the mailing to prevent paralegal students all over the country from howling, "How will he prove he mailed it then?!?!?!")

About 20 minutes after Barry leaves, one last straggler visits Sela's open house and offers $10,000 more than Barry is willing or able to pay. Sela immediately signs a contract and calls Barry to revoke her offer. Unfortunately, a revocation (like an offer or a rejection) is only effective when communicated. By the time Sela reaches

Barry, he has already mailed his acceptance. There is no longer an offer to revoke; there is a binding contract and the probability of a lawsuit. Sela could have prevented this situation by simply writing into her offer "acceptance effective only when received," "acceptance must be by personal delivery," or something similar. Unfortunately, clients often do not understand the need to control their contracts to prevent default law from creating an agreement they would not have wanted.

Whether an acceptance was "properly dispatched" depends on whether the means of acceptance was authorized. Some courts enforce the rule strictly and would find a faxed acceptance unauthorized if the contract called for mailed acceptance. Other courts consider, among other factors, whether an alternative method of communication was timely and whether the method used was the functional equivalent of the method described. If the offer does not specify a means of acceptance, it is assumed that the means by which the offer was communicated is appropriate for acceptance. Proper dispatch also required that the letter be correctly addressed and stamped.

The UCC states that unless otherwise unambiguously indicated by the language or circumstances, an offer "shall be construed as inviting acceptance in any manner and by any medium reasonable in the circumstances." The provision even gives the seller an option to either promise shipment or actually ship goods, in response to an offer to buy goods for prompt or current shipment. While these provisions allow for flexibility, they also create opportunities for disagreement.

In today's world people rarely communicate offer and acceptance by mail, but the mailbox rule can still create problems. A sender may be able to prove that a faxed or e-mailed acceptance was reasonable under the circumstances and was sent on a particular date, even though it was received much later or not received at all.

3. Mirror Image Rule

Mirror Image Rule
Acceptance must be
identical to offer

The common law also has the **mirror image rule** for acceptance. Suppose that Sela had written the agreement to call for closing and possession on May 15. Barry's dad wants to attend closing and knows he will be out of town on that date. Barry crosses that date out and inserts May 16, then mails the acceptance. Sela hadn't seemed to care much about the closing date during their discussion and, in fact, she did not care. The change, however, converts what was intended as an acceptance into a counter-offer. The acceptance is no longer the **mirror image** of the offer and Sela is off the hook.

Does this seem harsh? Does it reflect how modern businesses operate? Consider this situation:

Example

Lou handles purchasing for Taylor's small manufacturing business. On Monday morning, Taylor comes into the office, visibly upset. The company's biggest customer, Ryan, is expecting delivery of 1,000 frames on Friday for an important show. Taylor just discovered that the crate of fasteners needed to finish the frames was infiltrated by mice and moisture. The fasteners are rusty and cannot be used. Taylor thinks that the Ryan order cannot be finished on time and that the company will lose its biggest customer. Lou thinks quickly and says, "If I can get a crate of fasteners here by Wednesday, could you get some folks to work overtime and get it done?" "Brilliant," screams Taylor, "do that and you are in for a terrific bonus." Lou pulls out a yellow form, titled PURCHASE ORDER, in use since the Stone Age and never read by anyone since it was written by a lawyer many years ago. Lou fills in all of the important details—the model number of the fasteners, the quantity, the price, the delivery requirements and payment terms—and faxes it to the supplier. Lou never reads the small print on the bottom of the form, and neither does Pat, who takes the purchase order off of the fax machine at the supplier's office. After checking inventory, Pat pulls out a pink form, titled CONFIRMATION, in use since dinosaurs walked and also never read, and fills in the model number, quantity, price, delivery, and payment terms requested by the purchase order. Pat faxes the confirmation to Lou. Both parties think they have a contract. Counting on delivery, Taylor schedules overtime. Counting on having sold those fasteners, Pat tells another customer that the item is out of stock. BUT, at common law they would not have had a contract. The small print on the purchase order included a statement that "Supplier shall retain risk of loss with respect to the product until the product has been received within purchaser's building." On the other hand, the small print on the confirmation states "Supplier shall deliver the product to the loading dock at purchaser's place of business and shall have no further liability for loss after such delivery."

4. Battle-of-the-Forms Rule

Taylor and Ryan, however, are both merchants, so their contract for a sale of goods is governed by the UCC, which includes the **battle-of-the-forms rule**. Under the rule, the differences between an offer and acceptance do not necessarily mean that no contact has formed. In an effort to implement the intent of the parties, the rule looks to the language contained in the offer and acceptance, the conduct of the parties and whether the differences are caused by the addition of new terms or by contradictory terms.

> **Battle-of-the-Forms Rule** UCC rule, overrides mirror image rule when merchants use forms

The "battle of the forms" rule recognizes that business contracts often have us drowning in a sea of paperwork!

Because of the rule, parties involved in contract negotiations (or paralegals working for those parties) must carefully monitor any changes or additions to offers and raise appropriate objections immediately.

Assignment 3-4

Find the provision, in your state's enactment of the UCC, dealing with additional terms in acceptance or confirmation:

◆ In the battle-of-the-forms example, Supplier's acceptance contained a term "different" from that included in Taylor's offer; can the parties have a contract? What facts, not given in the fact scenario, might determine whether there is a contract?

- ◆ How does the UCC treatment of "additional terms" differ from its treatment of "different" terms?
- ◆ Suppose that the fasteners are delivered to the loading dock, but before they are taken inside, a sudden storm destroys the box and most of the contents are damaged. Will either the provision in the purchase order or the provision in the confirmation dictate liability?
- ◆ If neither the purchase offer nor the acceptance dictates liability, how might that be resolved? (This involves some "sleuthing" through the code.)

C.   Practical and Ethical Issues

Lawyers are often involved in negotiation (offer, counter-offer, and acceptance), particularly in settlement of cases, and face certain ethical questions regularly. The questions often revolve around the extent to which the lawyer can employ "benign" deception, bluffing, or trickery and the answers are not always clear.

The ABA Model Rules of Professional Conduct, Rule 4.1, states that in "the course of representing a client a lawyer shall not knowingly make a false statement of material fact or law to a third person," including the opposing party in a negotiation. Does the rule require that the lawyer correct an opponent's misunderstanding of the facts or law? The answer, as with many issues, is, "it depends." The comments to Rule 4.1 state:

> A lawyer is required to be truthful when dealing with others on a client's behalf, but generally has no affirmative duty to inform an opposing party of relevant facts. A misrepresentation can occur if the lawyer incorporates or affirms a statement of another person that the lawyer knows is false. Misrepresentations can also occur by partially true but misleading statements or omissions that are the equivalent of affirmative false statements. For dishonest conduct that does not amount to a false statement or for misrepresentations by a lawyer other than in the course of representing a client, see Rule 8.4.

Another important consideration is confidentiality. Rule 1.6 states, "A lawyer shall not reveal information relating to representation of a client unless the client consents after consultation." The rule generally "trumps" a lawyer's duty of truthfulness in statements to others, but Rule 4.1(b) provides an exception if disclosure is necessary to avoid assisting the client in a criminal or fraudulent act. For example, the client may prohibit a lawyer from revealing the highest acceptable settlement, but the lawyer cannot affirmatively lie about insurance coverage.

A lawyer can also face tort liability for misrepresentations during negotiation. A lawyer was found liable to an opposing party who settled a claim for a lower amount in reliance on a false representation about the insurance coverage available. *Fire Insurance Exchange v. Bell,* 643 N.E.2d 310 (Ind., 1994).

Other issues that can arise in negotiation:

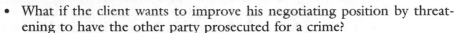

- What if the client wants to improve his negotiating position by threatening to have the other party prosecuted for a crime?
- What should a lawyer do if the lawyer becomes aware that the client is attempting to commit fraud?
- Insurance companies are often accused of quickly offering unfairly small settlements to people injured in accidents, before they have the chance to contact lawyers; what is the ethical position of a lawyer working for such a company?
- A prosecutor may wish to try to cut a deal with one of several co-defendants in order to build a case against the others; may she negotiate plea agreements with those defendants outside the presence of defense attorneys?

Assignment 3-5

Use your bookmarked cite for your state's ethical rules.

◆ Is there an ethical opinion (under Rule 4.1) concerning deception by silence or by failure to correct the other party's misunderstanding?
◆ Find the sections applicable to each of the three "other issues" above.

Review Questions

1. How does a court determine whether there has been a manifestation of mutual assent?
2. Identify all of the ways in which an offer can be terminated before acceptance.
3. Identify the presumptions created by the mirror image rule, the mailbox rule, and even the battle-of-the-forms rule. After examining those presumptions, do you think that they give an advantage to the offeror or offeree? Do you think that courts consider that advantage when called upon to interpret an ambiguous contract?
4. The battle-of-the-forms rule was created to facilitate creation of contracts, but businesses often don't like it. Why not? What do you think businesses commonly include in contracts to avoid the rule?
5. Discuss the issues raised by the following situation:
   Sal Student placed a phone order for new computer software for a drafting class by giving a credit card number and address over the phone. When the box arrived by mail, it contained a "box top user license," stating that: "Opening this box indicates acceptance of these

terms. If you do not accept the terms, you must return this box unopened within the next 30 days and your payment will be refunded." The license went on to disclaim all warranties, but Sal never read it. Sal tore open the box and spent the next two weeks trying to get the software to work. It never worked and the company refused to replace it or give a refund.

- Is software covered by Section 2-207?
- Does it make a difference that Sal is a consumer, not a merchant?
- Does it make a difference that the initial communication was oral and that the written communication was "accepted" by the act of opening the box?
- Is this situation extremely unfair? "Unconscionability" is discussed in the next chapter.

6. Discuss the legal issues raised by the following situation:

Your firm's client, Lee, owner of Lee's Landscaping (LL), has a problem. On April 2, LL gave its standard form contract to a potential client, Rene, for signature. The contract stated a price of $25,000 for the work specified by Rene. It was not signed by LL, but stated that Rene should sign the contract and return it to LL and that "this contract will be deemed accepted by LL when LL either returns the signed contract to homeowner or begins work." LL had intended the clause to provide flexibility. Its work is very dependent on weather and LL wants to be able to take advantage of good weather, even if it has not yet signed a contract and returned it to the homeowner.

Rene returned the signed document on April 4. The contract extends credit to Rene, so LL immediately ordered a credit report. Unfortunately, it was the busiest time of the year, and LL did not review and approve the report until April 10. On April 13, the area had its first dry day in two weeks. LL sent two trucks and four workers to Rene's property. When they arrived, Rene told the workers to leave. Another company had agreed to do the same work for less money.

- Is the situation likely covered by UCC or common law?
- Are there any missing facts about what happened between April 4 and April 13 that might influence your opinion?
- How would you characterize LL's actions on the morning of April 13?
- Would your opinions change if the nature of the contract changed, so that LL were a catering service that asserted that it would accept either by signing the customer's signed offer or by delivering food on the day of the party?

ACROSS

1. _____ image rule, common law requirement that acceptance be identical to offer
2. battle of the _____ rule, UCC, negates mirror image rule
6. subsequent _____ may terminate offer
12. promissory _____ might prevent revocation before acceptance
14. standard used to determine whether an offer was made
15. _____ -offer can terminate offer
17. at common law, an offer had to have _____ terms
18. UCC provides for _____ terms

DOWN

1. a person who regularly deals in the goods
3. a person pays to have an offer held open
4. auction without _____, seller may not refuse to sell to highest bidder
5. UCC provides for merchants _____ offer to remain open for a reasonable time
7. common law rule under which acceptance is effective when sent
8. generally does not constitute an offer
9. _____ of property may terminate offer
10. this action by offeree terminates offer
11. before acceptance, this action by offeror terminates offer
13. person to whom offer is made
16. _____ of offeror may terminate offer

4

Invalid Assent

This chapter explores wrongful conduct, mistakes, and overreaching in the formation of contracts and the remedies available. There is a strong tie-in between this material and issues of capacity, discussed in a later chapter, and some students may wish to look ahead to that material.

A. **Fraud**
B. **Misrepresentation**
C. **Mutual Mistake**
D. **Duress**
E. **Undue Influence**
F. **Unconscionability**
G. **Practical and Ethical Issues**

Sometimes offer plus acceptance does not add up to a contract. The apparent agreement may be invalid because of duress, fraud, mistake, or misrepresentation. Some of these defenses to contract formation, most notably fraud and some instances of duress and misrepresentation, can also be the basis of tort claims. This is significant because it means that the injured party may recover **punitive damages**, which are not normally awarded in contract cases.

Punitive Damages
Damages unrelated to loss, intended to punish

Punitive damages, discussed in depth in a later chapter, are not tied to actual loss, but are intended to punish bad behavior.

Claims of fraud and misrepresentation may also arise where the parties did not actually enter a contract with each other. Recall the mention of *Fire Insurance Exchange v. Bell*, 643 N.E.2d 310 (Ind., 1994), at the end of the last chapter. The lawyer who made a false statement about insurance coverage during settlement negotiations was found liable for fraudulent misrepresentation. The lawyer did not enter into any contract with the injured party, who accepted a low settlement in reliance on the false statement, but was, nonetheless, liable to that party.

A. Fraud

Fraud
False statement of material fact, made with intent to deceive, on which another reasonably relies, to his detriment

Fraud in the Execution
Fraud relates to the nature of the agreement

Fraud in the Inducement
Fraud relates to the party's motivation in entering the contract

Puffing
"Sales talk"

Silence as Fraud
A party has a duty to disclose and knowingly conceals the truth

Fraud is a false statement of material fact, made with intent to deceive, and justifiably relied upon by an innocent party, to his or her detriment. **Fraud in the execution** relates to the nature of the agreement. For example, Slimy Son-in-Law visits very sick Dad in the hospital and hands Dad a piece of paper, saying, "Sign here, Dad, this is your menu for tomorrow." In fact, it's a contract that allows Son-in-Law to buy Dad's lakefront home for half its real value. **Fraud in the inducement** relates to why the parties entered the contract. For example, I might agree to buy your car for $10,000 because I think it has only 20,000 miles on it; in fact, the odometer was not operating for more than a year and the real mileage is about 35,000. Nonetheless, I *did* know I was buying a car.

A statement of material fact is something that a reasonable person would care about in deciding whether to enter the contract. A reasonable person would care about the age of the roof, but would she care about the age of the towel bars? Sales-talk statements, such as "This is the best-handling car you will ever drive," are not generally considered statements of fact and are sometimes called **puffing**.

Can silence constitute fraud? Yes, if a party has a duty to disclose or is knowingly concealing the truth. Increasingly, sellers of homes and cars are required by statute or regulation to make disclosures about matters such as defects, mileage, etc. The common law has required disclosure in situations where one party knows the other is operating under a false belief and cannot discover the truth. For example, Seller wants to sell a house with a basement subject to bad flooding. Seller waits until August, historically a very dry month in her area, scrubs the basement until all odors are gone, installs paneling and carpeting, and creates a nice-looking living area. Buyer never thinks to ask about flooding.

Example

Obligation to Disclose
Who Would Have Guessed? Your state may have unique rules concerning disclosures:
RCW 64.06.022
Disclosure of possible proximity to farm.
A seller of real property shall make available to the buyer the following statement: "This notice is to inform you that the real property you are considering for purchase may lie in close proximity to a farm. The operation of a farm involves usual and customary agricultural practices, which are protected under RCW 7.48.305, the Washington right to farm act."

Intent to Deceive
Knowledge of falsity

Intent to deceive is proven by knowledge of falsity. Suppose that Buyer purchases a house in January. Unable to test the air conditioning, Buyer relies on

Seller's statement that the system is "fine." Buyer discovers, in July, that the system doesn't work and will have to be replaced at great expense. Assuming that Seller did know that the system was not working, how might Buyer prove that knowledge?

Justifiable reliance means that the parties to a contract are generally required to reasonably look out for themselves. Suppose that Buyer purchases a small print shop from his buddy from the chamber of commerce. Seller has assured Buyer that the business is "great," and that he has "really enjoyed it," so Buyer doesn't bother to check the books. In fact, the business lost money for the last two years. Were Seller's statements "material fact" or just opinion or puffing? Even if a court were to look at such statements as being factual, it would likely conclude that Buyer could not reasonably rely on such statements in making a major purchase.

Justifiable Reliance
Reliance on assertion is reasonable

B. Misrepresentation

Misrepresentation is a false statement made without intent to deceive, upon which a party justifiably relies to his detriment. How can a person make a false statement without intending to deceive? A person might speak without sufficient knowledge (carelessness) or in the sincere (but mistaken) belief that the assertion is true.

Misrepresentation
False statement made without intent to deceive, upon which a party justifiably relies to his detriment

Two important considerations in misrepresentation are whether the statement was "fact" and whether the injured party was justified in relying on the speaker. The two considerations are often intertwined and require careful consideration of the circumstances. Does the listener have reason to believe that the speaker knows actual facts? For example, Mrs. O'Leary's assertion that the vacant lot behind the house she is selling "is going to be a beautiful country club," is likely an opinion on which the buyer has no right to rely. On the other hand, a subdivision developer's statement to all buyers that his vacant property, behind the houses they are buying, will be developed as a country club has different implications. Even assuming that development of a country club became impossible for reasons beyond the control of the speaker, a buyer would be more likely to rely on statements by the developer and more likely to regard the statements as fact, rather than opinion.

Many states require a "special relationship" between the parties, such that the injured party was entitled to rely on the statement. Consider this example: Acme, a company that designs and manufactures small parts, uses its own unique software to design the specifications of those parts and to run the machinery that actually manufactures the parts. In obtaining bids for a new computer system, Acme asked each seller whether its product would run the software. Each seller responded that it would. Unfortunately, Acme did not have the contract reviewed by a lawyer and did not get that promise included in the contract. There was no way to test the claim until the new computers were installed and networked to the manufacturing equipment. The computers, once installed, will perform all other functions (word processing, e-mail, etc.) but will not run the drafting software so that it will communicate with the manufacturing equipment.

The seller honestly believed that the computers would run the software, but after months of effort, cannot get the system to function to Acme's satisfaction. Acme regards the system, for which it paid almost $1,000,000, as worthless; if the seller removes the computers and returns payments made by Acme, the loss may bankrupt the seller's company. Do computer vendors have a special relationship with their customers such that customers are entitled to rely on such assertions? What if the misrepresentation were an assertion, by an architect, that a 10th-story balcony would safely hold 1,500 lbs.? The "special relationship" may be based on professional expertise.

Assignment 4-1

1. Does your state require a mileage disclosure when a car is sold? Are home sellers required to make any disclosures? Use the Internet to find these answers. If you do not find answers in the online statutes, you may have to check with state agencies, such as the office of the attorney general or the office of the secretary of state.

2. Use computer-assisted legal research (CALR) to find and summarize, for class discussion, a case from your state involving misrepresentation by an applicant for insurance. Your search, in your state case law database might be [misrepresent! /p applica! /p insurance]; the use of the expander [!] will allow you to find variations, such as "the applicant misrepresented her use of tobacco," or "the application included a misrepresentation concerning use of tobacco." Did the court allow the insurance company to deny coverage based on the false statement? What was the most important factor in the court's decision?

C. Mutual Mistake

Mutual Mistakes
All parties are mistaken about a basic assumption

Basic Assumption of Fact
An assumption essential to the value of a transaction

Mistake is a difficult concept. If a party were able to avoid liability under a contract simply because of "buyer's remorse" or fear of financial consequences, contracts would have no real meaning. After all, a contract is all about allocating risk. The concept of mistake is, therefore, generally limited to **mutual mistakes** about the **"basic assumptions" of fact**, in cases where the parties have not specifically allocated risk with respect to assumptions. For example, Seller and Buyer both believe that the farm property is 160 acres. A survey discloses that it is 140 acres. Buyer may avoid the contract. This concerns a basic factual assumption and both parties were mistaken.

A mistake in judgment or concerning consequences, however, is generally not a basis for avoiding a contract. For example, a buyer may pay too much for a house because he didn't research the market; an injury victim may settle a claim without realizing how difficult life will be with limited arm mobility. A mistake about the law, *e.g.,* the tax consequences of a contract, is also generally insufficient to "get out" of a contract. Many contracts, by implication, allocate risk (and, therefore, responsibility) with respect to those assumptions. For example, a contractor agrees to replace a kitchen floor for a set price, without including any provision for unexpected difficulty. If the work is ultimately more than the contractor expected, he may have to accept the loss.

A **unilateral mistake**, where only one party is mistaken about a basic assumption, could rise to the level of fraud, if the other party has made a false statement or is concealing the truth. In addition, unilateral mistake of fact and mistake of law are grounds for avoiding a contract in some states, if there was a confidential or fiduciary relationship between the parties.

As you might expect, the Uniform Commercial Code (UCC) takes a more liberal approach and includes a concept called **"commercial impracticability."** A party may be excused from contract obligations if an unforeseen circumstance makes performance impracticable. This is discussed further in the chapter on contract performance.

Unilateral Mistake
Where only one party is mistaken about a basic assumption

Commercial Impracticability
A party may be excused from contract obligations if an unforeseen circumstance makes performance impracticable

Duress
A wrongful threat, intended to induce action by the other party

D. Duress

A contract may be invalid if it was entered into involuntarily, because of a "wrongful" threat. A threat does not have to be illegal to be wrongful. Physical force, or the threat of physical force, while rare, renders an agreement void. If an agreement is entered into because of economic threats or coercion, the contract may be voidable if the threat was improper. Keep in mind, however, that not all "threats" are improper and that people do have motivations for entering contracts. The fact that a person would rather have avoided the choice does not invalidate the contract.

Example

Pat's dog did substantial damage to neighbor Lou's garden. Pat has repeatedly promised to "make it right," but has not taken any action. Exasperated, Lou tells Pat, "If you don't sign this contract and promise to pay for the landscaper I've hired, I am going straight down to the courthouse and I am going to file a small claims complaint against you." Pat signs the contract and later decides not to pay. The contract is probably valid. A lawsuit is the mechanism that society has established for settling disputes such as this; Lou was simply offering the option of settlement before filing.

On the other hand, assume that on the day the damage was done, before Pat had any opportunity to repair the damage, Lou threatened to poison the dog. Pat signed a contract, agreeing to pay for expensive landscaping services, only out of fear. Pat might be able to claim duress.

Criminal Plea Agreement
An agreement in which a prosecutor and a defendant arrange to settle a criminal case against the defendant

Defendants, having accepted a plea agreement, sometimes claim duress (a plea agreement is a contract under which the defendant enters a plea in a criminal case in return for a reduction in the charges or penalty). A **criminal plea agreement** is unique in that it has two parts — the admission of guilt and the sentencing agreement — and it must be approved by a judge. If the judge rejects the sentencing agreement, withdrawal of the plea generally does not require any showing of duress. For an explanation of withdrawal of a plea when the judge has not rejected the sentencing agreement, see *United States v. Hyde*, 520 U.S. 670 (1997).

E. Undue Influence

Undue Influence
A dominant party takes advantage of that position in entering a contract with party under domination

Fiduciary Relationship
One party is obligated to act in the best interest of the other party

A special relationship can give one person **undue influence** over another; if the dominant party takes advantage of that position in entering a contract, the agreement may be voidable. Often, undue influence involves a **fiduciary relationship**, a relationship in which one party is obliged to act in the best interest of the other party.

Example

The doctor/patient relationship is a classic fiduciary relationship. Dr. Lou treats Pat Patient's severe diabetes; Pat believes that no other doctor could keep the condition under control. One day, Dr. Lou asks Pat to invest in a "pyramid scheme" in which Lou is deeply involved. A pyramid scheme involves paying money to those "up the chain" and counting on getting money as new people are brought into the scheme. Pat truly does not want to invest $1,000 in this plan, but does so out of fear that Lou will not continue the doctor-patient relationship.

Pat may have another basis for invalidating the contract: illegality, discussed in a later chapter.

Can a contract involving individuals in a special relationship be valid? Yes, if the agreement involves fair consideration, the dominant party made full disclosure, and the party in the "weaker" position must have had independent advice.

EXHIBIT 4-1
Clauses Negating Undue Influence

When parties on unequal power or in a special relationship enter into a contract, the agreement often recites that the "weaker" party has been informed of his rights and has been adequately represented. Such recitals might be found in a pre-marital contract, a contract between lawyer and client, or a plea bargain agreement like the one below, found on the website of the Department of Justice, http://www.usdoj.gov/ag/pleaagreement.htm.

From a Pre-Marital Agreement:

ACKNOWLEDGMENTS. Each party acknowledges that he or she has had an adequate opportunity to read and study this Agreement, to consider it, to consult with attorneys individually selected by each party, without any form of coercion, duress or pressure. Each party acknowledges that he or she has examined the Agreement before signing it, and has been advised by independent legal counsel concerning the rights, liabilities and implications of this document.

From a Plea Agreement:

The defendant represents to the Court that the defendant is satisfied that his attorneys have rendered effective assistance. The defendant understands that by entering into this agreement, the defendant surrenders certain rights as provided in this agreement. The defendant understands that the rights of criminal defendants include the following:

a. If the defendant persisted in a plea of not guilty to the charges, the defendant would have the right to a speedy jury trial with the assistance of counsel. The trial may be conducted by a judge sitting without a jury if the defendant, the United States, and the judge all agree.

b. If a jury trial is conducted, the jury would be composed of twelve laypersons selected at random. The defendant and the defendant's attorney would assist in selecting the jurors by removing prospective jurors for cause where actual bias or other disqualification is shown, or by removing prospective jurors without cause by exercising peremptory challenges. The jury would have to agree unanimously before it could return a verdict of either guilty or not guilty. The jury would be instructed that the defendant is presumed innocent, that it could not convict the defendant unless, after hearing all the evidence, it was persuaded of the defendant's guilt beyond a reasonable doubt, and that it was to consider each charge separately.

c. If a trial is held by the judge without a jury, the judge would find the facts and, after hearing all the evidence and considering each count separately, determine whether or not the evidence established the defendant's guilt beyond a reasonable doubt.

d. At a trial, the United States would be required to present its witnesses and other evidence against the defendant. The defendant would be able to confront those witnesses and the defendant's attorney would be able to cross-examine

---

EXHIBIT 4-1
(continued)

---

them. In turn, the defendant could present witnesses and other evidence in defendant's own behalf. If the witnesses for the defendant would not appear voluntarily, the defendant could require their attendance through the subpoena power of the Court.

   e. At a trial, the defendant could rely on a privilege against self-incrimination to decline to testify, and no inference of guilt could be drawn from the refusal of the defendant to testify. If the defendant desired to do so, the defendant could testify in the defendant's own behalf.

F.   Unconscionability

Unconscionable
A contract that is so unreasonable that it is "shocking"

A contract that is so unreasonable that it is "shocking" is referred to as **unconscionable**. Unconscionability can be procedural (*e.g.*, requirements "buried" in the contract) or substantive (*e.g.*, terms that are grossly unfair, but not hidden). The UCC provides that a court may refuse to enforce all or part of an unconscionable contract. Unconscionability often relates to inequitable consideration (*e.g.*, paying a grossly inflated price), or to contract provisions so unfair that they are considered to violate public policy; those specific situations are further discussed in later chapters. However, other aspects of a contract can also be unreasonable.

Commercial Contract
A contract between businesses

Bargaining Power
Ability to influence

Adhesion Contract
A take-it-or-leave-it contract in which one party has all of the bargaining power

   Courts rarely apply the doctrine of unconscionability to **commercial contracts** (between businesses) or to contracts involving sophisticated parties because the doctrine assumes unequal **bargaining power**, that one of the parties had no ability to reject the terms. A take-it-or-leave-it contract, in which one party had all of the bargaining power, is sometimes called an **adhesion contract**.

   In a typical unconscionability scenario, an unsophisticated consumer is presented with a "standard" printed contract to lease an apartment, buy insurance, buy a car, or take a loan. The consumer rarely attempts to read the contract and would likely be unable to understand its terms. The consumer (correctly) assumes that the terms are non-negotiable in any case. The "fine print" might disclaim warranties, take away the consumer's right to go to court, or describe the consumer's obligation as far beyond what the consumer understands.

   A claim of unconscionability raises many issues: Does an unsophisticated consumer really have "freedom of contract" when an entire industry uses essentially the same printed form? Are there legitimate reasons for using printed forms that actually benefit consumers by keeping prices lower? When a court applies unconscionability, is it taking away the incentive to read contracts or act as an educated consumer?

EXHIBIT 4-2

This material is complicated and hard to learn, but worth the effort. The two job listings below, chosen randomly from Chicago Daily Law Bulletin® show the demand for paralegals with knowledge of contract law. http://jobs.lawbulletin.com/rc_search_ads.cfm ©Law Bulletin Publishing Co.

Contracts Paralegal

Large Loop Corporation seeks a contracts paralegal for immediate hire. Qualified candidates must have at least four years of experience as a contracts paralegal. Responsibilities will include the preparation/receipt of executed contracts, negotiating, preparation of drafts/reports, research, due diligence and various duties as assigned. Previous equipment lease experience and a large firm or in-house background is highly preferred. Bachelor's degree and/or a paralegal certificate is required. This corporation offers competitive salary, excellent benefits and an in-house environment with a high regard for work-life balance. Please contact xxxx xxxxxxx at (312) xxx-xxxx and submit resumes to xxxxxxxxx@xxxxx.com.

Retail/Office Leasing Paralegal

Prestigious Chicago law firm seeks an experienced commercial real estate paralegal to work on retail and office leasing matters. Will review, revise and administer a high volume of retail and office leases. Pay to $70K. Must have at least 3 years of experience as a Commercial Real Estate Paralegal with a law firm or a corporate legal department. Bachelor's degree and/or paralegal certificate required. Please e-mail your resume to xxx@xxxxx.com and call her at (312) xxx-xxxx. (Loop; Real Estate/leasing; 3+)

Area of Practice: Contracts, Equipment Leasing
Location: Chicago Loop

G. Practical and Ethical Issues

What relationship better fits the definition of a fiduciary relationship than attorney/client? But does the existence of that relationship automatically mean that the client was subject to duress or undue influence or that an expensive fee agreement was unconscionable? Obviously not every lawyer-client contract is tainted. In a previous chapter, you read a case dealing with an attorney who did business with a client in a way that was unethical.

Read the *Alderman* case at the end of this chapter, in which the court rejects an assertion that the relationship was tainted, and the ethical opinion at the end of this chapter. In the *Alderman* case the client alleged duress and unconsionability as defenses against enforcement of a contract, based on threats to terminate representation. The case was not a disciplinary proceeding, but the court referred to the relevant ethical rule. In Colorado, the rule concerning terminating the attorney/client relationship is Rule 1.16, reproduced in Exhibit 4-3 with permission of the Colorado Bar Association, http://www.cobar.org.

Assignment 4-2

---

1. Based on the *Alderman* case, identify the factors that are important to a valid (not unconscionable) contract between attorney and client.
2. Find your state's ethical rule concerning termination of the attorney/ client relationship. Can a lawyer terminate the relationship if the client is unable to pay the fee (*e.g.*, unexpectedly lost his job)? Does the rule refer to making threats of termination?
3. A current "hot" unconscionability issue concerns contracts in which a consumer agrees to arbitration and gives up the right to go to court in the event of a dispute concerning the contract. Read the ethics opinion at the end of the chapter, which discusses the issue in the context of a contract between a lawyer and a client.
   a. The DC Bar had previously indicated that a mandatory arbitration provision in an attorney-client agreement was invalid unless the client was represented by a separate attorney. In this opinion, the Bar indicates that the arbitration provision is valid. What is different?
   b. The Bar seems to take the position that arbitration is beneficial in the situation discussed in the opinion. Why?
4. Do the Rules of Professional Conduct or the ethical opinions in your state address the issue of arbitration in a contract between attorney and client? If not, use CALR or Loislaw to find and summarize a case from your state in which the court addresses the issue.

EXHIBIT 4-3
Rule 1.16 Declining or Terminating Representation

(a) Except as stated in paragraph (c), a lawyer shall not represent a client or, where representation has commenced, shall withdraw from the representation of a client if:

    (1) the representation will result in violation of the rules of professional conduct or other law;

    (2) the lawyer's physical or mental condition materially impairs the lawyer's ability to represent the client; or

    (3) the lawyer is discharged.

(b) A lawyer may not request permission to withdraw in matters pending before a tribunal and may not withdraw in other matters unless such request or such withdrawal is because:

    (1) the client:

        (A) insists upon presenting a claim or defense that is not warranted under existing law and cannot be supported by good faith argument for an extension, modification, or reversal of existing law.

        (B) personally seeks to pursue an illegal course of conduct.

        (C) insists that the lawyer pursue a course of conduct that is illegal or that is prohibited by these rules.

        (D) by other conduct renders it unreasonably difficult for the lawyer to carry out the lawyer's employment effectively.

        (E) insists, in a matter not pending before a tribunal, that the lawyer engage in conduct that is contrary to the judgment and advice of the lawyer but not prohibited by these rules; or

        (F) deliberately disregards an agreement or obligation to the lawyer as to expenses or fees; or

    (2) the lawyer's inability to work with co-counsel indicates that the best interest of the client likely will be served by withdrawal; or

    (3) the lawyer's client knowingly and freely assents to termination of the lawyer's employment; or

    (4) the lawyer believes in good faith in a proceeding pending before a tribunal that the tribunal will find the existence of other good cause for withdrawal.

(c) When ordered to do so by a tribunal, a lawyer shall continue representation notwithstanding good cause for terminating the representation.

(d) Upon termination of representation, a lawyer shall take steps to the extent reasonably practicable to protect a client's interests, such as giving reasonable notice to the client, allowing time for employment of other counsel, surrendering papers and property to which the client is entitled and refunding any advance payment of fee that has not been earned. The lawyer may retain papers relating to the client to the extent permitted by law.

Review Questions

1. What is the significance of the fact that fraud can invalidate a contract and can also be the basis of a tort lawsuit?

2. What are the elements required to prove fraud? Can breach of contract itself ever constitute fraud? For example, Acme agrees to deliver items to Baker on a specified date. Acme does not deliver the items on that date and notifies Baker that it will not deliver the items. What fact(s) would Baker have to prove to succeed with a fraud claim?

3. Which members of society are most vulnerable to undue influence? Identify several relationships that might be considered fiduciary relationships.

4. Is an objective standard to determine unconscionability or duress possible? How can we distinguish between duress and "bad luck" that motivates entering a contract? Does a party who benefits from an unconscionable contract think it's shockingly unfair? Might that party refuse to deal with people under other terms? How far should courts go to protecting people who enter bad contracts?

5. Almost all of Dr. Carter's patients are covered by an HMO, through the two major employers in town. Dr. Carter really does not want to be under contract with the HMO; she thinks it takes away too much of her discretion in caring for patients. On the other hand, her patients will have to find new doctors if she does not contract with the HMO. From the HMO's perspective, its restrictions on referrals, etc. are necessary. Without the restrictions, it would have to raise its premiums above what most employers/patients would be willing or able to pay. Is Dr. Carter signing the HMO contract under duress? Are the HMO restrictions unconscionable? Is Dr. Carter an unsophisticated party without equal bargaining power?

6. When Kim filed for divorce, she really believed she would get sole custody of her child, Joey, because she had been a stay-at-home mother for five years while her husband worked long hours and frequently traveled on business. Things have not gone as expected. Kim has had to start working outside the home and is finding it difficult to balance work and parenthood. The court-ordered temporary support is lower than she expected and she is behind on paying bills. Worst of all, Kim's husband is planning to reveal to the judge that Kim had an addiction to prescription painkillers a few years ago, and once, while Kim was passed out, Joey (then 2 years old) wandered out of the house and was brought home by the police. Tired of the whole situation and depressed, Kim signs a settlement agreement under which she will share custody of Joey with her husband on an equal basis. Duress?

7. Discuss the legal implications of the following:
   Laurie, a beautician at Justin's, has a large client base. She is very talented and hopes to open her own shop when she saves enough money. For now, she is a content employee, paying off a student loan and charge account balances. One day, with no warning, Justin hands Laurie a contract. It recites her current terms of employment, with one

difference. The contract contains a statement that Laurie agrees not to open her own beauty shop or work for a competing shop within a 50-mile radius for a period of two years after leaving Justin's for any reason. Laurie does not want to sign the agreement. Justin says that Laurie must sign it right now or else she will be fired and have to leave immediately without access to her client records.

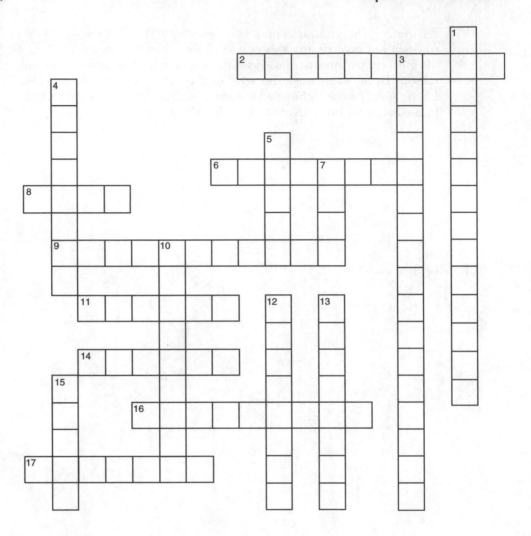

ACROSS

2. fraud in the _____ goes to party's motivation in entering contract
6. fraud may entitle injured party to _____ damages
8. "the roof is 9 years old" is a statement of material _____
9. "silent" fraud
11. person enters contract involuntarily, under threat
14. _____ mistake, a basis to invalidate contract
16. a relationship in which one party is obligated to look out for the best interests of the other
17. sales talk

DOWN

1. shockingly unfair
3. false statement without intent to deceive
4. both fraud and misrepresentation require proof of justifiable _____
5. a contract may be invalid because of _____ influence, one party essentially controls the other
7. fraud is a basis for invalidating a contract and can also be the basis of a _____ lawsuit
10. fraud in the _____; telling buyer she is signing a loan application when she is actually signing a purchase contract
12. threats of _____ force render agreement void
13. A false statement about a fact that is not important does not concern _____ fact
15. involves intent to deceive

CASE FOR ANALYSIS

ALDERMAN & ALDERMAN v. MILLBROOK OWNERS,
Connecticut Superior Court, Judicial District of Hartford
August 27, 2001

The plaintiff law firm was retained to represent defendant condominium owners' association with regard to environmental difficulties. Apparently the area had been contaminated; and the Department of Environmental Protection was engaged in enforcement actions. The law firm defended against the action by the government and instituted actions against alleged actual polluters, but those actions have thus far been unavailing. The law firm's billing exceeded original expectations, and in order to continue on, the defendant executed notes and security interests in favor of plaintiff. Plaintiff claims that the notes are in default, and seek relief. The gravamen of the defenses is that the conduct of the plaintiff law firm was overbearing and coercive, and for a variety of reasons the purported debt ought not be enforced.

[T]he second defense ... alleges that the parties entered into written attorney-client agreements . . . that promissory notes were executed by defendant and, at the same time, collateral assignments of common charges and security agreements were executed. . . . in addition to the notes, the defendant has paid more than $200,000 for the plaintiff's legal services. The second defense concludes with the language that "[t]he terms of the attorney-client agreement were unconscionable in that the amount and type of charges were excessive, duplicative, unethical and against public policy rendering said Entire Agreement void." . . . The fundamental test of unconscionability is whether the arrangement is so one-sided as to be unconscionable, in light of general commercial background under the circumstances. . . . Superior bargaining power in itself is not enough to strike down a contract as unconscionable. Additional elements must be present, such as, "a lack of meaningful choice as in the case of an industry wide form contract heavily weighted in favor of one party and offered on a take it or leave it basis, or exploitation by a stronger party who has control of the negotiations due to the weaker party's ignorance, feebleness, unsophistication as to interest rates or similar business concepts or general naivete." . . . The defense in this action simply recites several of the purported agreements, and then states in conclusory language that the charges were excessive, duplicative, unethical and against public policy . . . insufficient facts have been alleged to support a finding of unconscionability.

The plaintiff also seeks to strike the defense that allege[s] that plaintiff "threatened" that it would cease representing the defendant "and leave defendant exposed to liability" if defendant did not execute the notes. In fear of the threat, the defendant executed the notes. As a result, it is claimed, the notes were signed under duress. Duress is a defense rooted in traditional notions of contract law: if one of the parties to an agreement is motivated to agree because of a fear wrongfully induced by the other, then the agreement is not a true "meeting of the minds." The elements of duress have been stated to be: (1) a wrongful act or threat (2) that left the victim no reasonable alternative, and (3) to which the victim in fact acceded and that (4) the resulting transaction was unfair to the victim. . . . [T]he allegations . . . do not include reasonable inferences . . . that the "threat" was wrongful, that there was no reasonable alternative or that the resulting transaction was unfair. An attorney may withdraw if there is no "material adverse affect on the interests of the client"; §1.16(b) of the Practice Book, and there is no allegation that there was no reasonable alternative to continued representation by plaintiff.

***

SAMPLE ETHICAL OPINION

Opinion 218 D.C. Bar's Legal Ethics Committee, Washington D.C., by permission, 2006.

RETAINER AGREEMENT PROVIDING FOR MANDATORY ARBITRATION OF FEE DISPUTES NOT UNETHICAL

A retainer agreement providing for mandatory arbitration of fee disputes before the DC Bar Attorney-Client Fee Arbitration Board is not unethical provided the client is advised in writing of the availability of counseling by the staff of the ACAB and provided the client consents in writing to the mandatory arbitration.

Applicable Rules: 1.5 (Fees); 1.6(a)(5) (Confidentiality); 1.8 (Conflict of Interest)

Inquiry

In Opinion 211, we decided that a law firm retainer agreement that provided for mandatory arbitration of all disputes between the lawyer and law firm, including disputes concerning lawyer malpractice, was improper unless the client is counseled by another attorney prior to entering into the retainer agreement. We specifically reserved the question of whether a retainer agreement requiring arbitration limited to fee disputes only would be a violation of the Rules of Professional Conduct. Now we are asked to address that very issue.

The inquiry comes from the Attorney-Client Arbitration Board (ACAB, formerly known as the Fee Arbitration Board) which is concerned about the status under the new rules of agreements mandating arbitration of fee disputes in light of Opinion 211. The ACAB regularly receives requests for arbitration of fee disputes based on mandatory arbitration clauses providing for arbitration before the ACAB. We are informed that approximately per cent of the arbitrations handled by the ACAB involve mandatory arbitration agreements. Of these, the majority of the arbitrations are initiated by the client.

Discussion

No provision of the Rules of Professional Conduct specifically prohibits retainer agreements providing for mandatory arbitration of fee disputes between lawyer and client. Comment 15 to Rule 1.5 recommends that lawyers consider submitting to arbitration or mediation of fee disputes where procedures have been established by the Bar. Rule 1.6(d)(5) encourages the lawyer to minimize disclosure of client confidences in a fee collection action. The comments suggest that the lawyer should file John Doe pleadings and seek protective orders to protect client confidences. Arbitration, which is not open to the public, furthers the purposes of 1.6(d)(5) by protecting the client from a public airing of confidential matters.

Rule 1.8(g)(1) prohibits a lawyer from making "an agreement prospectively limiting the lawyer's liability to a client for malpractice[.]" In Opinion 211, we determined that Rule was not applicable as a prohibition on mandatory arbitration provisions in a retainer agreement. Even if 1.8(g)(1) were deemed to apply to arbitration provisions in a retainer agreement, a mandatory arbitration provision limited to fee disputes does not by its terms implicate Rule 1.8(g)(1) because a provision for mandatory arbitration of the lawyer's claim against the client for fees is not a prospective limitation of the lawyer's liability to the client for malpractice. The client's right to have malpractice claims determined by a court remains intact.

In Opinion 211, we determined that Rule 1.8(a) governs the use of mandatory arbitration provisions in retainer agreements. Rule 1.8(a) provides:

(a) A lawyer shall not enter into a business transaction with a client or knowingly acquire an ownership, possessory, security, or other pecuniary interest adverse to a client unless:

(1) The transaction and terms on which the lawyer acquires the interest are fair and reasonable to the client and are fully disclosed and transmitted in writing to the client in a manner which can be reasonably understood by the client;

(2) The client is given a reasonable opportunity to seek the advice of independent counsel in the transaction; and

(3) The client consents in writing thereto.

The retainer agreement before us in Opinion 211 required mandatory arbitration of all disputes before either the ACAB or the American Arbitration Association (AAA), required the client to consent to the jurisdiction of the D.C. Superior Court for all purposes connected with the arbitration, and provided a two-year statute of limitations within which arbitration must be started. We concluded that the complex nature of the arbitration provided for by the agreement could not adequately be disclosed to a lay client. Thus, we determined that mandatory arbitration agreements covering all disputes between lawyer and client are not permitted "unless the client is in fact counseled by another attorney." Id. at 9.

The concerns which led us to the conclusion we reached in Opinion 211 either do not exist where the retainer agreement provides for fee only arbitration or are adequately addressed by the procedures of the ACAB. For instance, the agreement in Opinion 211 provided for ACAB or AAA arbitration, but did not disclose AAA fees, nor that AAA arbitrators must be paid, and that in some instances the costs of AAA arbitration can be substantial. Here we address a fee agreement providing only for arbitration before the ACAB where the fees are only $25 and the arbitrators are not compensated.

More importantly, we believed the lawyer entering into a retainer agreement with a client for arbitration of all disputes, including malpractice, could not adequately explain the tactical considerations of arbitration versus litigation to the lay client—considerations such as lack of formal discovery, lack of a jury trial, and the closed nature of arbitration proceedings. We are informed that the staff of the ACAB is equipped to advise clients who are asked to sign retainer agreements with mandatory arbitration provisions of the nature of fee arbitration, the advantages and disadvantages, and the alternatives to fee arbitration. Moreover, the ACAB's procedures are relatively simple and its rules, which are also relatively simple to understand, are readily available to interested lawyers and their clients. We believe the counseling provided by the ACAB staff and the ready availability of the ACAB's rules are sufficient to adequately inform the lay client of the information necessary to make a decision about whether to agree to a provision for mandatory arbitration of fees.

We therefore conclude that a fee agreement providing for mandatory arbitration of fee disputes before the ACAB is ethically permissible provided the agreement informs the client in writing that counseling and a copy of the ACAB's rules are available through the ACAB staff and further that the lawyer encourage the client to contact the ACAB for counseling and information prior to deciding whether to sign the agreement. Moreover, the client must consent in writing to the mandatory arbitration. Rule 1.8(a)(3).

A final issue to be addressed relates to the possibility that a fee arbitration arising from a mandatory arbitration provision could preclude the client from later raising a malpractice claim against the lawyer. In many fee disputes the client's defense is inadequate representation. Would the client, after having raised such a defense in a fee arbitration based on a retainer agreement, be precluded on res judicata or collateral estoppel grounds from later prosecuting a malpractice claim? The rules of the ACAB provide that the result of the arbitration is an award (or the denial of an award) without any written factual findings or conclusions. Moreover, no recording or transcription is made of the testimony presented to the arbitrators. It is difficult to see how a client in such an arbitration could later be precluded from prosecuting a malpractice claim based on an adverse award in the arbitration. However, this raises a question of law and the Legal Ethics Committee does not make rulings on questions of law.

Because the legal effect of an arbitration award to the lawyer is unclear, we conclude that a lawyer relying on a mandatory fee only arbitration agreement may not ethically use the existence of an arbitration award in the lawyer's favor in an attempt to preclude a subsequent malpractice claim unless the lawyer has complied with the dictates of Opinion 211. Inquiry No. 91-1-2

Adopted: June 18, 1991

5

Consideration

This chapter explores one of the most complicated concepts in law: the distinction between a promise that is enforceable as a contract and an unenforceable "gift" promise. That distinction is consideration, the mutual benefit and detriment that characterize a contract.

Previous chapters may have given you the impression that contract law is a series of guidelines, rather than a set of rigid rules that can be easily memorized. That is an accurate assessment, but consideration is even more difficult to "pin down," particularly when the circumstances indicate a strong moral obligation to honor a promise.

A. Consideration: An Overview

Consideration
Each party to a contract must get something to which that party was not legally entitled before entering the contract, and each party must give up something to which that party was legally entitled before the contract

Consideration is the give-and-take that separates a contract from a gift; love and affection for the **donee**[1] are insufficient to transform a promised gift into a contract. If consideration is not present and has not been excused by law a promise is not enforceable. While the common law once included a concept that contracts "under seal" (sometimes called formal contracts) could be binding without consideration, many states and the Uniform Commercial Code (UCC) have abolished the theory. This may be the root of the current misconception that a promise made in writing is automatically valid.

Have you ever wondered why contests sponsored by sellers often state "no purchase necessary" or allow participants to enter using a "reasonable facsimile" rather than the form found on the product? By allowing participants to enter without the obligation to buy, seller/sponsors hope to avoid contract obligations.

Consideration is sometimes excused by law in cases involving promissory estoppel (discussed in previous chapters), promises to make charitable donations, promises to pay debts that are not legally enforceable (*e.g.,* because of bankruptcy or the statute of limitations), and some promises under which one person "guarantees" performance by another (such as co-signing a loan).

A practical way to look at the consideration requirement is that:

Each party to a contract must get something
We don't weigh the "something" and we don't always know what it will be at the outset.

To which that party was not legally entitled before entering the contract

Bargained-for
Each party is induced to enter contract by consideration offered by other party

*Legal scholars say that consideration must be "**bargained-for**."*
and each party must give up something to which that party was legally entitled before the contract.

With a bilateral contract that giving and getting is evidenced by promises; with a unilateral contract one party makes a promise and the other gives up something and becomes entitled to something upon performing the requested act. This definition works because it avoids confusion about what can serve as consideration. Let's take it apart:

"Each Party Must Get/Give Something" *but we don't weigh that "something."*

We cannot guess at a person's motivation in entering a contract. I might be willing to pay $500 for a ring that belonged to my grandmother, even though, objectively, it is worth only $50. The question is not whether the parties got a fair deal, but whether they got "something." That "something" does not have to benefit the party entering the contract, in the usual sense of that word.

---

[1]The donee is the recipient of a gift; the donor is the giver.

Example

The consideration I receive does not have to benefit me, in a non-legal sense. I really wish my brother would stop smoking and offer him $5,000 if he can quit for one year. He agrees to do it. In a practical sense, my brother is getting all the benefit if he can keep his promise. I did, however, get something to which I was not legally entitled before the agreement: his promise to stop smoking. What I am giving up is obvious: $5,000. My brother is giving up his legal right to smoke and getting my promise of $5,000. Note that my brother does have a legal right to smoke; if he were to promise to stop street racing he would not be giving up anything to which he is legally entitled.

B. Inequitable Consideration

On the other hand, consideration cannot be **illusory** (just an illusion). The parties must incur some real obligation. If I ask an artist to paint a portrait of my children and tell him that I will pay him $400, "if I like it," have I really incurred any obligation? My "liking" the painting is **subjective** and a court would not likely be able to judge whether the condition has been met.

Illusory
An illusion; stated consideration does not really obligate the party

Subjective Standard
Imposed or influenced by individual position or bias

In other situations, a court can impose a duty of "reasonable" behavior on an agreement that has the appearance of being illusory. For example, I might ask a teen-aged neighbor to mow my lawn this summer and tell him that I will pay $40 per mowing if he does a "good job." A court might be able to impose an **objective standard** on "good job," and might or might not be willing to do so, but nobody wants to go to court. The example illustrates the importance of avoiding ambiguity.

Objective Standard
Not influenced by personal opinion or bias

Generally a condition calling for approval by a party outside the contract is viewed as objective and, therefore, enforceable. For example, I might require that the painting of my living room walls be done to the satisfaction of my decorator. The court may assume that the decorator will employ objective professional standards and that real obligation has been incurred.

The examples given above involve common law contracts. As you might imagine, the UCC takes a moderate approach. This is illustrated by the "merchant's firm offer" rule, discussed in the previous chapter, under which an offer can be made irrevocable for a period of time, without consideration. The gap-filling provisions, for dealing with unstated quantity, delivery, time, and even price terms, can save contracts that might be considered illusory at common law. The obligation of good faith, applicable to "every contract or duty" covered by the Code, also saves contracts that might appear to be illusory on first glance.

Even with the more moderate approach of the UCC, the consideration requirement is not "just a formality." Consideration cannot be a **"sham."**

Sham Consideration
Stated consideration did not really occur

Example

Cal Collector and Dana Dealer sign an option contract, under which Dana agrees to hold an antique car for sale to Cal, at a specified price, for six weeks, while Cal attempts to find financial backing for an auto museum he wants to open. The contract states that Cal has paid $100 for the option, but Cal did not actually give Dana the money and has no intention of doing so.

Courts differ on when consideration crosses the line from being minimal to being a sham. What if the option contract stated consideration of one dollar and Cal actually gave Dana one dollar?

Nominal
Minimal

In some cases, the actual consideration might be unquestionably adequate (*e.g.,* $400,000 for a 3-bedroom house) but the parties might recite **nominal** consideration in the contract (*e.g.,* "for ten dollars and other good and valuable consideration . . .)."

Example

Recital
A formal statement

"**Recital**" of Consideration:

This type of formal assertion of consideration, written in archaic language, used to be found in most contracts.

NOW THEREFORE, in consideration of the premises and the mutual covenants set forth herein and for other good and valuable consideration, the receipt and sufficiency of which are hereby acknowledged, the parties hereto covenant and agree as follows:

Is it necessary? No, the actual obligations and promises set forth in the contract should establish the real existence (or lack) of consideration. Given the mixed results in cases exploring sham consideration, an attorney would be negligent to allow a client to depend on such a clause as a substitute for real consideration to support an agreement. Might it actually be harmful? Possibly; if such incomprehensible language is one of the first things the client sees in trying to read a contract, might the client decide not to try to read the rest of the document? If the client does not read the contract, how likely is compliance?

If consideration is "shockingly" unequal, a court may invalidate the contract as **unconscionable**. As noted in the previous chapter, situations in which one party has all of the power and the other is unsophisticated, economically disadvantaged, or in extreme need could also implicate duress or undue influence. The sample case at the end of the chapter illustrates an attempt to make such arguments, the unwillingness of a court to accept those arguments, and some ethical issues concerning contracts between lawyers.

There is a modern trend to protect those least able to protect themselves. Courts often review agreements for attorney's fees; most states have legislation limiting interest rates on consumer loans and providing protections for other types of agreements (*e.g.,* "payday loans"). This is discussed further in the chapter on LEGALITY.

C. Conditional Contracts

1. "Each Party Must Get/Give Something," *but the parties may not know, at the outset, what that "something" is.*

The requirement that one party gets and the other party gives "something" does not mean that the parties have to know exactly what that "something" will be at the time when they enter the agreement. Many contracts are conditional. A **condition precedent** is something that must happen before the contemplated transaction occurs. A **condition subsequent** is an event that might "undo" the contract.

Condition Precedent
Event that must occur before the contemplated transaction is completed

Condition Subsequent
Event that may "undo" an executed contract

Examples

A condition may protect a party when some uncertainty exists concerning his ability or desire to perform the contract. Bob wants to buy Sal's house, but is not sure he can get a mortgage. He writes an offer, including language that he will buy the house for $300,000, "if, within four weeks of acceptance of this offer, I can obtain a mortgage in the amount of $250,000 at an interest rate not higher than 9%." We don't know whether Bob will ultimately buy the house, but we know he is going to do "something." At the very least, he must apply for a mortgage, complete the necessary paperwork, etc. He has incurred SOME obligation. Getting a mortgage is a **condition precedent** to completing the sale, but the contract is valid even if that does not occur.

Laurel wants a great dress for her high school reunion and goes to an expensive, designer shop. The shop, which deals in one-of-a-kind items, does not normally accept returns. Laurel is, therefore, conflicted about buying a $900 dress without asking her husband's opinion of how it looks. The salesperson agrees that Laurel can put the dress on her charge account, take it home, and, if her husband does not like it, return it for a full refund. She writes the agreement (a **condition subsequent**) on the receipt. We don't know whether Laurel will keep and pay for the dress, but she has incurred SOME obligation. At the very least, she has to return the dress, in good condition.

---

2. Output, Needs, and Exclusive Dealing Contracts

Of course, the UCC takes a moderate approach (by now, you may see a pattern). The Code includes provisions relating to **"output," "needs,"** and **"exclusive dealing"** contracts that further illustrate that the parties need not know what "something" is at the outset and that a court can impose a requirement of "reasonable" performance.

Output Contract
Contract under which buyer agrees to purchase all that seller produces; court may impose requirement of reasonable performance

Needs Contract
Contract under which buyer agrees to purchase all of buyer's needs from seller (see exclusive dealing); court may impose requirement of reasonable performance

---

Examples

Parties entering a contract do not always know, at the outset, what they will need or be able to provide. Colonial Café enters into a contract with Janna's Bakery, under which Colonial will buy all of its baked goods from Janna's for one year and Janna will give Colonial a 10% discount off usual prices. This is a **"needs"** contract. Do we

Exclusive Dealing
Contract under which
parties agree to deal only
with each other with respect
to particular needs

know how much Colonial will buy? No; the whole town could go on the Atkins diet, drying up the market for baked goods. But we do know this: If Colonial buys any baked goods, it will buy them from Janna's and if Janna's sells baked goods to Colonial, it will give a discount. Each party has incurred "some" obligation. This could also be characterized as an **exclusive dealing contract**, because Colonial will only deal with Janna's for its baked goods. These agreements can have anti-trust implications, as discussed in the chapter on LEGALITY.

Leah, the owner of Unique Boutique, spots a clever little purse made out of a cigar box and finds out that its owner, Elise, made it. Elise makes the purses as a hobby and is happy to agree to sell Leah her entire **"output"** (all of the purses she makes) at $25 per purse for the next six months. She generally makes 2-3 purses per week. The law implies "good faith," so that Elise cannot, without being in breach, start drinking lots of coffee, staying up all night, and producing 20 purses per week, nor can she spend the next six months zoned out in front of the television, making one purse per month.

Assignment 5-1

Using your state's version of the UCC:

1. Identify the sections dealing with unconscionability, and
2. Identify sections dealing with output/needs contracts.

Contracts under Seal
Formal contracts

3. Does your state still recognize **contracts under seal** (also called **formal contracts**)?

D. Bargained-for

1. "To Which that Party Was Not Legally Entitled Before the Contract"

Legal scholars say that consideration must be "bargained-for," which is another way of saying that each party gets something that he was not entitled to "before the contract" and that each party is induced to "give" by what he will "get." A contract cannot normally be "inflicted" on a party by the delivery of consideration that party did not seek.

Legal scholars often say, "Past consideration is no consideration." Returning to the example at the beginning of this chapter, suppose that I learned that my brother had finally responded to my nagging and stopped smoking and I told him that I was so proud of him that I planned to give him $5,000. The promise is unenforceable because the giving and getting were not in response to each other.

Even judges sometimes struggle with the notion that past consideration is no consideration, particularly when there seems to be a moral obligation.

Consider this famous case: A lumber mill worker (Webb) was dropping a huge block from an upper level when the president of the company (McGowin) suddenly appeared below. To avoid crushing the other man, Webb went over the edge with the block, to change its path. Webb suffered crippling injuries. McGowin promised Webb payments and actually made the payments for the rest of his life, but when McGowin died, the executors of his estate stopped paying, claiming the promise was not supported by consideration. Ultimately, the estate was required to make the payments.

You can find *Webb v. McGowin*, an Alabama case, using computer-assisted legal research (CALR), but before you look it up, can you guess the distinction between the case and the situation in which I promised my brother $5,000 because he stopped smoking? Some "moral obligation" agreements, lacking consideration, can be upheld under the doctrine of promissory estoppel. Why not McGowin's promise? Promissory estoppel is based in reliance; Webb did not act in reliance on McGowin's promise. Although commentators have various theories, the case may simply reflect sympathy for a horribly injured party with no other recourse.

In fact, the law has carved out an exception for common "rescue" situations. Suppose that a patient arrives at a hospital by ambulance, unconscious and not accompanied by a relative or friend. Are the doctors who worked to save her life not entitled to compensation? Courts treat the situation as more a problem of offer and acceptance than of consideration and say that a contract can be implied by law. This was previously explained within the discussion of quasi-contract in an earlier chapter.

2. Pre-existing Obligations

Another important question is whether the parties got something new, something to which they were not already entitled. For example, Jo is having trouble in class. The professor says, "Come in during my office hours and I will tutor you for $30 per hour." Jo will likely not have to pay because the professor was under a pre-existing obligation to help students during office hours. In a sense, Jo has already paid for that, by paying tuition. Similarly, police officers are often prohibited from collecting rewards for finding missing people or property; they are already paid and legally obligated to find missing people and property. What if the obligation is owed to a party outside the contract? For example, if my brother had already promised to stop smoking, for which our father will pay $1,000, is my subsequent promise unenforceable? The answer differs from state to state.

In looking at whether the parties got something new, keep in mind that one of the main functions of a contract is to allocate risk.

Example

We enter contracts to secure a position. Hal Homeowner is renovating an old house and wants the slate entry floor replaced with ceramic tile. He picks the tile. The salesperson, Sal, comes to the house to measure and talk about installation. Sal says that the job will be fairly easy; they can remove the old floor and install the new one for an hourly rate of $40. Sal says the job will take 18-22 hours. Hal says that he needs a firm price, so that he can determine exactly what he can afford with respect to other repairs. Sal shrugs, "Suit yourself, you could probably get this done cheaper hourly." The two sign a contract that calls for removal of the slate and installation of the new tile for $1,000. When Sal's employee arrives to do the work, he discovers that the slate was improperly installed. The removal ends up taking 25 hours; the installation takes another 6 hours. Sal feels he is entitled to more than $1,000, but the contract allocated the risk of difficulty to the company. Hal did not get anything he was not already entitled to; Sal had a **pre-existing obligation** and was obligated to do the work regardless of the difficulty. In this situation, the contract allocated the risk and the result is "fair" because Hal had no idea what would be required; Sal is in the business and in a better position to evaluate the situation.

Cost-plus Contract
A way of sharing risk

Allowances
Contract total price includes "estimates" for components; if actual price of components differs from allowances, total contract price changes

Incentive Consideration
Consideration changes to motivate faster or better performance

In an effort to avoid the pre-existing obligation rule and to create a contract in which risk is shared, some business people will only work at an hourly rate or will give an estimate, rather than a firm price. Other possibilities for risk avoidance or risk sharing include **"cost-plus"** contracts (I will build the garage for the cost of materials plus an additional 20%) and contracts involving **components** (Builder gives a price of $400,000 for construction of a house, which includes a fixed price for some things and **allowances** for other components; *e.g.,* Buyer has $3,000 "allowance" for light fixtures; if Buyer chooses more expensive fixtures, Buyer will have to pay the additional cost). A contract might also be performance-based or include **incentives**; *e.g.,* Owner will pay Contractor $100,000 for labor if the structure is complete by May 1 and will pay an extra $10,000 if the structure is complete by April 15. In a later chapter, you will learn to examine contract language carefully and evaluate whether risk is being assigned to one party or the other.

E. Modification of Existing Contracts

Would this make a difference? When the job was half finished, Sal went to Hal and said, "Look, we just cannot finish this job at this price, I need you to sign a new deal." Worried that Sal would leave the job unfinished, Hal signed a contract agreeing to pay $1,400. Can Sal collect $1,400? In most states, the answer is no; that would amount to blackmail. The two had pre-existing legal duties to each other: Sal to do the job and Hal to pay. Signing a new piece of paper adds nothing. Under the traditional view, there is no consideration for the new contract.

If you look at situations in your own life, you may have a better understanding of this. Suppose that you bought your first new car a few months ago, for $19,000. The dealer now calls you and says, "We've just closed out our books for last year and we took a bad loss. We are re-evaluating all of our prices and we need about $800 more from you."

The UCC does not require consideration to support modification of an existing contract for the sale of goods, if the modification is made in good faith and in response to circumstances that would not have been reasonably foreseeable. Some states have followed this more liberal approach. Even in those states, however, a modification signed under economic duress, such as a threat to walk off the job, would likely be considered invalid.

But, consider this. Sal said, "We can't finish the job at this price and I need you to sign a new deal, but I don't want an unhappy customer. I know you wanted new baseboard, so I am going to throw that in to the deal, so that you will know that we want you to be happy." The two then sign an agreement under which Hal will pay $1,500 and the work will include installation of new baseboard, which would normally add about $100 to the price. Now, Hal IS getting something new: the baseboard. Remember, the law does not weigh consideration. It may not be fair, but Hal has now essentially agreed to pay $500 for baseboard.

An agreement to accept a payment or performance in exchange for a different payment or performance, required under a contract, is known as an **accord and satisfaction**. The accord is the agreement to accept something different and the satisfaction is the actual performance. Sal and Hal reached an accord, the new agreement ($1,500), and the satisfaction (installation of the baseboard) discharges the original agreement.

Consideration is not always money, an object, or a service. It can be the grant or release of a legal right.

Accord and Satisfaction
Agreement to accept and give payment or performance, different from that originally required by contract

---

Example

Jerry cleans offices evenings and goes to school during the day. One of Jerry's clients, Caveat Realtors, hasn't paid its cleaning bill in several months and now owes $800. Jerry finally tells Caveat that there will be no more cleaning and that the bill is going to be "turned over to a lawyer." The next day, Jerry receives a check from Caveat, in the amount of $500. Jerry really needs the money and decides to deposit it and go after the additional $300 later. On the back of the check, however, where Jerry would endorse it for deposit, Caveat has printed, "Payment in full for all cleaning, 3/1/06-5/1/06." Does Jerry give up all right to the additional $300 by signing the check?

Before you answer, consider this: My electric bill for this month is $220. I'd like to relieve myself of some of this outrageous expense by writing a check for $100 and, on the back, writing "Payment in full. . . ." Many modern businesses handle a high volume of checks and cannot inspect each individually.

Look at the situation in terms of the definition of consideration. Jerry and Caveat had a contract; weekly cleaning in exchange for $100 per week. Each gave and got something. The language on the back of the check is an attempt to **rescind** (terminate that contract before all of its terms are completely performed) and create a new contract under which Caveat gets something (three weeks of free cleaning). What does Jerry get in return? Jerry was already entitled to the $500.

In the view of most courts, just putting it in writing does not create an enforceable contract, but the states are not in total agreement about modification of contracts. Some states have developed various exceptions to allow the parties to modify a contract without new consideration if the modification appears to be fair or if the parties have acted on the modification. If Jerry were your firm's client, your supervising attorney might ask you to research your state's position before advising Jerry to cash the check.

Rescind
To terminate a contract before all of its terms are completely performed

---

Assignment 5-2

Waiver
Intentional relinquishment of right, claim, or privilege

The Jerry/Caveat situation is NOT covered by the UCC. If it were a contract for the sale of goods, the answer might be easier to find. In your state's version of the UCC, identify provisions relating to modification, **recission**, and **waiver**.

◆ Does the provision require that a modification be written?
◆ Is a **waiver** retractable? For example, Factory has a contract with Supplier, under which Supplier delivers a crate of bolts to the Factory loading dock each Monday. For several weeks Supplier was without a full-time delivery driver and delivered the bolts on Tuesdays. Factory accepted the Tuesday deliveries without complaint and, therefore, waived its right to insist on Monday delivery, but would now like to have Monday deliveries resume. Can Factory now insist on Monday delivery or was the agreement modified by the behavior of the parties?

Could Jerry avoid the dilemma by crossing out the "payment in full" language or writing "under protest," "without prejudice," or "all rights reserved" above his signature? You may already know the answer to this. It is not an issue of consideration; it is an issue of acceptance/counteroffer.

F.   Settlement of Disputes

Liquidated Debt
Debt that is not in dispute

Unliquidated Debt
Debt, the amount of which is in dispute; settlement of an unliquidated debt can constitute consideration

Is it possible that Caveat is giving something in exchange? If the $800 debt is a **liquidated debt**, the answer is probably no. A liquidated debt is a debt that is not in dispute. Suppose, however, that the reason Caveat had not paid was dissatisfaction with Jerry. Caveat has a valid claim that Jerry did not do the entire job several times, spilled furniture oil on a valuable rug, and broke some pottery. Caveat was planning to replace Jerry and, possibly, to file suit in small claims court. The debt is **unliquidated** if the amount is in dispute and the settlement of an unliquidated debt can constitute consideration. Jerry would be giving up the claim to $300; Caveat would be giving up its claims with respect to damage and inadequate service. People involved in disputes concerning accidents have to be particularly careful about accepting checks before they know the extent of their damages.

It is also possible that in some situations, the agreement to accept an amount less than the full debt could constitute a completed gift. A promise to make a gift is not enforceable, but once a gift is completed, it may not be withdrawn. So, for example, if Son owed Dad $800 and Dad said, "Give me a check for $500, write 'payment in full' on the back, and we'll consider it done," some courts may consider it a completed gift.

In some states the "liquidated debt" rule has evolved, along with the concept of waiver. For example, in some jurisdictions, a landlord's agreement to accept $700 per month instead of $900, as stated in the lease, followed by actual acceptance of the lesser amount, could constitute an enforceable waiver of the unpaid amount. When a client presents an issue, it is always worth researching the possibility of exceptions unique to your state.

Assignment 5-3

Use CALR to find and summarize a case, from your state or a neighboring state. Remember to use expanders to find variations such as "unconscionable" or "unconscionability" and "rented" or "rental." Find cases involving:

◆ Unconscionability in a rental agreement (housing or rental of personal property);
◆ Whether new consideration is required to support changes to an existing contract;
◆ Parties intentionally stating nominal consideration in a contract when it would be just as easy to state actual consideration. Research cases involving recitation of nominal consideration in real estate transfers and/ or cases in which a party is "leasing" property for a stated term and has the right to purchase the property at the end of the term for a nominal price. What motivations underlie these transactions?

G. Practical and Ethical Issues

You have learned that courts do not generally involve themselves in the adequacy or fairness of consideration. Unfortunately, however, courts are sometimes called on to review the fairness of legal fees (the consideration in a contract between an attorney and client), particularly in "fee reversal" cases, in which the "losing" party must pay the "winner's" attorney fees. In addition, fees are subject to an ethical rule.

Assignment 5-4

Examine your state Rule of Professional Conduct relating to fees. In the ABA Model Rules, it is Rule 1.5.

◆ Is a contingency fee arrangement prohibited for certain cases?
◆ Does the Rule require that certain fee agreements be written?

◆ What factors go into the determination of whether a fee is "reasonable"?
◆ What business practices can a law firm implement to help keep fees reasonable? How can paralegals help?
◆ Attorney A's aunt was in a major accident, but A does not handle personal injury cases and, therefore, refers his aunt to Firm B. Firm B is able to negotiate a settlement of $600,000 for A's aunt and earns a fee of $200,000. Under what circumstances may A take a referral fee?

Now find and examine your state Rule of Professional Conduct relating to restrictions on the right to practice. The Rule, (Rule 5.6 in the ABA Model Rules) is key to understanding the *Hurd* case at the end of the chapter. Read the Hurd case, which involves allegations of duress, unconscionability, and pre-existing duty in a contract between lawyers.

Assignment 5-5

◆ What facts did the court find most important in rejecting Hurd's claims?
◆ Why did the agreement in the *Hurd* case limit the extra payment to involuntary separation?
◆ Why would a law firm try to discourage lawyers from leaving?
◆ How might this concern motivate a firm to hire paralegals, rather than new lawyers, in some cases?

Review Questions

1. In what circumstances might an agreement be enforced without consideration?
2. What is illusory consideration and how does the UCC deal with situations that might, at common law, be viewed as illusory because they call for performance to the "satisfaction" of one of the parties?
3. What is a condition precedent? What is a condition subsequent? In each of these situations, we say that there was a valid contract even though the performance originally contemplated does not ultimately occur: Why?
4. Give an example of an accord and satisfaction.

5. Under what circumstances does the UCC allow enforceability of modification of an existing contract without consideration?
6. What is a liquidated debt?
7. What are the special requirements for a contingent fee arrangement under ABA Model Rule 1.5? What kinds of cases may not be handled on a contingency fee basis?
8. In discussing the factors that determine the reasonableness of a fee, the Rule refers to "the likelihood, if apparent to the client, that the acceptance of the particular employment will preclude other employment by the lawyer"; how might acceptance of a case preclude other employment?
9. Identify the issues raised by the following:

   Jay got a new Acme charge card because Acme advertised a low interest rate on unpaid balances. Jay transferred his balance from another credit card to the Acme card. After six months, Acme increased the rate and sent out a mailing that stated that, by continuing to use the card, the customer agreed to the rather significant change. Jay thought the mailing was just more junk mail and never read it. He continued to use the Acme card, paid the minimum payment for a couple of months, and after three months, finally noticed the change. The difference in the interest rate will cost Jay a substantial amount of money.

ACROSS

2. stated consideration does not really obligate party
7. _____ power, the ability of a party to negotiate
8. consideration changes to motivate faster or better performance
9. contract to buy company's entire production
10. police officers often cannot collect rewards because they have a pre- _____ duty
11. contract, e.g., we will buy all of our dairy products from Acme
13. condition _____ identifies an event that must occur before performance goes forward
16. contract might include _____, e.g., buyer has $3,000 for light fixtures

17. _____ debt not in dispute
18. UCC allows _____ of existing contracts without consideration
19. contracts between businesses

DOWN

1. to terminate the contract
3. condition _____ can undo the contract
4. "_____ consideration is non consideration"
5. consideration so unfair it is shocking
6. _____-and-satisfaction
12. stated consideration did not really occur
14. _____ dealing contract can have anti-trust implications
15. _____-plus, a way of sharing risk
16. a take-it-or-leave-it contract

MATTHEW A. HURD, Plaintiff-Appellant, v. WILDMAN, HARROLD, ALLEN AND DIXON, Defendant-Appellee. APPELLATE COURT OF ILLINOIS, FIRST DISTRICT

303 Ill. App. 3d 84; 707 N.E.2d 609; February 2, 1999, Decided

BACKGROUND

Plaintiff is an attorney licensed to practice in Illinois. Following graduation from law school in 1985, plaintiff became employed at Wildman, Harrold, Allen & Dixon (the firm), governed by a written partnership agreement. In 1992, plaintiff became a nonequity partner of the firm in its Chicago office.

Returning from his honeymoon, plaintiff, without consulting independent counsel, signed a release and separation agreement (release) drafted by a partner. The release provided, in part: "13. In consideration of the promises under this Agreement, [plaintiff], individually, and for successors, assigns, heirs, and agents, each and all of them, hereby unconditionally and forever release, acquit, and discharge the Firm, its partners, employees, agents, and attorneys from any and all claims, demands, liabilities, and causes of action of every kind, nature and description whatsoever which arise out of its/his/her/their conduct of the business of the Firm, whether known or unknown, or suspected to exist, which [plaintiff] ever had or may now have against the Firm, or any of the released causes of action arising from your partnership in the Firm, the Partnership Agreement, or any federal, state, or local laws or regulations, including but not limited to the Age Discrimination in Employment Act and law pertaining to breach of contract or wrongful discharge."

[A]lmost three years following execution of the release, plaintiff filed his complaint, alleging that the firm breached the partnership agreement, regarding involuntary withdrawal of partners, and sought $ 270,000 in separation benefits. The agreement provided: "If a partner's separation results from involuntary withdrawal or death, the firm shall pay to the separated partner . . . a sum equal to twice his or her Base Amount. . . ."

Count II of plaintiff's complaint contended that the firm breached its fiduciary duties to him by . . . unlawful withholding of plaintiff's last paycheck, "until [plaintiff] was coerced into signing a purported release in violation of the Wage Payment and Collection Act . . ." The firm contended that the partnership agreement demonstrated that plaintiff was not entitled to separation payments. The firm contended: (1) plaintiff's agreement contained a release that unambiguously released claims in counts I and II of his complaint; (2) plaintiff failed to plead facts sufficient to allege fraud, illegality or self-dealing to support a claim for breach of fiduciary duty; and (3) there were insufficient facts to justify a request for punitive damages.

The trial court found that plaintiff was not an "employee" pursuant to the Wage Payment and Collection Act . . . granted defendant's motion to dismiss.

On appeal, plaintiff contends that: (2) the release was executed under duress and was . . . unenforceable; (3) there was no additional consideration to support the release; and (4) breach of fiduciary duties by defendant.

The release is unambiguous. . . . Once defendant establishes existence of a release, legal and binding on its face, the burden shifts to plaintiff to prove it invalid. . . . However, a release may be voided where its execution was obtained through fraud, duress, illegality or mistake. Economic duress is a condition where one is induced by wrongful act or threat to make a contract under circumstances that deprive one of exercise of free will . . . To establish duress, one must demonstrate that the threat left the individual "bereft of the quality of mind essential to making a contract." . . . The acts or threats must be wrongful; however, the term "wrongful" is not limited to acts that are criminal, tortious, or in violation of a contractual duty. They extend to acts that are wrongful in a moral sense. . . . In "economic duress," the defense cannot be predicated upon a demand that is lawful or upon threatening to do that which a party has a legal right to do . . . [W]here consent to is secured merely because of hard bargaining or financial pressure, duress does not exist . . . party must demonstrate circumstances depriving him of exercise of free will to invalidate an agreement. Unless wrongful or unlawful pressure is applied, there is no economic duress . . .

[P]laintiff contends that execution of the release was under economic duress as the firm "withheld direct deposit of his draw until [plaintiff] executed the Agreement." Plaintiff's affidavit specifically indicated that plaintiff feared that checks he had written would bounce, that he would be evicted, and that he was depending upon his fellow partners for references. However, these allegations do not establish that plaintiff lacked the quality of mind essential to executing the release . . . subjective fears do not amount to economic duress . . . plaintiff has failed to show that the release was entered into because of duress. . . .

III

Plaintiff contends that the court erred in dismissing his complaint as there was no additional consideration to support the release. . . . The release called for plaintiff to vacate his office and further stated that the firm would: provide voice mail and secretarial services; pay plaintiff's regular "draw" in the same installments, regardless of whether plaintiff had begun practicing at another firm prior to [stated] date; pay plaintiff a tax "draw" of $8,125; offer plaintiff to purchase his office furnishings at book value; and allow plaintiff to remain on the firm's . . . insurance programs until. . . . [P]laintiff contends that there was no additional consideration because the firm was required to provide him the above under the preexisting duty rule. "A release must be based upon consideration which consists either of some right, interest, profit or benefit accruing to one party, or some forbearance, detriment, loss of responsibility given, suffered or undertaken by another." . . . Any act or promise that is a benefit to one or a detriment to the other is sufficient . . . consideration was bestowed upon plaintiff.

[I]nquiry into whether a contract is supported by consideration does not extend to the adequacy of consideration. . . . It is not [a] court's function to review the amount of consideration unless so grossly inadequate as to shock the conscience. . . . inadequacy of consideration, in the absence of fraud or unconscionable advantage, ordinarily is insufficient to justify setting aside a contract. . . . notwithstanding legal or ethical considerations the firm had to plaintiff, plaintiff agreed to "unconditionally . . . release Firm, from *any and all* claims. A promise to do something one is already obligated to do is no consideration . . . signing the release, plaintiff obligated himself to never file suit against the firm in exchange for benefits he was not entitled to . . . this was adequate consideration.

[P]laintiff ratified the agreement by his conduct. . . . "A party cannot be permitted to retain the benefits received under a contract and at the same time escape the obligations . . . If a releaser . . . retains consideration after learning that the release is voidable . . . constitutes a ratification of the release." A victim of fraud who, knowing of the fraud, "accepts the benefits flowing . . . for any considerable length of time ratifies the contract." Here, following execution of the release, plaintiff was compensated . . . received a tax "draw" . . . offered the opportunity to purchase his office furnishings . . . and was allowed to remain on the firm's . . . insurance programs. . . . After accepting this compensation, plaintiff waited close to three years to file suit. As a result, plaintiff ratified the purportedly unenforceable release . . .

Plaintiff contends that the court failed to consider breach of fiduciary duty [T]he release defeated plaintiff's claims. . . . Plaintiff has the burden of establishing that the defense is unfounded. . . . plaintiff has not met this burden . . . Accordingly, the judgment of the circuit court is affirmed.

6

◆ ● ◆

Legality

◆ ● ◆

This chapter explores the traditional grounds for finding a contract clause to be illegal, as well as the developing concept of "public policy," protection of consumers, and common provisions that may be unenforceable. The topic overlaps with issues of invalid assent, discussed in an earlier chapter, so students may want to review those concepts.

A. **Violations of Statutes**
    1. **Licensing**
    2. **Usury and Other Lending Laws**
    3. **Gambling**
    4. **Blue Laws**
    5. **Torts**
    6. **Public Policy**
B. **Exculpatory Clauses**
C. **Restraint of Trade**
D. **Practical and Ethical Considerations**

An agreement that calls for violation of a statute, commission of a tort, or actions that are contrary to public policy is unenforceable. The illegality of one part of an agreement does not always mean that the entire agreement is unenforceable. In some cases a court may find that the rest of the agreement can be enforced without the illegal provision; the illegal provision is **severable**. When a court

Severable
Remainder of agreement can be enforced without unenforceable provision contained in the agreement

121

Blue-Penciling
Court edits parts of a contract

In Pari Delicto
The parties are equally at fault.

"edits out" parts of a contract, it is sometimes called **blue-penciling**. In addition, courts have discretion to avoid harming an innocent party, if necessary. The term **in pari delicto** means that parties are equally at fault.

Example

In a lawsuit concerning construction of a residence, the judge learns that the builder was operating without a license, in violation of a licensing statute. The judge subsequently learns that the homeowners were also in violation of the law; they obtained financing assistance from the city by claiming to be first-time homeowners who intend to live in the house. In fact, they own and live in another house and plan to rent the new house as an income property. The judge may determine the relative "fault" of the parties in determining whether to enforce the entire contract, parts of the contract, or none of the contract.

A.   Violations of Statutes

For obvious reasons, agreements involving serious criminal conduct, such as buying illegal drugs or hiring a "hit man," are not enforceable. Other agreements that violate statutes in a less flamboyant way might include, for example, rental of property with a promise to exclude minorities. If the violation is **malum per se**, meaning inherently "bad," the agreement is likely unenforceable. Other statutory violations are not inherently bad and are less serious (**malum prohitum**). The results can vary. The *Baby M* sample case at the end of this chapter includes extensive discussion of statutory violations as well as the more general violations of public policy.

Malum per se
Inherently bad

Malum prohitum
Not inherently bad; less serious

1.   Licensing

If a licensing law is intended to protect the public, agreements in violation of the law are unenforceable. For example, Attorney Bell was disbarred last year. Bell's neighbor, Adams, was unaware of the disbarment and asked Bell to prepare a complicated will and trust agreement. Bell did the work and submitted a bill for $1,000. Adams will not have to pay. The agreement was illegal.

On the other hand, a license requirement may be only a way of raising money. For example, River City requires that all door-to-door sales people go to city hall and pay $10 for a peddlers' license. Unaware of the requirement, Betsy-the-Brownie-Scout goes to Attorney Bell's house to sell Girl Scout cookies. Bell, in a wicked mood because of the disbarment, orders $300 worth of the low-cal cookies that nobody wants. When Betsy delivers the cookies and tries to collect, Bell claims that the agreement was illegal because of the lack of a license. No wonder Bell was disbarred! The contract is likely enforceable.

2. Usury and Other Lending Laws

A **usurious** contract is one that charges an illegal rate of interest on a loan. States have different laws concerning the rate of interest that may be charged on various types of loans. **Consumer loans**, which do not involve businesses, and loans that do not involve regulated banks are most often regulated. Visit the "Lectric Law Library" to find the rate for your state (http://www.lectlaw.com/files/ban02.htm).

The interest rate on so-called "pay day" or "title" loans is a current "hot topic." A related matter is the disclosures made in lending. Visit the Federal Trade Commission (FTC) website, http://www.ftc.gov/bcp/conline/pubs/alerts/pdayalrt.htm, for an explanation of pay day loans, and for an explanation of Truth-in-Lending (http://www.ftc.gov/ogc/stat3.htm).

Some states and the FTC regulate other aspects of lending contracts also. For example, the FTC Credit Practices Rule prohibits "confession of judgment" clauses like the one below. Read the sample clause, which is written in a way that would be incomprehensible to most borrowers. Were you able to determine that, by signing, the borrower was giving up normal legal rights, such as the right to be notified that a lawsuit has been filed and the right to appear in court and raise defenses to the lawsuit? Did you realize that the borrower is agreeing to have judgment entered against him immediately and to be represented by any attorney chosen by the lender? For more information, visit www.ftc.gov/bcp/conline/pubs/buspubs/complcred.htm.

The consequences of violation of statutes relating to lending can be very different. In some cases, the lender might not be allowed to collect any interest (the court regards the illegal interest rate as severable); in others the lender might not be allowed to recover even the principal amount (the court finds the illegal provision not severable and the entire agreement unenforceable).

Usurious Contract
Charges an illegal rate of interest on a loan

Consumer Loan
Loan for personal or family purposes

EXHIBIT 6-1
Example of a **Confession of Judgment**, also called a "Cognovits"

To secure payment hereof, the undersigned jointly and severally irrevocably authorize any attorney of any court of record to appear for any one or more of them in such court in term or vacation, after default in payment hereof and confess a judgment without process in favor of the creditor hereof for such amount as may then appear unpaid hereon, to release all errors which may intervene in any such proceedings, and to consent to immediate execution upon such judgment, hereby ratifying every act of such attorney hereunder.

Confession of Judgment
A clause that permits immediate entry of judgment without notice or an opportunity to present defenses

---

Assignment 6-1

Using your state statutes, find out:
    Does your state require a license for making consumer loans?
    Does your state regulate pay day loans?

---

3. Gambling

Most states now permit some forms of wagering, for example at casinos or racetracks or through a lottery, but may prohibit various agreements relating to gambling. For example, states differ on whether gambling on credit is allowed. In a sense, taking insurance is a form of gambling and many states prohibit taking insurance on another person if you do not have a legitimate financial interest in that person (an **insurable interest**).

Insurable Interest
Legitimate financial interest in a person

Assignment 6-2

Pyramid Scheme
Multi-level arrangement in which money is made by recruiting new people

A **pyramid scheme** can be a form of gambling. The sample case at the end of the chapter involves a pyramid scheme. Visit the FTC website, http://www.ftc.gov/bcp/conline/features/mlm.htm, and write a one-paragraph definition of "pyramid scheme."

---

4. Blue Laws

Blue Law
Prohibits certain transactions on Sundays

Sunday Statute
Prohibits certain transactions on Sundays; see Blue Law

A "**blue law**," also called a "**Sunday**" **statute**, prohibits certain transactions on Sundays. These laws are less common now, but still exist. For example, a law prohibiting the sale of liquor on Sunday morning is common. Your state may have its own unique Sunday laws; for example, Illinois prohibits auto dealerships from operating on Sundays.

5. Torts

A **tort** is a civil wrong (not a criminal prosecution) that is sometimes based in statute and sometimes based in common law. If an agreement calls for commission of a tort, even if there is no statutory violation, it is likely unenforceable. For example, JB, a successful painter, agrees to make derogatory, false remarks about other brands of paint, such as "it runs," or "that brand takes 3 coats to cover anything" in return for special pricing on Bozo Paints. The state has no statute dealing with **slander** (false statements that hurt the reputation of another), but the agreement is probably illegal.

Slander
False statements that hurt the reputation of another

6. Public Policy

Even if no specific statute prohibits the terms of the agreement, a court can refuse to enforce the agreement if it is **contrary to public policy**, meaning that it is not good for society. Courts have discretion to determine public policy by looking at statutes, even if they are not directly applicable, and common law. Governmental entities are, in some states, prohibited from including certain types of clauses in their contracts because those clauses may be against public policy. For an example, see http://www.legal.uncc.edu/prohibitedclauses.html. A sample case at the end of this chapter, *In the Matter of Baby M,* provides an excellent example of a court analyzing a public policy issue. Certain types of contracts commonly involve consideration of public policy.

Contrary to Public Policy
Not good for society

EXHIBIT 6-2

Many people think that U.S. law does not adequately protect consumers against unfair clauses and that unfair clauses should be considered illegal or contrary to public policy.

In 1993 the Council of the European Communities adopted a Directive on Unfair Terms in Consumer Contracts, requiring that member states pass laws to protect consumers. In 2002 French courts requested that AOL remove clauses from its subscriber contracts, which it called "abusive" or even "illegal." Other internet service providers may face similar orders, based on clauses that allow the companies to unilaterally modify the contract, clauses that imply acceptance by the subscriber of changes to pricing, billing and general conditions and clauses that absolve the company from liability for interruptions or errors in the service.

The European Union (learn more at http://europa.eu/pol/cons/index_en.htm) is taking action to inform and protect consumers. Should the United States be doing more? Some states do more than others, for example, Florida has declared that exculpatory clauses (described below) are unenforceable in residential leases. (83.47, Fla. Stats)

B. Exculpatory Clauses

Exculpatory Clause
Provision that attempts to excuse a party from liability for that party's torts

Tortious
Constituting a tort

An **exculpatory clause** is a provision, in an agreement, that attempts to excuse a party from liability for that party's own **tortious** (constituting a tort) actions. If the clause attempts to excuse liability for intentional or reckless conduct, it is generally unenforceable.

Example

Jo, an aspiring model, enters into a contract with Bill, a photographer and publicist. The contract, which Jo did not read, included a statement that Bill would have no liability for any torts committed against Jo. Bill subsequently uses pictures of Jo on a website advertising pornography or, perhaps Bill becomes angry during a photo shoot and slaps Jo, breaking her nose. In either case, Bill's actions constitute an intentional tort. If Jo sues Bill, it is likely that a court will not enforce the exculpatory clause because Bill's actions were intentional.

If the exculpatory clause involves negligent torts, the court will look at a number of factors to determine whether it is enforceable. Those factors include:

- Was the clause conspicuous and clear? A disclaimer, on the back side of a valet parking receipt, not seen until after the valet drives away with the car, is less effective than a sign, at the entrance to a parking garage, proclaiming "we are not responsible for any damage . . ."

Arms-Length Transaction
Relationship where parties have equal power to negotiate terms

- What is the relationship between the parties and the relative "need" of the parties? In an **arms-length transaction** the parties have equal power to negotiate terms. That is not often true between employer and employee, doctor and patient, customer and electric company, or a landlord and tenant.
- To what degree can the parties protect themselves? Was the hazard obvious? Was it within control of one of the parties?

Hold Harmless Clause
One party agrees to compensate other for losses arising from contract; see Indemnification Clause

Indemnification Clause
One party agrees to compensate the other for losses arising from the contract; see Hold Harmless Clause

In considering exculpatory clauses, keep in mind that a contract only binds its parties. If Stevie takes a job as a driver for Acme Co. and signs an agreement stating that "Acme Co. shall not be liable for the consequences of my negligent driving," the agreement only covers the relationship between Stevie and Acme. Pedestrians and other drivers are not part of that agreement and may sue Acme. The contract clause may then operate as a **"hold harmless"** or **indemnification** clause, under which one party agrees to compensate the other for losses arising from the contract.

EXHIBIT 6-3
Example Exculpatory Clause

Do you think a typical vacationer, renting a boat, would read or understand the following?

Renter _____, his/her family, relatives, heirs, and legal representatives do hereby, waive, discharge and covenant not to sue Voyagaire Houseboats ... for any loss or damage, or any claim or damage or any injury to any person or persons or property, or any death of any person or persons whether caused by negligence or defect, while such rental equipment is in my possession and/or under my use....[1]

Example Indemnification in Contract Between Insurance Provider and Dentist

Dentist agrees to indemnify, defend, and hold harmless Iota Insurance, Inc., its directors, officers, employees and agents for any and all claims, liabilities, damages, losses, costs, fees and expenses arising from or in any way related to any dental or other service performed by Dentist and any employees, associates, contractors or agents of Dentist.

---

[1]The Minnesota Supreme Court held that this language violated public policy in its 2005 decision, *Yang v. Voyagaire Houseboats, Inc.*, 701 N.W.2d 783.

C. Restraint of Trade

The basic policy of the United States favors free trade; and contract provision that inhibits free trade is subject to scrutiny in court. The most common form of provision that might restrain trade (a party's ability to engage in business) is a **covenant not to compete**. Non-competes, as they are called, are not enforceable independently; they can only be enforced as part of larger, legitimate agreement.

When a non-compete clause appears in a contract for the **sale of a business**, it is generally enforceable, if it is reasonable in terms of time limit, geographic limitations, and scope of activity covered. What is reasonable depends on the nature of the business and what is necessary to protect the buyer's legitimate interests. In the sale of a business, both parties are normally represented by lawyers and can negotiate terms that both can live with.

Covenant Not to Compete
Provision under which party agrees to refrain from engaging in specified business activities ("non-compete")

Example

Paul's Family Restaurant is a really popular place in Springfield. Dell buys the restaurant for $800,000 because it is so popular. How will Dell feel if, a week after the transaction is closed, the seller puts up a sign on vacant land across the street: "Coming in 6 months ... the NEW Paul's, featuring your old friends, Chef Stella

& Host Dan." If Dell had been smart, the sales contract would have included a restriction: "Seller agrees that seller will not operate, work in, or represent any restaurant within 5 miles of the premises for a period of two years." Such a restriction would be reasonable. On the other hand, would it be reasonable to include a restriction for 10 years, or one that covered the entire U.S., or one that limited the sellers from participating in ANY business? Probably not . . .

The parties are not so equal when entering an **employment contract**. Employers do have valid reasons to restrict future employment: concerns that customers will move with the employee; concerns that the employee with take secret information to the new employer; and concerns about the cost of training new people. On the other hand, the employee's freedom to change jobs and ability to make a living are also very important. Courts are, therefore, particularly careful in analyzing restrictions on employees. Not only must such a restriction be reasonable in terms of time and geography, it must be related to the employer's legitimate interest. A restriction might be a general promise not to engage in competition with the employer or might be more specific and prohibit the use of certain information acquired as an employee, solicitation of the employer's customers, or "poaching" of other employees.

Assignment 6-3

Read the cases at the end of this chapter and discuss:

1. To what extent did the personal characteristics of the "Baby M" parties impact the decision and public perception? What if the surrogate had been a well-educated woman who had originally entered the contract in order to raise funds for experimental treatment of her husband's cancer? What if, instead of leaving with the baby, she had immediately sought judicial review? What if the biological father had a criminal record and an unstable marriage?
2. Do you think the court was considering implications for the future as well as the past histories of the parties? If surrogacy contracts were always enforceable, might wealthy women rent the wombs of poorer women to avoid weight gain, stretch marks, and medical risks of pregnancy?
3. Could the contract at issue in the *Cohen* case be considered punitive? Why? Do you think this influenced the court?
4. Did the law firm have legitimate interests that were injured by Cohen's departure? Could the firm have protected itself by any other means?

Courts will also consider the interests of people outside the contract and may refuse to enforce a covenant if, for example, it would mean that patients would have to travel 100 miles to continue to see the doctor they have been seeing. What is reasonable will, again, depend on the nature of the business and the interest the employer is trying to protect. In addition, courts may consider the impact of the restriction on those outside the contract: patients and clients. A sample case at the end of this chapter contains an analysis of a covenant's impact on a lawyer's clients.

Example

It is in the best interests of employers to make restrictive covenants reasonable so that they will be upheld. Lynn, a newly graduated interior designer, is offered a contract to work for Jones Brothers, a Milwaukee-area furniture chain. The job will involve meeting with corporate clients to design and choose furniture for corporate offices. A clause providing that: "If employee leaves Jones for any reason, including firing or layoff, employee may not work for any furniture or design business in the state of Wisconsin (including employee's own business) for five years" is likely unreasonable. It might leave Lynn unable to find appropriate employment and it likely goes beyond the employer's needs. A more reasonable restriction might read: "If employee leaves Jones for any reason, including firing or layoff, employee may not contact any clients of Jones for a period of two years, if employee had contact with the client while employed by Jones."

Another possible restriction is an **exclusive dealing agreement**. For example, Bari's Café agrees to buy its baked goods only from Herb's Bakery in exchange for a ten-percent discount; Bari's will deal with Herb's exclusively in buying baked goods. An exclusive dealing agreement may, in some situations, violate anti-trust laws and should be analyzed carefully.

Assignment 6-4

Your instructor will tell you which problems to do, so that your class gets reports on each of these issues. Summarize a case and report to the class, focusing on how a court in your state resolved the situation. In structuring your query, remember to use expanders and to brainstorm for synonyms (*e.g.,* "restrictive covenant," "non-compet!" "promise or covenant or clause /s compet!") Use your CALR subscription or Loislaw to find a case involving:

◆ A restrictive covenant in an employment contract (what did the court find reasonable/unreasonable);
◆ A restrictive covenant in the sale of a business (what did the court find reasonable/unreasonable);
◆ A contract in contemplation of cohabitation by unmarried individuals of opposite sexes;
◆ An exculpatory clause in a rental agreement.

For the following cases, focus on how the court avoided harm to an "innocent" party, if it regarded one party as more at fault.

◆ A party trying to collect for medical or legal services rendered in violation of a licensing law (luckily these are rare cases, you may have to search multiple states);
◆ A debt with a usurious rate of interest;
◆ A violation of laws regulating lenders (lender licensing, truth-in-lending);
◆ A contract to insure the life of another, where the beneficiary did not have an insurable interest;
◆ A gambling debt or agreement or a pyramid scheme;
◆ A lawyer facing civil liability (a malpractice or negligence action) or disciplinary action because of involvement with a contract that included provisions that were illegal or contrary to public policy. You may have to search all 50 states on CALR or Loislaw and look at your ethics opinions site to find this one!

Discussion

Tenant leased a warehouse and office space in a business park for a term of five years, but vacated after about half the term. The landlord was unable to find a new tenant and sued under a lease clause that stated: "In the event of termination of this Lease by reason of a violation of its terms by the Lessee, Lessor shall be entitled to prove claim for and obtain judgment against Lessee for the balance of the rent agreed to be paid for the term herein provided, plus all expenses of Lessor in regaining possession of the premises and the reletting thereof, including attorneys' fees and court costs, crediting against such claim, however, any amount obtained by reason of any such reletting." This is called an **acceleration clause**. What does it mean, in plain English? Do you think the court should enforce the clause as written? Can you think of a fair solution?

Acceleration Clause
Causes payments to become immediately due upon the happening of stated event

D. Practical and Ethical Considerations

The material in this chapter touches on several "hot" issues in the practice of law:

• Lawyers are prohibited from imposing restrictive covenants on each other. A covenant that might be valid in another employment agreement is likely invalid if it restricts a lawyer because it would, in fact, restrict clients in their choice of lawyers. Read the *Cohen* case in the samples that follow; contrast with the firm's agreement in the *Hurd* case at the end of the chapter on Consideration. Do the cases represent two different ways to achieve the same goal? Find the applicable Model Rule or the rule in your state.
• Lawyers are licensed on a state-by-state basis, so that a lawyer may be violating a licensing requirement in, for example:

- Attending a real estate closing for a long-term client buying a vacation home in a neighboring state;
- Responding to a question e-mailed from another state by a visitor to the firm's website;
- Working at the corporate law department in Chicago and giving advice to corporate employees across the country;
- Working in a neighboring state after her law office was destroyed by a hurricane.

ABA Model Rule 5.5 addresses multijurisdictional practice and the ABA Commission on Multijurisdictional Practice has a number of proposals to address these and other issues. For information on whether your state has adopted any of the proposals, visit http://www.abanet.org/cpr/mjp-home.html.

- Lawyers must protect client confidences, subject to exceptions relating to a client's criminal activity. Find your state's Rule of Professional Responsibility (ABA Model Rule 1.6) and identify the situations in which a lawyer is permitted to reveal information relating to representation of a client.
  - Does your state's rule require a lawyer to reveal information about a client under court order?
  - Is a lawyer required to reveal information about a client if that client has committed a very serious crime?
  - Is the ethical rule any different in situations involving fraud on a tribunal (perjury)?

Review Questions

1. What factors determine the enforceability of a restrictive covenant?
2. What factors determine the enforceability of an exculpatory clause?
3. What is an indemnification?
4. What can a court do if only part of an agreement is illegal or against public policy?
5. When might failure to have a required license NOT be a basis for invalidating a contract?
6. Given ABA Model Rule 1.6 and the rules discussed in previous chapters, what should a lawyer do in the following circumstances:
   a. Lawyer becomes aware that client, practicing as a chiropractor, is not a validly licensed chiropractor.
   b. Client is involved in a heated custody battle and it looks like client will win. Last week client's 2-year-old child was found wandering several blocks from other spouse's home, alone. Lawyer now learns that client actually took the child from other spouse's fenced backyard, took the child to a spot several blocks away, and, from a nearby public phone, placed the "anonymous" call alerting the police.

c. Would it make a difference if lawyer learned about the situation described above before it happened?

d. Would it make a difference if the lawyer learned about the above situation several years after it occurred?

e. Client wants to include an obviously unreasonable restrictive covenant in an employment contract, to prohibit employees from working for any competitor for six years.

f. Lawyer learns that the contract client has been using for years contains a false statement about client's credentials.

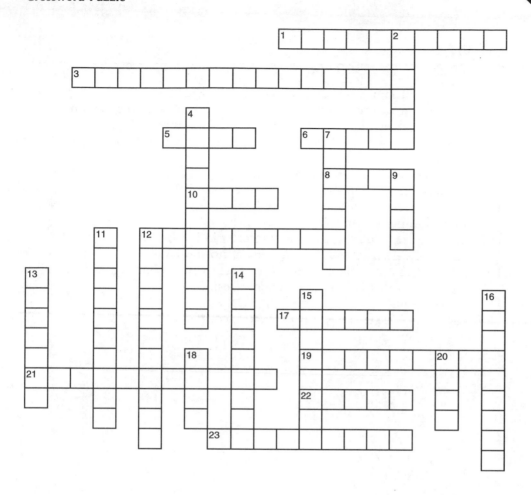

ACROSS

1. _____ of judgment allows immediate entry of judgment without notice or hearing
3. one party agrees to compensate the other for losses
5. _____-harmless, one party agrees to compensate other for losses
6. charging interest at an illegal rate
8. _____-length transaction; the parties had equal power to negotiate
10. in _____ delicto, parties equally at fault
12. _____-dealing arrangement; one party will deal with no others
17. even though no statute makes the conduct illegal, a court can refuse to enforce a contract on grounds of public _____
19. legal parts of agreement can be enforced without illegal part—which is _____
21. type of conduct least likely to be protected by an exculpatory clause
22. _____ per se, inherently bad
23. to be enforceable, a non-compete covenant must be reasonable in time and _____

DOWN

2. blue law prohibits transactions on _____
4. an exculpatory clause must be _____ and clear to be enforceable
7. false statements that hurt the reputation of another
9. a covenant not to compete is most likely to be enforced in _____ of a business
11. Courts carefully scrutinize non-competes in _____ contracts
12. a clause that attempts to excuse a party from liability
13. _____ scheme, a multi-level arrangement in which money is made by recruiting new people
14. _____ interest, a financial interest in person's life
15. _____ loan; borrower is person, not business
16. If a _____ law is intended to protect the public, agreements in violation of that law are likely unenforceable
18. a civil wrong
20. _____-penciling, a court edits a contract

CASES FOR ANALYSIS

IN THE MATTER OF BABY M, A PSEUDONYM FOR AN ACTUAL PERSON
SUPREME COURT OF NEW JERSEY

109 N.J. 396; 537 A.2d 1227
February 3, 1988, Decided

[Ed. note: This case has been heavily edited.]

[T]he Court is asked to determine the validity of a contract to provide a new way of bringing children into a family. For a fee of $10,000, a woman agrees to be artificially inseminated with the semen of another woman's husband; she is to conceive a child and after its birth surrender it to the natural father and his wife. The . . . natural mother will thereafter be forever separated from her child. The wife is to adopt the child, and she and the natural father are to be regarded as its parents. [T]his is called a "surrogacy contract," the natural mother called the "surrogate mother."

William Stern and Mary Beth Whitehead entered into a surrogacy contract. It recited that Stern's wife was infertile, that they wanted a child, . . . that through artificial insemination using Stern's sperm, Whitehead would become pregnant, carry the child, deliver it to Stern, and . . . terminate her rights so that Mrs. Stern could adopt. Mrs. Stern's status as a nonparty to the agreement presumably was to avoid the baby-selling statute. *N.J.S.A.* 9:3-54.

Stern agreed to pay Whitehead $10,000 after the child's birth, on delivery to him . . . to pay $7,500 to the Infertility Center. The Center . . . arranged the contract by bringing the parties together, explaining the process, furnishing the contractual form, and providing legal counsel.

The history of the parties' involvement suggests good faith. William and Elizabeth Stern were married in 1974, both were Ph.D. candidates. Due to financial considerations and Mrs. Stern's pursuit of a medical degree, they decided to defer starting a family until 1981. Mrs. Stern learned that she might have multiple sclerosis and that the disease in some cases renders pregnancy a health risk. Her anxiety appears to have exceeded actual risk, which current medical authorities assess as minimal. Nonetheless, fearing that pregnancy might precipitate blindness, paraplegia, or other debilitation, the Sterns decided to forego having their own children. Most of [Stern's] family had been destroyed in the Holocaust . . . he wanted to continue his bloodline . . . considered adoption, but were discouraged by the substantial delay apparently involved and by potential problems from their age and differing religious backgrounds.

Whitehead's response apparently resulted from her sympathy with others who could have no children; she also wanted the $10,000 to help her family. . . . Whitehead became pregnant. The pregnancy was uneventful and on March 27, 1986, Baby M was born.

Not wishing anyone to be aware of the arrangement, Mr. and Mrs. Whitehead appeared as the parents. Her birth certificate indicated her name to be Sara Whitehead and her father to be Richard Whitehead. Sterns visited the hospital unobtrusively to see the newborn.

Whitehead realized, almost from the birth, that she could not part with this child. She had felt a bond during pregnancy. Some indication of attachment was conveyed at the hospital. She apparently broke into tears and indicated that she did not know if she could give up the child. She talked about how the baby looked like her other daughter. . . . she turned child over to Sterns at the Whiteheads' home. . . .

Whitehead's despair frightened Sterns. She told them that she could not live without her baby, that she must have her, only for one week. Sterns, concerned that Whitehead might commit suicide, believing that Whitehead would keep her word, turned the child over to her. [F]our months later, the child was returned to the Sterns, having been forcibly removed from [a] home in Florida owned by Whitehead's parents. . . . She was brought to New Jersey. The prior order awarding custody to Sterns was reaffirmed. Pending judgment, Whitehead was awarded limited visitation.

Sterns' complaint, in addition to seeking custody, sought enforcement of the contract. Pursuant to the contract, it asked that the child be permanently placed in their custody, that Whitehead's parental rights be terminated, and that Mrs. Stern be allowed to adopt the child.

The trial took thirty-two days . . . expressing that the contract was valid, the trial court devoted its opinion to the baby's best interests . . . inconsistency is apparent. The contract calls for sole custody in Sterns, and termination of Whitehead's rights, regardless of evaluation of best interests. [T]he court awarded custody to Stern based on evidence and analysis as if no contract existed. Its rationalization was that while the contract was valid, specific performance would not be granted unless in the best interests of the child. The issues were as if Stern and Whitehead had had the child out of wedlock and disagreed about custody. The court's awareness of the irrelevance of the contract is suggested by its remark that beyond the question of best interests, "[a]ll other concerns raised by counsel constitute commentary."

The trial court concluded that statutes concerning adoption, termination of parental rights, and payment of money in adoptions, do not apply. It reasoned that because the Legislature did not have surrogacy contracts in mind, those laws were irrelevant . . . that surrogacy contracts are valid and that Stern's rights under the contract were constitutionally protected. . . . Whitehead appealed.

INVALIDITY AND UNENFORCEABILITY
OF SURROGACY CONTRACT

Our conclusion has two bases: direct conflict with existing statutes and conflict with public policies, as expressed in statutory and decisional law.

One of the contract's purposes, adoption through private placement, though permitted in New Jersey "is very much disfavored." Its use of money—and we have no doubt that money is paid to obtain an adoption and not for the personal services of Whitehead—is illegal and perhaps criminal. *N.J.S.A.* 9:3-54. [T]here is coercion: the mother's irrevocable agreement, prior to birth, to surrender the child . . . is unenforceable in private placement adoption. Even where the adoption is through an approved agency, formal agreement occurs only *after* birth after the mother has been offered counseling. *N.J.A.C.* 10:121A-5.4(c). Integral to these invalid provisions is the agreement, equally invalid, of the mother not to contest proceedings to terminate her parental rights, as well as her contractual concession, that the child's best interests would be served by awarding custody to the father and his wife—all of this before she has conceived, and, in some cases, before she has the slightest idea of what the natural father and adoptive mother are like.

The foregoing provisions directly conflict with New Jersey statutes, offend long-established State policies. . . . the entire contract is unenforceable. Stern knew he was paying for adoption of a child; Whitehead knew she was accepting money so that a child might be adopted; Infertility Center knew that it was paid for assisting in the adoption. The actions of all three worked to frustrate the goals of the statute. It strains credulity to claim that these arrangements amount to something other than a private placement adoption for money.

The prohibition of our statute is strong. Violation constitutes a high misdemeanor, *N.J.S.A.* 9:3-54c. The evils inherent in baby-bartering are loathsome. The child is sold without regard for whether the purchasers will be suitable parents. The natural mother does not receive counseling to assist her in making a decision that may affect her for a lifetime . . . monetary incentive may, depending on circumstances, make her decision less voluntary . . . adoptive parents may not be fully informed of the natural parents' medical history. . . .

[T]ermination of Whitehead's parental rights fails to comply with the stringent requirements. Our law provides for such termination only where there has been a voluntary surrender to an approved agency or to the Division of Youth and Family Services accompanied by a formal document acknowledging termination of parental rights, *N.J.S.A.* 9:2-16, -17; *N.J.S.A.* 9:3-41; *N.J.S.A.* 30:4C-23, or where there has been a showing of parental abandonment or unfitness. A termination may ordinarily take one of three forms: an action by an approved agency, an action by DYFS, or an action in connection with a private placement adoption. The standards for termination are substantially the same, except that whereas a written surrender is effective when made to an approved agency or to DYFS, there is no provision for it in the private placement context. *See N.J.S.A.* 9:2-14; *N.J.S.A.* 30:4C-23. . . . [W]here there has been no surrender to an approved agency or DYFS, termination of parental rights will not be granted absent a strong showing of abandonment or neglect. While the statutes make procedural allowances when stepparents are involved, the substantive requirement for terminating natural parents' rights is not relaxed one iota. *N.J.S.A.* 9:3-48c(1); . . . a "best interests" determination is never sufficient to terminate parental rights; the statutory criteria must be proved.

In this case a termination of parental rights was obtained not by proving statutory prerequisites but by claiming the benefit of contractual provisions . . . Since the termination was invalid, adoption by Mrs. Stern could not properly be granted. . . . There is no exception provided by law, and it is not clear that there could be any "order or judgment" validating a surrender of custody as a basis for adoption when that surrender was not in conformance with the statute.

Contractual surrender of parental rights is not provided for in our statutes. In the Parentage Act, *N.J.S.A.* 9:17-38 to -59, there is a provision invalidating any agreement "between an alleged or presumed father and the mother of the child" to bar an action brought for the purpose of determining paternity "[r]egardless of [the contract's] terms." *N.J.S.A.* 9:17-45. Even a settlement agreement concerning parentage reached in a judicially-mandated conference is not valid unless approved by the court. There is no doubt that a contractual provision purporting to constitute irrevocable agreement to surrender a child for adoption is invalid.

B. Public Policy Considerations

The contract's invalidity, resulting from conflict with the above statutory provisions, is further underlined when measured against New Jersey public policy. The basic premise, that natural parents can decide in advance which one is to have custody, bears no relationship to the law that the child's best interests shall determine custody. . . . The fact that the court remedied that aspect of the contract through the "best interests" phase does not make the contract any less offensive to the public policy of this State.

The surrogacy contract guarantees permanent separation of the child from one of its natural parents. Our policy, however, has long been that to the extent possible, children should remain with and be brought up by both of their natural parents. The surrogacy contract violates the policy of this State that the rights of natural parents are equal.

The only legal advice Whitehead received was provided in connection with the contract that she previously entered into with another couple . . . Whitehead was examined and psychologically evaluated, but . . . It is apparent that the profit motive got the better of the Infertility Center. [T]he evaluation . . . was not put to any use, for the psychologist warned that Whitehead demonstrated traits that might make surrender of the child difficult and that there should be further inquiry. To inquire further, however, might have jeopardized the Center's fee.

Worst of all, however, is the contract's total disregard of the best interests of the child. There is not the slightest suggestion that any inquiry will be made at any time to determine the fitness of the Sterns as custodial parents, of Mrs. Stern as an adoptive parent, their superiority to Mrs. Whitehead, or the effect on the child of not living with her natural mother.

This is the sale of a child, or at least the sale of a mother's right to her child, the only mitigating factor being that one of the purchasers is the father. . . . all parties concede that it is unlikely that surrogacy will survive without money. That conclusion contrasts with adoption; for obvious reasons, there remains a steady supply, albeit insufficient, despite the prohibitions against payment. The adoption itself, relieving the natural mother of the financial burden of supporting an infant, is in some sense the equivalent of payment.

Second, the use of money in adoptions does not *produce* the problem — conception occurs, and usually the birth, before illicit funds are offered. With surrogacy, the "problem," consisting of the purchase of a woman's procreative capacity, at the risk of her life, originates with the offer of money. Third, with the law prohibiting the use of money in adoptions, the financial pressure of unwanted pregnancy do not lead the mother to the highest paying, ill-suited, adoptive parents. She is just as well-off surrendering the child to an approved agency. In surrogacy, the highest bidders will become the adoptive parents regardless of suitability, so long as payment is permitted . . . it is clear that it is unlikely that surrogate mothers will be as numerous among those women in the top twenty percent income bracket as among those in the bottom twenty percent.

Putting aside the issue of how compelling her need for money may have been, and how significant her understanding of the consequences . . . consent is irrelevant. There are, in civilized society, some things that money cannot buy. In America, merely because conduct purchased by money was "voluntary" did not mean that it was beyond regulation and prohibition. . . . Employers can no longer buy labor at the lowest price, even though that labor is "voluntary," . . . or buy women's labor for less than paid to men for the same job, . . . , or purchase the agreement of children to perform oppressive labor, . . . or purchase the agreement of workers to subject themselves to unsafe or unhealthful working conditions, . . . There are values more important than granting to wealth whatever it can buy, be it labor, love, or life. Whether this principle recommends prohibition of surrogacy, which sometimes results in great satisfaction to all of the parties, is not for us to say. We note here only that, under existing law, the fact that Mrs. Whitehead "agreed" to the arrangement is not dispositive.

Nothing in this record justifies a finding to terminate Whitehead's parental rights under statutory standard . . . there was no intentional abandonment or very substantial neglect of parental duties without reasonable expectation of reversal in the future, the court never found Whitehead an unfit mother and stated that Whitehead had been a good mother to her other children. The decision to terminate Whitehead's parental rights precluded determination on visitation. Our reversal requires delineation of Whitehead's rights to visitation . . . this factually sensitive issue, never addressed below, should not be determined by this Court.

CONCLUSION

If the Legislature decides to address surrogacy, this case will highlight many potential harms. . . . The problem can be addressed only when society decides what its values and objectives are in this troubling, yet promising, area. . . . The judgment is affirmed in part, reversed in part, and remanded for further proceedings consistent with this opinion.

RICHARD G. COHEN, APPELLANT, V. LORD, DAY & LORD, RESPONDENT COURT OF APPEALS OF NEW YORK

75 N.Y.2d 95; 550 N.E.2d 410; 551 N.Y.S.2d 157 November 14, 1989, Argued December 19, 1989, Decided

[Ed note: Material omitted.]

A law firm partnership agreement which conditions payment of earned but uncollected partnership revenues upon a withdrawing partner's obligation to refrain from the practice of law in competition with the former law firm restricts the practice of law in violation of Disciplinary Rule 2-108 (A) of the New York Code of Professional Responsibility and is unenforceable as against public policy.

For almost 20 years plaintiff Cohen was a partner in the firm, Lord, Day & Lord (LD&L). In 1985, Cohen withdrew to become a partner in another New York City firm.

The LD&L partnership agreement recognized that withdrawing partners were entitled to a share of profits representing unpaid fees, and fees for services performed but not yet billed, at the time of departure. [T]o avoid the expense of detailed accounting, the agreement provided for departure payment, based on a formula, to be paid over a three-year period.

When Cohen requested his departure compensation, LD&L refused to pay, stating that Cohen had forfeited the money by electing to continue to practice law in competition with the firm. [T]he firm relied on the forfeiture-for-competition clause of the agreement: "Notwithstanding anything in this Article * * * if a Partner withdraws and *continues to practice law in any jurisdiction in which the Partnership maintains an office or any contiguous jurisdiction,* . . . he shall have no interest in and *there shall be paid to him no proportion of net profits collected thereafter, whether for services rendered before or after his withdrawal.* There shall be paid to him only his withdrawable credit balance on the books at the date of his withdrawal, together with his capital account."

Cohen sued . . . The firm complained that plaintiff took several LD&L clients and an associate attorney to his new firm. On LD&L's motion to dismiss the court ruled that the clause was unenforceable as violative of Disciplinary Rule 2-108 (A). The Appellate Division reversed, stating that the clause was valid as a "financial disincentive" and did not "prevent plaintiff from practicing law in any jurisdiction." We now reverse.

While the provision does not completely prohibit a withdrawing partner from engaging in the practice of law, the monetary penalty it exacts constitutes an impermissible restriction on the practice of law. **The forfeiture-for-competition provision would discourage and foreclose a withdrawing partner from serving clients who might wish to continue to be represented by the withdrawing lawyer and would thus interfere with the client's choice of counsel.**

DR 2-108 (A) of the New York Code, entitled "Agreements Restricting the Practice of a Lawyer," provides: A lawyer shall not participate in a partnership or employment agreement with another lawyer that restricts the right of a lawyer to practice law after the termination of a relationship, except as a condition to payment of retirement benefits. The purpose is to ensure that the public has the choice of counsel. ABA Formal Opinion No. 300 concluded it was unethical for an attorney to insert a restrictive covenant in a contract of employment with another attorney . . . stated: "Clients are not merchandise. Lawyers are not tradesmen. They have nothing to sell but personal service. An attempt, therefore, to barter in clients, would appear to be inconsistent with the best concepts of our professional status" [A] restrictive covenant * * * would be an attempt to 'barter in clients'. Efforts, direct or indirect, in any way to encroach upon the business of another lawyer, are unworthy of brethren at the Bar * * * prohibits every form of solicitation of employment. A former employee of a lawyer or a law firm would be bound to refrain from any effort to secure the work of clients of his former employer. Furthermore, he would be bound to preserve the confidences and not divulge the secrets, of any clients of his former employer. * * * Obviously, no restrictive covenant in an employment contract is needed to enforce these provisions of the Canons of Professional Ethics.

LD&L argues that DR 2-108 (A) and the ABA opinions condemn only blanket prohibitions on a lawyer's practice of law in a community, and that something denominated an economic disincentive, like its forfeiture-for-competition clause, does not prevent Cohen from practicing law. The argument docs not withstand scrutiny in these circumstances.

In *Matter of Silverberg* held unenforceable an agreement which provided that upon termination of the partnership, neither partner was to represent clients of the other for an 18-month period unless the client directed otherwise in writing. If a partner were to represent a client of the other, 80% of fees recovered were to be turned over to the client's original attorney. The court, stating that "[lawyers] should not traffic in clients," concluded that the agreement "amounts to a covenant restricting the practice of a lawyer" in violation of DR 2-108 (A) (75 AD2d, at 819).

[I]f financial penalties were not "restraints" there would be no need to exempt the specific category of retirement. Retirement benefits are set forth in exclusive section of the agreement—it expressly excludes withdrawing partners and refers back to the forfeiture-for-competition provision. Unlike retirement benefits, which extend to the death of the partner and then may even continue to the surviving spouse, departure compensation is temporally limited—all payments are to conclude three years following withdrawal. Finally, to treat departure compensation as a retirement benefit would invert the exception into the general rule, thus undermining the prohibition against restraints on lawyers practicing law.

Defendant also urges that forfeiture of compensation is justified because of economic hardship suffered by a firm when a partner leaves to join a competitor. While a law firm has interest in its survival and economic well-being and in maintaining clients, it cannot protect those interests by contracting for forfeiture of *earned revenues* during the withdrawing partner's tenure and participation and by, in effect, restricting the choices of the clients to retain and continue the withdrawing member as counsel.

Accordingly, the order of the Appellate Division should be reversed and the case should be remitted to Supreme Court for determination of the amount due plaintiff. *[Ed. note: Dissent and footnotes omitted.]*

7

Capacity

This chapter explores the special protections given to minors and incompetent parties when they attempt to enter into contracts. The material also touches on current issues relating to, and protection available outside the judicial system for, vulnerable members of society.

A. **Minors**
    1. **Minors as Agents for Adults**
    2. **Necessities**
    3. **Fraud**
    4. **Ratification**
B. **Mental Incompetence**
    1. **Determining Mental Incompetence**
    2. **Intoxication**
    3. **Analyzing Incompetence and Intoxication**
C. **Practical and Ethical Issues**

Some people are given special protection from contract mistakes in the form of the right to **avoid** (make void[1]) the contract. Those individuals included minors, the mentally incompetent, and some people under the influence of intoxicating substances. The law presumes competence and the burden of proving incompetence is on the party claiming the right to avoid the contract.

Avoid
Make a contract void; see disaffirm

---

[1]The distinction between a void contract, which is not enforceable and has no legal recognition, and a voidable contract, which is valid unless the party with the power to avoid (the minor or incompetent) chooses to disaffirm, is discussed in Chapter 2.

A.   Minors

Minor
A person who has not reached adult status, typically the day before his/her 18th birthday

Majority
The age of adult status (typically 18)

Infant
A minor

Guardian
Individual with legal responsibility for the minor

Administrator
Responsible for settling a person's financial affairs after death; also called executor

A **minor** is defined by statute in most states as a person who has not reached the day before his or her eighteenth birthdays (the age of **majority**). At common law, minors were called **infants** and "infancy" lasted until age 21. You may still find the term "infants" in use in many legal research materials. A minor (or the minor's **guardian** or **administrator**) generally has the power to avoid a contract, while the adult does not have the same power.

Example

Minors and adults do not have equal rights in a contract. While her husband, Bob, was out of town, Ann held a garage sale and sold an antique crystal vase to Jill for $200. Jill gave Ann $100 cash (all she had with her) and signed a promise to return with the other $100 later. Jill, who is actually 17, appeared to be in her early 20s and Ann never questioned her age. Jill took the vase home, where it fell off a shelf, shattering. Jill can avoid the contract and not have to pay the remaining $100. In a few states, Jill may even be able to get her $100 back. On the other hand, if Bob came home and told Ann that he loved that vase and is very angry that it is gone, Ann cannot avoid the contract and require Jill to return the vase.

Your immediate reaction might be that this is unfair and that it could cause businesses a lot of trouble. In fact, most minors do enter into contracts and it rarely causes businesses trouble. Not only are most minors unaware of their legal right to avoid, they would have difficulty enforcing that right. In addition, there are a number of exceptions to the protection.

EXHIBIT 7-1

Example:
   States have created various exceptions to the rights of minors to disaffirm contracts:

VERIFICATION OF SELF-SUFFICIENT MINOR STATUS
(15 through 17 years of age — California Civil Code 34.6)

For the purpose of obtaining diagnosis or treatment at the Campus Health Center, or by any physician or dentist associated with the clinic, the undersigned certifies that all of the following facts are true:

1) I am living separate and apart from my parents or legal guardian.

Place of Residence of minor (Number and Street)

City, State and Zip Code

EXHIBIT 7-1
(continued)

Place of Residence of Parent or Guardian

2) I am managing my own financial affairs regardless of source of income (so long as it is not derived from a source declared to be a crime by law).

_____

Name and Address of Bank

_____

Name and Address of Employer

_____

Other Source of Financial Support — Explain

3) I understand that I will be financially responsible for the charges incurred for my medical or dental treatment and care, and that I may not disaffirm this consent because I am a minor. I am _____ years of age, having been born on the _____ day of Month _____, Year _____.

Dated: _____ Signed: _____

Witness: _____

---

1. Minors as Agents for Adults

If a minor acts as an **agent**, for the benefit of and under the direction of an adult, the adult is the real party to the contract. This is what happens when a mom sends her teenager to the store to pick up milk and bread or even to buy school clothes. (Agency is more fully explained in a later chapter and a sample power of attorney, the document that creates the agency relationship, is reproduced later in this chapter.)

Imagine that Mom puts $25,000 in Son's account and sends the very mature-looking 17-year-old to buy an expensive car from an unsuspecting older man. The plan is to drive the car for about 10 months, avoid the contract, and get the money back. Will it work? Probably not; the seller will likely make the effort to research where Son got the money and be able to prove that Son was actually acting for Mom.

Agent
One who is authorized to act for or in place of another; representative

2. Necessities

There are laws limiting the power of avoidance with respect to certain contracts, such as student loans, some banking contracts, military enlistment, and

Necessities
Things indispensable to life; reasonably needed for subsistence, health, comfort, and education, considering the person's age, station in life, and medical condition

Emancipation
Minor is no longer under care/control of an adult

obligations that would be enforceable without a contract (such as to pay tort damages or support a child). In addition, a minor can have liability under contracts for **necessities** (also called necessaries). This is similar to the quasi-contract theory discussed in a previous chapter; the minor responsible for the reasonable value (remember the term "quantum meruit") of the goods or services received. What constitutes a necessity depends on the circumstances of the minor, particularly whether an adult is providing necessities. In some (but not all) states, **emancipation** (minor is no longer under care/control of an adult), marriage, or enlistment in the armed forces may either give the minor capacity or make the minor liable for more necessities. To see an interesting discussion of whether housing constitutes a necessity for a minor, read the sample case at the end of this chapter.

Example

It may appear that the law rewards "bad" behavior by minors. Ed, a handsome 17-year-old bad boy, signs a 12-month lease to rent a cheap, studio apartment for $400 per month. His friends help pay the rent and they use the apartment for drinking, smoking, womanizing, and gambling, until his mom finds out that they are not going to the library every night. Can Ed avoid the lease? Yes, in most states Ed can avoid the lease and have no further liability. In a few states, Ed may get a refund of some money he has already paid in rent because those states treat a minor's contracts as invalid from the beginning. Other states would allow Ed to avoid the lease, but might require him to make **restitution** — to restore the adult's financial position because the consideration itself (use of the apartment for several months) cannot be returned. On the other hand . . .

Fred, a hard-working 17-year-old, leaves home because of constant violence and neglect by his alcoholic, unemployed parent. Fred, who works 30 hours each week for a major retailer, looks like a man in his 20s. He signs a 12-month lease to pay $400 per month for a cheap studio apartment. After a few months, Fred is given an opportunity to go into a management training program sponsored by his employer, but he must relocate. Can Fred avoid the lease? The answer depends on the state: in many states, he cannot avoid the lease. Even if he can avoid the lease, it is highly unlikely that the landlord would have to return any part of the $2,400 in rent that Fred has already paid in any state. Fred is liable for the value he received because, otherwise, minors in his position might be totally unable to secure necessities like housing.

Restitution
Return of, restoration of, or compensation for

Restitution, requiring the minor to make compensation, is a complex issue. Most courts are more forgiving with minors as defendants (*e.g.*, landlord suing Ed for lost rental income after Ed stops paying rent) and more harsh with minors as plaintiffs (*e.g.*, Ed suing the landlord for a refund). Many courts require return of the consideration, if the minor still has it, but do not require restitution. For example, minor buys a car and stops making payments, minor may have to return the car; if, however, car has been destroyed in an accident, adult may be out of luck. In general, a minor cannot avoid the contract to improve his position. So, for example, a minor could not buy a car from S for $3,000, then sell the car to B for $3,000, then avoid the contract with S and demand the return of his $3,000 without making restitution.

EXHIBIT 7-2

What is the effect of emancipation in your state? The Vermont law:

12 V.S.A. §7156. Effect of emancipation

§7156. Effect of emancipation
(a) The order of emancipation shall recognize the minor as an adult for all purposes that result from reaching the age of majority, including:
(1) entering into a binding contract;
(2) litigation and settlement of controversies including the ability to sue and be sued;
(3) buying or selling real property;
(4) establishing a residence except that an emancipation order may not be used for the purpose of obtaining residency and in-state tuition or benefits at the University of Vermont or the Vermont state colleges;
(5) being prosecuted as an adult under the criminal laws of the state;
(6) terminating parental support and control of the minor and their rights to the minor's income;
(7) terminating parental tort liability for minor;
(8) indicating the minor's emancipated status on driver's license or identification card issued by the state.
(b) The order of emancipation shall not affect the status of the minor in the applicability of any provision of law which requires specific age requirements under the state or federal constitution or any state or federal law including laws that prohibit the sale, purchase or consumption of intoxicating liquor to or by a person under 21 years of age

---

3. Fraud

Would it make a difference if Ed had engaged in **fraud** (a false statement regarding a significant fact, intended to deceive an individual who then relies on the statement) by stating his age as 22 or, perhaps, showing false identification? In most states a minor can disaffirm despite misrepresentation or fraud; the states differ on the minor's obligation to make restitution in such situations. This is particularly complicated by the fact that a minor *is* liable for torts. Fraud is an intentional tort, as well as a defense to contract enforcement. Most courts will not allow a tort lawsuit for fraud if it would amount to allowing the adult to enforce the contract.

Fraud
False statement regarding a material fact, intended to deceive an individual who reasonably relies on the statement

4. Ratification

Would this make a difference? Shortly after moving in, Fred sent the landlord a notarized letter, stating that "although I am a minor, I intend to be

Disaffirm
Make a contract void; see Avoid

Ratify
To acknowledge or validate a contract after its execution

Express Ratification
To state or write intent to honor a contract or, if the contract has been executed, to acknowledge the contract

Implied Ratification
Intent to honor contract or acknowledgment of contract can be inferred from behavior or words

fully bound to this lease. I will not **disaffirm** (avoid) the lease." No difference; a minor has no power to **ratify** (confirm) before reaching the age of majority. After majority, ratification can be **express** (the minor states or writes an intent to honor the contract or, if the contract has been fully performed, acknowledges the contract) or can be **implied**. Implied ratification can take the form of continuing to use the property or service received under the contract for a time after reaching majority or it can arise from the minor's failure to disaffirm the contract within a reasonable time after majority. Interestingly, in some states, ratification does not take place simply because the minor has continued to uphold his part of the contract, for example, by making payments. A sample case, at the end of this chapter, includes an argument that the minor had ratified an agreement by waiting a significant period of time before disaffirming.

What happens if property continues to change hands after transfer by a minor? That depends on the type of property. The Uniform Commercial Code (UCC) provides that an innocent party takes goods free of the minor's power of disaffirmance; but in many jurisdictions a minor can reclaim real property, even from an innocent party.

Assignment 7-1

Has your state enacted the Uniform Transfers to Minors Act? It may be part of a group of laws relating to trusts and fiduciaries. The Act allows transfer of property to a custodian without having a guardian formally appointed. The custodian can manage the property and make payments on behalf of the minor. Transfer under the Act satisfies IRS requirements for qualifying a gift for exclusion from estate tax. The Act is an extension of the Uniform Gifts to Minors Act.

◆ What is the citation to the Act?
◆ Does the statute include a form to be used for transfers?
◆ Does the statute include a section exempting those who deal with the custodian from liability?

Another complicated issue concerns a parent's ability to enter into a contract for a minor. Because parents are generally required to provide for their children, there is no question of the parent's liability on contracts for goods and services to benefit a child. On the other hand, what if a parent signs a release from liability and a child is subsequently injured? In many states the field trip release forms signed by parents are ineffective! Courts seem to look to public policy to determine the validity of such a release. You may recall that such a contract, releasing a party from liability, is called an exculpatory agreement. Consider this: if a release also contained a clause under which the parent agreed to indemnify the school/club/park district, and the release was found to be invalid, might the indemnification be upheld? What would be the consequences of such a ruling? Why might it happen and what would be the public policy considerations?

Assignment 7-2

A. In your online state statutes, find the citation for one of the following:

◆ A statute concerning student loans to minors;
◆ A statute concerning the contractual rights of emancipated minors; or
◆ A statute concerning the contractual rights of married minors.

B. Using computer-assisted legal research (CALR), find, summarize, and report to the class, a case:

◆ Involving a minor's misrepresentation of age in entering a contract;
◆ Involving a contract with an intoxicated person (alcohol or drugs);
◆ Involving a person alleging mental incompetence to avoid a contract;
◆ Involving a release signed on behalf of a minor;
◆ Involving what constitutes a necessity; or
◆ Involving a minor's obligation to make restitution after disaffirmance.

Try to find a case from your state, but you may have to search all states. These cases are surprisingly rare.

C. Read the cases at the end of this chapter and discuss:

◆ Do you think these cases are unfair to the adults involved? Is there a difference between John McDonald's situation and Kim Young's situation?
◆ Do you think it should make a difference that these minors lived with the contracts they signed for several months?

B. Mental Incompetence

1. Determining Mental Incompetence

Mental incompetence is not synonymous with old age or physical disability. Mental incompetence is the inability to understand the nature and consequences of the transaction (the **cognitive** test) or inability to act reasonably with respect to the transaction (the **volitional** test). When a court employs the volitional test, it generally also asks whether the other party was aware of the person's mental condition and whether the contract was one a reasonable person would have made. Mental incompetence can arise from senility, mental illness, delirium, or mental retardation. The contracts of an individual who was incompetent at the time when the contract was entered are generally voidable; incompetence occurring after the contract is formed does not render the contract voidable.

Cognitive Test
Mental incompetence determined by inability to understand the nature and consequences of a transaction

Volitional Test
Mental incompetence shown by inability to act reasonably with respect to a transaction

Adjudicated Incompetent
Court has declared person incompetent

Non-adjudicated Incompetent
Incompetence has not been determined by court

Some states differentiate between **adjudicated** and **non-adjudicated** incompetents. It is difficult to obtain a court determination (adjudication) of incompetence and, in those proceedings, a guardian is appointed to protect the incompetent individual.

With respect to non-adjudicated incompetents and in states that do not make the distinction, courts generally look at whether the contract involved a necessity and the incompetent's state of mind at the time of entering the contract. Non-adjudicated incompetents (and incompetents in states that do not make the distinction) are generally required to make restitution when they avoid a contract, if the other party had no reason to know of the incompetence. Like minors, incompetents are liable for the reasonable value of necessities and are capable of ratifying contracts when they are competent.

Void
With no legal effect from the outset

In states that do make the distinction, the contracts of the adjudicated incompetent may be **void** that is, with no legal effect from the beginning.

Example

An adjudicated incompetent often has no liability for contracts. Jenn, an adjudicated incompetent 24-year-old, with the mental capacity of a 4-year-old, escapes from the house with her mother's purse. She goes into an art store and pays $300 cash for a glass vase, which she drops on the sidewalk immediately on leaving the store. In states that make the distinction, Jenn's guardian can obtain a full refund; Jenn has no obligation to the store. This is not unfair, if you consider that incompetence rising to the level necessary to obtain an adjudication would be obvious to most people.

---

2. Intoxication

Intoxicated
Under the influence of alcohol or drugs

Intoxicated individuals, under the influence of alcohol or drugs at the time of making a contract, are often classified with the mentally incompetent. While the law does not generally protect voluntary drunks from the consequences of their actions, it does not allow others to take advantage of intoxication. Courts look at the cause (bad reaction to prescription medication vs. illegal drugs or drinking to excess) and degree (often judged under the same standard as mental incompetence) of intoxication and the other party's awareness of the intoxication. In addition, courts look at whether the intoxicated person ratified the contract by failing to disaffirm promptly on becoming sober.

A person (the principal) who fears becoming incompetent (*e.g.*, the elderly, those diagnosed with degenerative diseases) will sometimes sign a power of attorney, to appoint another person to act as an agent. Agency is discussed in depth in a later chapter. A durable power of attorney is an appointment of an agent that remains valid despite the principal's loss of mental capacity. A sample power of attorney appears in Exhibit 7-3.

Explanation

The following form provides what is known as "statutory property power" and may be used to grant an agent powers with respect to property and financial matters. When a power of attorney in substantially the following form is used, including the "notice" paragraph at the beginning in capital letters and the notarized form of acknowledgment at the end, it shall have the legally binding effect intended under the statute. The validity of a power of attorney as meeting the requirements of a statutory property power shall not be affected by the fact that one or more of the categories of optional powers listed in the form are struck out or the form includes specific limitations on or additions to the agent's powers, as permitted by the form.

Using the form below will not invalidate or bar use by the principal of any other or different form of power of attorney for property. Nonstatutory property powers must be executed by the principal and designate the agent and the agent's powers, but they need not be acknowledged or conform in any other respect to the statutory property power.

NOTICE: THE PURPOSE OF THIS POWER OF ATTORNEY IS TO GIVE THE PERSON YOU DESIGNATE (YOUR "AGENT") BROAD POWERS TO HANDLE YOUR PROPERTY, WHICH MAY INCLUDE POWERS TO PLEDGE, SELL OR OTHERWISE DISPOSE OF ANY REAL OR PERSONAL PROPERTY WITHOUT ADVANCE NOTICE TO YOU OR APPROVAL BY YOU. THIS FORM DOES NOT IMPOSE A DUTY ON YOUR AGENT TO EXERCISE GRANTED POWERS; BUT WHEN POWERS ARE EXERCISED, YOUR AGENT WILL HAVE TO USE DUE CARE TO ACT FOR YOUR BENEFIT AND IN ACCORDANCE WITH THIS FORM AND KEEP A RECORD OF RECEIPTS, DISBURSEMENTS AND SIGNIFICANT ACTIONS TAKEN AS AGENT. A COURT CAN TAKE AWAY THE POWERS OF YOUR AGENT IF IT FINDS THE AGENT IS NOT ACTING PROPERLY. YOU MAY NAME SUCCESSOR AGENTS UNDER THIS FORM BUT NOT CO-AGENTS. UNLESS YOU EXPRESSLY LIMIT THE DURATION OF THIS POWER IN THE MANNER PROVIDED BELOW, UNTIL YOU REVOKE THIS POWER OR A COURT ACTING ON YOUR BEHALF TERMINATES IT, YOUR AGENT MAY EXERCISE THE POWERS GIVEN HERE THROUGHOUT YOUR LIFETIME, EVEN AFTER YOU BECOME DISABLED. THE POWERS YOU GIVE YOUR AGENT ARE EXPLAINED MORE FULLY IN SECTION 3-4 OF THE ILLINOIS "STATUTORY SHORT FORM POWER OF ATTORNEY FOR PROPERTY LAW" OF WHICH THIS FORM IS A PART (SEE THE END OF THIS FORM). THAT LAW EXPRESSLY PERMITS THE USE OF ANY DIFFERENT FORM OF POWER OF ATTORNEY YOU MAY DESIRE.

EXHIBIT 7-3
(continued)

IF THERE IS ANYTHING ABOUT THIS FORM THAT YOU DO NOT UNDERSTAND, YOU SHOULD ASK A LAWYER TO EXPLAIN IT TO YOU.

POWER OF ATTORNEY made this _____ day of _____ (month), _____ (year)

1. I, _____, (insert name and address of principal) hereby appoint: _____ (insert name and address of agent) as my attorney-in-fact (my "agent") to act for me and in my name (in any way I could act in person) with respect to the following powers, as defined in Section 3-4 of the "Statutory Short Form Power of Attorney for Property Law" (including all amendments), but subject to any limitations on or additions to the specified powers inserted in paragraph 2 or 3 below:

(YOU MUST STRIKE OUT ANY ONE OR MORE OF THE FOLLOWING CATEGORIES OF POWERS YOU DO NOT WANT YOUR AGENT TO HAVE. FAILURE TO STRIKE THE TITLE OF ANY CATEGORY WILL CAUSE THE POWERS DESCRIBED IN THAT CATEGORY TO BE GRANTED TO THE AGENT. TO STRIKE OUT A CATEGORY YOU MUST DRAW A LINE THROUGH THE TITLE OF THAT CATEGORY.)

Real estate transactions.
Financial institution transactions.
Stock and bond transactions.
Tangible personal property transactions.
Safe deposit box transactions.
Insurance and annuity transactions.
Retirement plan transactions.
Social Security, employment
   and military service benefits.

Tax matters.
Claims and litigation.
Commodity and option
   transactions.
Business operations.
Borrowing transactions.
Estate transactions.
All other property
   powers and transactions.

(LIMITATIONS ON AND ADDITIONS TO THE AGENT'S POWERS MAY BE INCLUDED IN THIS POWER OF ATTORNEY IF THEY ARE SPECIFICALLY DESCRIBED BELOW.)

2. The powers granted above shall not include the following powers or shall be modified or limited in the following particulars (here you may include any specific limitations you deem appropriate, such as a prohibition or conditions on the sale of particular stock or real estate or special rules on borrowing by the agent):_____

3. In addition to the powers granted above, I grant my agent the following powers (here you may add any other delegable powers including, without

EXHIBIT 7-3
(continued)

limitation, power to make gifts, exercise powers of appointment, name or change beneficiaries or joint tenants or revoke or amend any trust specifically referred to below): _____

(YOUR AGENT WILL HAVE AUTHORITY TO EMPLOY OTHER PERSONS AS NECESSARY TO ENABLE THE AGENT TO PROPERLY EXERCISE THE POWERS GRANTED IN THIS FORM, BUT YOUR AGENT WILL HAVE TO MAKE ALL DISCRETIONARY DECISIONS. IF YOU WANT TO GIVE YOUR AGENT THE RIGHT TO DELEGATE DISCRETIONARY DECISION-MAKING POWERS TO OTHERS, YOU SHOULD KEEP THE NEXT SENTENCE, OTHERWISE IT SHOULD BE STRUCK OUT.)

4. My agent shall have the right by written instrument to delegate any or all of the foregoing powers involving discretionary decision-making to any person or persons whom my agent may select, but such delegation may be amended or revoked by any agent (including any successor) named by me who is acting under this power of attorney at the time of reference.

(YOUR AGENT WILL BE ENTITLED TO REIMBURSEMENT FOR ALL REASONABLE EXPENSES INCURRED IN ACTING UNDER THIS POWER OF ATTORNEY. STRIKE OUT THE NEXT SENTENCE IF YOU DO NOT WANT YOUR AGENT TO ALSO BE ENTITLED TO REASON-ABLE COMPENSATION FOR SERVICES AS AGENT.)

5. My agent shall be entitled to reasonable compensation for services rendered as agent under this power of attorney.

(THIS POWER OF ATTORNEY MAY BE AMENDED OR REVOKED BY YOU AT ANY TIME AND IN ANY MANNER. ABSENT AMENDMENT OR REVOCATION, THE AUTHORITY GRANTED IN THIS POWER OF AT-TORNEY WILL BECOME EFFECTIVE AT THE TIME THIS POWER IS SIGNED AND WILL CONTINUE UNTIL YOUR DEATH UNLESS A LIMITATION ON THE BEGINNING DATE OR DURATION IS MADE BY INITIALING AND COMPLETING EITHER (OR BOTH) OF THE FOLLOWING:)

6. ( ) This power of attorney shall become effective on _____ (insert a future date or event during your lifetime, such as court determination of your disability, when you want this power to first take effect)

7. ( ) This power of attorney shall terminate on _____ (insert a future date or event, such as court determination of your disability, when you want this power to terminate prior to your death)

(IF YOU WISH TO NAME SUCCESSOR AGENTS, INSERT THE NAME(S) AND ADDRESS(ES) OF SUCH SUCCESSOR(S) IN THE FOLLOWING PARAGRAPH.)

EXHIBIT 7-3
(continued)

8. If any agent named by me shall die, become incompetent, resign or refuse to accept the office of agent, I name the following (each to act alone and successively, in the order named) as successor(s) to such agent: _____

For purposes of this paragraph 8, a person shall be considered to be incompetent if and while the person is a minor or an adjudicated incompetent or disabled person or the person is unable to give prompt and intelligent consideration to business matters, as certified by a licensed physician. (IF YOU WISH TO NAME YOUR AGENT AS GUARDIAN OF YOUR ESTATE, IN THE EVENT A COURT DECIDES THAT ONE SHOULD BE APPOINTED, YOU MAY, BUT ARE NOT REQUIRED TO, DO SO BY RETAINING THE FOLLOWING PARAGRAPH. THE COURT WILL APPOINT YOUR AGENT IF THE COURT FINDS THAT SUCH APPOINTMENT WILL SERVE YOUR BEST INTERESTS AND WELFARE. STRIKE OUT PARAGRAPH 9 IF YOU DO NOT WANT YOUR AGENT TO ACT AS GUARDIAN.)

9. If a guardian of my estate (my property) is to be appointed, I nominate the agent acting under this power of attorney as such guardian, to serve without bond or security.

10. I am fully informed as to all the contents of this form and understand the full import of this grant of powers to my agent.

Signed _____
(principal)

(YOU MAY, BUT ARE NOT REQUIRED TO, REQUEST YOUR AGENT AND SUCCESSOR AGENTS TO PROVIDE SPECIMEN SIGNATURES BELOW. IF YOU INCLUDE SPECIMEN SIGNATURES IN THIS POWER OF ATTORNEY, YOU MUST COMPLETE THE CERTIFICATION OPPOSITE THE SIGNATURES OF THE AGENTS.)

Specimen signature of agent (and successors)	I certify that the above signature of my agent is correct.
_____	_____
(agent)	(principal)
I certify that the above signature of my successor agent is correct.	Specimen signature of successor agent
_____	_____
(principal)	(successor agent)
Specimen signature of successor agent	I certify that the above signature of my successor agent is correct.
_____	_____
(successor agent)	(principal)

EXHIBIT 7-3
(continued)

(THIS POWER OF ATTORNEY WILL NOT BE EFFECTIVE UNLESS IT IS NOTARIZED AND SIGNED BY AT LEAST ONE ADDITIONAL WITNESS, USING THE FORM BELOW.)

State of _____
County of _____

The undersigned, a notary public in and for the above county and state, certifies that _____, known to me to be the same person whose name is subscribed as principal to the foregoing power of attorney, appeared before me and the additional witness in person and acknowledged signing and delivering the instrument as the free and voluntary act of the principal, for the uses and purposes therein set forth and certified to the correctness of the signature(s) of the agent(s).
Dated: _____

(SEAL) _____
Notary Public

My commission expires _____

The undersigned witness certifies that _____, known to me to be the same person whose name is subscribed as principal to the foregoing power of attorney, appeared before me and the notary public and acknowledged signing and delivering the instrument as the free and voluntary act of the principal, for the uses and purposes therein set forth. I believe him or her to be of sound mind and memory.
Dated: _____ (SEAL)

_____
Witness
(THE NAME AND ADDRESS OF THE PERSON PREPARING THIS FORM SHOULD BE INSERTED IF THE AGENT WILL HAVE POWER TO CONVEY ANY INTEREST IN REAL ESTATE.)
This document was prepared by: _____

3.   Analyzing Incompetence and Intoxication

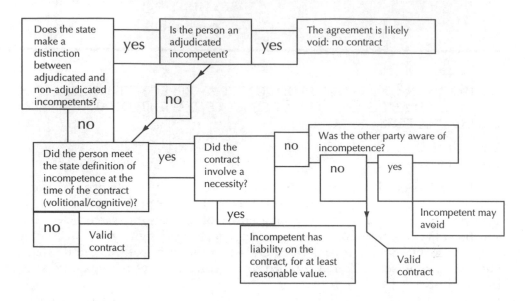

C.   Practical and Ethical Issues

As our society ages, contracts that take advantage of senior citizens are becoming a major problem. The elderly are often competent, but very vulnerable. Some of the problems involve "scams" that are fraudulent; for example, a scam artist drives a truck with a sign identifying it as belonging to a home inspector from house to house, knocking on doors and telling residents that their chimneys may be blocked in a way that presents a danger of asphyxiation. Scam artist offers to fix the problem immediately for $100. After getting the money, scam artist does nothing more than climb onto the roof and stick a broom into the chimney. Other problems arise from predatory practices; for example, Terry Telemarketer knows that Ella Elderly lives alone and is very lonely. Terry calls Ella several times a week, knowing that Ella can be talked into buying anything, even though she cannot afford to spend the money.

Sadly, there is often little that can be done after these practices are discovered. Scam artists disappear quickly; a non-fraudulent contract, entered into by a competent senior citizen, is likely valid, even if it was the result of targeting seniors. Governmental bodies are increasingly taking action to educate senior citizens and their families about these practices in advance and to investigate complaints. Some helpful sites sponsored by the federal government:

- http://www.firstgov.gov/
- Senate Special Committee on Aging: http://aging.senate.gov/public/index.cfm?FuseAction=Home.Home
- U.S. Dept. of Health & Human Services, Administration on Aging: Consumer Protection and the Elderly: http://www.aoa.gov/prof/notes/notes_consumer_protection.asp

Many states also have resources. For example, Illinois has a Department on Aging, with a special program to train bank personnel to detect, prevent, and report financial exploitation: http://www.state.il.us/aging/1abuselegal/abuse_financial.htm#bsafe. The Illinois Attorney General also has information about predatory practices and filing consumer complaints: http://www.ag.state.il.us/consumers/index.html.

Assignment 7-3

Another issue is dealing with clients who lack capacity. The relevant ABA Model Rule is Rule 1.14. Find the rule for your state and answer the following:

◆ Does the attorney-client relationship automatically terminate when the lawyer determines that the client has diminished capacity?

◆ Is a lawyer required to seek appointment of a guardian or conservator immediately upon determining that the client has diminished capacity?

◆ What is a guardian ad litem; what is a conservator?

◆ Is the confidentiality requirement different with respect to clients with diminished capacity? When can a lawyer reveal information about a client with diminished capacity?

While the ethical rules relating to confidentiality, conflicts of interest, and dealing with a client under disability, also apply to minors as clients, a lawyer has to be especially careful to understand his or her role with respect to a minor. If the lawyer is court-appointed, the court may be asked to clarify. Some states make the distinction between a **guardian ad litem** (appointed to look out for the best interests of the child during the course of litigation) and an **attorney for the child**, whose role is to advocate the child's position. The best interests of the child do not always coincide with the client's wishes. For example, a teen-ager involved in a custody dispute might want to live with the parent who imposes no curfew and is very lax with discipline.

For examples of state standards for guardians ad litem, visit http://www.guardianadlitem.org/; http://www.courts.state.va.us/gal/home.html; or http://www.nccourts.org/Citizens/GAL/.

Guardian ad litem
Court-appointed person to advocate best interests of a child or incompetent during litigation

Attorney for the Child
Attorney whose role is to advocate the child's position

Assignment 7-4

◆ Find online resources available to help senior citizens and their families in your state.

◆ Substance abuse is a serious problem among lawyers. Most states now have **LAPs** (lawyers assistance programs) to provide confidential help to impaired lawyers. Find the website describing your state's program.

LAPs
Lawyers Assistance
Programs

Review Questions

1. What is the difference between an adjudicated and a non-adjudicated incompetent?
2. What is a necessity and why does it matter?
3. Under what circumstances can a minor enter into a contract enforceable by the other party?
4. Does it (should it) make a difference whether a minor is using minority as a weapon (*e.g., to sue an adult for the return of property*) or as a shield (*e.g., to defend self when being sued by an adult*)?
5. What is the difference between a guardian ad litem and an attorney for a child or incompetent? What are the special ethical rules applicable to dealing with an incompetent?

ACROSS

2. reaching the age of _____, a person becomes a legal adult
4. the contract of an adjudicated incompetent may be _____
6. in most states, a person under age 18 is a _____
8. Ratification can be express or _____
11. to make a contract good after-the-fact
13. being freed from parental control
14. a false statement on which another is intended to rely
15. although the law does not favor this condition, others may not take advantage
16. legally responsible for a minor or an incompetent
17. _____ test, was person able to act reasonably

DOWN

1. _____ test: was the person able to understand the nature and consequences of acts
3. one who acts on behalf of another
5. A minor may _____ a contract
7. Minors and incompetents have some liability for _____
9. A minor's contract is _____ at the minor's option
10. An _____ incompetent has been declared, by a court, to lack capacity
11. courts differ on whether minors must make _____ to compensate adults for their losses
12. a legal term for a minor

CASES FOR ANALYSIS

These cases demonstrate how differently courts look at "necessities," depending on the circumstances of the minor.

H & S HOMES, L.L.C., AND RUSS D'OLYMPIO V. JOHN F. MCDONALD SUPREME COURT OF ALABAMA

823 So. 2d 627 December 7, 2001, Released

[Ed. note: Material omitted.]

H & S Homes, L.L.C. ("H & S"), and D'Olympio are defendants in an action filed by John F. McDonald and Christina L. McDonald. H & S and D'Olympio appeal from denial of motions to dismiss and/or to compel arbitration and stay discovery as to John F. McDonald. We affirm.

FACTS AND BACKGROUND

On January 28, 2000, John and Christina McDonald, husband and wife, purchased a manufactured home from H & S [and] executed a separate agreement, in which they agreed to submit to binding arbitration all disputes arising from the transaction [which] was incorporated by reference into the purchase contract.

On February 26, 2001, the McDonalds filed this action against H & S and D'Olympio, general manager of H & S. McDonalds allege fraud, suppression, misrepresentation, deceit, negligence, wantonness, and conversion arising out of their purchase of the mobile home.

H & S filed a motion to dismiss and/or to compel arbitration, seeking to enforce the arbitration agreement, supported with a submission, which established that the McDonalds had signed the agreement and that their purchase had substantially affected interstate commerce. The submission also established that McDonalds had taken possession of the manufactured home, that they remained in possession of the home, and that they had made payments required under the contract.

McDonalds responded with their own submission. In his affidavit, John testified that he was 17 years old when he entered into the contract, that he provided a copy of his driver's license on the date of the purchase, and that on December 14, 2000 (nearly 11 months after taking possession of the home), he sent H & S a letter disavowing the contract based upon his minority status at the time of the purchase.

H & S responded that even if John was a minor at the time he signed the contract, he had since reached the age of majority and had ratified the contract by, among other things, continuing to live in the home, continuing to make the payments, and filing this lawsuit based upon the contract.

On May 15, 2001, the trial court entered an order, finding that the arbitration agreement was enforceable as to claims asserted by Christina. However, as to claims asserted by John, the trial court's order provided: "Pursuant to Alabama Code §30-4-16, his disability of non-age would have been removed when he became eighteen on February 28, 2000. . . . Of course, a minor can be held responsible for necessities. If housing is not a necessity, a question is raised as to whether the husband ratified the agreement by waiting nearly ten months to avoid the contract. These are questions of fact and it would be premature to dismiss and/or require arbitration as to John.

"Wherefore, it is hereby ORDERED as follows:

"1. That Motion to Dismiss And/Or Compel Arbitration is granted as to Christina and claims asserted by her are dismissed, with prejudice.

"2. That the Motion to Dismiss And/Or Compel Arbitration and Stay Discovery is denied as to John F. McDonald."

H & S and D'Olympio appeal the denial of their motions to compel arbitration as to John's claims.

We agree with the trial judge that the motions to compel arbitration of John's claims were properly supported. H & S presented evidence establishing that the contract contained a written arbitration agreement signed by John and evidence establishing that the purchase at issue had "substantially affected interstate commerce," as required to trigger application of the Federal Arbitration Act. . . . Because H & S properly supported their motion to compel arbitration, the burden shifted to John to present evidence to overcome those motions. . . .

Arbitration agreements are subject to the contract defenses other contracts are subject to, such as fraud, duress, and unconscionability. . . ." It is well settled by the authorities that infants are not liable on any of their contracts, except for necessaries. Harris v. Raughton, 37 Ala. App. 648, 649, 73 So. 2d 921, 922 (1954) (recognizing that the inquiry of what constitutes a "necessary" for an infant "must be related to the particular facts and circumstances of each case." Thus, infancy is a valid defense to the motion to compel arbitration of disputes arising out of a contract.

We conclude that, although the trial court denied the motions to compel, the orders essentially allowed the parties to conduct discovery regarding the contract defenses affecting the enforceability of the arbitration agreement. We agree with this result. We conclude that, at this juncture, John has presented sufficient evidence of a contract defense to overcome H & S's properly supported motions to compel arbitration and that the parties are entitled to proceed with discovery limited solely to John's claims of infancy, whether he effectively disavowed the purchase contract, whether the manufactured home constituted a "necessary" for John, and whether John ratified the contract after he reached the age of majority. We encourage H & S to refile motions to compel arbitration after the completion of discovery if, at that time, they believe those motions continue to have merit. Accordingly, we affirm the orders by the Montgomery Circuit Court. AFFIRMED. *[Ed. note: Dissent omitted.]*

KIM YOUNG V. PHILLIP WEAVER
COURT OF CIVIL APPEALS OF ALABAMA

883 So. 2d 234; December 12, 2003, Released

[Ed. note: Some text and footnotes omitted.]

Kim Young appeals from a judgment awarding damages to Weaver for alleged breaches by Young of an apartment lease between Young, as tenant, and Weaver, as landlord.

In the fall of 2001, Young, who at the time was 18 years old and had been living with her parents all of her life, decided that she "wanted to move out and get away from [her] parents and be on [her] own." Young and a friend, Ashley Springer, also a minor, signed a contract for the lease of an apartment with Weaver. No adult signed the lease as a guarantor. Young was employed on a full-time basis at a Lowe's hardware store located in Tuscaloosa at the time. Young paid a security deposit in the amount of $300; the rent for the apartment was $550 per month, and the lease was to expire on July 31, 2002.

Young and Springer moved into the apartment in September and, together, paid rent; Young moved out near the end of November. Young paid her portion of the rent for October and November, but stopped making payments after she moved out of the apartment.

On February 19, 2002, Weaver filed a claim against Young for unpaid rent and damage done by Young's dog. The court awarded $1,370 in damages. Young argues on appeal that the apartment was not a "necessity" and that, as a minor, she was not bound by the lease and owes Weaver nothing. We find this argument to be dispositive.

Under Alabama law, one who is unmarried and has not reached the age of 19 years is deemed to be a minor, i.e., subject to the disabilities of nonage (such disabilities may, in certain circumstances, be removed by a juvenile court). See §26-1-1, §26-13-1 et seq., §30-4-15, and §30-4-16, Ala. Code 1975. Among the disabilities of nonage is incapacity to make a binding contract: 'a minor is not liable on any contract he makes and that he may disaffirm the same.' . . . However, Alabama, like most other states, provides that persons providing 'necessaries' of life to minors may recover the reasonable value of such necessaries irrespective of the existence of a (voidable) contract respecting those necessaries. As stated by the Alabama Supreme Court 'when necessaries are furnished to one who by reason of infancy cannot bind himself by his contract, the law implies an obligation on the part of such person to pay for such "necessaries" out of his own property.' . . . Young does not seek reversal of the trial court's judgment on the ground that the use of the apartment after November 2001 was not "furnished" to her. Instead, her principal argument on appeal is that the apartment was not a necessity. We agree that this case must be disposed of in Young's favor on this basis.

A necessity has been defined as something " 'necessary to the position and condition of the [minor].' " . . . "every case stands upon its peculiar facts and reasonable necessities, according to the circumstances of each case; and there is no positive or iron-bound rule by means of which it may be determined what are or what are not necessaries." Determining whether the subject of a contract is a necessity to a minor entails a two-step analysis: first a court must determine whether the subject of the contract is generally considered a necessity. If the subject is so considered, then determine, on the particular facts of the case, whether the subject of the contract is, in fact, a necessity to that minor. The first inquiry is a question of law; the second inquiry entails a factual determination.

[I]n general, lodging is considered a necessity. Young contends that the apartment was not a necessity to her because, she argues, her parents kept her room waiting so that she could return to their home at any time. Young's father testified that every time he talked to his daughter, he asked her to move back in with them; he was willing to take Young back at any time. In essence, because

Young's parents were able and willing to house Young at the same time she contracted to lease the apartment, Young argues that in this case the particular lodging at issue was not a necessity.

In support, Young cites Harris v. Raughton, 37 Ala. App. 648, a minor bought an automobile . . . paid $90 cash as down payment . . . the car would not operate satisfactorily, so in about two days he returned it and demanded a refund. This was refused, and the automobile was left at appellants' place of business. . . . Raughton sued to recover his down payment. Raughton was married and had bought the automobile to use as transportation to and from his employment. Raughton owned a truck that he had been using for the same purpose and that he had not disposed of at the time he purchased the automobile. The court determined that, because Raughton had another vehicle, the automobile was not a necessity, and, Raughton was at liberty to void the contract for the automobile.

By analogy, Young argues that because she had a place to live still available to her at the time she signed the lease and during the time she lived in the apartment, the apartment was not a necessity. Several authorities from other states support this position.

Likewise, . . . [in another case], defendants were husband and wife and were minors at the time they purchased a house trailer. Both were employed . . . before they purchased the trailer, defendants were living with the parents of the husband. The Ohio Court ruled that . . . the trailer was not a necessity, reasoning that: " 'To enable an infant to contract for articles as necessaries, he must have been in actual need, and obliged to procure them for himself. They are not necessaries as to him if he was already supplied with sufficient articles of the kind, or if he had a parent or guardian who was able and willing to supply them. The evidence in this case indicates that, just as in cases discussed above, Young's parents were willing and able to provide lodging for their daughter at the time she rented the apartment.' "

Given the authorities cited and the particular facts of this case, we conclude that the trial court erred in its determination that the apartment was a necessity for Young . . . as a minor, Young is not legally bound under the lease. This result may seem unjust, but as the Supreme Court observed in Ex parte McFerren: "The above rule [that a minor may disaffirm a contract] may, at times, work a hardship. The law must, however, have a definite policy, and its rules must be fixed. The law has fixed its policy with reference to the protection of infants with regard to their contracts, and those who deal with them, except when actually supplying them with necessaries, deal with them at their peril." . . . Accordingly, the judgment of the trial court is reversed, and the cause is remanded for the trial court to enter a judgment in favor of Young. REVERSED AND REMANDED.

8

Statute of Frauds

This chapter explores those contracts that must be in writing to be enforceable and provides samples of agreements within those categories. Students will also learn how the law is adapting to deal with the reality that most documents created in the 21st century will never be printed on paper.

A. **Requirement of Writing**
B. **Narrow Interpretation of the Requirement**
C. **Written Evidence Other Than Written Contract**
D. **Contracts in Cyberspace**
E. **The Categories**
    1. **Promises in Anticipation of Marriage**
    2. **Contracts Not to be Performed within a Year**
    3. **Contracts Involving Land (Real Property)**
    4. **Contracts for Sale of Goods, $500**
    5. **Promises to Answer for the Debts of Another**
F. **Practical and Ethical Issues**

A. Requirement of Writing

As you know, most contracts are not written, but a few are not enforceable without a **writing**. Some types of contracts are more likely to be entered into based on emotion, rather than clear thinking, or are particularly susceptible to fraud, perjury, and failure of memory. The original Act for the Prevention of Fraud and Perjuries was enacted in England in 1677 to deal with those concerns by requiring written evidence of the agreement. Every state has adopted some form of what is now called the Statute of Frauds. Law students often use a mnemonic device to remember the major categories of contracts "within" the Statute in most states:

Anticipation of	Marriage	
Cannot be performed within one	Year	
	Land	real estate contracts
Promises by an executor to pay	Estate's debts	
Sales of	Goods over $500[1]	added by the UCC
	Suretyship[2]	

Many states have added categories, such as contracts promising to make a will with specified gifts, promises to lend money, ratification of contracts entered while a minor, assignments for the benefit of creditors, contracts authorizing an agent to buy or sell real estate, and contracts to pay commission to real estate contracts (remember the promissory estoppel sample case from chapter 1). The Uniform Commercial Code (UCC) also requires that other sales of personal property for more than $5,000 (§1-206), as well as certain leases of goods, **negotiable instruments**, and contracts creating **security interests** be written.

Of course, just remembering "MYLEGS" or the words the letters represent is overly simplistic. Before we get into the details of what those letters mean, let's look at some general principles.

Negotiable Instruments
A promise or order to pay, such as a check; can be passed along like cash

Security Interests
Interest in personal property to secure performance of an obligation; evidence of indebtedness

---

Assignment 8-1

Using either your state website or CALR, find the categories covered by the statute of frauds for your state. To formulate your search, consider this: the Statute of Frauds is a limitation on civil lawsuits. A civil lawsuit, based on a contract of a type covered by the statute, may not be pursued unless there is a writing, so the Statute limits the rights and remedies available in court.

B. Narrow Interpretation of the Requirement

In some cases, the Statute of Frauds is the legal "technicality" people love to hate: competent parties have made a legal agreement, supported by consideration, not tainted by fraud or any other problem, and there is plenty of evidence to prove that agreement, but the agreement is not enforceable because it is not in writing.

---

[1]2003 Amendments to UCC Article 2 would raise the amount to $5,000; check to see whether your state has adopted the change.
[2]Both promises by an executor to pay estate debts and suretyship are, in essence, promises to pay the debts of another.

Because of such cases, exceptions and "tricky" ways of reading the requirement have evolved in the courts. So, if you think that the definitions of the categories represented by MYLEGS are overly complicated, you are correct! Courts like to find ways to take agreements out of the categories covered by the Statute.

Most courts hold that if the Statute of Frauds is not raised as an affirmative defense[3], it is **waived**, meaning that the argument has been abandoned. The Statute may also be waived if the party who is not seeking enforcement admits in court or in court documents that an agreement existed. The Statute may not be raised after the contract has been fully performed and, in some cases may not be raised after one party has fully performed. Also keep in mind that if the otherwise valid contract is unenforceable because of the Statute of Frauds, some states allow recovery in quasi-contract or promissory estoppel.

Waived
Claims have been abandoned

C. Written Evidence Other Than Written Contract

Written evidence need only amount to an acknowledgment of agreement by the **party "to be charged,"** meaning the party trying to get out of the contract. The written evidence does not have to be a formal contract and does not even have to be an **integrated** statement of the agreement.

A memo or notes (including a collection of notes), in any form, can be sufficient, depending on the facts. The writing may be generated by a computer, or it may be scrawled on a napkin. The writing need not have been created at the time the contract was created; it need not be still in existence at the time of the lawsuit. It need not have been prepared with the intent of formalizing the contract. It need not even be delivered to the other party. The memo or note need only indicate that there is or was an agreement and state, with reasonable certainty, the identities of the parties, the subject matter, and the essential terms. Other terms can be provided by implication, other documents, or other evidence. The **signature** need not be the party's full name, correctly spelled; it can consist of initials, a signature stamp, a mark, or, in some cases, the use of letterhead.

Party to be Charged
Party attempting to avoid contract liability

Integrated Agreement
Agreement that is intended to be final and complete

Example

A written denial can satisfy the requirement. Sam Seller and his friend Billie Buyer shook hands on the deal: Billie would buy Sam's house for $250,000, with the closing on May 15, all appliances included, clean title, and no mortgage contingency. They planned to have Sam's lawyer write it up in a few days. After Billie left, however, another person visited Sam's open house and offered Sam $265,000. Sam immediately wrote and mailed a quick note:

---

[3]An affirmative defense is part of an answer to a complaint in which the defendant takes the offense and responds to the allegations with his own allegations.

> *Billie, I am going to have to back out of our deal to sell you my house for $250,000 — Pat came by and offered me $265,000 for basically the same deal, with the closing on May 15 and all the appliances. Since contracts for real estate have to be in writing, we didn't really have a contract, but I am sorry and hope that you aren't too angry. [signed] Sam.*

Upon receiving the note, Billie may have sufficient evidence to support enforcement of the agreement. Furthermore, even if Sam had written a similar note to a mutual friend (rather than to Billie), describing the agreement and expressing his regret, the note could serve as the evidence Billie would need to meet the Statute of Frauds requirement.

Assignment 8-2

◆ Many contracts are now formed without paper, via the Internet or terminals such as ATMs. The "signature" for such a contract might be a typed name, use of a personal identification number (PIN), a scan of a person's voice or retina, a signature with an electronic pen on a special tablet, or other means. Such contracts can satisfy the statute of frauds. Using your bookmarked site for state law, determine whether your state has adopted the **Uniform Electronic Transaction Act**; if so, summarize its terms. If it has not, federal law is applicable; find and summarize the **Electronic Signatures in Global and National Commerce Act**, the "e-signature act" 15 U.S.C. §7031, which promotes the use of paperless transactions. You may use the Cornell site: http://www4.law. cornell.edu/uscode/. Keep in mind that electronic signatures are not sufficient in some areas of law, such as the requirement for a signature on a will and the acts referenced above do not apply to all transactions requiring a signature under the UCC. The 2003 revisions to Article II (not adopted by any state as of this writing) make electronic signatures and records the equivalent of paper documents.

◆ The laws referenced above are "technology neutral" and do not dictate how the "signature" should be authenticated or how the integrity of the data should be protected. Consider when you have either entered a transaction online or simply wanted access to a website and have had to click "I AGREE" at the end of a long agreement, disclaimer, or license. Do you feel that simply clicking an icon should form a binding contract? Find a case discussing the issue. You may want to use CALR, but you can find many cases by using the free internet and searching [**click-wrap agreement**].

◆ Find and summarize a case from your state involving the Statute of Frauds and report to the class whether the court was willing to strictly

Click-Wrap Agreement
Agreement used in connection with software licenses; often found on the Internet as part of the installation process of software packages; usually requires user to manifest assent by clicking an "ok" button on a dialog box or pop-up window

apply the writing requirement or found a way to take the agreement out of the requirement.

D. Contracts in Cyberspace

In addition to problems with the signature and the take-it-or-leave-it nature of contracts ("adhesion" contracts, which leave no room for negotiation, are discussed at length in another chapter) on the Internet, "cyber contracts" present other issues:

Why do we generally feel secure with contracts we enter face-to-face? With face-to-face contracts, we have two clear avenues of enforcement. On an informal level, we know the other party is concerned about her reputation. If I hire a local builder to construct my deck and I am unhappy, word will spread; the builder's business may suffer. On a formal level, I can seek mediation or arbitration with the Better Business Bureau or a similar agency, or I can file a lawsuit.

These options may not exist with online contracts. We often do not know the real identity of the other party or that party's location; the other party may not be subject to the jurisdiction of our courts.

If the matter does reach a court, does the cyber contract have the same value as evidence as a paper contract? A face-to-face contract may have been witnessed or even notarized. It is unlikely that such third-party witnesses exist for an online contract. Passwords, cookies, and IP tracing may provide some security concerning the location and identity of a party, but are not perfect security against tampering.

While some websites attempt to create a system of enforcement based on reputation, there is nothing to stop an unscrupulous party from creating a new identity as needed. Your local builder cannot easily change his name and appearance to escape your wrath! In fact, there is nothing to stop a party from wrongfully disparaging another party's reputation.

Privacy is also an issue, beyond concern about identity theft. The local eccentric "trader" might gather, cleanup, and sell "junk" at a garage sale and stay "under the radar" with respect to the Internal Revenue Service. Doing so on a website might catch the attention of tax authorities.

In the future, more online contracts may be entered through third-party services that can operate like escrow services. For example, the service will not release payment to seller until buyer acknowledges satisfactory receipt of a product.

E. The Categories

Contracts that must be evidenced by a written instrument include the following.

1. Promises in Anticipation of Marriage

This category does not cover promises to marry, but other promises that assume that a marriage will take place. The category can even cover promises

Pre-nuptial
Agreement in anticipation of marriage; typically involves a promise to convey property when marriage occurs or concerns division of property in the event of a divorce; see Ante-nuptial

Ante-nuptial
Agreement in anticipation of marriage; typically involves a promise to convey property when marriage occurs or concerns division of property in the event of a divorce; see Pre-nuptial

made by parties other than the husband or wife. Such agreements are often called **pre-nuptial** or **ante-nuptial** or marriage settlement contracts, and typically involve a promise to convey property when a marriage occurs or an agreement about the division of property in the event of divorce.

"Pre-nups" are very common among those who have substantial assets before getting married or have been previously married and either have known the pain of property division or want to protect their assets for children from a previous spouse. In recent years, the press has often speculated about the terms of the pre-nup when a celebrity couple gets engaged or breaks up.

Many states have special requirements for pre-nups, which may include full disclosure of assets and even representation by separate lawyers. Compliance with these requirements may even have to be stated in the agreement itself. Be sure to check the requirements for your jurisdiction, when assisting with such a contract.

EXHIBIT 8-1
SAMPLE: Pre-Marital Agreement

---

1. The Parties, Jeanne McCoy ("Jeanne") and Michael C. Kalland ("Michael") *[note use of defined terms]* plan to marry in the near future and wish to establish their respective rights and responsibilities with regard to income and property. *[These paragraphs are recitals, giving background]*
2. Each of the Parties has been previously married and divorced; each has children.
3. The Parties are getting married because of their love for each other and do not wish to change their present financial circumstances.
4   Jeanne has identified all of her financial assets, property, liabilities, and sources of income on Exhibit A, attached hereto and made part of this Agreement.
5. Michael has identified all of his financial assets, property, liabilities, and sources of income on Exhibit B, attached hereto and made part of this Agreement.
6. Each Party has made full disclosure of his or her financial status in the attached Exhibits and has examined the Exhibit prepared by the other.
7. Each Party acknowledges that he or she has separate income and assets sufficient to provide for his or her financial needs.
8. The parties are in the process of purchasing a residence, which shall be held in tenancy in common; each party is contributing half of the cost of the purchase of the residence.
9. During the course of the marriage, the Parties shall share in the costs of housing, food, and utilities. Each Party shall be responsible for his or her own personal expenses, including, but not limited to, clothing,

---

EXHIBIT 8-1
(continued)

---

grooming, vehicles, travel, gifts, taxes on income, debt payment and medical care.

10. Each Party waives:
    a. all claim to assets listed on the Exhibit prepared by the other party and to any property or income resulting from those assets;
    b. all claim to any income, gift, or inheritance received by the other during the course of marriage;
    c. all rights to share in the other Party's estate upon death;
    d. all rights to any pension, profit sharing or retirement income of the other Party;
    e. all rights to support or maintenance in the event of separation or divorce.

11. Each Party has consulted with an independent attorney and is satisfied with his or her representation. *[note the various waivers and acknowledgments]*

12. Each Party acknowledges that he or she has been fully advised of the legal claims they might have in the absence of this Agreement and that courts have the authority to disregard this Agreement if necessary to avoid impoverishing a spouse.

13. This Agreement is entered into and shall be construed and enforced under the laws of the state of _____. *[13 is a choice of law clause; 14 is an integration clause]*

14. This Agreement constitutes the entire Agreement between the Parties and may only be modified by written agreement, signed by both Parties. In the event that any part of this Agreement is deemed unenforceable, it is the wish of the Parties that the rest of the Agreement be considered valid and enforceable.

Date   Signatures
Witness/Notary Seal

---

2.   Contracts Not to be Performed Within a Year

The writing requirement applies only if the promise, by its terms, would not permit performance within a year. If performance is possible within a year, even if unlikely and even if the parties do not anticipate performance within a year, the requirement does not apply. Nor does it matter how long performance actually takes, after the contract is made. Promises with an uncertain duration and promises with alternatives, one of which could be performed within a year, are not subject to the requirement.

Examples

- On October 1, 2006, a former U.S. President promises to speak at Yale's graduation in May 2008. This promise must be in writing; the calculation is made from the time when the agreement was made, not from the time when performance begins.
- Following an accident that left Pat Plaintiff with limited use of her right arm, Don Defendant agreed to give Pat $300 per month for the rest of her life, in exchange for dropping a lawsuit. This does not have to be in writing because it is possible that Pat will die within a year. Some states disagree and require that lifetime contracts be in writing, see McInerney v. Charter Golf, Inc., **176 Ill.2d 482 (1997)**

---

3. Contracts Involving Land (Real Property)

Easement
Limited right to use real property

A promise to transfer "any interest in land" is generally within the statute; therefore, real estate sales, leases (in most states only leases for more than a year), mortgages, options on land[4], and **easements** require a written instrument. The Statute of Frauds does not require a written instrument for an agreement to build or perform some other service on land.

4. Contracts for Sale of Goods for $500 or More

In most states UCC §2-201 requires a writing for the sale of goods for a price of $500 or more. Remember, the UCC does not cover contracts for services (such as employment) and that the UCC is always subject to amendment. In 2003 the National Conference of Commissioners on Uniform State Laws, together with the American Law Institute, promulgated amendments to Article 2 that include raising the Statute of Frauds amount for sale of goods to $5,000. Whether states will adopt the change remains to be seen. For more information, visit http://www.nccusl.org.

Example

Does the "bright line" test of price seem arbitrary? Ann is at the mall to buy a gift for her husband. On the clearance table in an electronics store, there is a hand-held mini-computer, which would normally sell for $900, but it is marked down to $450 because of a scratch on the case. The line to pay is long and Ann is in a hurry. She hands the computer to a salesperson, saying "hold this for me. I have to run down to Sears and get a gallon of paint. I will be back in 20 minutes to pay." The salesperson says, "OK, it's yours," but forgets all about and sets it on a table. Another customer

---

[4]An option is, essentially, a contract to hold an offer open (see Chapter 4).

buys it before Ann returns. Could Ann sue for breach of contract? YES (of course she has to prove that it happened — maybe that's not a problem, maybe she has a friend with her or maybe the salesperson admits to the exchange).

But, if the computer had been marked $600, the oral contract would not be enforceable.

The UCC specifies exceptions, including:

- contracts for goods to be specially manufactured for the buyer that are not suitable for sale to others in the normal course of business, if the seller has already made a substantial commitment;
- situations where the party "trying to get out of it" admits in testimony or a pleading that an agreement was made;
- situations where the goods have been received and **actually accepted**;
- situations where payment has been accepted.

5. Promises to Answer for the Debts of Another

Both the "E" (executor promises to pay debts of estate) and the "S" (**suretyship**) in MYLEGS fall under this category; they are **collateral promises**, not the primary promises of the contract.

Example

The difference between a surety and a co-signer can be very important. Son is buying his first new car; he signs a loan contract, promising to pay $250 per month (Son is primarily liable). Because Son is young and doesn't have a credit history, the lender requires **surety** (also called **guarantor**). Dad signs a promise to pay if Son doesn't pay. Dad's promise is collateral; he is only liable if son **defaults** (fails to pay). If dad was primarily liable (a **co-signer**, who signed the contract on equal terms with Son) or if Dad promised Son (not lender) "Don't worry, I will pay if you can't," the agreement would not fall within the Statute of Frauds. Some courts have taken this a step further and have taken contracts out of the statute if the main purpose of the person's agreement was his own benefit. If Dad and Son were to share the car, but had Son take the loan and Dad act as a surety, those states would find the Statute inapplicable.

An **executor** or **administrator** is the person who carries on the business of an **estate**, which is essentially the "business" of the finances of a deceased person or a person who has been declared incompetent. The executor is not usually personally liable for the debts of the estate and a promise to assume such responsibility must be in writing.

Example

People make promises in the heat of emotion and the statute of frauds can protect them. Cody's 25-year-old brother, Ron, died several days after hitting a tree with

Collateral Promise
Promise to guarantee the debt of another, made without benefit to the party making the promise

Surety
Liable for the payment of another's debt or the performance of another's obligation; see Guarantor

Guarantor
Agrees to be responsible for another's debt or performance under a contract if the other fails to pay or perform; see Surety

Default
Fail to meet obligations

Co-signer
One who participates jointly in borrowing

Executor
One who carries on the business of an estate; see Administrator

Administrator
One who carries on the business of an estate; see Executor

Estate
The entity for managing finances of a deceased person or an incompetent

his motorcycle. Ron had no medical insurance. After being appointed as executor of Ron's estate, Cody discovered that Ron had only about $5,000 in assets, but the outstanding hospital bill was $90,000. Cody tells the hospital staff, "You were so good to my brother, I will pay this even if it takes the rest of my life." Cody had no legal obligation to pay the debt, so this is not enforceable unless in writing. Do you recognize another problem in the example? There is no consideration. Cody's promise was an incomplete gift. If, however, there were consideration, the promise would have to be evidenced by writing.

Exhibit 8-2 contains a sample of a suretyship contract that would most likely be used to guaranty the performance of a contractor working on a big construction project. A **performance bond** surety agreement guarantees that a contract will be performed according to its terms and specifications. If a contractor defaults, these bonds generally obligate the surety to either finance the contractor, undertake the completion of the project, obtain a new contractor to the owner or pay the bond penalty. A **payment bond** surety agreement guarantees that a contractor will make appropriate, prompt and full payments for labor and material consumed on a project. A **maintenance bond** is intended to assure a project will remain free of defects in workmanship or materials for a specific period of time. This sample is very hard to read. For a future assignment, you will attempt to rewrite it in plain English. For the moment, read it to determine whether you can understand it. What type of bond does it represent?

EXHIBIT 8-2

KNOW ALL MEN BY THESE PRESENTS:

That we, _____, as Principal, and_____, as Surety, are hereby held and firmly bound unto _____ as Obligee in the penal sum of _____ ($_____) for payment whereof the said Principal and Surety bind themselves, their heirs, executors, administrators, and successors, jointly and severally, firmly by these presents.

The conditions of this obligation are such that whereas the Principal entered into a certain contract, hereto attached, and made a part hereof, with the Obligee, _____, dated _____, _____, for _____ (Project No. ___).

NOW THEREFORE, the condition of this obligation is such that, if the Principal shall faithfully perform the said Contract in accordance with the Plans and Specifications and Contract Documents, and shall fully indemnify and save harmless the Obligee from all cost and damage which the Obligee may suffer by reason of Principal's default or failure so to do and shall fully reimburse and repay the Obligee all outlay and expense which

---

EXHIBIT 8-2
(continued)

---

the Obligee may incur in making good any such default, then this obligation shall be null and void, otherwise it shall remain in full force and effect.

In the event that the Principal is declared in default under the said Contract, the Surety will within Fifteen (15) days of the Obligee's declaration of such default take over and assume completion of said contract and become entitled to the payment of the balance of the Contract Price. Conditioned upon the Surety's faithful performance of its obligations, the liability of the Surety for the Principal's default shall not exceed the penalty of this bond.

The Surety agrees to pay to the Obligee upon demand all loss and expense, including attorney's fees, incurred by the Obligee by reason of or on account of any breach of this obligation by the Surety.

Provided further, that if any legal action be filed upon this bond, venue shall lie in the county where the said Contract is to be performed.

Provided further, that the Surety, for value received, hereby stipulates and agrees that no change, extension of time, alteration or addition to the terms of the said Contract, or to the work to be performed thereunder, or the Specifications accompanying the same, shall in anywise affect its obligation on this bond, and it does hereby waive notice of any such change, extension of time, alteration or addition, to the terms of the said Contract or to the work or to the Specifications.

By signature hereon, if the amount of this bond exceeds $100,000, the Surety attests that at the time the bond was executed (Surety shall provide Obligee with evidence of the following):

(1) it was a holder of a certificate of authority from the United States Secretary of the Treasury to qualify as a surety on obligations permitted or required under federal law; or

(2) had reinsured any liability in excess of $100,000 by a reinsurer holding a certificate of authority from the United States Secretary of the Treasury.

IN WITNESS WHEREOF, the above bounden parties have executed this instrument under their several seals this _____ day of _____ in the year _____, the name and corporate seal of each corporate party being hereto affixed, and these presents duly signed by its undersigned representative pursuant to authority of its governing body

SIGNATURES AND WITNESSES.

F.   Practical and Ethical Considerations

The Statute of Frauds came into existence to prevent fraud and perjury, but might it actually promote perjury in some circumstances? One of the exceptions, recognized by most courts as taking an agreement outside the Statute of Frauds is an admission, in court or court documents, that an agreement existed.

Affirmative Defense
Part of an answer to a complaint in which defendant attempts to limit or excuse liability, based on facts outside those claimed by plaintiff

When a defendant responds to a complaint alleging breach of contract, the defendant can raise the Statute as an **affirmative defense**. An affirmative defense limits or excuses a defendant's liability, even if the plaintiff's allegations are proven, and is based on facts outside those claimed by the plaintiff. If the defendant is able to prove the Statute as an affirmative defense, the case can be dismissed before trial in most jurisdictions.

Example

Billie Buyer files suit against Sam Seller, alleging breach of a contract for the sale of Sam's house to Billie. Sam responds that no written agreement exists. Assuming that Sam never wrote the note described in the previous example, the lawsuit might be dismissed before trial.

Assignment 8-3

How should a lawyer prepare the client to answer if a case based on an oral contract is not dismissed or if the client is required to testify in another matter and might be asked about the existence of the oral agreement? Identify the relevant ethical rules, some of which have been discussed in previous chapters.

Review Questions

1. How should a defendant respond to a lawsuit based on a contract that falls within the Statute of Frauds but that is not evidence by a writing? Why is it essential that the defendant respond in the correct way?
2. Why do courts try to find exceptions to the Statute of Frauds?
3. Why might a court uphold a contract that was not reduced to writing and that would otherwise fall within the Statute of Frauds?
4. What are the characteristics of a writing sufficient to satisfy the Statute of Frauds?

5. What is the difference between primary liability and collateral liability for a debt?
6. What are the major categories of contracts that must be evidenced by a writing?
7. What is a "click-wrap agreement" and why are they problematic, for reasons other than the Statute of Frauds?
8. What special requirements may apply to pre-nuptial agreements?
9. The ABA Model Rules provide that one type of lawyer-client fee agreement *shall* be in writing. What type of agreement must be written?

ACROSS

2. UCC has exception for goods specially _____ if seller has made substantial commitment
5. type of signature acceptable for contracts formed online
7. requirement of valid writing, can be satisfied in various ways
10. easement or mortgage must be written because they convey interests in _____
12. another name for guarantor
13. contract falls within s/f if it cannot be performed within a _____
14. a guarantee of a loan is _____, not primary
16. the s/f was intended to prevent this
18. the "business" of handling deceased person's finances
19. Check is an example of a _____ instrument
20. Contracts for sale of _____ for $500 or more must be in writing

DOWN

1. S/F is _____ if not raised as an affirmative defense
3. also called administrator, handles financial affairs of deceased person
4. "party to be _____" is party trying to get out of the contract
6. s/f is inapplicable if the contract has been fully _____
8. a pre-_____ contract, anticipating marriage, within s/f
9. an agreement intended to be final and complete
11. failure to pay, as required by the contract
12. a _____ interest is an interest in personal property to secure payment of a debt
15. six letters stand for major categories covered by the s/f
17. contracts allowing agent to sell _____ estate or to pay such an agent commission generally must be written

9

Third Parties/
Secured
Transactions

In analyzing almost any contract problem, the first question is whether a contract ever formed. That question involves looking at agreement, consideration, legality, capacity, and whether the statute of frauds required a written instrument. If a contract did form, the next question is: What are the rights of the parties? This chapter explores how a contract affects parties who may not have been part of the original agreement or who may have been part of that agreement in a peripheral way.

People outside the original contract relationship can have rights with respect to the contract in one of three ways. An outsider might act as an agent for one of the parties. Outsiders might also be beneficiaries. Rights/obligations under the contract might be assigned or delegated to outsiders or an outsider might guarantee performance.

A. Agency

Agent
One who acts on behalf of another

Principal
Party for whom agent acts

An **agent** acts on behalf of another party, the **principal**. For purposes of this book, you will learn about agency as a means of entering into a contract. Many, possibly most, business contracts are created by an agent. Consider when you run into Wal-Mart to buy socks. You don't deal with members of the Walton family or other stockholders of the corporation that owns and sells you the socks; you deal with an agent. Businesses that operate as entities, such as corporations and limited-liability companies, must enter contracts through agents.

> Agency involves three parties: the principal, the agent, and the outside party. The agent is the mechanism, but the contract forms between the principal and the outsider.

---

1. Establishing Agency

Not everyone who acts on behalf of another is an agent. Agency requires consent of the principal and the agent. Does the consent have to be written? Not necessarily; the agency agreement must be written in cases where the statute of frauds applies directly, for example, appointment of an agent for a period of more than one year. In some states, the agency contract must be written because the contracts the agent will deal with must be written, because of the statute of frauds. A contract to sell real estate must be in writing, so a contract to employ a real estate agent must be in writing. This requirement is called the **equal dignity rule**. The document that creates an agency relationship is sometimes called a **power of attorney**.

A sample power of attorney for property can be found in Chapter 7.

An agent is not always an employee and agency need not be a compensated relationship. The agent may act as a "gift" to the principal. An agent might not even have contract capacity in some cases. Any teenager who takes Mom's car and money and buys a gallon of milk and a loaf of bread for the family is acting as an agent. The main characteristic of agency is the **control** exercised by the principal over the agent. The principal gives the agent authority to act in one of several ways.

Equal Dignity Rule
Requirement that agency contract be written, if contract to be established by agent must be written

Power of Attorney
Document creating an agency

Express Authority
Authority given by words or conduct

Implied Authority
Authority not expressed in writing or spoken words; arises from circumstances

a. **Express authority** is the authority given by words or conduct. Gale engages Andi Agent to sell a house. Andi has express authority to sell the house.
b. **Implied authority** is authority reasonably necessary to accomplish the express purpose. Andi has implied authority to advertise the house.

c. **Operation of Law** can create authority in an emergency situation. Rizwana was alone in the store where she is a sales clerk when a car hit and broke out the front window. The manager could not be found; Rizwana did not want to leave the store open to the elements and to thieves and ordered a company to board up the broken window, even though she was never authorized to make purchases for the store.

d. **Ratification** is acceptance of the agent's unauthorized actions after-the-fact. Ian told his new employee, Jana, that she could not make any purchases without his express permission. Ian was out of town for several days, when the fax machine failed. Jana went to the office supply store, where Ian has an account, and bought a new machine. The office supply store clerk was careless and did not check who had authority to order for Ian. When Ian returned, he could have refused to pay, but he did not object to the machine. He started using it and is now obligated to pay. Of course, Jana may be liable to Ian for breach of her obligations as an employee.

e. **Apparent authority** results from the principal's dealings with third parties, when the principal has given those third parties reason to believe that an agent has authority. Suppose, in the above example, Jana repeatedly ordered supplies and Ian paid every time, never raising an objection. The tenth time Jana placed an order, Ian decided to put his foot down and refuse to pay. He may be **estopped** from denying liability because he created the impression that Jana had authority to place orders. Similarly, if Jana *did* have authority to place orders, but Ian failed to notify the office supply store when he fired Jana, Ian might be liable for orders placed by Jana after her termination. For obvious reasons, apparent authority is always based on the principal's conduct; an agent cannot create his or her own authority.

Operation of Law
Rights and obligations are implied by law, for example, in emergency situations

Ratification
Acceptance of acts by agent after they occur

Apparent Authority
Principal's dealings with third parties have given them reason to believe that an agent has authority

Estop
To bar assertion of a claim or right that contradicts what has been said or done before

All of the above describe theories under which a principal can be liable on a contract entered by an agent. Normally the agent is not liable on that contract because the third party knows that the contract is really the principal's contract. If the third party does not know that, the agent might be liable.

Example

Disclosure is essential to protecting the agent from liability to the third party. Disney wants to establish a new theme park in the Midwest and contacts Laurel, a noted expert in commercial real estate in the area west of Chicago. Disney hires Laurel to acquire the needed land, but tells Laurel that she may not disclose Disney's interest. Such a disclosure would cause a sharp increase in price. Laurel starts immediately and first signs a contract to buy 160 acres from Farmer Brown. Laurel might either say nothing — Disney is an **undisclosed principal** — or might say "I am working for a corporation but cannot reveal its identity" — Disney is a **partially disclosed principal**. If Disney decides to change plans before the purchase is completed, Farmer Brown *can* sue Laurel. After all, if he is unaware of Disney, who else would he sue? Laurel may be all right, however, because Disney has a duty to indemnify her — discussed below.

Undisclosed Principal
Existence of agency relationship not known to third party

Partially Disclosed Principal
Existence of agency is known, identity of principal is not known

---

2. Agency Duties

Fiduciary Relationship
Relationship in which one person is under a duty to act for the benefit of the other on matters within the scope of the relationship

Agency is a **fiduciary relationship;** the principal and agent have special obligations to each other.

Principal's Duties to the Agent

- To **cooperate** in performance of agreed duties. For example, Hollis signed a six-month listing to sell her home, then her job transfer was cancelled. Having spent money advertising the house, the agent refused to cancel the contract. Hollis changed the locks so that agent could not show the house. Hollis may be liable to agent.

Indemnification
Compensation or reimbursement for a loss

- To **indemnify** (reimburse) the agent for expenses reasonably incurred in carrying out the agency.
- To **communicate** relevant information.
- To comply with any contract with the agent.

Agent's Duties to the Principal

- To **obey** lawful directions.
- To be able to **account** for the principal's money in the agent's care.
- To exercise **reasonable care**. While an agent is not expected to have a crystal ball and make only decisions with positive outcomes, the agent is expected to act with reasonable care — to conduct reasonable investigation and use common sense.
- To keep the principal **fully informed** — for example, a real estate agent cannot unilaterally decide that an offer is too low to even discuss with the principal.
- **Loyalty**, which encompasses:
  - Not using or disclosing confidential information obtained from or about the principal.
  - Not becoming involved in conflicting relationships without the principal's consent.
    - Outside Profits: Dana, department head of the paralegal program, has responsibility for choosing and ordering books. A publisher gives Dana a "gift" of $500.
    - Competing With Principal: While working as Hal's agent to find an investment property, Ana finds a duplex that is priced substantially below its value. Ana puts in her own bid to buy the property, which would have been an excellent investment for Hal.
    - Working for Competing Principals: Lyn is a sales rep for Jocko Sports and calls on stores in a four-state area to get those stores to carry the Jocko line of products. Lyn starts to represent a competing line, Team Stuff, and shows both lines when visiting stores.
    - Secret Dealing With Principal. While working to find Hal an investment property, Ana transfers a building she owns to a trust and then buys the building for Hal, not revealing her ownership.

Agency normally ends by agreement of the parties, the passage of an agreed time (*e.g.,* a six-month listing), completion of the purpose (*e.g.,* the house is sold), or the inability of one of the parties to perform (death, incapacity). In some cases termination of agency may be possible, but wrongful. For example, Jocko Sports gave Lyn a two-year contract as a sales representative, but breached the contract by firing Lyn after five months. Jocko is able to end the relationship, but may have liability for doing so. On the other hand, a principal may be unable to terminate an **agency coupled with an interest**, in which the agent has a financial "stake" in the transaction. For example, in order to obtain a special price, Lee signed a three-year contract with Onandoff Internet. For convenience, Lee authorized Onandoff to make a monthly charge to her credit card to pay for the service. Unfortunately, Onandoff took on far too many new customers and for weeks Lee was unable to get online. Frustrated, Lee signed up for a different service and called to cancel the monthly payment to Onandoff. Unfortunately, Lee appointed Onandoff as an agent to make those charges to the credit card and Onandoff has a financial interest — Lee may be unable to terminate the arrangement.

Agency Coupled with an Interest
Agent has a financial stake in the transaction

Examine this sample agency contract and look for provisions dealing with cooperation, communication, outside profits. Would this agreement have to be in writing to be enforceable?

EXHIBIT 9-1
Buyer-Broker Agency Agreement

THIS AGREEMENT is entered into this _____ day of _____, 20_____, by ("Buyer"), and _____, ("Broker").

1. Buyer desires to employ Broker to locate and negotiate the purchase of real property on behalf of Buyer and Broker desires to accept such employment and to use best efforts to find a suitable property for Buyer;
2. Broker is duly licensed as a real estate broker in the State of _____ and maintains an office, properly equipped and staffed to render the services contracted for in this agreement.
3. Buyer desires to purchase property in _____ County, State of _____, with specifications and intended use set out in Exhibit "A", attached and made a part of this agreement, ("Property").
4. Buyer warrants that he has the financial ability to purchase such a Property, at the price and on the terms and conditions set out in Exhibit "B", attached and made a part of this agreement.
5. Broker shall use best efforts to find a suitable Property, shall advertise the desires of the Buyer, and has right to locate and negotiate the purchase of a suitable Property at the price and terms set out in Exhibit "B", or at any different price and terms as may be hereafter accepted by the Buyer

EXHIBIT 9-1
(continued)

6. The term of this Agreement shall be _____ months, beginning on the date of signing by both parties, and ending at noon on _____, 200_____,

7. Broker shall inspect prospective properties and obtain complete information before presenting the property to Buyer for consideration.

8. Buyer shall not, during the term of this Agreement, or any extension hereof, contract to buy any property, without providing the Broker with full details of any such action in writing.

9. If Broker identifies a suitable Property during the term of this Agreement and Buyer contracts to buy that Property, Buyer shall pay to Broker, at the time of closing of the purchase of the Property, a commission of _____ (_____%) percent of the purchase price for the Property.

10. Broker may represent and receive commissions from both Buyer and Seller of the Property.

11. If Buyer locates Property solely through his own efforts, Buyer may enter into a contract for the purchase of the Property without liability to Broker for commission in any amount; however, at the time of closing, Buyer shall reimburse Broker for all documented, reasonable out-of-pocket expenses incurred by Broker during the term of this Agreement. Within twenty four (24) hours of initial contact with any such prospective seller, Buyer shall provide Broker with the property description, and contact information for the owner of the Property, and the circumstances under which Buyer obtained knowledge of the Property.

12. This Agreement may be terminated by either party, prior to a contract for purchase being executed, upon written notice to the other party. If this Agreement is terminated by Buyer, Buyer agrees to reimburse Broker for all documented, reasonable out-of-pocket expenses incurred by Broker prior to termination.

13. Broker, a cooperating broker, or an authorized escrow agent may accept and hold, money paid by Buyer as a deposit with regard to any Property located pursuant to this Agreement, under the laws of _____; in the event of forfeiture by a prospective seller, all such sums shall be immediately returned to Buyer.

14. This Agreement in no way guarantees the location or purchase of a Property.

15. Broker (may) (may not) use the name of Buyer in locating and negotiating a purchase.

16. If provisions of this Agreement shall for any reason be held to be invalid, such invalidity shall not affect any other provision of this Agreement.

17. This Agreement contains the entire agreement of the parties and no oral statements or prior agreements shall have any force and effect.

EXHIBIT 9-1
(continued)

This Agreement shall not be modified except by a writing executed by both parties.

18. This agreement, and all transactions contemplated hereby, shall be governed by the laws of _____. The parties agree to submit to the jurisdiction and venue of a court located in _____ County, _____. If litigation arises out of this Agreement the parties agree to reimburse the prevailing party's reasonable attorney's fees, court costs, and other expenses, whether or not taxable by the court as costs, in addition to other relief to which the prevailing party may be entitled. In such event, no action shall be entertained by any court of competent jurisdiction if filed more than one year after the date the cause(s) of action actually accrued regardless of whether damages were then calculable.

19. The agreements contained herein are binding upon the parties and their respective heirs, successors, legal representatives and assigns.

20. This Agreement will not be recorded in the public records of any county.

Signatures, witnesses and exhibits omitted.

B. Contract Beneficiaries

As implied by the name, a **third-party beneficiary** benefits from the contract. Whether a beneficiary has enforceable rights under the contract depends on the intent of the original parties. To determine the intent of the parties, courts look at whether they were aware of the third party and whether the relationship makes intent to benefit likely.

Third-Party Beneficiary
Not a party to a contract, but benefits from contract

Examples

A third party does not have the right to enforce a contract if the contract was not intended to benefit that third party. Hugh Homeowner was thrilled to learn that his neighbor, Nils, signed a contract to sell his house to Yuri Yuppie. Nils has never taken care of the property and, as a result, the value of Hugh's property has suffered. Hugh knows Yuri intends to paint the house immediately, have professional landscapers work on the yard, and dispose of the trash on the porch. One day Yuri tells Hugh that Nils is "backing out" of the sale because moving will be so difficult. Yuri does not want to spend the time and money to go to court and plans to simply find another house to rehab. Although Hugh would, in fact, have benefited from performance of

Incidental Beneficiary
A third-party beneficiary, not intended to benefit from contract, does not acquire rights under contract

Donee Beneficiary
A third-party beneficiary, intended to benefit from contract performance, as a gift

Creditor Beneficiary
A third-party beneficiary, to whom a contract party is indebted, and who is intended to benefit from the performance of a contract

the contract, he was not an intended beneficiary and cannot enforce the contract or seek a remedy, based on the breach, in court. Hugh was an **incidental beneficiary**.

While visiting his insurance agent about his homeowners' insurance, Val buys a life insurance policy on an impulse and names his wife as beneficiary. Val forgets to tell his wife about the policy and she discovers it about a year later, after Val's sudden death in an accident. Val's wife was not even aware of Val's contract with the insurance company, but she can enforce it once she has knowledge. A court will assume that Val had intent to make a gift benefiting his wife, based on the relationship. Val's wife is a **donee beneficiary**.

Suppose that Val's house was destroyed in a fire and his mortgage lender wanted payment under the homeowner's policy. Mortgage lenders generally require that they be specifically named on such policies as beneficiaries. Even if lender were not named, it could seek to enforce the contract. A court would assume intent to benefit the lender because of Val's legal obligation to the lender. The lender is a **creditor beneficiary**.

In either example, the insurance company could assert defenses that would be valid against the original contract party, such as fraudulent information in the application for insurance or failure to pay premiums.

EXHIBIT 9-2
Sample: Mortgage clause requiring that borrower make lender a creditor beneficiary

Property Insurance. Borrower shall keep the improvements now existing or hereafter erected on the Property insured against loss by fire, hazards included within the term "extended coverage," and any other hazards including, but not limited to, earthquakes and floods, for which Lender requires insurance. This insurance shall be maintained in the amounts (including deductible levels) and for the periods that Lender requires. What Lender requires pursuant to the preceding sentences can change during the term of the Loan. The insurance carrier providing the insurance shall be chosen by Borrower subject to Lender's right to disapprove Borrower's choice, which right shall not be exercised unreasonably. Lender may require Borrower to pay, in connection with this Loan, either: (a) a one-time charge for flood zone determination, certification and tracking services; or (b) a one-time charge for flood zone determination and certification services and subsequent charges each time remappings or similar changes occur which reasonably might affect such determination or certification. Borrower shall also be responsible for the payment of any fees imposed by the Federal Emergency Management Agency in connection with the review of any flood zone determination resulting from an objection by Borrower....

EXHIBIT 9-2
(continued)

All insurance policies required by Lender and renewals of such policies shall be subject to Lender's right to disapprove such policies, shall include a standard mortgage clause, and shall name Lender as mortgagee and/or as an additional loss payee. Lender shall have the right to hold the policies and renewal certificates. If Lender requires, Borrower shall promptly give to Lender all receipts of paid premiums and renewal notices. If Borrower obtains any form of insurance coverage, not otherwise required by Lender, for damage to, or destruction of, the Property, such policy shall include a standard mortgage clause and shall name Lender as mortgagee and/or as an additional loss payee.

In the event of loss, Borrower shall give prompt notice to the insurance carrier and Lender. Lender may make proof of loss if not made promptly by Borrower. Unless Lender and Borrower otherwise agree in writing, any insurance proceeds, whether or not the underlying insurance was required by Lender, shall be applied to restoration or repair of the Property, if the restoration or repair is economically feasible and Lender's security is not lessened. During such repair and restoration period, Lender shall have the right to hold such insurance proceeds until Lender has had an opportunity to inspect such Property.... If Borrower abandons the Property, Lender may file, negotiate and settle any available insurance claim and related matters. If Borrower does not respond within 30 days to a notice from Lender that the insurance carrier has offered to settle a claim, then Lender may negotiate and settle the claim. The 30-day period will begin when the notice is given. In either event, or if Lender acquires the Property under Section 22 or otherwise, Borrower hereby assigns to Lender (a) Borrower's rights to any insurance proceeds in an amount not to exceed the amounts unpaid under the Note or this Security Instrument, and (b) any other of Borrower's rights (other than the right to any refund of unearned premiums paid by Borrower) under all insurance policies covering the Property, insofar as such rights are applicable to the coverage of the Property. Lender may use the insurance proceeds either to repair or restore the Property or to pay amounts unpaid under the Note or this Security Instrument, whether or not then due.

Whether an injured party is an intended beneficiary is particularly important with respect to warranties. At common law, lack of **privity** (not being a party to the contract relationship) often prevented injured parties from taking advantage of warranties in a contract. If Dad bought a car, which was subsequently in an accident because of a defect, could family members collect damages from a seller with whom they had no contract relationship? Could Dad sue the manufacturer, or only the dealership with which he had a contract? The common law differs from state to state. While injuries to a person or property are normally addressed

Privity
Being a party to the contract

by tort law, and privity is not an issue, damages that are purely economic (*e.g.*, lost income) are still addressed by contract law. As you might imagine, the Uniform Commercial Code (UCC) addresses the issue.

Assignment 9-1

◆ Aunt Liz hired attorney Neil to write her will, leaving her estate in trust to two nieces, Ann and Beth. Unfortunately, Neil established the trust in a way that put the entire burden of taxes on Ann's share. Liz has died and Ann feels Neil breached a contract to create a trust to benefit the two nieces equally. Can Ann sue? Was she a third-party beneficiary under the contract between Liz and Neil. Use computer-assisted legal research (CALR) to find a case discussing whether a non-client can be a beneficiary under a contract to employ a lawyer.

◆ Search the Internet and find the Uniform Statutory Form Power of Attorney Act. Has your state adopted a form based on the Act?

◆ Research and report to the class as to whether your state recognizes a **durable** power of attorney or a **springing power of attorney**, which "springs" into effect upon the happening of a stated event, e.g., "When my doctor certifies that I am unable to make my own decisions . . ." For more information about these powers of attorney, visit http://www.aarp.org/families/legal_issues/legal_guides/a2004-03-24-li_selfhelppowerofattorney.html.

◆ In adopting the UCC, each state chose from three alternatives concerning who can be a third-party beneficiary to warranties included in a sale of goods. Find the alternative enacted by your state.

Durable Power of Attorney
Creates an agency relationship that remains in effect during the grantor's incompetency

Springing Power of Attorney
Comes into effect at a later date

C. Assignment and Delegation

Assignment
A transfer of property or rights

Delegation
Assignment of obligations

The transfer of a party's rights under a contract is called **assignment**; the transfer of duties is **delegation**. The two often go together.

1. Assignment

Assignment is assumed to be allowable unless the contract specifically and validly prohibits assignment, the right being assigned is highly personal, or assignment is prohibited by law. For example, some states prohibit assignment of future wages or of a personal injury claim. An assignment may not substantially change the risks, rights, or duties under the contract. Changing the address to which a payment is made is not substantial, but attempting to change the amount of the payment would be a prohibited substantial change. Courts tend to rule in favor of allowing assignment.

Example

Assignment of contracts for financing is very common. Family Home is a small, independent appliance store. In order to compete with the "big boys," Family must offer financing to customers who do not have credit cards. When Family sells a freezer and the buyer signs a note to pay $50 per month for the next 24 months, Family cannot afford to "hold the paper." Family's cash flow would not permit it to have several hundred accounts outstanding and be able to buy new inventory. Family therefore "sells the paper" to Acme Acceptance. Acme pays Family $1,800, and Family assigns the note promising 24 payments of $50. Acme is happy because it will earn $600 by taking monthly payments. Family is happy because it sold a freezer at a profit and is able to replenish inventory. Customer is not inconvenienced; she is simply given a new address to which the payments should be sent. Family is the **assignor**, Acme is the **assignee**, and customer is the **obligor**.

Assignor
One who transfers rights to another

Assignee
One to whom rights are transferred by another

Obligor
One who owes an obligation.

Gratuitous
Done without compensation; a gift

A valid assignment must provide for notice to the obligor. Whether an assignment is revocable may depend on whether it was **gratuitous** (a gift) or for consideration as well as the degree to which the parties have acted on the assignment. Always check state law in such a situation. Whether the assignment can be cancelled or revoked may also depend on whether the assignment was oral or written. Is an oral assignment valid? Yes, unless the statute of frauds applies. For example, assignment of a contract to purchase real estate would have to be in writing.

Normally the assignee has the right to enforce the contract immediately upon valid assignment. The Family-Acme-Customer transaction may be a secured transaction, however, and special concerns arise. What if the freezer does not work and Family Home refuses to fix or replace it? Is Customer limited to suing Family while continuing to make payments to Acme? The answer is generally no.

Mortgage
Security interest in real estate

Real Property
Land and buildings

Collateral
Assets pledged by a borrower to secure a loan or other credit, and subject to seizure in the event of default

Lien
An encumbrance against property, typically to secure payment of a debt

Foreclose
Take property to satisfy debt

You are probably familiar with the concept of a **mortgage** against **real property** (land and buildings) to secure a loan; the property serves as **collateral**. The lender has a **lien** and can **foreclose** (take the property) if the borrower fails to pay. Because the lender is generally not also the seller of the property, the issue of defenses based on problems with the property does not come up often. To discover whether real property is subject to a mortgage, check the recorder for the county in which the property is located.

When the seller retains a security interest in personal property, as in the Family-Acme situation, the situation is not the same as a mortgage. Secured interests in

Chattel
Moveable items, also called
personal property

personal (**chattel**) property are covered by Article 9 of the UCC. The end of this chapter contains an overview of the most important provisions.

2.   Delegation

You may remember that personal impossibility is not usually an excuse for contract performance. For example, Pat enters a contract to paint Lou's house. A week later Pat is in an accident, has a broken arm, and cannot paint. Performance is not objectively impossible, so what can Pat do? Pat can delegate. Most contract duties are delegable, but delegation does not relieve the delegator (Pat) of liability. As with assignment, delegation may be prohibited by the terms of the contract or may violate the law or public policy. Delegation is also prohibited if the other party has a substantial interest in personal performance. Painting a house is not a service that requires a particular individual, and Lou would probably be unsuccessful in objecting to delegation. If Pat were an artist, under contract to paint Lou's portrait, or a lawyer, under contract to draft Lou's will and trust, the service would be "personal" and Lou could object to delegation.

EXHIBIT 9-3
Sample: Clause Prohibiting Assignment and Disclaiming Agency

ASSIGNMENT/SUBCONTRACTING
The Contractor may not assign this contract or any part thereof, or assign any of the sums to be paid hereunder, nor shall any part of the work done or material furnished under this contract be sublet without the Owner's express written consent.

The Contractor may not enter into subcontracts for any of the work contemplated under this contract unless included in the specific provisions of this contract. Any such subcontract must acknowledge the binding nature of the contract and must incorporate this contract, including any attachments. Contractor is solely responsible for the performance of any subcontractor. Contractor shall not have the authority to contract for or incur obligations on behalf of the Owner.

---

3.   Novation

Chattel
Moveable items, also called
personal property

A **novation** under which a new party takes over all of the rights and duties of the original party occurs if the original party is totally discharged from liability under the contract.

A common assignment-delegation situation arises when the original tenant under a lease wants to bring in a new tenant. The most common issue is whether the original tenant is excused by having assigned all of her rights and delegated all of her duties (a novation) or remains responsible on the lease because the sublease did not amount to a new contract. Often the lease will deal with the issue directly by limiting the right to sublease (*e.g.,* requiring landlord's approval) and stating that the original tenant is not excused. Some states have statutes to protect residential tenants in this situation.

Typical language found in a sublease form:

Under this sublease agreement, the Principal Tenant (who signed the original rental agreement) remains responsible to the Landlord for all terms and conditions of the lease. For example, if the Subtenant does not pay rent or causes damages, the Principal Tenant remains liable to the Landlord for these damages. For these reasons, many Principal Tenants require a security deposit from their Subtenant, and have the Subtenant pay the rent to them rather than to the Landlord. The Principal Tenant stands in the relationship to the subtenant as a landlord and has the right to terminate the tenancy of the subtenant with proper legal notice. Also note that this form of agreement anticipates that permission to sublet is required by the landlord or his agent and is valid only if signed by the Landlord.

A sample Assignment/Novation appears in the next chapter.

4. Joint and Several Liability and Guarantors

In the chapter concerning the statute of frauds, you learned about suretyship (Chapter 8 includes a sample of a surety contract), guarantors, and co-obligors, who become part of a contract by "guaranteeing" the performance of a primary party. In some situations the party guaranteeing performance is not liable until the primary obligor has defaulted and, in order to "collect" on the guarantee, the other party has to establish default by the primary obligor. In other situations the party guaranteeing performance is "primarily" liable on the contract along with the "main" party. If parties are both primarily liable, they may be jointly liable or do they have **"joint and several liability,"** meaning that each of them could be individually responsible for the entire obligation. A co-obligor or surety under a contract may have rights, in addition to liability under the contract, particularly the right to notice if the primary party is in default.

Joint and Several Liability Co-obligors can be sued together or any one can be liable for the entire obligation

---

Examples

The difference between primary and secondary liability is key to determining who can be sued and when they can be sued. Jenn "co-signs" on a lease so that her brother can have his own apartment. After a few months, brother stops paying rent because the landlord has not made needed repairs. Can the landlord immediately bring action against Jenn or must he first take action against brother and establish his default? May landlord sue Jenn without suing brother? The answers depend on whether the language of the contract makes Jenn only secondarily liable and, if she is primarily liable, whether she has joint and several liability.

Tim and Tom rented an apartment together. The landlord checked credit on each of them and had them sign a 1-year lease, with rent at $600 per month. Tim lost his job and moved back home to live with his parents. Tom has not been able to find another roommate and believes he should not be responsible for Tim's share of the rent because the landlord knew he was renting to two separate adults. What do you think? The clause in Exhibit 9-4 appeared in the lease.

EXHIBIT 9-4
Miscellaneous

In all references to LESSEE herein, the singular shall be deemed to include the plural and the masculine, the feminine. Where this LEASE is signed by more than one person as LESSEE, all such persons shall be jointly and severally liable for the payment of rent and any additional rent and the performance of all covenants and agreements to be kept by LESSEE hereunder.

D.   Secured Transactions Under the UCC

Inventory
Goods held for sale or lease

Instruments
Formal written documents

Securities
Evidence of investment in a common scheme

Attachment
Creation of an enforceable security interest

Perfect
To register or record an instrument so that the public is on notice of its terms

Some, but not all, states have adopted a revised version of Article 9. Depending on your state, its version of Article 9 may cover security interests in goods, **inventory** (goods held for sale or lease to customers), **instruments** (checks, notes, certificates of deposit), **securities** (investment in a common scheme, such as ownership of stock in a company), and other property (accounts and intangible property, such as patents and copyrights).

Attachment, or the creation of an enforceable security interest, occurs when the parties make a security agreement, if:

- the lender (the secured party) has given something of value, and
- the debtor has some legal rights in the property serving as collateral, and
- the debtor authenticates a document describing the collateral or the lender takes possession of the property.

The security interest automatically applies to any proceeds if the debtor sells or otherwise disposes of the collateral and can apply to property acquired after the agreement is entered. Once a security interest has attached, the lender can seize the collateral from the debtor if the debtor fails to pay as agreed. What happens if the collateral is no longer in the possession of the debtor or if the debtor attempts to use the same property as security for additional loans? To protect itself from such situations, the lender should **perfect** its security interest.

The most common way to perfect a security interest is to file a financing statement with the appropriate state agency. Perfection can also occur when the secured party takes possession of the collateral until the debt is paid. If the collateral consists of **consumer goods**, items used primarily for personal, family, or household purposes, and the loan was a **purchase money security interest** (a loan to buy the collateral items — as in the Family Home/Customer/Acme example), the security interest is automatically perfected, without any filing and without possession.

Liens against highway vehicles, all terrain vehicles and motorboats (these vehicles have certificates of title) are typically *not* UCC filings. To find liens against titled vehicles, search your state division or registry of motor vehicles.

If a security interest is perfected, it follows the collateral even if the collateral is sold or otherwise transferred, except when it is purchased by a **good-faith buyer in the course of ordinary business**. Let's assume that all of the freezers in Family Home's inventory were collateral for financing from Family's supplier. Customer buys a freezer, unaware of the security interest (therefore in good faith) and dealing with a business that routinely sells freezers (course of ordinary business). Customer takes the freezer free from the security interest.

On the other hand, if Family's competition, Adams' Appliances, knew that Family Home was in financial trouble and bought all of Family's inventory (a **bulk sale**), the freezers would continue to be collateral even after Adams' bought them. It is, therefore, essential that buyers protect themselves from buying property that might remain subject to a perfected security interest. They protect themselves by doing a UCC search, through the appropriate state agency, to identify security interests recorded against goods not in possession of a consumer.

Consumer Goods
Items used primarily for personal, family, or household purposes

Purchase Money Security Interest
Lien against property to secure a loan used to acquire that property

Good Faith Buyer in the Course of Ordinary Business
A buyer who acts honestly, gives value, and has no notice of other claims

Bulk Sale
Sale of major part of inventory, not in ordinary course of business

Assignment 9-2

As assigned by your instructor

♦ Determine whether your state has any statute that limits a landlord who wants to prohibit sublease or assignment of a residential lease.

♦ Find and report on a case from your state involving one party trying to prevent delegation by the other party.

♦ Sometimes a third party plays another role with respect to a contract: the third party induces one of the original parties to breach the contract. Find and report on a case from your state involving "interference with a contract relationship."

♦ Determine how a UCC search is done in your state and write a short report. This site may help you get started: http://www.coordinatedlegal.com/SecretaryOfState.html

♦ Report on how you would determine whether real estate in your county is subject to liens. Be specific, give addresses, etc.

♦ Report on how liens against vehicles are handled in your state. Does such a lien appear on the title document itself? What is the process for searching the title to a titled vehicle?

E. Practical and Ethical Issues

Third parties can be a concern in the lawyer-client relationship.

Example

Attorneys must be careful to not let third parties interfere with their obligations to a client. Marie, the owner of a successful restaurant, has been a client of your firm for many years. With her own personal and business matters, as well as her connections in the community, she has been a major source of business for the firm. Marie's son, Freddie, married Joan five years ago, against Marie's wishes. The two are now divorcing. They have never done well financially. Freddie works part-time at the restaurant and Joan has stayed home with their two young children. Marie has provided them with a house and cars, as well as money.

Marie has paid a $5,000 retainer to have the firm represent Freddie. Freddie initially stated that he and Joan had reached agreement that he would have custody of the children with limited visitation for Joan. Joan planned to return to her home state, about 500 miles away, and Freddie said that he would pay all of Joan's living expenses for a couple of years, "while she got on her feet." The money would, of course, come from Marie. Freddie said that the firm should work out the details about the payments, visitation, and other matters, then put the agreement in writing.

About a month later, Freddie came to the office alone, without an appointment, and in an agitated state. He stated that he could never be a good parent because of his drug addiction and that he really wants Joan to take the kids to her family and make a new start. He claimed that the original plan was his mother's idea and that she cannot be told why things have changed. Marie is adamant that the children must stay in this area and that she must have a substantial role in raising them.

Let's take it a step further. Assume that Marie finds out that Freddie is no longer seeking custody and comes into the firm, demanding an explanation. Marie also wants her $5,000 retainer back. The money was initially deposited in a clients' funds escrow account, but only $800 remains. The balance has been transferred to the firm's business account and has been spent on office expenses, such as utility bills. Marie claims that the firm was wrong to cash the check at all, much less take the money before the "work was done" according to her wishes. Freddie is claiming that Marie is not entitled to any of the money, because it constituted a gift to him.

Assignment 9-3

Identify all of the firm's ethical concerns and possible solutions, based on your state's Rules of Professional Conduct. You have dealt with some of the relevant rules in past lessons. In addition to considering those rules, find and analyze rules concerning Conflicts of Interests with Current Clients; Professional Independence; and Safekeeping of Property.

Review Questions

1. Identify the ways in which an agency relationship can be created. In what types of situations must the agency be created in writing?
2. Identify the duties of an agent to a principal and of a principal to an agent.
3. What is an agency coupled with an interest and how is it different from other agency relationships?
4. How are third-party beneficiaries categorized and which types have the right to enforce the contract?
5. Under what circumstances is assignment prohibited? When is delegation prohibited?
6. What does it mean to "perfect" a security interest?
7. Explain "durable power of attorney."
8. How are bulk sales treated differently with respect to security interests?

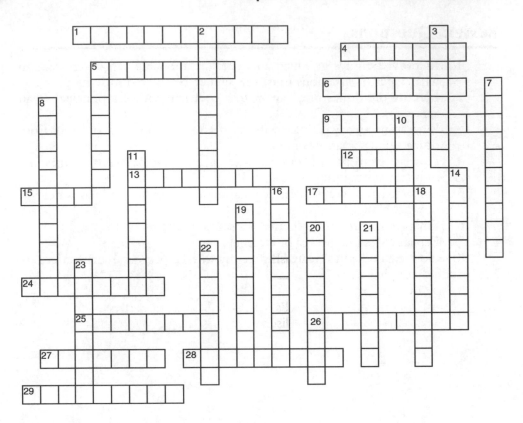

ACROSS

1. acceptance of unauthorized acts after the fact
4. equal _____ rule requires that some agency contracts be in writing
5. _____ money security interest, a loan to buy collateral items
6. third party beneficiary because of financial interest
9. type of third party beneficiary with no right to enforce
12. a security interest in property
13. a good faith purchaser in the course of _____ business is protected from liens
15. _____ sale of all inventory
17. authority reasonably necessary to accomplish express purpose
24. principal is _____ estopped from denying apparent authority
25. party who receives an assignment
26. reimburse
27. being part of contract relationship
28. good held for sale or lease
29. an agent acts on behalf of a _____

DOWN

2. to pass on contract rights
3. power of _____ creates agency
5. a lender should _____ security interest to protect against third parties
7. property subject to security interest
8. checks, notes, etc.
10. third party beneficiary as a gift
11. security interest in real property
14. agency by operation of law occurs in _____
16. creation of a security interest
18. to pass on contract duties
19. to take the collateral
20. agency is this type of relationship
21. agency coupled with an _____ may not be readiy terminated
22. authority created by principal's acts/words to third parties
23. original party to contract is discharged, new party takes duties

10

Performance:
Required or
Excused?

Having determined whether a contract formed and, if so, who has rights under that contract, the next step is to determine whether obligations under that contract are still owed or have been discharged. This chapter explores identifying breach, excuses for non-performance, and related issues.

A. **Discharge Due to Unmet Condition**
B. **Discharge by Agreement**
C. **Discharge by Operation of Law**
D. **Impossibility**
E. **Breach As Excusing Performance**
    1. **Common Law**
    2. **Perfect Tender Under the UCC**
F. **Other Performance Issues Under the UCC**
G. **Anticipating Breach**
H. **Practical and Ethical Issues**

If a contract did form, what happens when a party does not meet one or more of the obligations? A later chapter will discuss the remedies available when a party is in breach of contract. This chapter will focus on whether there was a breach.

Discharge
Release

Failure to perform obligations set forth in a contract is not a breach if performance has been **discharged**, meaning excused.

---

*Failure to perform a contract involving a governmental entity can have particularly serious consequences. A "whistleblower" may be able to obtain an award for exposing fraud or misuse of government funds, by initiating a **qui tam** lawsuit.*

Qui Tam
Lawsuit in which a whistleblower can obtain reward for exposing misconduct involving government contracts

A.   Discharge Due to Unmet Condition

Some excuses that discharge the obligation to perform have been discussed in previous chapters. For example, there may have been an unmet condition precedent. If a contract states, "I will buy your house if I can obtain a mortgage," and the buyer is unable to obtain a mortgage, the buyer is discharged. Whether a contract provision is a condition precedent or only a promise, not a basis for discharge, can be a complex issue. Suppose Rocha Painting signs a contract to paint the exterior of Joan's house, with "painting to begin on May 1," but painting has not begun as of May 2 because Rocha does not have sufficient staff. Rocha promises to send a crew no later than May 4 but Joan wants to cancel the whole agreement. The issue is whether the May 1 start date was a condition precedent so that Joan might be excused from the contract or was only one of Rocha's promises, so that Joan is bound to the contract but may be entitled to damages for the delay. When a contract does not clearly indicate whether a provision is a condition or a promise, courts employ the rules of construction described in the previous chapter. Good legal advice should help the parties clarify their intentions during negotiations and state those intentions in the contract.

EXHIBIT 10-1
Sample, Condition Precedent

MORTGAGE CONTINGENCY: This Contract is contingent upon Buyer obtaining an unconditional written mortgage commitment (except for matters of title and survey or matters totally within Buyer's control) on or before _____, 20_____ for a _____ (type) loan of $ _____ or any lesser amount as Buyer is willing to accept. The initial interest rate shall not exceed _____% per annum, amortized over not less than _____ years. Buyer shall pay any loan origination fee and/or discount points not to exceed _____% of the loan amount. Seller shall pay any loan origination fee and/or discount points not to exceed _____% of the loan amount. Fees or points to be paid by Buyer shall be applied first, with Seller to pay remaining fees or points, if any. Buyer shall pay the

---

**EXHIBIT 10-1
(continued)**

---

cost of application, usual and customary processing fees and Closing costs charged by lender. Buyer shall submit a written loan application within five business days after acceptance of this Contract. Failure to do so shall constitute default under this Contract. If Buyer, having applied as specified above, is unable to obtain a loan commitment and serves written notice to Seller within the time specified, this Contract shall be null and void and earnest money refunded to Buyer upon written direction of the Parties to Escrowee. If written notice is not served as specified, Buyer shall be deemed to have waived this contingency and this Contract shall remain in full force and effect. Any condition in the mortgage commitment requiring sale of Buyer's existing real estate shall not render the commitment conditional. If Seller at Seller's option and expense, within thirty (30) days after Buyer's notice, procures for Buyer a mortgage commitment or notifies Buyer that Seller will accept a purchase money mortgage upon the same terms, this Contract shall remain in full force and effect. In such event, Seller shall notify Buyer within five (5) business days after Buyer's notice of Seller's election to provide or obtain such financing, and Buyer shall furnish to Seller or lender all requested information and shall sign all papers necessary to obtain the mortgage commitment and to close the loan.

B. Discharge by Agreement

The parties may have discharged the contract by release or **recission** (a mutual agreement to cancel), modification of the old agreement, an accord and satisfaction, or a **novation** — a new contract, involving new parties, which cancelled the old. Remember, new contracts generally must be supported by new consideration.

Recission
A mutual agreement to cancel

Novation
New contract, involving new parties; cancels earlier contract

---

**EXHIBIT 10-2
Sample**

ASSIGNMENT AND NOVATION AGREEMENT
This "Agreement" is made on _____ by _____. ("Assignor"), having its principal place of business at _____ and _____ ("Assignee"), having its

EXHIBIT 10-2
(continued)

principal place of business at _____ and _____ ("ABC"), having its principal place of business at _____.

1. Assignor and ABC are parties to a Contract for _____, dated _____, which remains in full force and effect, the "Contract");

2. Assignor desires to transfer and assign to Assignee its rights, duties and obligations under the Contract and Assignee desires to acquire the Contract from Assignor for consideration set forth below and on terms and conditions hereinafter set forth;

3. Assignor desires to be discharged from the performance of the obligations enumerated in the Contract and ABC is willing to release Assignor from the obligations of the Contract and to consent to Assignee assuming such obligations;

4. Assignor hereby assigns, transfers, conveys and delivers to Assignee, effective as of _____, 200 _____ (the "Effective Date"), all of Assignor's right, title and interest in, to and under the Contract and Assignee hereby accepts such assignment and agrees to assume, from and after the Effective Date, all of Assignor's rights, duties and obligations in, to and under the Contract.

5. Assignee shall reimburse Assignor for and hold Assignor harmless against any obligation to perform any of the assigned duties and obligations included in the Contract.

6. Assignor, Assignee and ABC hereby agree that this Agreement shall constitute a novation of the obligations of Assignor under the Contract. Accordingly, all of the rights, duties and obligations of Assignor under the Contract are hereby extinguished. ABC recognizes Assignee as Assignor's successor in interest in and to all of Assignor's rights, duties and obligations in, to and under the Contract.

7. In consideration of this assignment, Assignee is paying to Assignor an aggregate purchase price of _____ Dollars ($) in cash, and paying to ABC a fee of _____ Dollars ($) in cash, by wire transfers to accounts specified by Assignor and ABC, simultaneous with the execution of this Agreement.

8. This Agreement shall inure to the benefit of and be binding upon the parties hereto and their successors and assigns, and matters herein with respect to the Contract shall inure to the benefit of ABC and its successors and assigns from and after the Effective Date.

IN WITNESS WHEREOF, the undersigned have executed this Agreement as of the date first written above.

C. Discharge by Operation of Law

A party may also be discharged by the death or incapacity of a party under contract to perform personal services or **insolvency** (bankruptcy). A court may find that a contract is unenforceable, for example, because it violates public policy or because performance has become illegal (*e.g.,* change in zoning makes construction of gas station illegal). Performance may also be excused if one party is preventing the other party's performance; consider whether the party has **tendered** performance — that is, been ready, willing, and able to perform.

Insolvency
Unable to pay debts

Tender Performance
Party's indication that he is ready, willing, and able to perform

D. Impossibility

A court may discharge a contract if performance becomes impossible, in an objective sense. **Objective impossibility** means the impossibility is not personal. For example, if a house is destroyed by a hurricane, a contract to paint that house cannot be performed by anyone. On the other hand, if the painter discovers that he underbid the job and would lose money by painting the house at the contract price, or if the painter over-booked and cannot meet the dates in the contract, the problem is personal or subjective.

Objective Impossibility
Impossibility in an objective sense; not personal

Courts rarely discharge a party who entered a contract that turns out to be a bad deal. If the problem arose from bad judgment, the party is almost always bound to the contract. It is possible for a court to discharge a party in cases of **commercial impracticability** if an event that was not anticipated by either party would make performance extraordinarily difficult and unfair for one party. For example, a company under contract to ship material out of New Orleans in November 2005 might have been excused under the doctrine of commercial impracticability because of hardships imposed by hurricane damage.

Commercial Impracticability
An event, not anticipated by either party, that makes performance extraordinarily difficult and unfair for one party

An event not anticipated by either party might also result in **frustration of purpose**. Frustration of purpose means that the contract has no remaining value for one party. In either case, the problem must result from an event that was truly unexpected and must go beyond financial difficulty. For example, if a school had chartered buses to take students to New Orleans for an event scheduled for November 2005 and, because of damage from Hurricane Katrina, the event was cancelled, a court might have found that frustration of purpose justified excusing the school from paying for the bus charter contracts.

Frustration of Purpose
Contact has no remaining value for party due to an unanticipated event

Because courts do not often discharge parties for impossibility and commercial impracticability, many contracts include **force majeure** provisions.

Force Majeure
Contract provision excusing performance for an event such as "act of God," fire, labor dispute, accident, or transportation difficulty

EXHIBIT 10-3
Examples: Force Majeure Clauses

Neither party shall be liable in damages or have the right to terminate this Agreement for any delay or default in performance if the delay or default is caused by conditions beyond control of that party, including, but not limited to Acts of God, Government restrictions (including, but not limited to, denial or cancellation of any export or other necessary license), war, insurrection or any other cause beyond the reasonable control of the party whose performance is affected. Neither party shall be liable for any failure or delay in performance under this Agreement (other than for delay in the payment of money due and payable hereunder) to the extent said failures or delays are the proximate result of causes beyond that party's reasonable control and occurring without its fault or negligence, including, without limitation, failure of suppliers, subcontractors, and carriers, or party to substantially meet its performance obligations under this Agreement, provided that, as a condition to the claim of nonliability, the party experiencing the difficulty shall give the other prompt written notice, with full details following the occurrence of the cause relied upon. Dates by which performance obligations are scheduled to be met will be extended for a period of time equal to the time lost due to any delay so caused.

Remember, contract law is primarily default law (it applies only if the parties have not stated their intentions to the contrary) and the parties can write the contract they want. A clause permitting cancellation or delay in the event of "act of God, fire, labor disputes, accidents or transportation difficulties" will generally be enforced unless a party is trying to use it in a way that essentially gives him the option to perform or not, depending on whether it is in his best interests.

Assignment 10-1

- ◆ Find the citations to sections in your state's version of the Uniform Commercial Code (UCC) dealing with conditions precedent (non-happening of presupposed condition) and commercial impracticability.
- ◆ **Find the appropriate sections and report what happens** when goods are destroyed after a sales contract has formed. The answer depends on whether the risk of loss has passed from the seller to the buyer. The UCC contains assumptions about risk of loss, in the absence of agreement. These assumptions depend on whether there has been a breach of contract, who has possession of the goods, and what type of

transaction is involved. For this assignment, assume that there is no agreement, that there has been no breach of contract, and that the transaction is a **sale-or-return**. A sale-or-return is similar to a **consignment** — the seller has delivered the goods to a buyer who will resell them or return them to the seller. In a sale-or-return situation, the buyer takes **title** (ownership) of the goods until selling or returning them; in a consignment, title remains with the seller.

◆ The answer may also depend on whether the goods were **identified** when the contract formed — that is, designated as the particular goods being sold. *Find the UCC provision concerning destruction of goods identified to the contract* before the risk of loss passes. Other goods are **fungible,** meaning interchangeable

Sale-or-Return
Seller delivers goods to buyer who resells or returns them to seller; buyer takes title until sale or return

Consignment Merchant
Merchant holds goods for sale, does not take title

Title
Ownership

Identified
Goods designated as the particular goods being sold

Fungible
Interchangeable

E. Breach as Excusing Performance

1. Common Law

One party's performance can be discharged by the other party's breach of the contract. For example, Norma agreed to sell Travis her house and had the paperwork and the keys ready on the agreed date, but Travis arrived without the money. Norma is obviously not obligated to give him the deed and keys.

Some contracts require **perfect performance**, with no deviations. Perfect performance is also called **strict performance**. In general, a contractual obligation to pay a specified amount of money requires strict performance. If Travis had agreed to pay $600,000 for the house and showed up with cashier's checks for $550,000 and an "IOU" for $50,000, Norma would not be obligated to deliver the deed.

With respect to other duties, however, the common law generally does not assume that perfect performance is required unless the parties have stated that it is required and the expectation is reasonable. Not every breach merits complete discharge. For example, if Norma had just completed construction of a $500,000 custom house for Travis and Travis discovered that Norma had painted several rooms the wrong colors, Travis would not be entitled to walk away from the contract.

With respect to duties requiring services, **substantial performance** is required. A party who has substantially performed is entitled to the contract price, minus the value of the defects. In the custom house example, Norma would be entitled to $500,000 minus the cost of repainting the rooms incorrectly painted.

If a contract requires substantial performance, the court will discharge the other party only if the performance was so bad as to amount to **material** or **major breach**. If the house Travis expected was to have been a two-story colonial, facing east on a corner lot, but Norma confused the plans for two jobs and build a modern ranch facing north, Travis would be entitled to discharge and, possibly, to an additional remedy (discussed in a later chapter).

Perfect Performance
No deviations from contract; see Strict Performance

Strict Performance
No deviations from contract expectations; see Perfect Performance

Substantial Performance
Only minor deviations from contact specification; acceptable in most service contracts

Major or **Material Breach**
Substantial breach of contract, usually excusing other party from further performance

What is substantial performance and to what extent is the breaching party entitled to payment for the imperfect performance? Courts generally look at the following:

- Whether the contract is divisible—for example, Pat agrees to plow Hannah Homeowner's driveway after each snowfall this season for $40 per visit. Pat visits and plows 12 times, but her truck is destroyed in an accident and she is unable to plow after the last two snowstorms of the season. The 12 visits have independent value for Hannah, even though the contract was not completed. On the other hand, a partially finished basement remodeling job may have no independent value.
- Whether the unfulfilled promise was dependent on some performance by the other party—for example, is an insurance company obligated to pay a claim if the insured party failed to pay the last premium? Is a builder required to complete remodeling if the homeowner has not acquired fixtures as promised?
- Whether the end product can be used for its intended purpose.
- The benefit received by the non-breaching party; was the breach major or minor?
- The degree of hardship to the breaching party.
- Whether money damages can be used to compensate for defects.
- Whether the party whose performance was imperfect acted in good faith. The Restatement defines good faith as remaining faithful to the "agreed common purpose and justified expectations of the other party." Good faith involves consideration of whether the breach was intentional.
- The consequences of any delay. Parties often include a provision stating that "**time is of the essence**," meaning that any delay constitutes breach. If they do not include such a provision, an injured party may be able to recover damages only if there is proof of damages attributable to the delay. Even if parties do include such a provision, some courts regard it as "boilerplate" and look at whether there has been real harm.

Time Is of the Essence
Any performance delay constitutes breach

EXHIBIT 10-4
Example: This typical time-is-of-the-essence provision also includes a "non-waiver" provision

---

Time is of the Essence. Time is of the essence with respect to all provisions of this Agreement that specify a time for performance; any delay with respect to specified times for performance shall constitute a material breach of this contract. The failure of a party to enforce this provision with respect to failure to comply with a specified time for performance shall not affect that party's right to require strict compliance with the specified times for performance at any time thereafter. Waiver of any breach or default shall not constitute a waiver of any subsequent breach or default or waiver of this provision.

Satisfaction Clauses

Some contracts require performance to the "satisfaction" of a party. Courts will determine whether to apply an objective test or subjective test based on the type of performance required. A court is likely to apply a subjective standard (was this individual actually satisfied) when performance and satisfaction are of a personal nature, for example, painting a portrait. On the other hand, performance may be something that can be judged by common standards of utility or marketability, such as painting office walls. In such cases a court is likely to apply an objective (reasonable) standard. Do you think courts also look at unjust enrichment in these situations? Note that once the office walls are painted, they remain painted whether the customer says he is satisfied or not; the customer who is not satisfied with a portrait does not get the portrait. Such factors may play a role. Some contracts call for satisfaction of an outsider, for example, construction to the satisfaction of the architect. Courts tend to uphold such clauses as written and require the outsider's statement of satisfaction.

Satisfaction Clause
Contract provision requiring performance to the satisfaction of a specified individual

---

EXHIBIT 10-5

The following language appeared in a construction clause:
"All work shall be done subject to the final approval of the Architect or Owner's authorized agent, and his decision in matters relating to artistic effect shall be final, if within the terms of the Contract Documents . . . should any dispute arise as to the quality or fitness of materials or workmanship, the decision as to acceptability shall rest strictly with the Owner, based on the requirement that all work done or materials furnished shall be first class in every respect. What is usual or customary in erecting other buildings shall in no wise enter into any consideration or decision."

After the owner rejected siding installed by a subcontractor because of its appearance, the builder removed and replaced the siding and refused to pay the subcontractor. Although the language appears to allow the owner to reject work for purely subjective reason, the appeals court upheld a jury instruction that the "general rule applying to satisfaction in the case of contracts for the construction of commercial buildings is that the satisfaction clause must be determined by objective criteria. Under this standard, the question is not whether the owner was satisfied in fact, but whether the owner, as a reasonable person, should have been satisfied with the materials and workmanship." The court indicated that it would be possible to contract for subjective approval, but that the language in the contract did not achieve that result.[1]

---

[1] *Morin Building Products Company, Inc. v. Baystone Construction Inc.,* 717 F.2d 413 (7th Cir. 1983).

Assignment 10-2

As directed by your instructor, find and summarize for class discussion a case from your state involving:

◆ the meaning of "good faith" in an insurance contract;
◆ substantial performance of a contract to construct a building;
◆ a "time-is-of-the-essence" clause (discussed below); or
◆ a "satisfaction clause."

---

2. Perfect Tender Under the UCC

Perfect Tender Rule
Buyer has reasonable time to reject goods that fail, in any respect, to conform to the contract

The UCC differs from the common law in that, under the **perfect tender rule**, a buyer has a reasonable time to reject goods that fail, in any respect, to conform to the contract. The rule seems harsh when compared to the common law doctrine of substantial performance, but the Code does include provisions to lessen the impact.

Trade Usage
Industry standards for permissible deviations from specifications

Course of Dealing
What has been done by the parties in the past

Cure
Seller delivers conforming goods before contract deadline, after buyer rejects non-conforming goods

- The parties may draft a contract that permits some degree of deviation from the specifications for the goods; this is common in some industries.
- Courts must consider **trade usage**; some industries have standards for the level of permissible "flaws" in products.
- Courts also consider **course of dealing**, what has been acceptable to the buyer in the past.
- If a buyer does reject nonconforming goods, the seller may have the opportunity to **cure** by delivering conforming goods before the contract deadline. The Code even extends the time for cure to a "further reasonable time," in some circumstances.

Example

These rules are part of how the UCC accommodates the "real world" of modern business. Acme Uniforms contracted to provide City Hospital with 1,000 sets of green "scrubs" for personnel, to be delivered on May 1. On April 20, Acme realizes that its inventory is insufficient because of roof damage at a warehouse. Not wanting to leave a big customer empty-handed, Acme ships 500 sets of green scrubs and 500 sets of blue scrubs. On April 25 City Hospital notifies Acme that it does not want the blue scrubs. City Hospital can accept some of the goods and reject others. If Acme can get green scrubs to the hospital by May 1, there is no breach. If Acme had a reasonable belief that City would accept blue scrubs, the time may even be extended beyond May 1. In addition, if City Hospital has accepted mixed colors several times in the past, there may be no breach.

Once the buyer accepts the goods, the perfect tender rule does not apply. The buyer generally has the right to inspect the goods before paying or accepting. Once the buyer has accepted the goods, the buyer may revoke that acceptance if there was a legitimate reason for accepting them in the first place (*e.g.*, the seller had promised to cure or the defects were not visible) and there is a nonconformity that substantially impairs the value of the goods. Acceptance may not be revoked because of minor deviations from conformity.

In some situations the Code implies acceptance. The buyer is viewed as having accepted the goods if, after having a reasonable opportunity to inspect, the buyer indicates that the goods conform to the contract or that the goods are accepted in spite of nonconformity, fails to reject them, or does some act that indicates ownership (*e.g.*, reselling the goods).

The perfect tender rule applies to timing as well as conformity of goods. Under the UCC, time is of the essence except in installment contracts. So, delivery of goods on May 2 would be a total breach if delivery had been promised for May 1.

F. Other Performance Issues Under the UCC

For contracts concerning the sale of goods, the UCC describes performance expectations when the parties have not done so in the contract. For example, the Code contains provisions dealing with the time, place, and manner of **tender** (making goods available to the buyer); definitions of shipping terms; assumptions about warranties (mentioned in previous chapters); and other matters.

Tender
To make available

Assignment 10-3

Use your state's version of the UCC to list the following, as assigned by your instructor, giving cites to sections:

◆ the section number of the perfect tender rule;
◆ the section number of the provision allowing a party to demand assurances (described below)
◆ the place of delivery, when none is specified;
◆ the difference between a CIF contract and a C & F contract;
◆ what is meant by ex-ship;
◆ the seller's obligation if the goods are in the possession of a **bailee**;

A **bailee** is a person, other than the owner, who is in possession of goods under an arrangement called a bailment.

Bailee
Person, other than owner, who is in possession of goods under an arrangement called a bailment

---

G. Anticipating Breach

If one party (A) believes that the other party (B) is going to breach the contract, is A excused from performing A's obligations? A may believe that it would be better to "cut her losses."

Repudiation can occur by a statement that a party cannot or will not perform or by a party's voluntary act that makes substantial performance impossible or apparently impossible. For example, Association has a contract to hold a conference at Swank Hotel next month and learns that Swank has just begun a major remodeling project. Guest rooms, conference rooms, and the banquet facility are not expected to be ready for occupancy before the conference dates. A common example of a condition that may make performance appear to be impossible is insolvency. The UCC has specific rules dealing with insolvent buyers and sellers.

Repudiation occurs before the other party has performed, otherwise, it is simply breach. For example, if buyer has fully paid for delivery of a product and seller indicates that delivery is impossible, it is simply breach of contract. On the other hand, if buyer is to pay after delivery and seller states that delivery is impossible, it is repudiation. The situation is also called **anticipatory breach**. The rights of the other party depend on the circumstances.

Anticipatory breach must be clear-cut; it cannot be based on assumption or inference. Under the UCC, if a party has reasonable grounds to believe that the other will not perform, that party may demand **assurances**; failure to give adequate assurances within a reasonable time operates as a repudiation so that the "**insecure party**" may suspend his own performance.

If the contract is not covered by the UCC, the insecure party may have a variety of options, including continuing under the contract, demanding assurances, suspending performance, or canceling the contract. The insecure party's rights depend on state law.

When repudiation occurs, the other party generally has a duty to make reasonable attempts to **mitigate** — limit the damages. For example, Banquet Hall has the Smith-Jones wedding scheduled for next Saturday. Supply House calls on Monday and tells the manager that, because of a fire, it will be unable to provide chicken breasts for the reception. Can Banquet Hall just ignore the situation, hope for the best, and, after the Smith-Jones disaster, sue Supply House? Probably not — Banquet must attempt to mitigate by getting the chicken breasts from another source. To mitigate, the buyer may **cover**, by obtaining substitute goods if reasonably available. Damages are still available and will be discussed in a later chapter.

Repudiation
A party's words or actions indicating intention not to perform the contract

Anticipatory Breach
Belief that other party will not perform

Assurance
A pledge or guarantee that gives confidence or security

Insecure Party
Party has good-faith belief that performance by other party is unlikely

Mitigate
Limit or reduce damages

Cover
Buyer obtains substitute goods

Example

Mitigation language found in a contract to hold a conference at a hotel:

"If the hotel is able to sell any of the guest rooms canceled, that portion of the damages will be refunded based upon the number of guest rooms resold."

H. Practical and Ethical Issues

When a contract is breached, the non-breaching party often suffers financial harm and may feel "wronged" in a way that goes beyond financial compensation. This is particularly true when the breach is intentional. Imagine that your wedding reception was to take place at Bella Banquets, four weeks from next Saturday. The invitations have been sent, you expect 180 guests. Last night Bella, experienced a fire. The damage could be repaired in time for your reception, but only at an expense far greater than the profit expected. In addition, Bella has, for a long time, planned a major renovation. This seems like a good time to do it. Bella notifies you that it will not be hosting your reception. You will not be able to find an equivalent location in the next four weeks and will have to notify all of your guests. While you will be entitled to financial compensation, you will probably not be satisfied by an award of money.

Nonetheless, the law regards breach of contract as a business matter. Sometimes clients decide to breach a contract simply because it makes financial sense to do so. Can a lawyer ethically advise a client to breach a contract? Can a lawyer assist a client in an intentional breach of contract? Read the ethical opinion at the end of the chapter for guidance.

Review Questions

1. Identify the ways in which performance can be excused by agreement.
2. Identify the ways in which performance can be excused by operation of law.
3. How does the UCC perfect tender rule differ from common law?
4. Which UCC provisions lessen the impact of the perfect tender rule?
5. Under what circumstances is acceptance of goods implied under the UCC?
6. What options does a contract party have if that party believes that the other party will breach the contract?
7. Under what circumstances would it be unethical for an attorney to assist a client in breaching a contract?

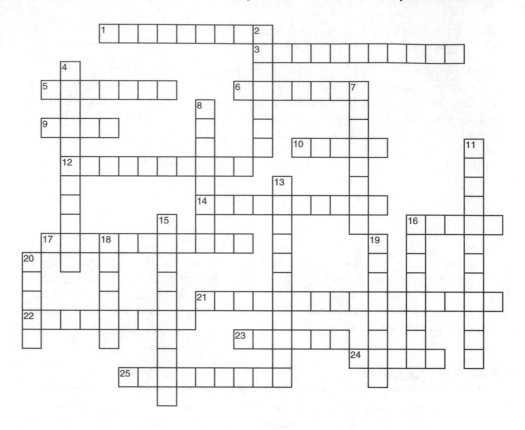

ACROSS

1. released from contract obligations
3. _____ performance; acceptable in most contracts for services
5. courts will look at course of _____ in applying perfect tender rule
6. UCC requires _____ tender in sale of goods
9. seller delivers nonconforming goods, which are rejected, then delivers conforming goods by required date
10. usage of _____ is considered in applying perfect tender rule
12. if goods have been _____ to the contract and are destroyed before delivery, contract may be discharged
14. party may demand _____ in anticipatory breach situation
16. _____ majeure provision — excuses performance for acts of God, etc.
17. like a sale or return
21. commercial _____; unanticipated event makes performance unreasonably difficult for one party
22. impossibility is judged by _____ standard
23. in possession of goods, not owner
24. to obtain substitute goods
25. an agreement to cancel contract

DOWN

2. time is of the _____, clause requiring strict performance of deadlines
4. an indication that the party does not intend to fulfill the contract
7. a party who is ready, willing, and able to perform has _____ performance
8. _____ damages, limit losses
11. _____ breach; belief that other party will not perform
13. _____ of purpose, unanticipated event leaves party no purpose for contract
15. like bankruptcy
16. goods that are interchangeable
18. _____ performance = perfect
19. new contract, new parties, canceling old contract
20. material breach = _____ breach

CASE FOR ANALYSIS

ILLINOIS STATE BAR ASSOCIATION
ISBA Advisory Opinion on Professional Conduct

ISBA Advisory Opinions on Professional Conduct are prepared as an educational service to members of the ISBA. While the Opinions express the ISBA interpretation of the Illinois Rules of Professional Conduct and other relevant materials in response to a specific hypothesized fact situation, they do not have the weight of law and should not be relied upon as a substitute for individual legal advice.

THIS OPINION WAS <u>AFFIRMED</u> BY THE BOARD OF GOVERNORS JANUARY 1991. PLEASE SEE THE 1990 ILLINOIS RULES OF PROFESSIONAL CONDUCT, RULE 1.2.

Opinion Number 728 March 1981 Topic: Assisting a client in a breach of contract.

Digest: It is proper for an attorney to advise a client on the consequences of a breach of contract and to prepare documents that accomplish such a breach after the client has made an informed decision to breach, provided the attorney is not a party to a plan or scheme to enter into a contract with the intent to breach the same as to a material condition.

Ref: Illinois Code of Professional Responsibility Rule 7-101 and Rule 7-102

FACTS

A client borrows money on residential real estate and gives an institutional lender a mortgage and note. A condition of the mortgage is that the property not be sold, assigned or otherwise transferred. The remedy of the mortgagee in the event of a violation of that provision would be to declare the entire debt due and payable. Subsequently, the client entered into a contract of sale to a third party which provided that the parties would not give a copy of the contract of sale to the institutional mortgagee. This contract of sale was drawn by the attorney for the client. In a prior conversation, attorney advised his clients to circumvent the due on sale clause. The client's attorney had subsequently stated that he will continue to advise clients to enter into similar real estate contracts in order to avoid due on sale covenants and he maintains this practice is professionally ethical as long as he gives informed advice to his client of the purpose and existence of the due on sale clause.

QUESTION

Is it professionally proper for an attorney to advise his client of the consequences of breaching a contract and to assist the client if the client elects to commit a breach of the contract based upon full knowledge of the consequences of such a breach?

OPINION

It is the opinion of the Committee that it is proper for an attorney to advise a client of the consequences of breaching a contract where full disclosure is made to the client of the legal ramifications and consequences. If the client makes an election that he can not or will not comply with the terms of his contract after competent legal advice of the consequences of a breach of contract, the attorney may assist the client in preparing documents to implement the client's election. Our answer is expressly predicated upon an assumption that the breach of the contract of sale in contravention of the due on sale clause is not a crime. Obviously, our answer would be different if it were. It is also assumed that full disclosure and competent professional advice was given to the client.

Rule 7-101 of the Code of Professional Responsibility effective July 1, 1980, states:

"(a) A lawyer shall not intentionally (1) fail to seek the lawful objectives of his client through reasonably available means permitted by law . . ."

and further: "(b) In his representation of a client, a lawyer may refuse to aid or participate in conduct that he believes to be unlawful, even though there is some support for an argument that the conduct is legal."

furthermore under Rule 7-102 it is stated:

"(a) In his representation of a client, a lawyer shall not (7) counsel or assist his client in conduct that the lawyer knows to be illegal or fraudulent . . ." and further under that rule:

"(b) A lawyer who receives information clearly establishing that (1) his client has . . . perpetrated a fraud upon a person . . . shall promptly call upon his client to rectify the same . . ."

It is the opinion of the committee that the terms "reasonably available means permitted by law," "legal," "unlawful," "fraudulent," "fraud" or "illegal" generally relate to actions which are criminal in nature and for which the law provides sanctions. A breach of contract which is not a crime does not rise to this prohibition.

All clients have the right to legal counsel and the right to advice on the consequences of a breach of contract. A client is entitled to informed advice as to the potential consequences of a breach of contract as opposed to the consequences of compliance with the contract terms.

The economic survival of a client may well depend upon failing to fulfill a contract. The relative consequences of breach or compliance are to be weighed by the client after informed advice. If the client elects to breach a contract after being fully informed, it is not unethical for his attorney to prepare documents to implement the client's decision.

On the other hand, it is the opinion of the Committee that it would be professionally improper for an attorney to knowingly aid a client to enter into a contract where the attorney is aware of the client's plan to breach a material provision of the contract at the time the contract is executed and to thereafter assist and counsel the client in carrying out such a scheme. Such conduct would amount to a fraud at the inception and it would be unethical for an attorney to participate in such a plan.

11

Remedies

Assuming that performance has not been excused, but that performance is not forthcoming, what are the consequences? This chapter explores alternatives to litigation, handling litigation, and the possible outcomes of litigation.

    A. Alternative Dispute Resolution
    B. Litigation
    C. Remedies: Theory
        1. Damages
        2. Equitable Remedies
    D. Tort Law vs. Contract Law
    E. Practical and Ethical Issues

Most parties enter into a contract with good intentions, seeing the agreement as mutually beneficial and intending to perform as expected. Occasionally something goes wrong; it might be beyond the control of the parties, the result of carelessness, or a decision based on the least damaging of several options. Sometimes the failure to meet expectations or the subsequent breakdown in the relationship is the result of lack of information about options and consequences. The Uniform Commercial Code (UCC) can be a resource to the parties and help them salvage the situation or avoid litigation by providing a number of self-help remedies. The parties to a sales contract can know what is available to them and expected of them, just by looking at the Code. As discussed in the chapter on Performance, some examples of what the UCC has to offer are as follows:

- The Code specifies the measure of damages when a buyer repudiates the contract or does not accept goods and for when the seller repudiates or fails to deliver. The general theory of damages is discussed below; the Code provides methods of calculation.
- The Code sets forth the buyer's duties with respect to rejected goods and the buyer's right to "**cover**" by obtaining other goods (also discussed in a previous chapter).
- A buyer may accept nonconforming goods; the Code sets forth the measure of damages.
- The Code calls for "**substituted performance**" when agreed-upon facilities have become unavailable.
- A seller who discovers that buyer is insolvent has specified rights to reclaim goods, stop delivery, salvage, or resell the goods.

Cover
Good faith, reasonable effort to obtain goods from another source

Substituted Performance
§2-614, use of commercially reasonable substitute facility

Sometimes the parties are not able to resolve the matter by reference to the UCC. Sometimes the Code does not apply and negotiations fail. In such cases, the parties may have to resort to more formal means of resolving their dispute.

A.   Alternative Dispute Resolution

A recent trend is to participate in **Alternative dispute resolution** (**ADR**). There are many types of ADR; mediation and arbitration are commonly used in contract law disputes. In **mediation**, a third party (the **neutral**) helps the parties understand each other's positions and may suggest solutions, but any agreement ultimately comes from the parties. In **arbitration**, the neutral hears both sides and then imposes a decision.

Alternative Dispute Resolution
To settle a dispute other than by litigation, including arbitration and mediation; called ADR

Mediation
Neutral helps parties understand each others' positions and may suggest solutions, but agreement ultimately comes from the parties

Neutral
A third party in ADR, mediator or arbitrator

Arbitration
A neutral hears both positions and imposes a decision

Court-annexed ADR
Use of the court system's own mediators or arbitrators before going to trial

Many courts now require **court-annexed** ADR—going through the court system's own mediators or arbitrators before going to trial before a judge. In contract law, however, it is quite common for the parties to include an ADR requirement in the contract, regardless of whether the court system would require it.

ADR can have many advantages: it generally results in resolution much faster than going to court, is often far less expensive than trial, and keeps the conflict out of court and can salvage the relationship between the parties. Also, the neutral can be an expert in a field that might be a complete mystery to an average judge (*e.g.*, having a structural engineer as an arbitrator in a construction contract dispute). If the parties have a long-term or valuable relationship, such as a landlord and tenant in a 25-year commercial lease, these are extremely important considerations.

ADR can also have disadvantages. In recent years, there have been many cases arguing that ADR requirements that deprive consumers of their "day in court" are unconscionable. A legal professional drafting, reviewing, or negotiating a contract for a client should carefully consider the following:

- Where will ADR take place and is that location inconvenient to the client?
- What is the timeline for ADR and is a period of discovery (evidence gathering) allowed?
- How is the neutral to be chosen and paid; is the neutral truly neutral?

- Under what rules will the hearing be conducted and do those rules obligate the parties to cooperate in discovery before the hearing?
- Are both parties equally bound to engage in ADR; is a specific type of notice required to trigger the ADR obligation?
- Does the clause attempt to make the result **binding (binding arbitration)** or do the parties retain the right to go to court to challenge the result?
- If a particular neutral is named—particularly if that neutral is a governmental agency—what is the backlog and how long would the parties have to wait for a hearing?

Binding Arbitration
Parties give up the right to challenge arbitration result in court

You should be aware of the Federal Arbitration Act (see www.law.cornell.edu/ uscode/uscode09/usc_sup_01_9_10_1.html), and state arbitration laws. See www. mac.doc.gov/nafta/usarb.htm for a summary of the federal law and list of state laws.

B. Litigation

If the parties do have the right to go to court, it is common for the contract to include a statement about where the matter will be litigated **(jurisdiction)** and which state's law will apply **(choice of law)**. Often one party will try to gain the upper hand by requiring litigation in a state convenient to that party or by requiring application of law more familiar or advantageous to that party, despite the fact that, without such a provision, the matter would be litigated in another place under other law. Constitutional and public policy considerations may prohibit application of a choice of law provision that would cause application of the law of a jurisdiction with no relationship to the parties or the transaction.

Jurisdiction
Area within which judicial authority may be exercised

Choice of Law
Contract language that defines which state's law will apply in case of litigation

Some disputes result in **parallel litigation**, or cases that proceed in more than one state or in both state and federal courts. Such cases require the paralegal to be extremely well organized; law firms engaged in parallel litigation generally use case-management software.

Parallel Litigation
Single dispute results in cases in more than one state or in both state and federal courts

It is also common for a contract to include a **notice of claims provision**, requiring that a party give the other party written notice within a specified time before filing suit. Such a requirement has the effect of shortening the **limitations period** for bringing suit (also called statute of limitations). The impact of a notice requirement is magnified if the particular type of contract is governed by a shorter limitations period in the relevant state. Medical service contracts and construction contracts, for example, may have shorter limitations periods than other contracts. At the very least, the parties should understand the requirements of the notice of claims provision.

Notice of Claims Provision
Contract language requiring one party to give the other party written notice a specified time before filing suit

In drafting pleadings for contract law litigation, you must keep in mind the elements and defenses of contract law learned in this course. You must also understand the court rules for your jurisdiction. Those rules are also important in assisting with **discovery** (pre-trial investigation of facts by questioning, inspection, etc.) in contract litigation. **Electronic discovery (e-discovery)**, involving recovery of e-mail, drafts of documents, internal memos, and more, from computers,

Discovery
Pre-trial investigation of facts by questioning, inspection, etc.

E-Discovery
Electronic recovery of e-mail, and documents from computers, servers, and hand-held PDAs

servers, and even hand-held personal digital assistants (PDAs) has changed the nature of the paralegal's role from clerical to technical.

To see how the federal court rules of procedure deal with some contract litigation issues, visit http://www.law.cornell.edu/rules/frcp/index.html and look at Pleadings, Rule 9 — Pleading Special Matters. For more specific information about filings cases in federal courts, visit http://www.uscourts.gov/rules/distr-localrules.html and find the local rules for federal courts in your area.

You have studied contract law for several weeks and, by now, realize that it is complicated. Despite the complexity of the law, juries consisting of people with no legal training are often the decision-makers with respect to the factual issues in contract cases. How do juries know enough about the framework of the law to make those decisions? They are given jury instructions. Paralegals are frequently asked to locate appropriate jury instructions for submission to the judge. A sample of a jury instruction involving the affirmative defense of duress, studied in a previous chapter appears in Exhibit 11-1.

EXHIBIT 11-1
With permission, from www.state.ak.us/courts/insciv/24.08D.doc

---

24.08D AFFIRMATIVE DEFENSE — DURESS

The defendant [plaintiff] claims that the agreement upon which the plaintiff [defendant] relies is void because the defendant [plaintiff] was under duress at the time [his] [her] [its] promise was made.

The defendant [plaintiff] made [his] [her] [its] promise under duress if you decide that the following things have been proved by clear and convincing evidence:

(1) the defendant [plaintiff] involuntarily accepted the plaintiff's [defendant's] terms because the defendant [plaintiff] believed [he] [she] [it] had no reasonable alternative but to accept those terms;

(2) the defendant [plaintiff] had no other reasonable alternative; and

(3) the defendant [plaintiff] had no other reasonable alternative because of coercive words or conduct by the plaintiff [defendant] that was criminal, tortious or morally wrong.

A fact is proved by clear and convincing evidence if the evidence induces belief in your minds that the fact is highly probable. It is not necessary that the fact be certainly true or true beyond a reasonable doubt or conclusively true. However, it is not enough to show that the fact is more likely true than not true.

If you decide that each of these things has been proved by clear and convincing evidence, then the agreement between plaintiff and defendant is void and you must return a verdict for defendant [plaintiff].

Otherwise, the agreement is not void and you must decide some additional things that I will explain to you.

Use Note

The burden is on the party seeking to void the contract to prove these elements by clear and convincing evidence. Helstrom v. North Slope Borough, 797 P.2d 1192, 1197 (Alaska 1990). But cf. Witt v. Watkins, 579 P.2d 1065, 1070 n.16 (Alaska 1978) (Lighter burden may apply where employee executed personal injury release with employer.)

If the allegation is that the plaintiff's conduct was criminal or tortious, consideration should be given to instructing the jury on the elements of the claimed crime or tort.

Comment

In Helstrom v. North Slope Borough, 797 P.2d 1192, 1197 (Alaska 1990), the Alaska Supreme Court identified three elements that must be satisfied before a contract can be voided for duress:

(1) one party involuntarily accepted the terms of another;
(2) circumstances permitted no other alternative; and
(3) such circumstances were the result of coercive acts of the other party.
(Case discussion omitted)

Not all states have jury instructions online. For more information about jury instructions in general and some links to state jury instructions, visit http://www.llrx.com/columns/reference19.htm.

Your state may have some jury instructions online even if no links are provided on the Law Library Resource Exchange site. For further information, search the website for your state court system or the highest court in your state system or the website for your state bar association.

Assignment 11-1

As assigned by your instructor:

◆ Find the website for your local state trial court. Does the court have an arbitration or mediation program? If so, get the details: Is it mandatory? What types of cases are covered? Who are the neutrals? What does it cost?
◆ Find jury instructions, in use in your state, dealing with affirmative defenses to breach of contract.
◆ Contact the clerk of your local court and find out how you can obtain a sample of a complaint and/or answer filed in a breach of contract case. If possible, obtain the sample and share it with your classmates.
◆ Using your online state statutes or computer-assisted legal research (CALR), determine the limitations period (statute of limitations) setting the time limit for bringing a case alleging breach of contract.

You may find different periods applicable to oral contracts and written contracts. If you have trouble finding the site, visit http://www.law. cornell.edu/topics/state_statutes.html#1commercial.

◆ Find the statute of limitations for cases involving contracts for sales of goods, under your state's enactment of the UCC.

◆ Research case management software and write a report on the functions available.

◆ Find your state code of civil procedure in the online statutes, then examine your local court rules (probably on the website for your local state trial court or the clerk of that court). Are there any particular rules for filing contract cases? For example:

　◆ Is the plaintiff required to attach a copy of any written contract to the complaint?

　◆ If the plaintiff is asking for payment, is it necessary to allege that payment has been demanded and denied?

　◆ Are there any special requirements for pleading a condition precedent?

　◆ Does a complaint have to state specifically that the parties did have capacity?

　◆ Are there any particular requirements for pleading fraud or mistake?

Legal Remedy
Award of money; also called Damages

C. Remedies: Theory

Damages
Award of money; also called Legal Remedy

Case at Law
A case requesting damages (money)

Equitable Remedy
Award that is non-monetary and involves court orders; see Case in Equity and Chancery Case

Case in Equity
Courts can issue orders based on fairness; see Equitable Remedy

Chancery
A chancery court can order acts performed

Election of Remedies
Injured party's choice between remedies available for a single actionable occurrence

In awarding a remedy in a case based on breach of contract, the court can look at three concerns: the parties' expectations, what the parties did in reliance on the contract, and what should be restored to the parties. Two of the concerns focus on past conduct and one concerns itself with a theoretical future: what would have happened if the contract had not been breached. With these concerns in mind, a court can fashion a legal remedy or an equitable remedy that is reasonable.

A **legal remedy** is an award of money, also called **damages**; a case requesting damages is called a **case at law**. An **equitable remedy** is non-monetary; it involves court orders. Equitable remedies are decided by a judge, not by a jury. A case involving equitable remedies is sometimes called a **case in equity** or a **chancery** case. Courts award equitable remedies only under limited circumstances, when a legal remedy would not be adequate. Awards of damages fit into several categories, described below.

A sample case at the end of this chapter includes a discussion of the evolution from separate courts for law and equity to a combined system. Historically, the injured party had to choose among available remedies. In the sample case the injured party had transferred title to his home in exchange for a promise of lifelong care. The other party breached that promise. Under the old view, the injured party would have had to choose between seeking a court order returning title to his home or an award of money damages. The more modern view allows non-breaching parties to seek remedies in both categories, unless the remedies are inconsistent or would be unjust. The UCC specifically rejects **election of remedies** in cases involving breach of a sales contract.

1. Damages

Compensatory damages are intended to put the non-breaching party in the position she would have been in if the contract had been fully performed. Because this is a forward-looking theory, compensatory damages are sometimes called **expectation damages**. Sometimes it is not a difficult calculation. For example, if Banquet Hall ordered 200 stuffed frozen chicken breasts for an awards dinner at $3.00 apiece, learned on the day before the dinner that Supply House would be unable to deliver, and was able to cover by purchasing 200 breasts from another source at $3.50 apiece, direct compensatory damages would be $100. It's rarely that simple, however.

Example

Banquet Hall may have had **incidental damages**. For example, Banquet Hall had to have an employee come in on her day off to make calls, find another supplier, and place an order. The $50 cost is not directly related to the contract, but it may be part of the award. The court will also look at **costs avoided** because of the breach. For example, assume that Supply House had a $50 delivery charge, in addition to its $600 charge for the goods. If the new source does not charge for delivery, Banquet Hall has avoided that cost. The UCC identifies incidental damages in breach of sales contracts involving goods.

Incidental and consequential damages do not flow directly from the contract. When Supply House entered the contract to provide chicken breasts, the contract clearly contemplated the cost of supplying chicken breasts; the contract probably made no mention of the cost of having an employee work to find an alternate source. These types of damages are, therefore, limited to what the breaching party could have reasonably foreseen. The party claiming indirect damages must be able to prove the amount with reasonable certainty; courts will not award damages that are too speculative or unforeseeable.

Consequential damages may include injuries to other property or people that were **foreseeable** at the time of the contract. For example, Pat buys a new washing machine, has it installed, and throws a load of laundry in before leaving for work. The machine had a defect; there was a breach of the contract warranty. Unfortunately, the defect was in the part that told the machine when to stop filling. Pat comes home several hours later and finds extensive water damage. The UCC specifies that consequential damages include injuries to property proximately resulting from breach of warranty.

Consequential damages (sometimes called **special damages**) can also be lost profits. For example, Pat ordered 200 holiday-theme sweaters for his boutique at a cost of $20 per sweater. He planned to sell the sweaters at $40 per sweater. The supplier failed to deliver. Is Pat entitled to the $4,000 profit he anticipated? That depends on the likelihood that he would have made the profit. Courts award only damages that can be proven with reasonable certainty. How long has Pat been in business? What is his history of holiday sales? The certainty of lost profits is a particular problem in cases involving new businesses; some states have statutes or

Compensatory Damages
Damages intended to put non-breaching parties in the position they would have occupied if the contract had been fully performed

Expectation Damages
Damages intended to put non-breaching parties in the position they would have occupied if the contract had been fully performed; see Compensatory Damages

Incidental Damages
Losses reasonably associated with or related to actual damages; indirect damages

Costs Avoided
Expenses non-breaching party will not incur

Consequential Damages
Losses that do not flow directly and immediately from an injurious act

Foreseeable
That which a reasonable person would anticipate

Special Damages
Losses that do not flow directly and immediately from an injurious act, but are indirect; see Consequential Damages

common law doctrines dealing with the issue. As you might imagine, parties often desire to limit liability for consequential damages.

Example

The American Institute of Architects has drafted the following language under which both the contractor and the owner waive claims against each other for consequential damages:

On the part of the owner, a waiver of damages in respect of "rental expenses, for losses of use, income, profit, financing, business and reputation and for loss of management or employee productivity or of the services of such persons" and on the part of the contractor, a waiver of damages in respect of "principal office expenses including the compensation of personnel stationed there, for losses of financing, business and reputation, and for loss of profit except anticipated profit arising directly from the work."

Reliance Damages
Damages awarded for losses incurred by plaintiff in reliance on the contract; puts party in position that would have been occupied if the contract had not been made

If it appears that Pat's anticipated profit was speculative, the court may award **reliance damages** to put him in the position he would have been if the contract had not been made. Perhaps Pat should be awarded the $500 he spent on advertising to sell the sweaters. Reliance damages are usually the only damages awarded in promissory estoppel cases, discussed in an earlier chapter.

Present Worth Doctrine
The value, in "today's money" of payments to be made in the future

Also keep in mind that, under the **present worth doctrine** (also called **present value doctrine**), payments required to be made in the future must be reduced to their present worth. For example: employee has a three-year contract and is to be paid $70,000 in the first year, $75,000 in the second year, and $80,000 in the third year. During the first year of employment, employer fires employee in breach of the contract. Employee has already been paid $50,000. Employee cannot recover the full $175,000 of salary unpaid under the contract right now; a court must reduce the amount to its present value. Money has time value. If the employer must pay the full sum now, he will lose the interest or investment income he might have otherwise earned with the money before paying it as salary to employee.

Example

Because of the uncertainty surrounding calculations of damages, parties frequently limit damages in their contracts. Have you ever taken film to be developed? Think about the print on the envelope in which you deposit the film. That is your contract. What are you entitled to if the developer loses or destroys your film? In all likelihood you are agreeing that your damages will consist of replacement rolls of film. Imagine the possibilities: What if the pictures were the only existing pictures of a historic event? The UCC specifically allows parties to limit remedies, unless the limitation would be unconscionable.

Liquidated Damages
Damages agreed to in advance of breach, in the contract itself

Liquidated damages are damages agreed to, in advance of breach, in the contract itself. For example, Owner has agreed to move out of his current home on May 15 and, in the contract with the builder of his new house, inserts a clause that the house must be ready for occupancy by May 15, with a provision that damages for delay will be $200 per day. Of course, both parties have to agree and, in some cases it is to their advantage to agree. It avoids the difficulty of determining actual damages. Courts will enforce liquidated damages clauses that are reasonable and that do not appear to be an attempt to "punish" the breaching party. Sophisticated parties now commonly include incentives, such as "$400,000 if ready for occupancy by May 15; $390,000 if ready by June 1." The UCC specifies that a "reasonable" provision for liquidated damages is enforceable.

Example

Liquidated damages clause in a contract for dormitory housing.

If, after taking occupancy of a room, the student cancels this housing contract as described in Paragraph 12 above, the student shall pay liquidated damages in the amount of $10.00 (Ten Dollars) per day for the remainder or unexpired portion of the term of the academic agreement, not to exceed $500.00 (Five Hundred Dollars).

Punitive damages (also discussed in a previous chapter) are not generally available for breach of contract. It does not matter that the breach was intentional. If, however, the breach of contract involved wrongful conduct that would be independently actionable under tort law, punitive damages may be available. Examples include fraud (intentional false statements), duress, or breach of fiduciary duty. The purpose of punitive damages is to punish and deter wrongful behavior that went beyond breach of contract, rather than to compensate the injured party. So, in cases involving wrongful behavior, a court may award punitive damages even though the injured party has been fully compensated for any loss.

A non-breaching party is entitled to **nominal damages** even if no financial loss resulted from the breach or if the loss cannot be proven with reasonable certainty. Cases seeking only nominal damages are rare because of the cost of going to court. Parties with the resources to do so sometimes bring a suit to establish their positions for future contract relationships. More commonly, however, nominal damages are awarded to a party who sought compensatory damages because the court decides that the party either suffered no real loss or was unable to prove his loss.

A party might also want to recover **costs** and **attorney's fees** in the event of litigation. Costs include filing fees, fees for service of process, and similar charges incurred in going to court. For some types of contract litigation (*e.g.,* consumer fraud cases) a statute may provide for payment of "prevailing party's" fees and costs by the other party. In other cases the contract itself may call for payment of successful party's fees and costs. Absent such a clause or statute, the parties must pay their own attorneys' fees, regardless of whether they win or lose. Some courts allocate costs among the parties, even without a contract provision. An award of attorney's fees is sometimes called **fee recovery** or **fee reversal**.

Nominal Damages
Minimal amount of damages awarded, even if no financial loss resulted from the breach or if the loss cannot be proven with reasonable certainty

Costs
Examples include filing fees, fees for service of process and similar charges incurred in litigation

Attorney's Fees
Payment, to attorney, for services

Fee Recovery or **Fee Reversal**
An award of attorney's fees

Example

Attorney's fees and costs provision.

In the event of litigation relating to the subject matter of this Agreement, the non-prevailing party shall reimburse the prevailing party for all reasonable attorney fees, costs, and expenses of litigation resulting from such litigation.

Finally, in calculating damages, a court will also consider whether the injured party could have reasonably avoided any of the loss. The UCC specifically addresses **mitigation of damages**. As you may imagine, the parties may not agree on whether mitigation was reasonably possible. One of the sample cases at the end of the chapter demonstrates how mitigation offsets damages.

Mitigation of Damages
An attempt to reduce the harm

2.   Equitable Remedies

Courts have discretion with respect to equitable remedies and will not enter orders mandating specified actions if an award of damages would adequately compensate the injured party. Courts also avoid equitable remedies if parties outside the contract would have to be involved (*e.g.*, property has been resold), if the injured party has delayed in a way that is unfair to the other party (**laches**), if the remedy would cause unreasonable hardship, if the terms of the contract are unclear, or if the contract involves unfairness.

Laches
Injured party delays in seeking remedy in a way that is unfair to the other party

Specific Performance is a court order requiring a party to perform her contractual obligations. It is most commonly awarded in cases involving **unique property**. For example, if seller refuses to sign a deed after signing a contract to sell his house, a court will order him to do so. Could Banquet Hall have obtained an order of specific performance for the undelivered chicken breasts? Probably not; chicken breasts are not unique property and are readily available from other sources. Specific performance is not appropriate for contracts involving personal services. Forcing a person to perform work against her will would be similar to slavery and it would be very difficult to ensure the quality of the work.

Specific Performance
Court order requiring a party to perform contract obligations

Unique Property
An item that is not readily available from other sources

An **injunction** is a court order requiring or prohibiting specific actions. For example, Lee has an option to purchase Pat's farm at any time during the next year. Lee learns that Pat is planning to convey the farm to Terry. Lee can obtain an injunction to prevent the transfer. An injunction can be awarded in a personal service contract situation, for example, to prevent an employee under contract to one employer from going to work for another.

Injunction
Court order requiring or prohibiting specific actions

Restitution (also discussed in a previous chapter) is restoration to the position occupied by the injured party before the contract was entered. It usually requires return of consideration and is commonly applied in situations where damages cannot be calculated with the certainty required by the court or situations involving an unenforceable or voidable contract. Restitution is sometimes available to the party in breach of the contract.

Restitution
To return property or its value

Examples

Examples of Restitution

Jan conveyed title to her empty lot to Carl Contractor for construction of a custom house. The contract requires Jan to get a mortgage and pay Carl, who will transfer the lot and house back when construction is complete. Carl fails to begin construction as required by the contract. Jan wants her lot back.

Carl Contractor orally agreed to begin construction on a house for Jill in 15 months and took a deposit of $10,000. The contract is unenforceable under the statute of frauds (not to be performed within one year) and Jill may seek restitution for the return of the deposit. In this type of situation, restitution is used to prevent unjust enrichment; it's a quasi-contract situation.

Jan signed a contract to sell her lot for $75,000 and took a $15,000 deposit from Bill. Bill later tells Jan he cannot complete the purchase. Jan then sells the lot to Connie for $80,000. Bill may be entitled to return of his money, despite his breach.

The UCC provides for restitution and **replevin** in specified circumstances. Replevin is recovery of goods from one who is wrongfully in possession of those goods.

Reformation (also discussed in a previous chapter) is the "rewriting" of a contract, also called "blue-penciling," and is rare. It is most often employed in cases of mutual mistake, when the court attempts to make the contract reflect the real intentions of the parties, or in cases of unconscionability, where the court wants to give the injured party the benefit of the contract without the burden of the unfair provision.

Replevin
Recovery of property from one who is wrongfully in possession

Reformation
Rewriting contact; called Blue-penciling

EXHIBIT 11-2

UCC Self-Help Remedies, Seller (depend on the nature of Buyer's breach)	UCC Self-Help Remedies, Buyer (depend on nature of Seller's breach)	Damages: Consider ability to prove with reasonable certainty, foreseeability, mitigation	Equitable Remedies: Available only if damages inadequate; consider balance of equities
Recission: cancel the contract or accept substituted performance	Recission: cancel the contract or accept substituted performance	Compensatory: puts non-breaching party in position would have occupied if contract had been fully performed. (loss of value – costs avoided + incidental + consequential)	Injunction: prohibits actions
Withhold or stop delivery	Cover: obtain substitute goods	Liquidated: agreed in advance, must be reasonable	Restitution: restores non-breaching to position occupied before contract, *e.g.*, return of property

EXHIBIT 11-2
(continued)

UCC Self-Help Remedies, Seller (depend on the nature of Buyer's breach)	UCC Self-Help Remedies, Buyer (depend on nature of Seller's breach)	Damages: Consider ability to prove with reasonable certainty, foreseeability, mitigation	Equitable Remedies: Available only if damages inadequate; consider balance of equities
Resell goods	Replevin: recover goods identified to contract, in possession of another	Nominal: a small amount, available if loss was negligible or not adequately proven	Specific Performance: requires party to perform contract
	Security Interest: in goods in buyer's possession that do not satisfy contract requirements	Punitive: available only if tort (*e.g.*, fraud) involved in breach	Reformation: court "rewrites" contract, rare
If the above-listed remedies are inadequate, seller may sue for damages; see column 3	If listed remedies inadequate, buyer may seek damages (column 3), or equitable remedy, *e.g.*, specific performance	Reliance: restores (in a financial sense) non-breaching party to position occupied if contract not made	

D. Tort Law vs. Contract Law

Because breach of contract usually does result in some "harm" parties sometimes try to frame their cases as tort actions, rather than (or, in addition to) contract actions. This can be an effort to obtain an award of damages not generally available for breach of contract. For example, a party hoping for an award of punitive damages might allege the tort of fraud. Bringing a tort suit might also be necessary if a situation is not covered by contract law. For example, a third party might interfere with the performance of a contract between others and cause a breach; the appropriate action is not for breach of contract, but for tortious interference with contract. In other cases, a party might want to frame his case as contract case or as a tort case because of the statute of limitations applicable to the case or because of particular standards that might be applied to the case.

In general, if the lawsuit is based on breach of a duty imposed by society (*e.g.*, the duty to drive in a safe manner) it is a tort case; if it is based on a breach of a duty voluntarily assumed as part of a contract (*e.g.*, an obligation to complete a warehouse by a certain date) it is a contract case.

Some situations fit into both areas of law. For example, a seller might breach a contract by delivering a defective product, which causes harm to a person or property. The situation may be covered by the contract warranties (discussed in previous chapters). Warranty actions are often inadequate as a remedy in such situations because warranties can be disclaimed, limited, or modified. In addition, depending on the jurisdiction, a warranty action might not provide a remedy because the injured party was, himself, negligent in a way that contributed to the injury; misused the product; or was not in **privity of contract** (not a party to the contract and, perhaps, far removed from the contract relationship).

The most recent evolution in this area of law is the imposition of **strict liability** (liability regardless of fault) on sellers of products. While the law differs from state to state, a merchant seller (in the business of selling the product) is generally liable for injuries arising from the sale of a product in a defective condition that is unreasonably dangerous. The product must have been in the defective condition when it left the control of the defendant. The injured party is not required to prove that the seller was careless or negligent or how the product came to be defective. The proximate cause of the injury can be a manufacturing defect, a design defect, or failure to warn. The goals of the law are to give consumers (who may not have medical insurance) maximum protection, to put the financial burden on those who profit from selling the profit, and to motivate manufacturers to produce safe products. Because of the burden this legal theory imposes on sellers, some states allow consideration of the injured party's negligence or misuse of the product and some states have imposed limits on awards of damages.

Privity
The relationship between the parties to the contract

Strict Liability
Liability regardless of fault

E. Practical and Ethical Issues

Attorneys are motivated to hire paralegals not only to get work done efficiently, but also because paralegals are a profit center. In recent years, fee reversal cases (discussed in this chapter) have made well-educated paralegals a particularly valuable part of an efficient law office.

When there is no fee reversal issue, whether the attorney bills the client for paralegal time, as a separate item on the bill is purely a private matter; there is no court involved.

Example

Client consults lawyer about negotiating and drafting a contract to sell a business. Lawyer estimates that the work will take about 10 hours and says "My hourly rate is $250; my paralegal's hourly rate is $80." "WHAT!" client exclaims, "you are going to bill me separately for your paralegal?" Lawyer shrugs and says, "Suit yourself. If you'd prefer to not work with a paralegal I will do all the work myself. Your bill will be about $2,500. If you do work with my paralegal and he does half the work, it will be about $1,650." Suddenly, client wants to work with the paralegal.

Why is this arrangement beneficial for the lawyer? The lawyer makes a profit on the paralegal. If the paralegal's salary, benefits, office space, etc. cost the lawyer about $40 an hour, half of the billing rate is profit. In addition, if the lawyer is busy, she can spend the five hours that are "freed up" by the paralegal's work on another client matter. Is there anything unethical about this? No, this is a private contract to which the client has agreed and the lawyer is in business to make a profit, like any other employer.

In a fee reversal case the situation is a little different. The party who ultimately pays the lawyer did not choose the lawyer, did not agree to the hourly rate, and did not have an opportunity to monitor the work as it was done. In order to make sure that the billing is fair, the court making a fee recovery award reviews the bill. This is demonstrated by one of the sample cases at the end of this chapter. If the court determines that the bill was unfair, it will cut the bill. This motivates lawyers to delegate work to those with lower billing rates.

Imagine that the bill submitted to the court included 40 hours of time for summarizing depositions, at $400 an hour. The court might decide that this type of work did not have to be done by a lawyer with a billing rate of $400 and cut the bill to $100 per hour. The firm has learned a valuable lesson: Next time, use a paralegal for deposition summaries! Most courts not only allow separate billing for paralegals in fee reversal cases, they encourage it by scrutinizing the bill. This is not universally true; always check the precedent in the particular court system.

Of course, unscrupulous lawyers might start including billing for photocopying, filing, and other low-level clerical work as "paralegal work." As a result, many courts scrutinize not only the type of work done, but also the credentials of the paralegals who did the work.

Assignment 11-2

Read the cases at the end of the chapter.

◆ Do you think the nature of the defendant's actions in the *Madrid* case influenced the court's decision that both an equitable remedy and an award of damages were appropriate? Might the court have reached a different conclusion if the defendant had not taken advantage of the elderly homeowners in such an extreme way, or is the concept of separating law and equity generally obsolete?

◆ In the *Edington* case, the court deducted from plaintiff's award the amount she earned working for Glock after Remington terminated her contract, but did not deduct the amount she earned from a real estate company. Why? The court cut both the hours claimed and the hourly rates in the attorneys' fees award. Why?

Courts employ particular measures for damages in particular cases. As assigned by your instructor, find cases from your state, summarize and report to the class how the court measured damages in cases involving:

◆ A contractor's delay in completing construction.

◆ Lost profits in a situation involving a **franchise** (contract granting the right to operate under a brand name, such as McDonald's, Burger King, Taco Bell, Dunkin Donuts, or Aamco); does your state have a rule concerning new businesses? *Note: a sample franchise contract appears in the appendix for use in an assignment in a later chapter.*

◆ An employer's or employee's breach of an employment contract.

◆ Mitigation of damages in a situation where the injured party was able to sell the product or service to another customer and claims that the new contract should not offset the damages for breach because it would have been able to fulfill the new contract even if the buyer had not breached.

◆ A construction defect; if possible find a case where correction of the defect would constitute "economic waste."

◆ A claim for emotional distress damages.

◆ Attorney's fees with paralegal fees billed separately in a breach of contract matter.

◆ Find your state's consumer protection/fraud act. Use your bookmarked state statutes, CALR, or the website for the attorney general of your state. Does the statute provide for awards of attorney fees? Arbitration?

> **Franchise**
> Contract granting the right to operate under a brand name

Review Questions

1. What are the two main means of ADR? What is meant by court-annexed ADR?

2. Buyer ordered 200 white lab coats in a variety of sizes. Seller, who lost a substantial amount of inventory as the result of a storm, shipped 200 blue lab coats in various sizes. How does the UCC characterize seller's actions? What essential fact is missing? What options are available to buyer under the Code?

3. Under what circumstances will a court award an equitable remedy? Identify some equitable remedies?

4. Under what circumstances will a court award punitive damages for breach of contract?

5. What type of damages are awarded in promissory estoppel cases? Under what circumstances is this same type of damages awarded in a breach of contract case?

6. Under what circumstances will a court award incidental or consequential damages?

7. Under what circumstances will a court uphold a clause providing for liquidated damages?

8. What "details" should be clarified before a client commits to participation in arbitration?

9. How does an attorney benefit from billing a client for paralegal time, at a rate lower than would be billed for attorney time?

10. Consider your state's consumer fraud statute and the sample cases, What is the purpose of fee award statutes? Do you think courts ever award punitive damages because there is no statute or contract provision to serve as a basis for an award of attorney fees?

11. After reading the second sample case, identify the factors a court uses, in a fee reversal case, to determine whether attorney's fees are reasonable.

ACROSS

1. court-_____ ADR is increasingly common
3. _____ period, time for bringing suit
10. area of law in which courts issue orders based in fairness
11. _____ damages look to where injured party would be if contract were fully performed
12. damages agreed in advance
13. contracts sometimes dictate the _____ where a case will be litigated
18. _____ damages; e.g., extra transportation costs
22. lost profits are a type of _____ damages
23. another term for a monetary award
24. retrieval of goods from person wrongfully in possession
25. court order prohibiting specified actions

DOWN

2. _____ damages, even if no loss proven
4. another term for a mediator or arbitrator
5. filing fees, etc.
6. specific performance available for contracts involving _____ property
7. damages awarded only if conduct was also intentional tort
8. with _____ arbitration the parties give up the right to challenge the result in court
9. to restore party to previous position
14. re-writes the contract
15. _____ damages put injured party in position occupied before contract formed
16. cutting losses resulting from breach
17. another term for equity
19. _____ performance requires party to fulfill contract obligations
20. _____ provision may require written notice before filing suit
21. _____ remedy, an award of money

CASES FOR ANALYSIS

SAMPLE CASE 1: Punitive damages and restitution combined

JOSE L. MADRID a/k/a JOE L. MADRID, Plaintiff-Appellee, v.
MEDARDO MARQUEZ, Defendant-Appellant.
COURT OF APPEALS OF NEW MEXICO

131 N.M. 132; 2001 NMCA 87; 33 P.3d 683;
September 19, 2001, Filed

Based on certain oral representations, Jose Madrid and his wife Celia, now deceased, transferred the title to their home to Marquez. When Marquez attempted to evict the Madrids from their home, the Madrids filed suit against Marquez and others alleging fraud, breach of contract, outrage, and prima facie tort, and requested recission and equitable reformation. The district court found in favor of Madrid and ordered alternative relief: Madrid could reimburse Marquez for his expenditures related to the transfer and upkeep in the amount of $56,261.96 and rescind the deed, or Madrid could retain a life estate in the real estate with a remainder interest in Marquez. The district court also awarded Madrid $20,000 in punitive damages. Marquez appeals arguing: (1) the district court improperly awarded punitive damages; (2) there was not substantial evidence supporting the award or the finding of an oral agreement; (3) the statute of frauds bars enforcement of the oral contract. We affirm.

Madrid and Marquez were neighbors. In early 1997, Madrids took out a mortgage. By mid 1997, they were having difficulty in making the payments . . . were suffering from medical problems. Marquez was aware of the financial and medical problems [and] offered to allow Madrids to remain in their home rent free for the remainder of their lives and to care for them in return for a deed to the Madrid home. The Madrids accepted. Marquez arranged for a closing at which Madrids executed a deed [that] contained no language with regard to the promised life estate. Marquez refinanced the property and paid off the existing Madrid mortgage. Marquez began harassing, and intimidating the elderly and ill couple and attempted to force the Madrids from their home. The Madrids contacted an attorney and this litigation ensued.

Marquez's primary argument is that punitive damages cannot be recovered without recovery of compensatory or nominal damages. *cites omitted* correctly states the general law of New Mexico regarding punitive damages, none of the cases cited consider whether punitive damages may be awarded in equity. This is a case of first impression in New Mexico . . . we believe justice is better served by allowing award of punitive damages in equity cases where conduct of the wrongdoer warrants punitive damages to deter clearly unacceptable behavior.

Punitive damages are "sums awarded in addition to any compensatory or nominal damages, usually as punishment or deterrent levied against a defendant found guilty of particularly aggravated misconduct, coupled with a malicious, reckless or otherwise wrongful state of mind." . . . the award does not measure a loss suffered by the plaintiff. Historically, the judicial system in the United States [had] separate courts of law and equity. Punitive damages could be awarded only in a court of law. [M]ost jurisdictions now have a merged system of courts of law and equity. New Mexico has a merged system.

During the evolution of the combined system, a split of authority developed regarding the award of punitive damages in equity. Marquez urges the majority rule that no punitive damage awards are made in equity because punitive damages are awarded for vengeance or punishment, and equity is not the place for such a remedy. Other jurisdictions follow a more modern trend and award punitive damages in equity to facilitate judicial administration, to deter misconduct, and to completely serve justice. . . . We find the modern approach more persuasive. Requiring an award of compensatory damages as a prerequisite to an award for punitive damages is a technical rule that should not be applied blindly.

New Mexico law allows a plaintiff who establishes a cause of action in law, to recover punitive damages as long as the wrongdoer's conduct is willful, wanton, malicious, reckless, oppressive, grossly negligent, or fraudulent and in bad faith . . . misconduct must be addressed regardless of whether the case is brought in law or equity. This case is a prime example of why punitive damages should be awarded. Marquez's fraudulent conduct induced Madrids to transfer their house. Marquez harassed, threatened, and intimidated. He made continuing promises . . . but never put it in writing. He attempted to evict the Madrids. Marquez's behavior is precisely the kind of behavior that warrants an award of punitive damages.

Marquez argues that the Statute of Frauds bars enforcement. [H]e would limit our consideration of events to those occurring after closing and have us ignore discussions and acts of the parties before the closing. The purpose of the Statute of Frauds is to protect the parties, not to allow one party to defraud the other. The district court enforced an oral promise based on partial performance and properly fashioned a remedy that allowed Madrids to have the benefit of their bargain or rescind the entire agreement. Substantial evidence supports the determination, and we reject Marquez's argument that a written agreement was necessary to convey a life estate to the Madrids.

CASE 2: Mitigation of damages, calculation of damages, award of paralegal fees

EDINGTON V. COLT'S MANUFACTURING COMPANY, INC. SUPERIOR COURT OF CONNECTICUT, JUDICIAL DISTRICT OF HARTFORD, AT HARTFORD

November 25, 2002, Filed

[P]laintiff was retained by defendant pursuant to a written contract for the purpose of providing public relations services in her capacity as a professional gun shooter . . . she was expected to enter competitive shooting contests. This contract was renewed several times, the last one at issue . . . for a 3-year period from

January 1, 1999 through December 31, 2001. Defendant terminated the contract as of January 4, 2000 by letter dated January 26, 2000.

Plaintiff instituted this action to recover sums due her under the contract, potential bonus payments from which she was foreclosed, the value of guns and miscellaneous services which should have been furnished to her and reasonable attorneys fees.

Plaintiff claims she lost $35,000 each year for 2000 and 2001 by reason of payments due her under the contract, a bonus payment shortfall of $20,000 and a loss in receipt of guns, parts and services due her in the amount of $8,000 . . . she claims attorneys fees and costs in the amount of $40,289, subsequently revised to $51,878.

If an employee is wrongfully dismissed while working under a fixed term contract, e.g. three years, he may recover the salary due for the remainder of the term plus whatever fringe benefits or commissions could be reasonably expected, minus amounts earned elsewhere . . . Plaintiff is entitled to recover $70,000 for the two years remuneration due her under the contract.

Defendant [is] claiming plaintiff failed to mitigate damages by failing to make reasonable efforts to secure employment, most notably failing to accept employment offered to her by the defendant in a period of negotiations which took place from February through May 2000.

A wrongfully discharged employee's right to an award is limited by the doctrine of mitigation and failure to use reasonable diligence in seeking another comparable job may be considered in mitigating damages. The period of back pay may terminate when there is an unconditional and bona fide offer of reinstatement to the same or equivalent position. An offer of reinstatement does not limit liability of the employer unless the position offered complies with the terms of the breached contract. . . .

Nor has defendant produced any substantial evidence . . . In fact plaintiff obtained some alternative employment in 2001. Defendant claims further mitigation because plaintiff was not required to incur traveling and lodging expenses which she ordinarily incurred as part of her employment. Colt was not obligated to reimburse her for these expenses but sometimes it did. . . . Damages to the plaintiff should be reduced by her expenses saved in consequence of the breach of contract. . . . The court finds that $1,219 per event represented the more reasonable average because the $1,709 charge appears to be extraordinarily excessive. The court finds further that, on average, one half of the requests for reimbursements were honored. Based on a minimum of seven events a year, at an average cost of $1,219, half of which was reimbursed, it is found that over a two year period, plaintiff saved $8,540 in expenses which she would ordinarily have paid, and this amount should be applied in mitigation of her damages.

[T]he contract provides for bonuses if she won or placed in the first three competitions she was engaged to enter, ranging from $1,000 to $3,000. Plaintiff claims $20,000 in lost bonuses based on a per year average of $10,000. Defendant argues that the average amount of bonuses she earned over five years preceding 2000 was $6,450. The evidence of her bonuses received in the past five years is a more reliable indication of what she might have earned in 2000 and 2001, and she is awarded $12,900 for failed bonuses.

Defendant claims that money earned from other services, including from Peachtree Realty in 2000 in the amount of $1,035 and from Glock in 2001, in the amount of $34,564.02 should be deducted from her recovery. The unusual nature of plaintiff's employment, was that of a performer, and did not require any fixed period of time or hours. However, her alternate employment with Glock, a competitor to defendant, would have been barred by her contract with defendant and her compensation from Glock, in the amount of $34,564, should be deducted from her recovery.

Paragraphs 9(b), (c) and (d) provide for guns, parts and services to be provided by defendant . . . which she did not receive. The . . . value of the guns and parts that would have been provided to her in 2000 and 2001 was $8,000 . . . it is not appropriate to credit her for guns and parts during the year she was employed by Glock which presumably provided her with other guns and parts. Accordingly, she should be credited in the amount for $4,000 for the loss of these items.

Plaintiff claims reasonable attorneys fees of $40,289 based on the contract which states: In the event that the terminated party wishes to litigate whether a material default has occurred, the prevailing party in such litigation shall be entitled to recover reasonable attorneys fees and costs from the other parts [sic]. . . . Since this contract was drawn by defendant, any ambiguity in this clause should be resolved in favor of plaintiff. It is a fair conclusion that attorneys fees are awardable to the plaintiff, the prevailing party in this case.

At trial plaintiff's claims for $40,289 in attorneys fees was based on 64.5 hours of partner time at $300 per hour; 57.50 hours of associate time at $250 per hour; and 75.50 hours of paralegal time at $75 per hour. Subsequently, plaintiff revised these claims to 69.6 hours for partners, 87.5 hours for associates and 110.5 hours for paralegals, presumably for the addition of trial hours. Taking into consideration average rates in Hartford County, the difficulty of the case and the fact that this action resembled a collection action in which the principal debt was not contested, although a vigorous defense was raised based on mitigation of damages, the court has adjusted this claim as follows:

Partners	50 hours at $250/hour	$12,500
Associates	50 hours at $200/hour	$10,000
Paralegals	50 hours at $50/hour	$2,500
		$25,000

No award is made for punitive damages . . . plaintiff is entitled to damages of $43,796, based on the following computation. In addition, Plaintiff is awarded $25,000 for attorneys fees, for a total of $68,796.

Base Pay	$70,000
Lost bonuses	12,900
Guns and parts	4,000
	$86,900
Less Glock earnings	$34,564
Unused travel	8,540
Net Damages	$43,796

12

Contract Interpretation

What happens when the parties disagree about what is required by a contract? In the worst cases, the parties have to resort to alternative dispute resolution (**ADR**, mediation or arbitration, discussed in detail in the previous chapter) or the courts. This chapter first introduces the common component parts of a contract, then focuses on the **rules of construction** that are applied to resolve such disputes. Knowing these rules is critical to drafting a contract that will not result in disputes.

ADR
Alternative dispute resolution (discussed in Chapter 11)

Construction (rules of)
Rules that are applied to resolve contract disputes and to determine parties' intentions

---

A. **Components of a Written Contract**
 1. **Identifications**
 2. **Recitals**
 3. **Consideration**
 4. **Definitions**
 5. **Body**
 6. **Signatures and Acknowledgments**
B. **Parol Evidence Rule**
C. **Rules of Construction**
D. **Practical and Ethical Issues**

Remember, these rules of construction are "default rules" and apply when the parties do not adequately describe the expectations and obligations in the contract. The Uniform Commercial Code (UCC) includes many default provisions, some of which you studied in an earlier chapter, concerning offers (the gap-filling or open terms provisions). Good lawyers and paralegals give careful thought to every provision, rather than allowing the default provisions to create the contract.

A.　Components of a Written Contract

1.　Identifications

This section, generally at the top of the first page, gives the title, identifies the parties, and states the date of signing. It may indicate how the parties will be identified throughout the rest of the contract. It should never include confusing identifications, such as "party of the first part."

Example

EMPLOYMENT CONTRACT

This employment contract is made on March 15, 2007, ("Contract Date"),[1] between Fox Valley Investors Coop, LLC, an Illinois limited liability company, ("FVIC"), 1012 River Road, St. Charles, IL 60174 and Chris Zehelein, 329 Duncan Ave., Elgin, IL 60120 ("Employee").

Assignment 12-1

When drafting or implementing a contract involving a business, it is important to determine:

◆ Is the business a sole proprietorship, a corporation, a limited partnership, a general partnership, or a limited liability company;
◆ Accurate contact information and address;
◆ Whether the contract gives the correct name; and
◆ Whether the business is in good standing.

Find the website for the agency responsible for registration of business entities in your state. This is usually the Office of the Secretary of State. Although many online services offer corporate searches for a fee, it is important that you use the official site to get accurate, up-to-date information without paying a fee. Using your state's site, search for corporations in your state that include your last name in their names.

Defined Term
Short-hand way of referring to a person, place, thing, or event that might otherwise require a lengthy description

---

[1]Reference to any person, place, thing, or event can be made easier by creating a **defined term,** essentially a short-hand way of referring to that person, place, thing, or event, that might otherwise require a lengthy description.

2. Recitals

Short statements that give background or explain the reasons for the contract, recitals are not technically part of the contract. Recitals do not contain essential terms, requiring a party to do or not do anything, but they can play an important role in contract interpretation. In older contracts, recitals often begin with the word "whereas."

Example

1. FVIC is engaged in the business of providing online training for employees of its clients and requires the services of a web page designer.
2. Employee is a web page designer, previously employed by Elgin Community College.
3. Employee terminated his employment at Elgin Community College in order to accept employment by FVIC.

---

3. Consideration

As you know, a contract is not valid without consideration, which means that each party must get something she or he was not legally entitled to before entering the contract and each must give up something to which s/he was legally entitled before the contract. A written contract may contain a "formal" statement of consideration at its beginning, such as: "for ten dollars and other valuable consideration, receipt of which is acknowledged, the parties agree. . . ." Remember, however, that stating a dollar amount as a formality is not necessary, because courts do not generally weigh consideration. The mutual agreements and obligations stated in the body of the contract should be sufficient to support the contract.

Example

4. Employee has left his former employment and agrees to work as a web designer, as described in the employee handbook ("Handbook"), attached to this contract as Exhibit A and **incorporated by this reference**, for the period beginning April 1, 2007 and ending on April 1, 2008 (the Term of Employment"), at the salary and with the benefits stated in the Handbook.
5. FVIC agrees to compensate Employee in accordance with terms stated in the Handbook for the Term of Employment.

---

4. Definitions

If a contract is complex, involving multiple parties, events, locations, or objectives, it is often most efficient to include a list of all defined terms at the beginning, to avoid the distraction of integrating the definitions into the text. It is extremely important that the **defined terms** be used consistently. Even if the

Recitals
Short statements that provide background or explain the reasons for the contract; not technically part of a contract

Incorporation by Reference
A reference to an outside document, making that document part of a contract

contract does not contain a separate section for definitions, adequate definitions are essential. Even common terms may require definition. Consider a standard homeowner's insurance policy that excludes coverage for injuries incurred as the result of conducting business on the premises. Suppose that the homeowner's daughter is babysitting a neighbor's child (anticipating payment) when the child is hurt by a pan of boiling water falling from the stove. Would the policy cover the child's medical care?

Assignment 12-2

◆ Draft a definition of the term "business" that would exclude coverage for the incident described above; draft a definition that would cover the incident.

◆ MadCity University has always had a clause in its housing contract that allows school officials to evict a student from the dormitories for various activities involving (among other things) illegal drugs, smoking, open fires, and use of any "hazardous" substance. Last year, two students distributed peanuts in hidden spots throughout the study lounge as a "joke." A third student, severely allergic to peanuts, became violently ill. MCU is convinced that the students knew the likely consequences of their actions, but were unsuccessful in evicting the students on the "hazardous substance" provision. Draft a definition that would cover the situation.

◆ Professor Vietzen's syllabus includes a statement that late assignments are penalized 3 points per day. Identify the possible ambiguities and draft a definition to clarify.

◆ Your firm's client, Dina Developer, wants to establish a high-end, quiet subdivision. She wants a contract and covenants that will allow home-owners to conduct quiet home occupations, such as an architect who might meet clients in a home office once or twice a week, but wants to prohibit disruptive home businesses that will involve lots of noise or traffic. Draft a definition of home occupation that will meet Dina's needs.

Example

6. "Out of Office Work" means work performed by Employee, for the benefit or at the request of FVIC, at a location other than FVIC's offices or the employee's home, when performed at that location at the request of FVIC. Expenses related to Out of Office Work shall be compensated as described in Exhibit B, attached.

7. "Volunteerism" refers to participation in FVIC's programs for community service, as described on the company website, as it may be from time-to-time amended.

5. Body

The body of the contract describes the obligations of the parties and the consequences of failure to meet those obligations. When you receive a contract that has been signed, you do not have control of the contents, but should look for certain characteristics (described in the next chapter) to help you understand and implement the agreement. If the contract does not have these characteristics, *e.g.*, good organization and labeling, you may have to create a work copy or an outline to help yourself understand it. When you participate in creating a contract, you can make it user-friendly by remembering these traits.

Example

I. FVIC'S PROPERTY RIGHTS

16.   Intellectual Property. All material developed by Employee in the course of his employment shall be the property of FVIC. Employee shall sign all necessary assignments and other paperwork, as necessary to secure patent, copyright, or trademark rights in such material for FVIC.

17.   Trade Secrets. Employee shall not divulge any information concerning any FVIC product or clients to anyone either during or after termination of his employment with FVIC and shall not use such information for his own benefit.

18.   Competition. Employee shall not, during the Term of Employment or for a period of one year after the end of that term, perform work in any capacity for any of the competing companies listed on Exhibit B, attached to this contract and incorporated by this reference.

19.   Remedies for Violation of FVIC Property Rights. Employee acknowledges that, in the event of breach of any of the covenants in paragraphs 6-8 above, FVIC shall be entitled to monetary damages as well as injunctive relief.

II. EMPLOYEE'S RIGHTS

20.   Transfer. If FVIC notifies Employee that Employee has been transferred to another geographic location, Employee may, by written notice, terminate this contract. Employee shall continue to perform his contractual duties for five working days after the date on which FVIC receives such written notice. In the event of termination because of transfer, FVIC shall compensate Employee for days actually worked plus the sum of Ten Thousand Dollars ($10,000) and shall have no further liability to Employee.

21.   Failure to Renew. If, at the end of the Term of Employment, FVIC does not offer to extend Employee's employment on substantially the same terms . . .

---

6.   Signatures and Acknowledgments

To avoid any appearance that pages were switched, signatures should not be on a page separate from the text of the agreement. Some lawyers include a spot to allow the parties to initial each page to avoid claims that pages were switched. Never remove the staples from a signed contract unless your supervising attorney specifically directs you to do so.

Corporate signatures must comply with state law and may require a seal, attestation, or other formalities. Always make sure that the person signing on behalf of a business has authority to do so; this may require review of the documents that created the business (partnership agreement, articles of incorporation/by-laws, organizational agreement).

Example

Date: _____

Frank Transue, CEO	Chris Zehelein
Fox Valley Investors Coop, LLC,	329 Duncan Ave.
1012 River Road	Elgin, IL 60120

Witness   Witness

Notary Public
Person authorized by state to administer oaths, certify documents, attest to the authenticity of signatures, and perform other official acts

Record
To record a document is to file it with the official charged with keeping documents such as deeds and judgments

Self-Proving Document
Complies with formalities and can serve as testimony in court

Signatures may have to be witnessed by a **notary public**, if the contract will be **recorded**. Contracts concerning the title to real estate are often recorded, so that ownership can be determined by a search of the public records. In addition, contracts that are notarized may be considered "**self-proving**," meaning that they can serve as testimony in court.

Assignment 12-3

Many law firms require their paralegals to become notaries public so that they can witness signatures. Find information about becoming a notary in your state (again, probably the Secretary of State) and answer the following:

◆ What are the functions a notary can serve (Administer oath? Authenticate documents? Witness signature?)
◆ Is a notary required to keep a log book, with a record of each time s/he performs one of these functions? What is the bond requirement?

B. Parol Evidence Rule

A contract may lack some of the components described above or it may have all of those components and still leave room for disagreement, requiring use of the rules of construction. Before applying those rules, it is necessary to determine what constitutes "the contract" and whether it requires construction. The **parol evidence rule** is employed in making those determinations.

As you know, some contracts are comprised of several written instruments, others are evidenced by a single written document, and others involve no writing. Parties often engage in extended oral and written negotiations, with offers and counteroffers being made, accepted or declined, withdrawn, or forgotten. Once the parties agree on terms and reduce that agreement to writing, it is assumed that what went on during negotiations is irrelevant. The written contract is protected from "attack" by the parol evidence rule. The rule concerns evidence. If a contract has been put in writing, evidence of things said before the writing is not admissible to vary, contradict, or add to its terms. Like all legal matters, however, it is not as simple as it appears.

Parol Evidence Rule
A writing, intended by the parties to be a final embodiment of their agreement, cannot be modified by evidence that adds to, varies, or contradicts the writing

---

Example

Sam spent two days looking at models of condominium units and negotiating to buy a unit in a building still under construction. At the end of the second day, exhausted, Sam finally signed a contract to buy a two-bedroom unit for $188,000. Sam was too tired to read the contract, which called for closing and possession in April. During his final inspection in April, Sam was surprised to find that the unit did not have a refrigerator. Sam says that the sales agent orally promised a refrigerator before writing up the contract, but now Sam realizes that it was not listed in the written contract. The sales agent says he remembers talking about a refrigerator, but does not remember promising that the refrigerator would be included at the $188,000 price. Sam's friend Pat, who was with Sam during the negotiations, is willing to testify that it sounded like the refrigerator would be included, but will the testimony be allowed?

1. Was this an **integrated** contract, intended to be a final and complete statement of the agreement? If the contract included a phrase, such as "*options as agreed*," or did not list any of the options, Sam might argue that it was not the complete agreement. Many contracts include a **merger clause**, stating that the document is the complete and final statement of agreement. Because a written contract does not have to take any particular form, the status of a document that does not include any reference to outside agreements or a merger clause may be unclear. Might it be simply a proposal or have all parties agreed? Does the document address the disputed term at all; would such an agreement normally include some provision for dealing with the disputed term?

Integrated
Final and complete agreement

Merger Clause
Contract provision stating that the document is the complete and final statement of agreement

---

Sample Merger Clause:

This Agreement and the exhibits and schedules referred to herein constitute the final, complete, and exclusive statement of agreement between the parties with respect to the subject matter of this Agreement. This Agreement supersedes all prior and contemporaneous understandings or agreements between the parties. This Agreement may not be contradicted by evidence of any prior or contemporaneous statements or agreements. No party has been induced to enter into this Agreement by, nor is any party relying on, any representation, understanding, agreement, commitment or warranty outside those expressly set forth in this Agreement.

2. Is the oral evidence intended to contradict the written contract or simply to **explain an ambiguity or apparent mistake**? If the contract contained a scrawled notation, "*promised buyer R,*" or "*option package B,*" Sam might argue that he is not trying to change or add to the contract, but only to explain it. Whether the oral evidence is an attempt to change or an attempt to explain is often unclear and some courts look at whether the disputed term is consistent with the rest of the agreement.

3. Is the evidence intended to show fraud, duress, mistake, misrepresentation, unconscionability, illegality, incapacity, or other **facts that would make the agreement void or voidable**? In such a situation, the intent is not to change the written contract, but to show that it might not be enforceable. If Sam had said, "I am too tired to read this and sign it now," and the sales agent had responded, "Don't worry it includes everything you want, even the refrigerator," Sam might be able to argue that the contract was tainted by fraud. *Read the sample case at the end of this chapter for an example of a court allowing parol evidence in a case of mistake.*

Subsequent Agreement
A separate, later agreement that changes or modifies the original agreement

4. Was there a separate or **subsequent agreement** that changed or modified the agreement? Of course, a new agreement generally has to be supported by new consideration. Perhaps, after signing the contract for $188,000, which included upgraded kitchen counters, Sam and the salesperson made an agreement under which Sam would give up the upgraded counters in exchange for installation of a refrigerator.

5. Does the evidence indicate the existence of a **condition precedent**, so that the agreement might never have become effective? Again, this is not an attempt to change the written agreement, but evidence that the agreement did not bind the parties.

The UCC takes a liberal approach to application of the parol evidence rule and specifically allows evidence of the course of dealing, usage of trade, or course of performance to explain or supplement a final written agreement. The Code also allows evidence of consistent additional terms unless the written instrument was intended to be complete and exclusive.

Example

Sam buys four or five new mobile homes (personal property, rather than real property) from the same manufacturer each year for several years. This year, Sam signs an order for five mobile homes and fails to notice that it does not refer to refrigerators. Under the Code, Sam would be allowed to present evidence of the course of dealings between the parties, even without proving that the signed agreement was incomplete or ambiguous. Even if the parties had never done business together, Sam might be able show that inclusion of refrigerators was either customary in the industry or consistent with and not excluded by the signed agreement.

Assignment 12-4

Find the UCC provision concerning parol or extrinsic evidence.

C. Rules of Construction

Once a court identifies what constitutes the agreement and that the agreement is ambiguous it can apply **rules of construction** to try to determine the intent of the parties. Among the rules courts apply in interpreting contracts, in no particular order:

1. In choosing between two reasonable interpretations of a contract term, courts will interpret the contract against the party who drafted it. This is normally the offeror, who had the benefit of the mirror-image rule at common law.

2. When one interpretation will result in a lawful and effective contract and the other will result in no contract or a contract that is not workable, courts generally favor finding an effective contract.

3. Previous dealings between the parties are very important in establishing intent.

4. Words are given their commonly accepted meanings unless a different intention is clear and courts will not accept evidence of a different meaning when the words of the contract are unambiguous. If I sign a contract agreeing to sell you my 2004 truck, and later try to argue that we were really talking about my 2004 car, the court will probably not accept evidence that I always called my car "the truck." The contract appears unambiguous. Then again, what if I own a 2004 car and a 2002 truck?

5. Courts attempt to ascertain the intentions of the parties by looking at the purposes of the agreement and all of the surrounding circumstances. Let's assume that I own a 2002 car and a 2004 truck. The contract is ambiguous and the court would likely be willing to hear evidence that I knew you needed the truck in order to haul lumber for a construction project.

6. The written document is interpreted as whole and any disputed terms are interpreted so as to make them consistent with the rest of the agreement. If there are several documents that are part of a single transaction, those documents are looked at together. Perhaps you and I signed a contract under which you are building a dock and boathouse at my vacation property. That contract contains a statement that I am willing to sell you a truck for hauling lumber.

7. Specific terms govern over general terms and technical terms are generally given their technical meanings. If the agreement described a 2004 Ford truck with 25,000 miles on the odometer in one paragraph and referred to "the car" in other paragraphs, the specific description of the truck would govern.

8. Terms that were negotiated individually govern over boilerplate. **Boilerplate** refers to standard terms, included in most contracts, often pre-printed on a form or taken from a form book, not individually negotiated.

9. Hand-written terms govern over pre-printed terms and "spelled out" figures govern over numbers.

Assignment 12-5

◆ Find the UCC provisions concerning construction of contracts.
  ◆ What guidance does the Code provide when there is a conflict with respect to warranties in a contract?
  ◆ What does the Code say about situations in which the contract does not say when or how the buyer will pay for goods?

D. Practical and Ethical Issues

Many contracts end up in litigation because of mistakes that should have been caught during careful proofreading. Even lesser mistakes cause the writer to lose credibility. It is especially common for people who use text messaging, instant messenger or other forms of online or text-based communication to "slip up" and use informal (and incorrect) shortcuts, such as "thru" rather than "through" or "threw."

Common spelling/grammatical errors that may be missed by spell-check

- It's (a contraction meaning it is), when the intention was its (the possessive pronoun).
- Statue, when the intention was statute.
- Trail, when the intention was trial.
- Judgement, rather than judgment.
- Defendent, rather than defendant.
- Homonyms (words that sound alike), such as to, two, too; there, they're, their; then, than; or who's, whose.

Other common errors relate to numbering. If a contract goes through several drafts, a previously correct reference to "notice as described in paragraph 13 of this Agreement" may have become incorrect. Numbers may be inadvertently skipped or duplicated.

If a contract is adapted from a form previously used for another client, references to the parties and terms of that contract may remain in place unnoticed. Adaptation of a contract may also result in grammatical mistakes. For example, the earlier contract may have involved two buyers, while the current contract involves a single buyer. The result could be subject/verb or noun/pronoun inconsistency, such as "Buyer have paid earnest money" or "Buyer shall be entitled to return of their earnest money if. . . ."

Read the sample case at the end of this chapter, taking particular note of the testimony of the attorneys. Imagine the cost of litigating this problem, which most likely arose from a typographical/proofreading error. Obviously, one attorney has potential malpractice liability. A 2005 article in the American Bar Association publication *Law Practice Today* states that four out of five attorneys will experience at least one malpractice claim in their careers (http://www.abanet.org/lpm/lpt/articles/mgt04052.html).

Lawyers frequently rely on paralegals for proofreading. If possible and permitted by your instructor, exchange papers with a classmate before submitting your next graded assignment. Proofread each other's papers to see how different it is to proof a document written by someone else. Here are some tips to help you avoid the kind of problem that led to this case:

- Avoid proofreading your own work. If you must proofread your own work, allow enough time so that you can set the document aside, ideally for more than 24 hours, before you proof it.
- Proofread from paper, not from your computer screen.
- Proofread at a time of day when you feel alert.
- If possible, read aloud or have someone else read aloud to you.
- To ensure that you look at each word and don't "slide" ahead, keep a piece of paper under each line as you read or touch your finger to each word.
- Proofread in a location that is quiet and free of all distractions.
- For particularly important documents, proofread twice. Read the document once, focusing on meaning and implementation; read it a second time to look for spelling and grammatical errors.
- Some people find that reading backwards, word-by-word, is most effective for finding spelling and grammatical errors.
- Do a final "skim" to check headings, page numbers, and other "structural components" that may have been missed.

Assignment 12-6

1. Read the sample case at the end of this chapter and explain, in your own words, why the court did not apply the parol evidence rule to bar testimony.

2. A short (and very bad) construction contract appears at the end of this assignment. Identify the mistakes, ambiguities, and other problems with the contract.

3. A long (and not so bad) franchise contract is reproduced in Appendix B. Proofread it to identify any errors and write a letter to the client, Pete Avaadra, based on the following excerpts from a conversation Pete had with your boss. Your letter should identify the paragraphs in which you found your answers. Pete is an older man, eccentric, and not well educated. He built the business from a single storefront operation to a chain of 30 restaurants. He is ready to launch a franchise business with restaurants all over the U.S. Your firm has prepared the franchise contract, from a form used for a previous client. Here is what Pete said:

> "You know our trademark? The big 'A' with a pizza spinning on top? I'm thinking of changing it. People keep telling me it looks like some kind of spider. When I sign these franchises, am I locking into using that same trademark for however many years?
>
> "I'm worried about the secret recipe getting out. What if one of these operators tells me that he's buying a mixer and that the manufacturer needs to know the recipe to make the mixer strong enough? If this is some shady operator, do I have to give out the recipe so that this guy can get the mixer he wants? Also, you know I make them buy certain things from certain suppliers. Well, suppose I make them buy, let's say, dishwasher detergent, from a certain supplier and it's bad. Maybe it causes damage to the glasses. Am I liable for that?
>
> "Sometimes these guys think I am granting them a monopoly. They open a place and then they get all bent out of shape when I let another guy open a place a mile away. I need to be able to do that. Are we clear on that? But, on the other hand, I don't want them to open something like a 'Pat's Pizza' across the street after they're done with me.
>
> "I'm really sick of slow-pays; do I have any kind of automatic payment thing in place? Also, when I try to figure out what these guys owe me, well, sometimes they own more than one business. They tell me it's too hard to keep separate records. You know, they get better deals, say, having one cleaning service do both of their pizza operations and maybe their donut place too. So, how can I know I am getting an accurate picture of what they are making so that I get my cut?
>
> "OK, so a lot of times, it's more than one person signing on. You know, it might be brothers or friends or whatever. Anyway, one guy might be serious about it, while the other is just helping out. Well, the guy who's less interested sometimes walks away from the situation. Then you have the other guy claiming that he is going to honor his end of the deal but that he can't pick up the slack from the one who's out of the picture. So I ask, if one guy walks away, is the other guy 100% responsible?"

EXHIBIT 12-1

Construction Contract
This contract is entered into on March 13, 2007,
between Jane E. Lehmann, 325 River Bluff Road, Elgin, IL 60120
("Owner") And Robert J. Schell, doing business as Schell Corp.,
P.O. Box 451, Elburn, IL ("Builder")

WHEREAS:

- Lehmann owns property at 776 Diane Ave., Elgin IL and wishes to build a house on that property.
- Builder is in the construction business and has agreed to build a house on Lehmann's property.
- The house will be built according to the attached blueprints and specification list and the final price shall be $475,000.00.

TERMS:

1. Schell shall complete construction on or before September 1, 2006. Construction shall be considered complete when the city issues a certificate of occupancy. The Owner may not occupy the property before the final price is paid.

2. Jane shall pay the purchase price in installments: $50,000 upon signing this contract; an additional $100,000 when the roof is complete; $500,000 when the windows are installed, and the balance upon issuance of a certificate of occupancy.

3. Builder shall comply with all applicable building codes and municipal regulations, but makes no warranty with respect to materials installed in the house, such as roofing, furnace, appliances, windows, and cabinetry. Any warranties must come directly from the seller or manufacturer of the items. It is understood that Schell will not perform all work himself, but will employ subcontractors for work such as plumbing, electrical wiring, and excavation.

4. The price does not include landscaping or a driveway, but only includes those things listed on the blueprints or specifications.

5. During the course of construction, the house shall be kept insured against fire or other casualty.

6. Builder shall pay all subcontractors promptly and shall provide Owner with signed lien waivers.

7. Builder has the right to show the house to prospective customers as a sample of his work.

8. At the time of the third payout, Smith shall make a formal inspection of the property and shall submit to Schell, in writing, a list of deficiencies and defects.

EXHIBIT 12-1
(continued)

9. Shell shall provide any paperwork required by Owner's lender in order to obtain payouts during the course of construction and shall maintain liability insurance to compensate in the event of any injury to a worker or visitor at the building site.

10. If the Owner makes any changes in the plans or specifications, the Builder shall add the cost to the price and the owner shall pay the amount of the change promptly.

_____   _____

Jane E. Lehmann   Robert J. Schell

Review Questions

1. What part of a contract often begins with "WHEREAS" and what is the purpose of this section?
2. What is incorporation by reference?
3. What types of contracts require notarization?
4. What is a merger clause?
5. Assuming that the parol evidence rule does apply, for what purposes might evidence of oral agreements made before the written contract still be used?
6. Courts sometimes favor one of the parties in interpreting a contract. Which party is favored?
7. Identify at least five other rules courts use in interpreting contracts.

ACROSS

2. courts try to determine _____ of the parties
3. _____ terms, e.g. ("Owner")
4. clause states this is final and complete agreement
6. evidence of a condition _____ not barred by parol evidence rule
7. a contract intended to be entire statement of agreement
8. evidence of _____ agreement not barred by parol evidence rule
11. parol _____ rule protects written contracts from attack
12. another term for parol evidence
15. proofreading is best done from a document on this
18. signatures on behalf of _____ may require a seal or other formalities
21. courts construe contract against party who _____ it
22. in contract interpretation, court looks as document as a _____
23. give background for contract
24. facts that would indicate contract was _____ or voidable may be admissible
25. courts favor finding an _____ contract
26. courts give words _____ accepted meanings

DOWN

1. spelled-out figures govern over
2. beginning of contract, introduces parties
5. recitals often begin with this word
6. self-_____ documents can serve as testimony
9. terms govern over general terms
10. _____ terms are given their _____ meaning
13. a contract to be _____ may have to be notarized
14. don't remove these from a signed contract
16. individually negotiated terms govern over
17. _____ dealings, important in contract interpretation
19. parol evidence may be allowed to explain
20. a notary can witness a signature or administer an _____

CASE FOR ANALYSIS

This case demonstrates how a court deals with a contract that does not comply with the real intentions of the parties.

In re MARRIAGE OF THEODORE DANIEL JOHNSON, JR., Petitioner-Appellant, and SHAWNA SUE JOHNSON, Respondent-Appellee

Appellate Court of Illinois, Fourth District

237 Ill. App. 3d 381; 604 N.E.2d 378; 1992 178 Ill. Dec. 122
November 12, 1992, Filed

Theodore and Shawna were married on August 21, 1982. . . . have two children, Stefanie and Teddie. Theodore and Shawna were granted a dissolution of marriage on May 23, 1989, upon Theodore's petition for dissolution.

As part of the judgment of dissolution, they were granted joint custody of the children with Shawna having physical custody and Theodore being allowed reasonable visitation. Paragraph H of the marital settlement agreement stated: "The parties own a marital residence * * * Respondent shall have the exclusive possession and the use thereof, and . . . Petitioner shall forthwith surrender all keys . . . . parties shall sell the property upon the earliest of the following to occur: (1) *Petitioner's* remarriage, (b) the emancipation of their younger child, or (c) their agreement to do so." (Emphasis added.)

Theodore remarried . . . filed a motion to enforce the judgment . . . recited the facts of the judgment and specifically paragraph H. Theodore alleged he had remarried and had made demand on Shawna to . . . sell the property. Shawna had failed to respond, Theodore sought an order by the court to force the sale of the property pursuant to the agreement.

Shawna filed a petition . . . to modify the judgment . . . alleged that at all negotiations prior to the dissolution, as well as at the time the dissolution was awarded, the parties had agreed that it would be her remarriage which would trigger the sale of the residence. Shawna asserted the language in paragraph H of the agreement, which stated Theodore's marriage was the event to trigger the sale of the marital residence, was a clerical error.

Theodore had hired Greaves to represent him in the divorce proceedings with Shawna and had authorized Greaves to enter into settlement negotiations. The paramount concern to Theodore during the negotiations was the welfare of the parties' children. Theodore wished to minimize any disruptions . . . in his children's lives . . . Shawna's major concern was whether she would be able to meet her expenses. . . . Theodore agreed to grant her possession of the residence so that she and the children had an adequate place to live.

Theodore . . . admitted at one point he wished that Shawna's having a male guest sleeping overnight at the house would trigger sale of the house. He recalled other proposed terms regarding the splitting of the profits . . . as well as division of who would pay mortgage, taxes, and insurance. Theodore admitted that during negotiations, a proposed term of the agreement would be that Shawna's remarriage would trigger the sale of the residence.

Shawna's attorney drafted a judgment of dissolution which he thought contained the verbal agreement and sent a copy to Greaves. Theodore was handed the agreement at the courthouse on the day the judgment of dissolution was granted, at which time he signed it. Shawna was not present . . . had already signed the agreement. Theodore testified that the terms of the agreement were what he had previously agreed to.

Theodore's affidavit indicated "I did not wish to remain liable for . . . indebtedness on the former marital residence at a time when I married and sought to make a fresh start." Theodore guessed he adopted this rationale at the time he signed because "the agreement says what it says." On cross-examination, Theodore admitted he did not remarry until nearly 1½ years after the dissolution. Theodore testified it was not his intention to provide a place indefinitely for his wife and any live-in friend nor was it his intention to remain liable on the mortgage on that residence in the event he remarried and was unable to get financing on his own home. Theodore stated he read the agreement "front to back" before he signed it and it accurately stated his intentions.

Shawna testified the first time she became aware that it was Theodore's remarriage which would trigger the sale was when she received a letter regarding his demand . . . that Theodore's remarriage triggering the sale was never discussed . . . and that the agreement was that her remarriage would trigger the sale. Shawna believed the agreement merely contained a clerical error. She did not catch the word "petitioner" instead of "respondent" because she was unfamiliar with legal jargon.

Burt Greaves testified . . . . Shawna's attorney, Hensley, prepared and submitted to him, after the final settlement negotiation, the judgment of dissolution. Greaves approved it as to form. He acknowledged that during the negotiations, he and Hensley exchanged correspondence. When Greaves received the proposed judgment, he believed it represented the agreement the parties had reached . . . that Shawna's remarriage would be the event to trigger the sale. Greaves testified the remarriage of Theodore as a triggering event to sell the residence was "never discussed."

Hensley opined that he made an error when he drafted the judgment . . . that, throughout the entire negotiation as well as after the settlement, the issue of Theodore's remarriage triggering the sale was never raised . . . he would have counseled her not to sign the agreement if such a suggestion had been made.

The trial court concluded that Theodore read the agreement and signed it knowing what it stated . . . Shawna failed to prove that a mutual mistake occurred . . . her petition was denied. Shawna filed her post-trial motion to have the court vacate its denial . . . and a motion to amend her petition to include allegations of unilateral mistake accompanied by fraud. . . . Following a hearing the trial court granted Shawna's post-trial motion.

At the hearing on the amended petition, Theodore testified . . . that the document . . . is not reflective of the verbal agreement they reached . . . at no time did he ever propose to Hensley or Shawna that the house should be sold upon his remarriage . . . after the settlement conference, the parties had agreed that the house would be sold on the earliest of three things: (1) their agreement to sell the house; (2) their youngest child reaching 18 years of age; or (3) Shawna's remarriage.

The trial court concluded . . . the document . . . contained a scrivener's error. Neither of the attorneys noticed the error. Theodore did notice the difference, understood it, and signed the document despite knowing it was different than what had been verbally agreed upon. The court concluded . . . the agents of the parties made a mutual mistake of fact. The court granted Shawna's petition . . . Theodore filed his notice of appeal.

Theodore asserts the trial court erred in considering parol evidence relating to negotiations . . . [that] consideration of the letters between the attorneys prior to the final conference and the testimony of the witnesses as to what was agreed upon was improper since the agreement is unambiguous and the parties' intent must be gleaned solely from it.

Under the "parol evidence rule," if the instrument appears complete, certain, and unambiguous, then parol evidence of a prior or contemporaneous agreement is inadmissible to vary the terms of the instrument. (*Hartbarger v. SCA Services, Inc.* (1990), 200 Ill. App. 3d 1000, 1009, 558 N.E.2d 596, 601) It is well settled that the parol evidence rule is no bar to the admission of evidence on the question of mutual mistake, even when the instrument is clear and unambiguous on its face. Thus, parol evidence may be used to show the real agreement between the parties when a mistake has been made and the evidence is for the purpose of making the contract conform to the original intent of the parties. Parol evidence may be admissible to show the concerns of the parties prior to and contemporaneous with the signing of the written agreement.

A mutual mistake which may be established by parol evidence is a mistake common to both parties; thus, when there is a mutual mistake, the parties are in actual agreement but the agreement in its written form does not express the parties' real intent. Parol evidence is admissible to establish the fact of fraud or mistake. . . . When a mutual mistake or fraud is alleged, parol evidence is admissible to show the true intent and understanding of the parties.

The trial court properly considered parol evidence to show the real agreement between the parties and their intentions. . . . In order to entitle a party to reformation of a contract, he must show a mistake by both parties or a mistake by one party which is known and concealed by the other party. A "mutual mistake of fact" exists for purposes of the reformation of a written instrument, when the contract has been written in terms which violate the understanding of both parties. Shawna sustained her burden of proof to show a mutual mistake of fact by the parties. . . . Even Theodore agreed that at the conference, it was Shawna's marriage which would trigger the sale of the residence. . . . indicates that he was aware there was a mistake, and that the agreement reflected something that was not the agreement of the parties. . . . Affirmed.

13

Working with Contracts

In some situations, a law office has not been involved in negotiating or drafting a contract, but is only called upon to implement its provisions. A paralegal's ability to read and understand the contract is essential. The last chapter discussed the physical layout of a contract and the usual component parts. This chapter completes the process; students will learn the steps for implementing an executed contract and the process for assisting in the creation of a contract.

A. Incoming Contracts

Often, particularly if you work in a corporate law department, you will not be called upon to implement or litigate a contract drafted by someone else. That "someone" may be the opposing party or may be out of the picture and not available for consultation about ambiguities. Understanding the contract will require use of the skills and rules learned in the last chapter and knowledge of how a contract is negotiated and drafted.

A paralegal working in contract compliance or implementation or even in contract litigation should have a system for dealing with the contract at issue (see Exhibit 13-1).

EXHIBIT 13-1
Checklist for Incoming Contracts

a. Make work copies that you, the lawyer, and others can mark up. Do **not** unstaple the original; keep it, in pristine condition, in a safe place.

b. Read the contract, making notes as needed, especially concerning ambiguities, issues with regulatory agencies, and discuss those with your supervisor.

c. Identify important dates and actions. If you are implementing the contract, look for dates for matters such as required notices. Enter the dates and actions on your (and your firm's) calendar or docket, giving yourself enough advance warning before each date requiring action. Enter other parties' obligations too, to monitor compliance. Update as needed. If you are assisting in litigation, make a timeline of required dates as stated in the contract and dates on which the parties acted.

UCC Search
Activity conducted to find security interests in personal property that have been recorded under UCC Article 9

d. Obtain documents on the status of the businesses involved (e.g., certified copies of formation documents).

e. Note all requirements involving outsiders. If implementing a contract, place or calendar orders; if litigating, verify compliance and obtain copies, e.g.:
   1. Title search
   2. Certificates of insurance
   3. Copies of business licenses
   4. Survey
   5. Inspections/environmental disclosures
   6. Loan payoff documents
   7. **Uniform Commercial Code (UCC) search**
   8. Any other agency approvals

Escrow
Account held for the benefit of others, into which parties typically deposit documents, instructions, and funds for a transfer of property

Assignment
Transfer of interest in property or some right (contractual entitlement) to another

f. If implementing a contract, list documents you will create and begin work, e.g., escrow instructions, financial settlement statements, deeds, **assignments** . . . If litigating a contract, obtain copies of those documents if they have been created.

EXHIBIT 13-1
(continued)

---

g. Start a "closing binder" or "trial notebook" or an equivalent file so that all of the documentation can be found easily.

> A UCC search is conducted to find security interests in personal property that have been recorded under UCC Article 9. For example, bank gives a builder a loan to buy an expensive backhoe. The bank files a **UCC financing statement** (a lien), typically with the Secretary of State, listing the builder as debtor and the backhoe as collateral. If the builder tries to sell the backhoe, the UCC filing will show the buyer that the bank has a right to collect what it is owed from the proceeds of sale. If the builder tries to borrow more money using that same backhoe as security, the filing shows the new lender that at least part of the value of the backhoe belongs to another lender. When builder pays off the loan, the bank will file a release and the property will be free and clear. Lenders protect financial interests through UCC filings on consumer goods, commercial and farm equipment and products, fixtures, public-finance transactions, manufactured homes, timber to be cut and as-extracted minerals. This is discussed further in other chapters.
>
> Escrow: an account held by an individual or company (e.g., bank or title company) into which parties deposit documents and funds for a transfer of property (e.g., money, mortgage, promissory note, escrow instructions, a financial breakdown). When funding is complete and all required documents are in place, the escrow agent records the deed and disburses funds to the seller.
>
> Assignment: the transfer of an interest in property or some right (such as contract benefits) to another; for example, a building lease might be assigned to the new owner of the tenant business.

UCC Financing Statement Evidence that property is security for debt, typically filed with the Secretary of State

---

B. Creating a Contract

1. Negotiations

A lawyer is in the best position to serve the client when the lawyer is given the opportunity to participate in negotiation and draft the contract. Paralegals are often involved in contract negotiations and must be especially careful to avoid overstepping the invisible line and "practicing law." With that limitation in mind, however, many lawyers would be lost without the assistance of a paralegal to keep the process and the results organized. Organization is particularly important and difficult when several contracts are being negotiated for a single transaction or when a single contract has multiple parties. You may need to keep a chart or spreadsheet to keep track of the details. Some additional ideas are as follows:

- Start getting organized by creating a **checklist of provisions** typically included in a contract of the type you will be working with. You can look at formbooks (discussed later in this chapter) and samples (from your supervisor or your client) to create a checklist.
- If your supervising attorney has not done so, you can use the checklist to **interview the client** and gain a thorough understanding of the client's goals and intentions, timeline, and the "chain of approval"[1] for the contract. You can also use the formbooks or client interview to start to learn the terminology that may be unique to the particular type of business involved.
- Locate and become familiar with statutes and regulations applicable to the parties or transaction and, if the contract involves a governmental entity, with laws such as the Truth in Negotiations Act, 10 U.S.C. 2304, and governmental cost accounting guidelines.
- **Organize** the provisions into an outline of related topics, *e.g., Duties and Conditions; Breach and Remedies; Enforcement.* This will be the framework for negotiation and drafting.
- Maintain your own **form file**; keep a copy of every contract you work on, to serve as a reference for what works and what does not work.
- Perhaps 95% of all contracts now originate in an electronic format and many of those are never printed. This can lead to sloppiness in keeping track of what is the most current version of the agreement. Even if the contract is printed, it is important to keep **track of its evolution**. Use the **redlining** or **track changes** feature in your word processing software and make sure every new draft is dated.
- If the document is being sent back and forth by e-mail, you may want to "lock" the document you send so that **changes cannot escape your attention**. Some word processing programs have a lock feature; some firms send drafts as PDF-format read-only files.
- You can also use the "merge and track changes" feature in word processing software to compare the version of a contract you sent with the version you got back. Being aware of changes and additions is particularly important with contracts governed by the UCC because of the battle-of-the-forms rule.
- Review the language of any letters of intent or "agreements in principle" exchanged during negotiations with the supervising attorney to ensure that the client does not inadvertently create unwanted obligations.

Redline
Feature in word processing software that enables changes in a document to be tracked

2.   Drafting: Forms and Boilerplate

In preparing a contract, most lawyers and paralegals start with a form, a sample of a contract prepared by someone else. Forms can be found in formbooks in any

---

[1] In a business setting, it is common for mid-level employees to negotiate a contract, but people "up the chain of command" may have to approve and/or execute the contract.

law library, can be purchased in office supply stores (landlords frequently buy single-page form leases), and online. The important thing to remember is that a form is just a starting point. There is no such thing as "one size fits all" in law. A form can provide you with a checklist, to help you be sure you haven't overlooked anything, and can suggest particular wording, but if you do nothing but fill in blanks, you are committing malpractice. You need to read every word and ask whether it applies to the situation and whether it is good or bad for your client and make appropriate deletions, additions, and changes. Even with a printed form from an office supply store, you can and must cross out terms you don't like and insert new terms.

Most forms contain **boilerplate**, or standard terms that are included in every contract. Even boilerplate must be analyzed to determine whether it benefits or hurts the client. Common boilerplate clauses include statements concerning the law that will apply in the event of litigation (Illinois? California?), that terms should be read so that a male reference includes females and that singular includes plural (would the client want this if the contract is intended to provide a special benefit to a particular person?), or that in the event that one part of the contract is found to be invalid, the rest of the contract shall remain in effect (this is called a **severability clause** or a **saving clause** and *may not* be what the client wants).

Boilerplate
Standard terms included in most contracts

Severability Clause
Contract provision that in the event that one part of the contract is found to be invalid, the rest of the contract shall remain in effect

---

Example: Severability Clause

If any provision of this Agreement is held unenforceable by any court of competent jurisdiction, then such provision will be severed or modified to reflect the parties' intentions. All remaining provisions of this Agreement shall remain in full force and effect.

Assignment 13-1

Find an online source of legal forms and report to the class the cost of a typical form, whether you were able to determine who prepared the form, and whether the forms appeared to be useful.

The language used in a contract must have the precise level of specificity needed to communicate the intentions of the parties. To achieve that level of specificity, you must become familiar with the rules of contract interpretation, discussed in the previous chapter, and some writing guidelines. As you start to choose or write the individual paragraphs in the contract, remember KISS — keep it short and simple.

a. *Characteristics of a Good Contract*

A good contract is:

Well-Organized and Easy to Read

    a. Related matters should be kept together.
    b. Sections, and sometimes even paragraphs, should have headings so that people attempting to find specific provisions can do so easily.
    c. If the contract is long, it should have an index.
    d. There should be no big blocks of print or extremely long sentences. If necessary, break subjects into sub-topics or bullet points to ensure **visual accessibility**.

Thorough in Identifying Actors, Consequences, and Remedies

    e. Every required action should identify the party required to take that action.
    f. The contract should address the "who, what, when, where, why, and how" of each obligation of each party. As you know, contract law is "default law." The law will fill in any details not covered in the contract, perhaps to the detriment of your client. If a contract states that a person should do, or not do, something, it should also state what will happen if that person does not comply with the contract. Look at every provision and ask yourself, what if this does not happen?

Internally Consistent

    g. A well-written contract never contains contradictory terms. Carefully read the contract as if you were the opposing party, looking for inconsistency and holes.
    h. Make sure that the numbering system for paragraphs and sections makes sense, is consistent, and that references remain correct as the contract goes through changes during negotiations.

Clear

    i. Keep in mind that the parties often try to comply with the requirements of the contract without the benefit of legal advice. The contract should be understandable to the average person, who was not present during negotiations and who may not like the agreement.
    j. People who are obligated by the terms of a contract may be looking for any possible excuse to avoid that obligation. Again, test the contract by putting yourself in the position of the opposing party and looking for any ambiguities that might give you a "loophole."

The proper use of formbooks and checklists (such as the ABC checklist that follows) will help you produce contracts that are well organized and thorough. To ensure that your contract is clear and does not include loopholes, avoid legalese and other writing problems described below.

b. Formbooks and Checklists

Formbooks and boilerplate are useful because they make you consider and address matters that the client probably did not consider or mention. Get in the habit of looking for (when reading a contract) or considering (when drafting a contract) (see Exhibit 13-2).

EXHIBIT 13-2

- **A**ssumptions; do recitals state the purpose and background of the agreement?
- **B**inding authority; who will sign, title and address of signatory, check status of any business entities and authority to bind the entity. Is notarization required?
- **C**hanges; when and how may the parties modify the agreement?
- **D**elegation/assignment; may parties **delegate** (pass contractual obligations to another) or assign (pass entitlements to another)?
- **E**xpress conditions; conditions precedent, subsequent (see consideration chapter).
- **F**inancing; liens, mortgages; are all payment amounts and terms clearly stated along with information about penalties, taxes, and interest?
- **G**uarantors, if any.
- **H**old harmless/indemnification; is a party agreeing to reimburse for losses suffered as a consequence of specific conduct?
- **I**ntegration; is this the entire agreement, or are there outside documents?
- **J**oint and several liability?
- **K**in (ok, it's a stretch); is the agreement binding on heirs, successors?
- **L**imitations on liability, limitations/standards for performance, *e.g.*, if landlord shall pay tenant's moving expenses in the event of early termination, is there any limit on the expense?
- **M**itigation (see Remedies chapter); are parties required to "cut losses" in the event of breach?
- **N**on-competition/restrictive covenants (see legality chapter) confidentiality clauses and trade secrets.
- **O**wnership and risk of loss; who holds title to subject property at various stages? *E.g.*, if a buyer is making installment payments, at what point does buyer become owner?

Delegation
Pass contractual obligations to another

EXHIBIT 13-2
(continued)

- **P**erfect performance; to what extent can performance deviate from specifications? Are all performance terms, such as quantity and descriptions, unambiguously stated?
- **Q**ueries and notices; where are inquiries and notices sent? Under what circumstances must a party provide the others with notice of specific events?
- **R**emedies; does every possible breach have a remedy? Liquidated damages? Is ADR required? Is mediation or arbitration in client's best interest; where will it occur; how will arbitrator be chosen; do parties retain right to go to court?
- **S**everability; is this an "all or nothing" deal?
- **T**ime; is time "of the essence," or are delays acceptable? Are all dates clearly stated?
- **U**sage of terms; are terms used in ways different than generally understood?
- **V**enue, Jurisdiction; in case of litigation, and choice of governing law.
- **W**arranties; Review UCC implied warranties that may arise if not disclaimed and consider express warranties that client may want or give.
- E**X**cuses; on what grounds will the contract terminate, *e.g.*, death, bankruptcy?
- **Y**ield; if contract involves money that may earn interest, stock that may earn a dividend, or property that may earn rent; does the contract address the issue?

Assignment 13-2

Warranty and risk terms are particularly critical in contracts involving sales of goods. Visit your state's enactment of the UCC and find the provisions concerning warranties.

- ◆ Explain, in your own words, what is meant by the implied warranty of merchantability.
- ◆ How can a seller exclude the warranty of merchantability?
- ◆ Under what circumstances does a warranty of fitness for a particular purpose arise?
- ◆ List the ways that an express warranty may be created.

Now, find the "risk of loss" provisions relating to shipping.

- ◆ Explain, in your own words, what is meant by the abbreviations FOB and FAS.

◆ What does the UCC assume if the parties do not address the risk of loss during shipment?

Use computer-assisted legal research (CALR) to find and summarize, for class discussion, a case from your jurisdiction involving one of the UCC implied warranties.

As you probably know, jobs appropriate for people with paralegal credentials do not always have the title "paralegal" or "legal assistant," particularly when those jobs are within corporations. Use a job search site and report to the class about jobs described as contract compliance, contract administration, or contract manager.

---

c. Legalese

Legalese
Overly formal, often archaic language sometimes used in legal documents

While some legal terms have unique meaning, many are simply pompous and confusing. Before you use "legalese," ask yourself whether the term could be replaced with a plain English word without losing unique meaning. Also ask yourself whether you understand the term and never use a term you do not understand.

Examples

Terms with Unique Meaning
Consideration
Delegate
Assign
Severable
Financing Statement

Pompous Legalese
Party of the First Part
Hereinafter
Aforementioned
Forthwith
Thence
Heretofore
Herewith
Hereby

---

d. Active Voice

Active Voice
The subject of the sentence acts

Passive Voice
Subject is acted upon

With active voice, the subject of the sentence acts: "The builder shall obtain liability insurance before beginning construction." With **passive voice**, the subject is acted upon: "Liability insurance shall be obtained before construction begins." Active voice usually makes sentences shorter and easier to understand. More importantly, active voice may clarify expectations. If the passive voice example appeared in a contract, isn't it possible that both the builder and the owner would assume that the other party is responsible for obtaining insurance? The result might be catastrophic — no insurance.

e. Parallel Construction

Each phrase within a sentence should follow the same grammatical structure. Not parallel: "The employee's responsibilities shall include: identification of new potential customers; training support staff; and to minimize loss." Parallel: "The employee's responsibilities include: identifying new potential customers; training support staff; and minimizing loss."

f. Sexism and the Plural Pronoun

A good writer consciously avoids sexist language, and, for example, will write "police officer" rather than "policeman," except when referring to a specific male individual. Sometimes, however, that good intentions can lead to bad grammar: "Every buyer must pick their own carpet." There are several ways to avoid the singular/plural problem. You could use the plural consistently: "All of the buyers must choose their own carpet" or switch to second person: "As a buyer, you must choose your carpet." Unless it changes the meaning, you could omit the pronoun: "Each buyer must choose carpet." You can also use "his or her" or "he or she" in moderation.

g. Misplaced Modifiers

"The employee must, at all times, keep a complete record of all customer contacts on his desk." Need the record include only those contacts kept on his desk? Sometimes two sentences are better than one: "The employee must keep a complete record of all customer contacts. The record must be available on the employee's desk at all times."

The employee in question undoubtedly understood what was meant in the first example. Consider, however, that the employee might not want to have understood it. The employee is now leaving to start his own business and wants to be able to claim he is not prohibited from having contact with his former employer's customers because they are not in the record.

h. Padding

Many of us learned bad habits in high school, when we padded our essays to reach the teacher's requirement for length. In law, despite the tradition of long, impenetrable documents, fewer words make for better writing. Verbosity often makes the contract harder to understand and less accurate.

Why do we see so many wordy, incomprehensible forms?

In ancient England, few people could read or write and paper was an expensive commodity. On those rare occasions when a person needed to reduce a matter to writing (writing a will or an important contract), a scrivener would prepare the document. The scrivener was paid on a "per word" basis and had a strong interest in writing: "I give, devise, bequeath, and convey to my son Brian, any and all interest I may have in my horse Nell or any other horse I may own at the time of my death," rather than "I give my horse to Brian." From this tradition evolved the forms we see today!

A common example of verbosity at its worst is the use of future tense: "Landlord shall have the right to inspect." If this "shall" be the case, when will it begin? It is simpler and more accurate to say, "Landlord has the right to inspect" or "Landlord may inspect." Similarly, it is simpler and clearer to say, "Tenant shall procure insurance," rather than "The parties agree that tenant shall procure insurance." Always proofread several drafts, trying to eliminate unnecessary words, phrases, and sentences.

Examples

Wordy	Better
Due to the fact that	because
At that point in time	then
In accordance with	under
File an action	sue
Subsequent to	after
Prior to	before
Written document	document
For the purpose of	to
In lieu of	instead
In spite of the fact that	although
With the exception of	except
With reference to	about
Afford an opportunity	allow
Have a tendency to	tend
Have an impact upon	affect

Assignment 13-3

Read the interview transcript in Appendix A. Using that transcript, do the following, as assigned by your instructor:

1. Using formbooks in a law library and on the Internet, find forms for contracts involving performers. It is best to use formbooks or sources

dedicated to legal forms, but even using a search engine, like Google, will produce results. For example, searching for "performers contracts" led to samples at

http://midhudson.org/program/PerformersContracts.htm

http://web.mit.edu/slp/money/pdf/oncampus_performercaterer.pdf

http://meetingsnet.com/religiousconferencemanager/mag/
    meetings_ stage_checklist_speaker/index.html

http://contracts.onecle.com/type/2.shtml

http://smallbusiness.findlaw.com/business-forms-contracts/
    contracts/industries/travel/index.html

2. Outline clauses that should be included in this contract, organized in a logical way, and information that will be needed, but was not obtained in the interview.

3. Pick clauses from the forms that meet this client's needs and put them together, according to your outline, making changes as needed to meet this client's needs

4. The paralegal in this scenario was not well prepared and allowed the client to steer the interview and, possibly, missed important information. A good way to prepare for an interview is to look at forms in advance. Other great online sources of forms: http://www.ilrg.com/forms/ and http://www.uslegalforms.com. Look at sample forms and prepare a list of questions to interview a client for one of the following. You may not find a sample for the exact situation, but looking at contracts for similar situations will help.

   a. A client is going to allow a college student to live in her house in exchange for 15 hours per week of child care.

   b. A client is going to provide hand-painted sweatshirts to a local gift store, which will sell them on behalf of the client. Before starting work on this, be sure you understand the definition of **consignment**.

   c. The client is your former co-worker, a paralegal who has decided to work free-lance (as an **independent contractor**) and wants a contract to present to the lawyers who will be using his services. Consider the ethical rules in deciding on topics.

5. Using the information below, concerning paralegal Susan, do the following, as assigned by your instructor:

   a. Prepare a checklist of issues to be addressed by the contract (in teams or individually).

   b. Negotiate specific terms (based on the checklist).

   c. Draft one or more of the specific provisions negotiated.

   d. Prepare a contract for Susan.

   e. Review and evaluate outlines, provisions, or contracts written by others, based on thorough coverage of issues, legal adequacy, ambiguity, mechanical errors (grammar, spelling, organization), and whether the work product too strongly favors one party.

   f. Write a "reflection" on the negotiation and drafting process and the strengths and weaknesses of their final product.

Consignment
An arrangement under which goods are placed for sale, but title does not transfer to the seller

Independent Contractor
One hired to undertake a specific project using his own methods (not an employee)

EXHIBIT 13-3
Meet the Client

Local Woman Honored for Charity Work

Susan L. Barrett, a paralegal with the Naperville firm of Kostelny, Hallock & Brown, was honored at a ceremony in Chicago on May 4, Law Day, for her work with the Pro Bono Center for Disability and Elder Law. Ms. Barrett, a graduate of University of Iowa and of the Elgin Community College Paralegal Program, is shown with federal judge Marvin Aspen. The Center, known as CDEL, provides free legal services to low-income senior citizens. Volunteers, like Ms. Barrett, conduct phone interviews with clients to obtain relevant information for review by volunteer attorneys. Ms. Barrett, whose husband is an accountant, has two young children and also volunteers with the Shop-With-A-Cop program.

* * *

After this article ran in Chicago-area newspapers, Ms. Barrett was contacted by a recruiter and urged to apply for the job described below. The company has offered her the job, at $62,000, which is more than she currently earns, but Susan has concerns about the long commute, missing her children's school events, and the amount of travel. The company is concerned about longevity. The company plans to invest substantial time and money in training Susan by sending her to seminars. In the last five years, three paralegals have left this job to work for competing businesses, which pay better but are unwilling to train. The company is willing to negotiate everything except salary, pension, and health benefits (pension and insurance are described in a booklet Susan received during the interview).

Job Overview	*Job Description*
Company: Xxxxxxxxxx	**Classification:** Full Time
Location: US-IL-Chicago	**Compensation:** $50,000 to $65,000 per year

---

EXHIBIT 13-3
(continued)

Job Overview	Job Description
Base Pay: 50,000 - 65,000/Yr	International corporation with busy Chicago office needs a corporate paralegal with international corporate governance experience. Ideal candidate will have the following experience: work with local counsel to prepare annual report filings and board meeting minutes in foreign countries; administer actions of the Board of Directors over foreign companies; maintain corporate records for foreign companies; create off-shore entities;other corporate governance issues as requested. Foreign travel required.
Type: Full-Time Employee	
Industry: Legal	
Mgmt: No	
Job Type: Professional Services Legal	
Req'd Ed: Paralegal degree/cert	College degree and/or paralegal certificate required.
Req'd Exp: 3+ years	Candidate must have 3+ years of corporate experience.
Req'd Travel: Yes	If you are interested in this opportunity, please contact xxxxxxxxxxxx

---

C. Ethical and Practical Issues

Paralegals and lawyers have unique ethical concerns in contract negotiation. Paralegals and their supervising attorneys must be careful that the paralegal's role does not "cross the line" into unauthorized practice of law. While the line is not clear, some states are making efforts to give lawyers and their assistants more guidance, so that lawyers can make more efficient use of paralegals and keep costs down. For example, the Indiana Rules of Professional Conduct include a special section on Use of Non-Lawyer Assistants (http://www.in.gov/judiciary/rules/prof_conduct/).

Assignment 13-4

Discuss the following fact situations. If your state has a good definition of unauthorized practice of law, use that definition. Otherwise, you may want to visit the Indiana State Bar Association site (http://www.inbar.org/content/news/article.asp?art = 197).

◆ Paul Paralegal is a "contract specialist" for a large corporation. The corporation does not have a legal department or a lawyer on staff. Paul's job includes ordering supplies from various companies. In doing so, Paul negotiates terms, chooses an appropriate contract from several forms in his files, fills in blanks and sometimes writes his own language, and sends the contract to his boss for signature. Is this the unauthorized practice of law?

◆ Pam Paralegal works for a law firm that specializes in debt collection. She communicates with debtors by phone and mail in an effort to obtain payments. The firm gives her wide discretion. For example, a debtor may owe $10,000; Pam can negotiate with the debtor and can accept a payment of as little as half of the original debt without consulting her supervisor. Pam is motivated to obtain the highest possible payment because she is paid a percentage of what she brings in. Is Pam involved in unauthorized practice of law? Do you see any other ethical problems? Do you think there might be other laws involved?

While prohibitions on unauthorized practice indicate that the lawyer must have ultimate responsibility for the contract, even the lawyer does not have complete authority and must act on the client's decisions.

Assignment 13-5

Use your bookmarked state ethics site. Attorney Al has been negotiating a contract for Chris Client, who is selling a business. The negotiations have not gone well. This morning the opposing party called Al with an offer that was so bad it was insulting. Al does not even want to waste time telling Chris about the offer; Al is concerned that Chris will become upset or angry. May Al simply reject the offer without contacting Chris?

Review Questions

1. What are the four most important characteristics of the body of a contract?
2. How is a UCC search conducted?
3. What is an escrow arrangement?
4. How can a paralegal keep track of changes made to drafts of a contract during the negotiation process? How can a paralegal ensure that the other side does not make changes that go unnoticed?
5. Give examples of typical boilerplate clauses.
6. What is a severability clause?
7. What is the most helpful function of forms and formbooks?
8. Why is it especially important to know the warranty provisions of the UCC when you are working with a contract that is subject to the UCC? Would it be sufficient to simply omit any unwanted warranties from the written contract?

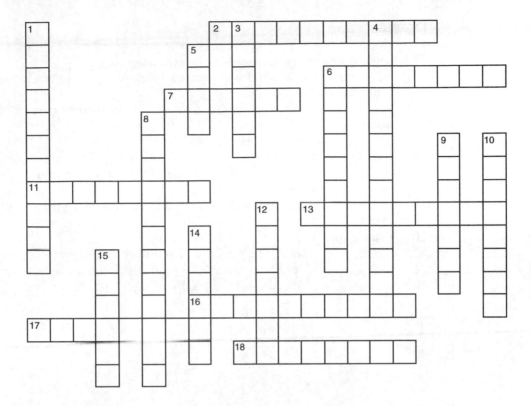

ACROSS

2. passing on contractual obligations
6. a contract that is to be _____ generally must be notarized
7. a UCC _____ is done to determine whether there are liens against personal property
11. pompous and confusing language
13. a UCC _____ statement is filed to make a public record of personal property being used as collateral
16. passing along your contractual entitlements
17. a misplaced _____ can change the meaning of a sentence
18. paragraphs at the beginning, giving background to contract

DOWN

1. standard language common to most contracts
3. an account into which documents and money are deposited to complete a transaction
4. _____ by reference makes an outside document part of the contract
5. another term for a security interest
6. tracking changes as a document is negotiated
8. a _____ clause addresses whether the rest of the contract remains valid if part is found to be invalid
9. _____ term, a shorthand way for reference to a person, place, or event
10. proper spelling, order entered by a judge
12. _____ voice, the subject is acted upon
14. a _____ public may witness a signature, authenticate a document
15. _____ voice is best for legal writing

CASE FOR ANALYSIS

CINCINNATI BAR ASSOCIATION v. CROMWELL
SUPREME COURT OF OHIO

82 Ohio St. 3d 255; 695 N.E.2d 243
March 25, 1998, Submitted June 24, 1998, Decided

ON FINAL REPORT OF THE BOARD OF COMMISSIONERS ON THE UNAUTHORIZED PRACTICE OF LAW OF THE SUPREME COURT OF OHIO, NO. UPL 96-3.

On August 1, 1996, relator, Cincinnati Bar Association, filed a complaint alleging that respondent, Elwood L. Cromwell III of Cincinnati, Ohio, although not licensed to practice law in any state or other jurisdiction of the United States, and not registered as an attorney at law with the Supreme Court of Ohio, had rendered legal services for others and therefore was engaged in the unauthorized practice of law. After respondent answered, the matter was submitted to the Board of Commissioners on the Unauthorized Practice of Law of the Supreme Court of Ohio ("board") on stipulated facts.

Respondent, a resident of Cincinnati, had never received a license to practice law in any jurisdiction and is not registered as an attorney with the Supreme Court of Ohio. During 1994 and part of 1995, respondent conducted a business under the name Paralegal Service Group, which operated without the supervision of an attorney. In May 1994, Dawn Brown engaged respondent and paid him a retainer of $50, with an additional $200 to be paid upon settlement, to pursue her claim against an insurance company arising out of an automobile accident. Respondent then wrote to State Farm Insurance Company, stating that he had been retained to negotiate a settlement for Brown and that he hoped it would not be necessary to turn the case over to an attorney for further legal action. He also wrote to Sports Therapy, Inc., presumably a creditor of Brown, to advise it that he was negotiating a settlement for Brown, and in September 1994, he drafted a settlement agreement with respect to the matter. Then Brown fired respondent and he refunded her retainer.

In January 1995, Calvin Ward engaged respondent to represent him with respect to a motor vehicle accident and paid him a retainer of $50. On Ward's behalf, respondent contacted the Windsor Group, an insurance company, with respect to a settlement. Respondent also received referrals from other individuals to retain him as their representative with respect to personal injury claims, and to review correspondence related to divorce.

The board concluded that respondent's actions, including communicating with insurance companies on behalf of Brown and Ward, and communicating with a creditor and preparing a settlement agreement on Brown's behalf, constituted the unauthorized practice of law in Ohio. The board recommended that respondent be prohibited from engaging in such practices in the future.

Per Curiam. We adopt the findings and conclusions of the board. As the board correctly noted, the practice of law includes representing others with regard to their causes of action for personal injury, communicating with insurance companies about claims, making representations to creditors on behalf of third parties, and advising persons of their rights, and the terms and conditions of settlement *Cincinnati Bar Assn. v. Fehler-Schultz (1992), 64 Ohio St. 3d 452, 597 N.E.2d 79; Stark Cty. Bar Assn. v. George (1976), 45 Ohio St. 2d 267, 74 Ohio Op. 2d 425, 344 N.E.2d 132.* Not having been registered to practice law in Ohio, respondent, by his actions, was engaged in the unauthorized practice of law in Ohio. Respondent is hereby enjoined from engaging in any further activities that might constitute the unauthorized practice of law. Costs taxed to respondent. *Judgment accordingly.*

Appendix A

◆ ◆ ◆

Sample Client Interview
for Assignment

◆ ◆ ◆

Marty Gupta has been Attorney Janna Hart's client for many years. Two years ago Marty formed a corporation, M.G., Inc., that bought and remodeled a building in Elgin, Your State, to operate a café. The café, Marty's Place, has been very successful and Marty now wants to offer entertainment on some evenings. Marty made an appointment to discuss creation of a contract form. Ms. Hart had an emergency court call on another matter and asked her paralegal, Guillermo, to handle the interview. This is a transcript; Guillermo is identified as G and Marty is M.

G: Marty Gupta? Hi, I'm Guillermo Ruiz; please call me Bill. I'm going to talk to you about what you need in your contract.

M: Hi. Are you the new lawyer? I expected to see Janna.

G: No, I'm Janna's paralegal. Janna had an emergency and didn't want you to have to wait on this.

M: Paralegal? Are you a law student?

G: No, I graduated from a paralegal program. I assist Janna with research and putting together information and I work on documents. I won't be taking Janna's place as your legal advisor. Today I am just going to get the basic information about what you want and then I will pull together a few forms and we can start the process. It will be Janna who gives you the finished work and tells you how to use it. Having me today actually saves you money. I know you already have our fee sheet. The hourly rate for talking to me is about half the hourly rate for Janna (grinning) so you might want to see more of me!

M: (laughing) You have a point about that!

G: So, tell me what kind of contract you need.

M: Well, you know my business, Marty's Café? It's just down the street.

281

G: Yes, I eat lunch there pretty often.

M: OK, that's where I've seen you before! Well, we are starting to get a pretty good evening crowd and I was thinking getting some entertainment on a regular basis on Fridays and Saturdays. Maybe sometimes a dance band or a DJ. We have some pretty good folk singers around here. I want to have a contract to use when I hire them. I am kind of worried about advertising, you know, spending the money, then having the act not show up or whatever. I looked into it and I have to figure it would cost me at least $500 for each date to advertise when I am having entertainment.

G: OK, So you want to make sure you have a firm commitment . . .

M: Right, these folks are artists, not business people, and they can be a little difficult. I also want to make sure they know they have to show up on time and can't leave early. Oh, another thing, I want to get the person I want or the band I want. I don't want them sending a friend instead.

G: Let me guess . . . you've already had a couple of acts in and had some problems.

M: You've got that right. One guy was supposed to play guitar and he got there and decided to do a comedy routine! Well that fell flat. Then another one, a woman, she spent most of the evening trying to sell a CD she recorded. We've had a couple of them show up drunk or maybe stoned and one almost started a fight with a customer.

G: That's incredible! You would think they'd want to make a good impression so they would be asked back.

M: Good impression . . . that is another thing. I don't want any of the guys showing up to do a show not wearing a shirt or shoes . . . and the women too . . . I did have one show up in a bikini top and a wrap skirt.

G: Wow. OK, what else concerns you?

M: Believe it or not, safety. That's an old wooden building, you know. We can't have them up there smoking or lighting candles or anything like that.

G: Got that. OK, now what is the deal with hiring these folks? Will it be long term? Might you have the same band for several weeks?

M: Not at all. I might ask an act back if it's good, but no guarantees. I want it clear that this is not like being hired for a job. One time deal, they pay their own taxes, whatever . . .

G: OK, so they are independent contractors and . . .

M: What is that?

G: An independent contractor is someone who is self-employed. You hire him to do some work for you, but he isn't your employee.

M: So, if I use that term, I am protected against all liability to these people? I don't want to be paying their hospital bills if they fall off the stage and don't have any insurance.

G: (shaking his head and smiling) Now you know nothing in law is that simple! There are a number of things we can do to try protect you from liability, and Janna is going to decide what will work best and go over that with you. I don't want to overstep my bounds here and start giving you legal advice. But don't worry; Janna will give some serious thought to your liability concerns.

M: Well, ok . . . but I am nervous. I do have some employees and I carry insurance for them, but these performers are different.

G: How does it work with paying them?

M: I don't want to pay them until after the performance. I can give them a check on the night they perform, after they are done. I am always there. Sometimes they want cash, but I can't guarantee that.

G: Do you ever give them a deposit up front?

M: Well, I never have. Not yet. I suppose I might have to if I wanted to get a group that is in demand. You know what? I don't want to do that. Hey, here is a question. What about the music they sing? Could I be sued if they were violating copyright or something?

G: I'll let Janna know you want to talk about that and consider it for the contract.

M: C'mon, just tell me. Could somebody sue me if one of these guys gets up and sings somebody else's music or, I dunno, copies a comedy routine? You know, what about these DJs? What kind of permission do they have to get to play the recordings if they do it as a business?

G: (laughing) Wow, you are a tough one! I'll do some research on that and have Janna get to you with an answer. So, back to the facts. You mentioned something about a stage. Do you have any equipment or lighting you provide?

M: Alright, I can see you won't crack under pressure (laughing). There are some can lights above the stage, but some of these folks bring their own. You should see some of the setups they have. Sometimes it takes them an hour to get ready and another to get it taken down.

G: Do you let them in early for that? Does it interfere with your business?

M: They can come early or stay late, but I don't pay for that time if it's hourly. Usually it's not hourly. Usually they just have a price. Some are hourly. Anyway, they can get the stuff in through the alley door. Actually, I have to insist on that. They sometimes don't like it because it involves using some steps. But they can't bring that stuff in through the dining room, where people are eating.

G: OK, that about covers it. I'll get to work on this and you can expect to hear from us in about a week.

Appendix B

◆ ◆ ◆

Franchise Agreement

◆ ◆ ◆

PETE'S "A" PIZZA, INC.
TABLE OF CONTENTS

XXIII.   ACKNOWLEDGMENTS
XXIV.   APPLICABLE LAW: VENUE

FRANCHISE AGREEMENT

THIS AGREEMENT ("Agreement") is made this _____ day of _____, 20____, by and between Pete's "A" Pizza, Inc., a Delaware corporation, having its principal place of business at 1700 Spartan Drive, Elgin IL 60123 ("Franchisor") and _____, [jointly and severally if more than one], ("Franchisee").

Franchisor has developed and owns a unique and distinctive system ("System") for development and operation of retail pizza restaurants featuring proprietary pizza and related menu items developed by Franchisor;

Distinguishing characteristics of the System include, without limitation, the name "Pete's 'A' Pizza"; distinctive interior design and layout, decor, and furnishings; confidential food formulae and recipes used in the preparation of food products, specifications for baking pizzas and other items; specialized menus; standards and specifications for equipment, layout, products, operating procedures, and management programs, all of which may be changed, improved, and further developed by Franchisor from time to time;

Franchisor identifies the System by means of trade names, service marks, trademarks, logos, emblems, and other indicia of origin, including, but not limited to, the mark "Pete's 'A' Pizza", the symbol reproduced on Exhibit A, attached hereto, and such other trade names, service marks, trademarks and trade dress as are now, or may hereafter, be designated by Franchisor for use in connection with the System (collectively, "Marks");

Franchisor continues to develop, use, and control the Marks in order to identify for the public the source of services and products marketed thereunder and to represent the System's high standards of quality, appearance, and service;

Franchisee desires to be assisted, trained, and licensed by Franchisor as a franchisee and licensed to use the System and to continuously operate one Pete's "A" Pizza at a location specified in Section 1.01 herein ("Franchised Location");

Franchisee understands the importance of the System and high and uniform standards of quality, cleanliness, appearance, and service, and the necessity of opening and operating Pete's "A" Pizza in conformity with the System;

THEREFORE, the parties hereto agree as follows:

I. GRANT OF FRANCHISE

1.01. Franchisor grants to Franchisee a franchise to open and operate a Pete's "A" Pizza, ("Franchised Unit"), at one location only: _____ upon terms and conditions contained in this Agreement and a license to use in connection therewith Franchisor's Marks and System. Franchisee may not operate the Franchised Unit at any site other than the Franchised Location.

1.02. Except as otherwise set forth herein, (a) the franchise granted to Franchisee is non-exclusive, and grants to Franchisee the right to establish and operate the Franchised Unit at only the specific location set forth hereinabove, (b) no exclusive, protected or other territorial rights in the contiguous area or market of such Franchised Unit or otherwise is hereby granted or to be inferred and (c) Franchisor has the right to operate and grant as many other franchises, anywhere in the world, as it shall, in its sole discretion, elect.

Franchisee acknowledges that, over time, Franchisor has entered, and will continue to enter, into franchise agreements with other franchisees that may contain provisions, conditions and obligations that differ from those contained in this Agreement. The existence of different forms of agreement and the fact that Franchisor and other franchisees may have different rights and obligations does not affect the parties' duty to comply with the terms of this Agreement.

II. DURATION

2.01. Except as otherwise provided in this Agreement, the initial term of this Franchise Agreement (the "Term") shall expire on the fifth (10th) anniversary of the date of commencement of operation of the Franchised Unit. The date of commencement of operation of the Franchised Unit shall be the date verified by Franchisor and delivered to Franchisee in using the "Notice" form attached as Exhibit "A". Franchisee shall operate the Franchised Unit and perform hereunder for the full Term of this Agreement.

2.02. Franchisee may, at its option, renew this franchise for two (2) additional periods of five (5) years each, provided that, at the time of each renewal:

A. Franchisee gives Franchisor written notice of such election to renew not less than six (6) months nor more than twelve (12) months prior to the end of the then-current term. Failure by Franchisee to timely provide Franchisor the required notice constitutes a waiver by Franchisee of its option to remain a franchisee;

B. Franchisee executes Franchisor's then-current standard form of franchise agreement, which may include, without limitation, a higher royalty fee and a higher advertising contribution, if any, than that contained in this Agreement; and the term of which shall be the renewal term as specified in Section 2.20, but shall contain no further renewal rights;

C. Franchisee is not in default under this Agreement or any other agreements between Franchisee and Franchisor (or any affiliate of Franchisor), and Franchisee has fully and faithfully performed all of Franchisee's obligations throughout the term of this Agreement; Franchisee is not in default beyond the applicable cure period under any real estate lease, equipment lease or financing instrument relating to the Franchised Unit; Franchisee is not in default beyond the applicable cure period with any vendor or supplier to the Franchised Unit; and, Franchisee shall not have been in default beyond the applicable cure period under this Agreement or any other agreements between Franchisor and Franchisee more than 3 times during the period 12 months before the date;

D. Franchisee has paid or otherwise satisfied all monetary obligations owed by Franchisee to Franchisor and its subsidiaries and affiliates and any indebtedness of Franchisee which is guaranteed by Franchisor, and Franchisee has timely paid or otherwise satisfied these obligations throughout the term of this Agreement;

E. Franchisee agrees, at its sole cost and expense, to renovate, refurbish and modernize the Franchised Unit, within the time required by Franchisor, including design, equipment, signs, decor items, fixtures, furnishings, trade dress, color scheme, presentation of Marks, supplies and other products and materials to meet Franchisor's then-current standards, specifications and design criteria for Burger Barn, as contained in the then-current franchise agreement, Manual (as defined herein), or otherwise in writing, including, without limitation, such structural changes, remodeling and redecoration and such modifications to existing improvement as may be necessary to do so.

F. Franchisee executes a release and a covenant not to sue, satisfactory to Franchisor, of any and all claims against Franchisor and its subsidiaries and affiliates, respective past and present officers, directors, shareholders, agents and employees, in corporate and individual capacities, including, without limitation, claims arising under federal, state and local laws, rules and ordinances, and claims relating to, this Agreement, any other agreements between Franchisee and Franchisor and operation of the Franchised Unit.

G. Franchisee shall pay to Franchisor a renewal fee equal to fifty percent (50%) of Franchisor's standard initial franchise fee in effect at the date of renewal.

H. Franchisee and the Franchised Unit shall be in compliance with the then-current System training requirements.

I. Franchisee has the right to remain in possession of the Franchise Location, or other premises acceptable to Franchisor, for the Renewal Term and all monetary obligations owed to Franchisee's landlord must be current.

J. As determined by Franchisee in its sole discretion, Franchisee has operated the Franchised Unit in accordance with this Agreement and the System (as set forth in the Manual).

III. FEES

3.01. Franchisee shall pay to the Franchisor the following:

A. A franchise fee of _____ Dollars ($_____) payable upon execution of this Agreement by Franchisee. Such franchise fee shall be fully earned by Franchisor upon execution of this Agreement by Franchisee and is in addition to any development fees paid to Franchisor by Franchisee.

B. A recurring, non-refundable royalty fee of five percent (5%) of Gross Sales (defined herein) during the term of this Agreement, due on or before the tenth (10th) day of each of thirteen (13), four (4) week annual periods ("Periods") on the Gross Sales of the preceding Period (or on such other basis as may be set forth in the Manual). Upon thirty (30) days prior notice, Franchisor may require Franchisee to authorize Franchisor to make electronic debits from Franchisee's operating account to pay the royalty fee.

3.02. In addition to the payments provided for in Section 3.01 Franchisee, recognizing the value of advertising and the importance of standardized promotion to the goodwill and public image of the System, shall pay to the national creative and production fund (NCP Fund) a recurring, non-refundable contribution ("Contribution") an amount to be determined by Franchisor, in its sole discretion, not to exceed three percent (3%) of the Gross Sales of the Franchised Unit, payable on or before the tenth (10th) day of each Period, for the preceding Period (or on such other basis set forth in the Manual). Upon thirty (30) days written notice, Franchisor may require Franchisee to authorize Franchisor to make electronic debits from Franchisee's operating account as a means of paying the Advertising Fund Contribution. The Contribution shall be used by the NCP Fund for national, regional, and/or local advertising and promotional materials and market research for the System, under the following conditions and limitations:

A. The NCP Fund, all contributions thereto, and any earnings thereon, shall be used only to pay costs of maintaining, administering, directing, producing and preparing market research, advertising, marketing materials and/or promotional activities for the System. Franchisee shall pay the Contribution by separate check made payable to the NCP Fund. All sums paid by the Franchisee to the NCP Fund shall be maintained in an account separate from other funds of Franchisor and shall not be used to defray any of Franchisor's expenses except as provided herein, and as Franchisor may incur in activities reasonably related to the administration or direction of the NCP Fund and advertising and marketing programs for franchisees and the System. The NCP Fund and its earnings shall not otherwise inure to the benefit of Franchisor. Franchisor shall maintain a separate bookkeeping account for the NCP Fund. Franchisor, upon request, shall provide Franchisee with an annual accounting of receipts and disbursements of the NCP Fund.

B. Selection of media and locale for placement shall be at the sole discretion of Franchisor.

C. It is anticipated that all contributions to and earnings of the NCP Fund will be expended for market research, costs of creating and producing advertising materials, marketing and/or promotional purposes and reimbursement to Franchisor of costs directly related to the management of the NCP Fund (including personnel costs) during the taxable year in which contributions and earnings are received. If, however, excess amounts remain in the NCP Fund at the end of a taxable year, all expenditures in the following taxable year(s) shall be made first out of accumulated earnings from previous years, next out of earnings in the current year, and finally from contributions.

D. The NCP Fund is not, and shall not be, an asset of Franchisor. Although the NCP Fund is intended to be of perpetual duration, Franchisor maintains the right to terminate the NCP Fund; provided, however, that the NCP Fund shall not be terminated until all monies in the NCP Fund have been expended for the purposes stated herein.

E. Advertising and marketing are intended to maximize public awareness of Franchised Units and the System. Franchisor has no obligation to insure that any individual Franchisee benefits from placement of advertising or marketing in its local market. Franchisee acknowledges that its failure to derive any such benefit shall not be cause for nonpayment or reduction of the required contributions to the NCP Fund.

3.03. If any monetary obligations owed by Franchisee to Franchisor are more than seven (7) days overdue, Franchisee shall, in addition to such obligations, pay to Franchisor a sum equal to one and one-half percent (12%) of the overdue balance per month, or the highest rate permitted by law, whichever is less, from the date said payment is due.

3.04. "Gross Sales" means all revenues generated by Franchisee's business conducted upon, from or with respect to the Franchised Unit, whether such sales are evidenced by cash, check, credit, charge, account, barter or exchange. Gross Sales includes, without limitation, monies or credit received from sale of food and merchandise, from tangible property of every kind and nature, promotional or otherwise, and for services performed from or at the Franchised Unit, including without limitation such off-premises services as catering and delivery. Gross Sales does not include sale of food or merchandise for which refunds have been made in good faith to customers, sale of equipment used in the Franchised Unit, or sales, meals, use or excise tax imposed by a governmental authority directly on sales and collected from customers; provided that the amount of such tax is actually paid by Franchisee to such governmental authority.

3.05. Franchisee shall spend at least Three Thousand and No/100 Dollars ($3,000.00) for grand opening advertising of the Franchised Unit during the first two (2) months following its opening, which advertising must be approved, in advance, by Franchisor.

IV. ACCOUNTING AND RECORDS

4.01. Accurate Records. Franchisee shall maintain and preserve, for at least three years from the dates of preparation, full, complete and accurate books, records and accounts in accordance with generally accepted accounting principles and in form and manner prescribed by Franchisor from time-to-time in the Manual. The records shall include, without limitation, cash register sales tape (including non-resettable readings), tax returns, deposit slips and other evidence of Gross Sales and other business transactions.

4.02. Royalty Reports. Franchisee shall submit weekly reports on forms prescribed by Franchisor, accurately reflecting all Gross Sales during the preceding week and such other forms, reports, records, financial statements or information as Franchisor may reasonably require by the Manual, or otherwise in writing.

4.03. Quarterly Statement. Franchisee shall, at its expense, submit to Franchisor quarterly, within thirty (30) days following the end of each quarter during the Term hereof, an unaudited financial statement with such detail as Franchisor may reasonably require ("Quarterly Statement") together with a certificate executed by Franchisee stating that such financial statement is accurate. Upon Franchisor's request, Franchisee shall submit to Franchisor, with each Quarterly Statement, copies of state or local sales tax returns ("Tax Returns") filed by Franchisee for the period included in the Quarterly Statement. If Franchisee prepares financial statements on the basis of thirteen (13), four (4) week periods ("Periods"), the Quarterly Statements shall be submitted within thirty (30) days following the end of the third, sixth, ninth, and thirteenth Periods.

4.04. Annual Statements. Franchisee shall, at its expense, submit within ninety (90) days following the end of each calendar or fiscal year, an unaudited financial statement for the preceding calendar or fiscal year, together with a certificate executed by Franchisee certifying that such financial statement is accurate ("Annual Statements") and such other information in such form as Franchisor may reasonably require. Upon written request from Franchisor, the foregoing Annual Statement shall include both a profit and loss statement and a balance sheet, and shall be prepared in accordance with generally accepted accounting principles. If Franchisee defaults under this Agreement, Franchisor may require, upon written notice, that all Annual Statements submitted thereafter include a "Review Report" prepared by an independent Certified Public Accountant.

4.05. Other Reports. Franchisee shall also submit for review or auditing, such other forms, financial statements, reports, records, information and data as Franchisor may reasonably designate, in form and at times and places reasonably required by Franchisor, upon request and as specified from time-to-time in the Manual or otherwise in writing. If Franchisee has combined or consolidated financial information relating to the Franchised Unit with that of any other business, Franchisee shall simultaneously submit forms, reports, records and financial statements (including, but not limited to the Quarterly Statements and Annual Statements) which contain detailed financial information relating to the Franchised Unit, separate from the financial information of such other businesses. Franchisee authorizes all of its suppliers and distributors to release to Franchisor, upon Franchisor's request, any and all of its books, records, accounts or other information relating to goods, products and supplies sold to Franchisee and/or the Franchised Unit.

4.06. Equipment. Franchisee shall record all sales on cash registers or other point-of-sale equipment approved by Franchisor ("POS Equipment"). Franchisor has the free and unfettered right to retrieve any data and information from P.O.S. Equipment and computers as Franchisor, in its sole discretion, deems appropriate, with the telephonic cost of the retrieval to be borne by Franchisor, including electronically polling the daily sales, menu mix and other data of the Franchised Unit.

4.07. Right of Audit. Franchisor or its designated agents have the right at all reasonable times to audit, review and examine by any means, including electronically through the use of telecommunications devices or otherwise, at its expense, the books, records, accounts, and tax returns related to the Franchised Unit. If any such audit, review or examination reveals that Gross Sales have been understated in any report to Franchisor, Franchisee shall immediately pay to Franchisor the royalty fee and Contribution due with respect to the amount understated upon demand, in addition to interest from the date such amount was due until paid, at the rate of one and one-half percent (1.5%) per month. If any understatement exceeds two percent (2%) of Gross Sales as set forth in the report, Franchisee shall, in addition, upon demand, reimburse Franchisor for any and all costs and expenses connected with such audit, review or examination (including, without limitation, reasonable accounting and attorneys' fees). The foregoing remedies shall be in addition to any other rights and remedies Franchisor may have.

V. MARKS

5.01. The franchise granted to use Marks applies only to use in connection with the Franchised Unit at the location designated, and includes only such Marks as are designated or which may hereafter be designated, in the Manual or otherwise in writing as a part of the System (which may or may not be all of the

Marks pertaining to the System), and does not include any other mark, name, or indicia of origin of Franchisor now existing or which may hereafter be adopted or acquired by Franchisor.

5.02. Franchisee shall not use the Marks as part of Franchisee's corporate or other business name. Franchisee shall not hold out or otherwise use the Marks to perform any activity or incur any obligation or indebtedness in such manner as might, in any way, make Franchisor liable therefor, without Franchisor's prior written consent. Franchisee shall execute any documents and provide other assistance deemed necessary by Franchisor to obtain protection for the Marks or to maintain the continued validity of such Marks; and Franchisor may substitute different Marks for use in identifying the System and the franchised businesses operating thereunder, and Franchisee agrees to immediately substitute Marks upon receipt of written notice from Franchisor.

5.03. Franchisee acknowledges Franchisor's exclusive right to use the mark Pete's "A" Pizza for restaurant services, food products, building configuration, and other Marks of the System. Franchisee shall not to represent that it has any ownership in the Marks or the right to use the Marks except as provided in this Agreement. Franchisee's use of the Marks shall not create in its favor any right, title, or interest in the Marks, and all such use shall be for the benefit of Franchisor. Use of the Marks outside the scope of this license, without Franchisor's prior written consent, is an infringement of Franchisor's exclusive right. During the term of this Agreement and after the expiration or termination hereof, Franchisee shall not, directly or indirectly, commit an act of infringement or contest or aid in contesting the validity or ownership of Franchisor's Marks, or take any other action in derogation thereof.

5.05. Franchisee shall promptly notify Franchisor of any suspected infringement of, or challenge to, the validity of the ownership of, or Franchisor's right to use, the Marks. Franchisor has the right to control any administrative proceeding or litigation involving the Marks. If Franchisor undertakes the defense or prosecution of any litigation relating to the Marks, Franchisee agrees to execute any and all documents and to do such acts and things as may, in the opinion of counsel for Franchisor, be necessary to carry out such defense or prosecution. Except to the extent that such litigation is the result of Franchisee's use of the Marks in a manner inconsistent with the terms of this Agreement, Franchisor shall reimburse Franchisee for out of pocket costs in doing such acts and things, except that Franchisee shall bear the salary costs of its employees.

5.06. Franchisee's license with respect to the Marks is non-exclusive and Franchisor retains the right: To grant other licenses for the Marks, in addition to licenses already granted to franchisees; To develop and establish other franchise systems for the same, similar, or different products or services utilizing marks not now or hereafter designated as part of the System, and to grant licenses thereto, without providing Franchisee any right therein; and To establish other systems for the sale of similar or different products using the same or similar Marks, without providing Franchisee any right therein.

5.07. All goodwill associated with the System and identified by the Marks shall inure exclusively to the benefit of Franchisor and is the property of Franchisor, and upon expiration or termination of this Agreement or any other agreement, no monetary amount shall be assigned as attributable to any goodwill associated with any of Franchisee's activities in the operation of the Franchised Unit granted herein, or use of the Marks.

5.08. Because every detail of the System is important to Franchisee, Franchisor, and other franchisees in order to maintain high and uniform standards of quality and services, and hence to protect the reputation and goodwill of all of them, Franchisee covenants:

B. To adopt and use Marks licensed hereunder only as proscribed by Franchisor;

C. To observe reasonable requirements with respect to trademark registration notices as Franchisor may from time to time direct in the Manual or otherwise in writing.

5.09. In order to preserve the validity and integrity of the Marks and to assure that Franchisee is properly employing them in operation of the Franchised Unit, Franchisor or its agents may at any reasonable times inspect Franchisee's operations, premises, and Franchised Unit and make evaluations of services provided and products sold and used therein. Franchisee shall cooperate with Franchisor's representatives in such inspections and render such assistance to the representatives as may reasonably be requested.

VI. OBLIGATIONS OF CORPORATE OR PARTNERSHIP FRANCHISEE

6.01. If Franchisee, or any successor to or assignee of Franchisee, is a corporation, or limited liability company:

A. Franchisee shall furnish, upon execution or subsequent transfer of this Agreement, a copy of the Franchisee's Articles of Incorporation, Certificate of Incorporation, Bylaws and a list of shareholders showing the percentage interest of each, and shall thereafter promptly furnish a copy of any and all amendments or modifications thereto;

B. Franchisee shall promptly furnish, on a regular basis, with certified copies of such corporate records material to the Franchised Business as Franchisor may require from time to time in the Manual or otherwise in writing; and

6.02. If the Franchisee, or any successor to or assignee of Franchisee, is a partnership, limited partnership or limited liability partnership, Franchisee shall furnish, upon execution or transfer of this Agreement, a copy of Franchisee's Articles of Partnership, if any, and Partnership Agreement, and shall thereafter promptly furnish a copy of any and all amendments or modifications thereto.

VII. MANUAL

7.01. To protect the reputation and goodwill of Franchisor and the System and maintain uniform standards of operation under Franchisor's Marks, Franchisee shall conduct the Franchised Business in accordance with Franchisor's

Manual (all manuals created or approved for use in operation of the Franchised Business, and all amendments and thereto, the "Manual"). The Manual shall remain the sole property of Franchisor. Franchisee shall at all times treat the Manual, and information contained therein, as confidential, and shall use reasonable efforts to keep such information confidential. Franchisee shall not, without Franchisor's prior written consent, duplicate, copy, record, or otherwise make the Manual available to any unauthorized person or entity.

7.02. So that Franchisee may benefit from new knowledge information, methods and technology in the operation of the System, Franchisor may from time-to-time revise the Manual and Franchisee agrees to adhere to and abide by all such revisions.

7.03. Franchisee shall keep its copy of the Manual current and up-to-date, and in the event of dispute as to the contents of Franchisee's Manual, the terms of the master copy of the Manual maintained at Franchisor's home office, shall be controlling.

7.04. The Manual is intended to further the purposes of this Agreement, and is incorporated, by reference, into this Agreement. Except as otherwise set forth in this Agreement, in the event of a conflict between the terms of this Agreement and the terms of the Manual, the terms of this Agreement shall control.

VIII. TRAINING

8.01. Franchisee, a partner of Franchisee if Franchisee is a partnership, or a principal shareholder of Franchisee if Franchisee is a corporation, must complete, to Franchisor's satisfaction, the Orientation Program ("OP") prior to opening the first Franchise Unit operated by Franchisee. OP shall consist of five (5) days of workshops, seminars and pizzeria management training conducted at a training facility designated by Franchisor.

8.02. In addition to completing the OP, Franchisee (or a partner or principal shareholder of Franchisee), and two (2) designated management employees of Franchisee, must attend and complete, to Franchisor's satisfaction the Pete's management training program ("MTP"), prior to opening the Franchised Unit. MTP shall consist of four (4) weeks of in-store operations training at a facility designated by Franchisor (a "Certified Training Facility"). A management employee of Franchisee that successfully completes MTP, shall be certified by Franchisor as a "Certified Manager".

8.03. Franchisee shall maintain the number of Certified Managers designated by the Franchisor in the employ of the Franchised Unit, which in no event shall be less than two (2). If Franchisee or any Certified Manager ceases active employment at the Franchised Unit, Franchisee must enroll a qualified replacement in the MTP program within thirty (30) days of cessation of such individual's employment.

IX. DUTIES OF THE FRANCHISOR

9.01. Franchisor will make available to Franchisee standard plans and specifications to be used only in the construction of the Franchised Unit. No modification to or deviations from the standard plans and specifications may be made without the written consent of Franchisor. Franchisee shall obtain, at its expense, architectural and engineering services to prepare surveys, site and foundation plans, and to adapt the standard plans and specifications to local or state laws, regulations or ordinances. Franchisee shall bear the cost of preparing plans containing deviations or modifications from the standard plans.

9.02. Franchisor shall provide consultation and advice to Franchisee as Franchisor deems appropriate with regard to construction or renovation and operation of the Franchised Unit, building layout, furnishings, fixtures and equipment plans and specifications, employee selection and training, purchasing and inventory control and other matters as Franchisor deems appropriate. Franchisor will make available to Franchisee such continuing advisory assistance in the operation of the Franchised Business, in person or by electronic or written bulletins made available from time to time, as Franchisor may deem appropriate.

9.06. Franchisor will continue efforts to maintain high and uniform standards of quality, cleanliness, appearance and service at all Pete's "A" Pizza restaurants, to protect and enhance the reputation of the System and demand for the products and services of the System. Franchisor will establish uniform criteria for approving suppliers; make reasonable efforts to disseminate standards and specifications to prospective suppliers upon request by the Franchisee, provided that Franchisor may elect not to make available to prospective suppliers the standards and specifications for food formulae or equipment deemed by Franchisor to be confidential; and may conduct periodic inspections of the premises and evaluations of the products used and sold at the Franchised Unit.

X. DUTIES OF THE FRANCHISEE

Because every detail of the System is important to Franchisor, Franchisee and other franchisees in order to develop and maintain high and uniform operating standards, to increase demand for Pete's products and services, and to protect the reputation and goodwill of Franchisor, Franchisee agrees that:

10.01. Franchisee shall maintain, at Franchisee's expense, the premises of the Franchised Unit and fixtures, furnishings, signs, systems and equipment ("improvements") thereon or therein, in conformity with Franchisor's standards and image and make such additions, alterations, repairs, and replacements thereto (but no others, without prior written consent) as may be required by Franchisor, including but not limited to the following:

A. To keep the Franchised Unit in the highest degree of sanitation and repair, including, without limitation, such periodic repainting, repairs or replacement of impaired equipment, and replacement of obsolete signs, as Franchisor may reasonably direct;

B. To meet and maintain the highest governmental standards and ratings applicable to the operation of the Franchised Business;

C. At its sole cost and expense, to complete a full renovation, refurbishment and modernization of the Franchised Unit, within the time frame required by Franchisor, including design, equipment, signs, interior and exterior decor items, fixtures, furnishings, trade dress, color scheme, presentation of trademarks and service marks, supplies and other products and materials, to meet Franchisor's then-current standards, specifications and design criteria for, including without limitation, such structural changes, remodeling and redecoration and such modifications to existing improvements as may be necessary to do so (hereinafter, a "Franchised Unit Renovation"). Franchisee shall not be required to perform a Franchised Unit Renovation if there are less than three years remaining on the term of this Agreement and/or the lease for the premises occupied by the Franchised Unit. Nothing herein shall limit Franchisee's other obligations to operate the Franchised Unit in accordance with Franchisor's standards and specifications for the System including, but not limited to, the obligations set forth in this Section X.

10.02. Franchisee shall operate the Franchised Unit in conformity with such uniform methods, standards, and specifications as Franchisor may from time to time prescribe in the Manual or otherwise in writing, to insure that the highest degree of quality, service and cleanliness is uniformly maintained and to refrain from any deviation therefrom and from otherwise operating in any manner which reflects adversely on Franchisor's name and goodwill or on the Marks, and in connection therewith:

A. To maintain in sufficient supply, and use only such ingredients, products, materials, supplies, and paper goods as conform to Franchisor's standards and specifications, and to refrain from using non-conforming items, without Franchisor's prior written consent;

B. To sell or offer for sale only products and menu items that have been approved for sale in writing by Franchisor, meet Franchisor's uniform standards of quality and quantity and as have been prepared in accordance with Franchisor's methods and techniques for product preparation; to sell or offer for sale the minimum menu items specified in the Manual or otherwise in writing; to refrain from any deviation from Franchisor's standards and specifications for serving or selling the menu items, without Franchisor's prior written consent; upon thirty (30) days written notice from Franchisor, to sell or offer for sale only such beverages produced by Franchisor's Designated Beverage Supplier (as defined in Section 10.03 below); and to discontinue selling or offering for sale such items as Franchisor may, in its discretion, disapprove in writing at any time;

C. To use the premises of the Franchised Unit solely for conducting the business franchised hereunder, and to conduct no other business or activity thereon, whether for profit or otherwise, without Franchisor's prior written consent;

D. To keep the Franchised Unit open and in normal operation during such business hours as Franchisor may prescribe in the Manual or otherwise in writing;

E. To permit Franchisor or its agents, at any time during ordinary business hours, to remove from the Franchised Unit samples of any ingredients, products, materials, supplies, and paper goods used in the operation of the Franchised Unit, without payment therefor, in amounts reasonably necessary for testing by Franchisor or an independent laboratory, to determine whether such samples meet Franchisor's then-current standards and specifications. In addition to any other remedies it may have under this Agreement, Franchisor may require Franchisee to bear the cost of such testing if any such ingredient, products, materials, supplier or paper goods have been obtained from a supplier not approved by Franchisor, or if the sample fails to conform to Franchisor's specifications;

F. To purchase, install and construct, at Franchisee's expense, all improvements, furnishings, signs and equipment specified in the approved standard plans and specifications, and other furnishings, signs or equipment as Franchisor may reasonably direct from time to time in the Manual or otherwise in writing; and to refrain from installing or permitting to be installed on or about the premises of the Franchised Unit, without Franchisor's written consent, any improvements, furnishings, signs or equipment not first approved in writing as meeting Franchisor's standards and specifications;

G. To comply with all applicable federal, state and local laws, regulations and ordinances pertaining to the operation of the Franchised Business; and

H. Allow Franchisor and its agents to enter the premises of the Franchised Unit at any time during ordinary business hours to conduct inspections; cooperate with Franchisor's representatives in such inspections as they may reasonably request; and, upon notice from Franchisor or its agents, and without limiting Franchisor's other rights, take steps necessary immediately to correct deficiencies detected during any such inspection, including, without limitation, immediately desisting from the further use of any equipment, promotional materials, products, or supplies that do not conform with Franchisor's then-current specifications, standards, or requirements.

10.03. Franchisee shall purchase all ingredients, products, materials, supplies, and other items required in the operation of the Franchised Business which are or incorporate trade-secrets of Franchisor, as designated by Franchisor ("Trade-Secret Products") only from Franchisor or suppliers designated by Franchisor; and upon thirty days written notice that Franchisor has designated an exclusive beverage supplier for beverage products sold within the System ("Beverage Products"), Franchisee shall purchase all such Beverage Products only from Franchisor's designated beverage supplier ("Beverage Supplier").

10.04. Franchisee shall purchase all ingredients, products, materials, supplies, paper goods, and other items required for the operation of the Franchised Business, except Trade-Secret Products and Beverage Products, solely from suppliers who demonstrate, to the continuing reasonable satisfaction of Franchisor, the ability to meet Franchisor's reasonable standards and specifications for such items; who possess adequate quality controls and capacity to supply Franchisee's needs promptly and reliably; and who have been approved in writing by Franchisor and such approval has not been revoked. If Franchisee desires to purchase such items from an unapproved supplier, Franchisee shall submit a request for approval, or shall request the supplier to seek approval. Franchisor shall have the right to require, as a condition of approval, that its representatives be permitted to inspect the supplier's facilities, and that samples from the supplier be delivered, at Franchisor's option, either to Franchisor or to an independent laboratory designated by Franchisor for testing prior to granting approval. A charge not to exceed Franchisor's reasonable cost of inspection and the actual cost of testing shall be paid by the supplier or Franchisee. Franchisor reserves the right, at its option, to reinspect the facilities and products of any such approved supplier from time to time and to revoke its approval upon failure of such supplier to continue to meet any of the foregoing criteria.

10.05. Franchisor disclaims all express or implied warranties concerning any approved products or services, including, without limitation, any warranties as to merchantability, fitness for a particular purpose, availability, quality, pricing or profitability. Franchisee acknowledges that Franchisor may, under appropriate circumstances, receive fees, commissions, field-of-use license royalties, or other consideration from approved suppliers based on sales to franchisees, and that Franchisor may charge non-approved suppliers reasonable testing or inspection fees.

10.06. All local advertising by Franchisee shall be in such media, and of such type and format as Franchisor may approve; shall be conducted in a dignified manner; and shall conform to standards and requirements as Franchisor may specify. Franchisee shall not use any advertising or promotional plans or materials until Franchisee has received written approval, pursuant to the procedures and terms set forth in Section 10.07.

10.07. All advertising and promotional plans proposed to be used by Franchisee, except plans and materials that have been previously approved, shall be submitted for written approval (except with respect to prices) prior to use. Franchisor shall use its best efforts to complete its review of proposed advertising and promotional plans within fifteen (15) days after Franchisor receives such plans. If approval is not within fifteen (15) days after receipt by Franchisor of plans, Franchisor shall be deemed to have disapproved.

10.08. Franchisee shall, at Franchisor's request, require all of its supervisory employees, as a condition of their employment, to execute an agreement prohibiting them, during the term of their employment or thereafter, from communicating, divulging, or using for the benefit of any person, persons, partnership, association, corporation or other entity any confidential information, trade secrets, knowledge, or know-how concerning the System or methods of operation of the Franchised Unit which may be acquired as a result of their employment with Franchisee or other franchisees. A duplicate original of each such agreement shall be provided by Franchisee to Franchisor immediately upon execution.

XI. INSURANCE

11.01. Insurance Program. Franchisee shall procure and maintain, at Franchisee's expense, an insurance policy or policies protecting Franchisee and Franchisor, and their officers, directors, agents and employees, against any loss, liability, or expense whatsoever from personal injury, death or property damage or casualty, including, fire, lightning, theft, vandalism, malicious mischief, and other perils normally included in an extended coverage endorsement arising from, occurring upon or in connection with the construction, operation or occupancy of the Franchised Unit, as Franchisor may reasonably require for its own and Franchisee's protection.

11.02. Insurance Requirements. Policies shall be written by an insurance company satisfactory to Franchisor, and shall include, at a minimum the following coverage:

A. Workers' Compensation Insurance, with statutory limits as required by the laws and regulations applicable to the employees of Franchisee who are engaged in the performance of their duties relating to the Franchised Unit, including any pre-opening training programs, as well as such other insurance as may be required by statute or regulation of the state in which the Franchised Unit is located.

B. Employer's Liability Insurance, for employee bodily injuries and deaths, with a limit of $500,000 each accident.

C. Comprehensive or Commercial General Liability Insurance, covering claims for bodily injury, death and property damage, including Premises and Operations, Independent Contractors, Products and Completed Operations, Personal Injury, Contractual, and Broadform Property Damage liability coverages, with limits as follows: Occurrence/Aggregate Limit of $1,000,000 for bodily injury, death and property damage each occurrence and $2,000,000 for general aggregate or Split liability limits of:

$1,000,000 for bodily injury per person
$1,000,000 for bodily injury per occurrence
$500,000 for property damage

D. Comprehensive Automobile Liability Insurance, if applicable, covering owned, non-owned and hired vehicles, with limits as follows: Combined Single Limit of $500,000 for bodily injury, death and property damage per occurrence or Split liability limits of:

$500,000 for bodily injury per person
$500,000 for bodily injury per occurrence
$250,000 for property damage

E. All Risk Property Insurance, on a replacement cost basis, with limits as appropriate, covering the real property of Franchisee and any real property which the Franchisee may be obligated to insure by contract. Such real property may including building, machinery, equipment, furniture, fixtures and inventory.

11.03. All such policies of insurance shall provide that they shall be canceled, modified or changed without giving thirty (30) days prior written notice to Franchisor. No cancellation, modification or change shall affect Franchisee's obligation to maintain the insurance coverages required by this Agreement. Except for Workers' Compensation Insurance, Franchisor shall be named as an Additional Insured on all such required policies. All liability insurance policies shall be written on an "occurrence" policy form. Franchisee shall be responsible for payment of any and all deductibles from insured claims under its policies of insurance. Franchisee shall not satisfy requirements of this Article XI until certificates of such insurance, including renewals, have been delivered to and approved by Franchisor. Franchisee shall not self-insure any of the coverage required by this Agreement, or non-subscribe to any State's applicable workmen's compensation laws without written consent of Franchisor. Franchisor may, at any time, increase minimum limits of insurance coverage or otherwise modify the insurance requirements upon written notice in the Manual. If Franchisee shall fail to comply with any of the insurance requirements herein, upon written notice to Franchisee by Franchisor, Franchisor may, without any obligation to do so, procure such insurance and Franchisee shall pay Franchisor, upon demand, the cost thereof plus interest at the maximum rate permitted by law, and a reasonable administrative fee designated by Franchisor.

11.04. Insurance obtained by Franchisee shall be primary to Franchisor's own insurance and the limits of such shall be exhausted before any benefits (defense or indemnity) may be obtained under any other insurance (including self-insurance) providing coverage to Franchisor. If payments are required under Franchisor's own insurance policies or self-insurance (whether for defense or indemnity) before applicable coverage limits for insurance policies obtained by Franchisee are exhausted, then Franchisee agrees to reimburse, hold harmless and indemnify Franchisor and its insurers for such payments. Franchisee shall notify its insurers of this Agreement and shall use best efforts to obtain an endorsement on each policy it obtains stating as follows:

> The applicable limits of this policy shall be applied and exhausted before any benefits may be obtained (whether for defense or indemnity) under any other insurance (including self-insurance) that may provide coverage to Franchisor. All insurance coverage obtained by Franchisor shall be considered excess insurance with respect to this policy, the benefits of which excess insurance shall not be available until the applicable limits of this policy are exhausted.

11.05. No Limitation on Coverage. Franchisee's obligation to obtain and maintain the foregoing policy or policies of insurance in the amounts specified shall not be limited in any way by reason of any insurance which may be maintained by Franchisor, nor shall Franchisee's performance of that obligation relieve it of liability under the indemnity provisions set forth in Section XVIII of this Agreement.

XII. CONFIDENTIAL INFORMATION

12.01. Franchisor shall not communicate, divulge, or use for the benefit of any other person, persons, partnership, association, corporation or other entity, any confidential information, knowledge or know-how concerning the construction and methods of operation of the Franchised Business which may be communicated to Franchisee, or of which Franchisee may be apprised, by virtue of Franchisee's operation under the terms of this Agreement. Franchisee shall divulge such confidential information only to such employees of Franchisee as must have access to it in order to exercise the franchise rights granted hereunder and to establish and operate the Franchised Unit pursuant hereto and as Franchisee may be required by law, provided Franchisee shall give Franchisor prior written notice of any such required disclosure immediately upon receipt of notice by Franchisee in order for Franchisor to have the opportunity to seek a protective order or take such other actions as it deems appropriate under the circumstances.

12.02. Any and all information, knowledge, and know-how, including, without limitation, drawings, materials, equipment, recipes, prepared mixtures or blends of spices or other food products, and other data, which Franchisor designates as confidential, and any information, knowledge, or know-how which may be derived by analysis thereof, confidential, except information which Franchisee can demonstrate came to Franchisee's attention prior to disclosure

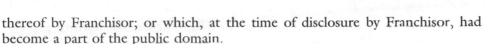

thereof by Franchisor; or which, at the time of disclosure by Franchisor, had become a part of the public domain.

XIII. COVENANTS

13.01. Franchisee covenants that, except as otherwise approved in writing by Franchisor, Franchisee or, alternatively, one designated management employee if that employee assumes primary responsibility for the operation of the Franchised Unit, shall devote full time, energy and best efforts to management and operation of the Franchised Business.

13.02. Franchisee will receive valuable specialized training and confidential information, including without limitation, information regarding the operational, sales, promotional, and marketing methods, procedures and techniques of Franchisor and the System. Franchisee covenants that, during the term of this Agreement, Franchisee shall not, directly or indirectly, for itself or on behalf of, or in conjunction with, any person, persons, partnership, association or corporation or other entity:

A. Divert or attempt to divert any business or customer of the business franchised hereunder to any competitor by direct or indirect inducements or otherwise, or to do or perform, directly or indirectly, any other act injurious or prejudicial to the goodwill associated with Franchisor's Marks and the System;

B. Employ or seek to employ any person who is, at that time, employed by Franchisor or by any other Pete's franchisee, or otherwise, directly or indirectly, induce such person to leave his or her employment therewith; or

C. Own, maintain, operate, engage in, or have any interest in any fast food restaurant that specializes in the preparation and/or sale of pizza or other food products substantially similar to those sold within the System. During the term of this Agreement, there is no geographical limitation on this restriction.

13.03. Franchisee shall not, regardless of the cause for termination, either directly or indirectly, for itself, or through, on behalf of, or in conjunction with any person, persons, partnership, association, corporation or other entity:

A. For a period of two (2) years following termination or expiration of this Agreement, own, maintain, engage in, or have any interest in any fast food restaurant which is located within a radius of ten (10) miles of the location specified in Section I, or the location of any other Pete's under the System, whether owned by Franchisor or any other franchisee, in existence as of the date of expiration or termination of this Agreement; or

B. For a period of one (1) year following termination or expiration of this Agreement, employ or seek to employ any person who is, at the time, employed by Franchisor or by any other franchisee, or otherwise, directly or indirectly, induce such person to leave his or her employment therewith.

13.04. At Franchisor's request, Franchisee shall obtain execution of covenants similar to those set forth in this Section (including covenants applicable upon the termination of a person's relationship with Franchisee) in a form satisfactory to Franchisor, including, without limitation, specific identification of Franchisor as a third party beneficiary of such covenants with the independent right to enforce them, from any or all managers of Franchisee who have received or will receive training from Franchisor; officers, directors, and holders of a direct or indirect beneficial ownership interest of five percent (5%) or more in Franchisee. Failure of Franchisee to obtain execution of a covenant required by this Section shall constitute a material breach of this Agreement. A duplicate original of each such covenant shall be provided by Franchisee to Franchisor immediately upon execution.

13.05. Each of the foregoing covenants shall be independent of any other provision of this Agreement. If all or any portion of a covenant in this Section is held unreasonable or unenforceable, Franchisee shall be bound by any lesser covenant subsumed within the terms of such covenant that imposes the maximum duty permitted by law, as if the resulting covenant was separately stated in and made a part of this Section.

13.06. Right to Reduce Covenants. Franchisor may, in its sole discretion, reduce the scope of any covenant set forth in Sections 13.02 and 13.03, without Franchisee's consent, effective immediately upon receipt by Franchisee of written notice thereof, and Franchisee shall comply with any covenant as modified, which shall be fully enforceable notwithstanding the provisions of Section XXII.

XIV. TRANSFERABILITY OF INTEREST

14.01. Transfer by Franchisor. Franchisor may transfer or assign its interest in this Agreement to any person, persons, partnership, association, corporation, or other entity. If Franchisor's assignee assumes all obligations of Franchisor hereunder and sends Franchisee written notice of the assignment so attesting, Franchisee shall promptly execute a release of Franchisor and its affiliates from claims or liabilities under this Agreement.

14.02. Transfer by Franchisee. Franchisee's rights and duties under this Agreement are personal and have been granted in reliance on Franchisee's business skill and financial capacity. Neither Franchisee, nor any successor to Franchisee, nor any individual, partnership, corporation or other entity which owns any interest in the Franchisee or in this Franchise Agreement, shall sell, assign, transfer, convey, donate, pledge, mortgage, or otherwise encumber any direct or indirect interest in this Agreement or in any legal entity which owns the Franchised Business without the prior written consent of Franchisor. Acceptance by Franchisor of any fee or other amount accruing hereunder from any third party shall not constitute Franchisor's approval of such party as a transferee or of the transfer of this Agreement to such party. Any purported assignment or transfer, by operation of law or otherwise, not having the written consent of Franchisor, shall be null and void, and shall constitute a material breach of this Agreement, for which Franchisor may then terminate without opportunity to cure pursuant to Section 15.02.E.

14.03. Conditions for Consent. Franchisor shall not unreasonably withhold consent to any transfer, when requested; provided, however, that prior to the time of transfer;

A. All of Franchisee's accrued monetary obligations to Franchisor and its subsidiaries and affiliates shall have been satisfied;

B. Franchisee shall have agreed to remain obligated under the covenants contained in Section XIII hereof as if this Agreement had been terminated on the date of the transfer;

C. The transferee is of good moral character and reputation, in the reasonable judgment of the Franchisor;

D. The Franchisor shall have determined, to its satisfaction, that the transferee's qualifications meet the Franchisor's then current criteria for new franchisees;

E. Franchisee and transferee shall execute a written assignment, in a form satisfactory to Franchisor, under which the transferee shall assume all obligations of Franchisee under this Agreement and Franchisee shall unconditionally release all claims Franchisee might have against Franchisor;

F. Transferee shall execute the then-current form of Franchise Agreement and other then-current ancillary agreements as Franchisor may reasonably require. The then-current form of Franchise Agreement may have different provisions including, without limitation, higher fees and Contributions than contained in this Agreement. The then-current form of Franchise Agreement will expire on the expiration date of this Agreement and will contain the same renewal rights, if any, as are available to Franchisee herein;

G. Transferee shall at its sole expense, complete a Franchised Unit Renovation, within the time required by Franchisor, unless a Renovation was completed within three years prior to transfer and perform such other work as may be required by Franchisor.

H. Transferee and such other individuals as may be designated by Franchisor in the Manual, must have successfully completed the training then in effect for new franchisees.

I. If the transferee is a partnership, the partnership agreement shall provide that further assignments or transfers of any interest in the partnership are subject to all restrictions imposed upon assignments and transfers in this Agreement;

J. Franchisee shall, at Franchisor's request, execute a written guarantee of transferee's obligations under the Agreement, which shall not exceed a period of three years from the date of transfer.

K. The Franchisee shall pay to Franchisor a transfer fee of Five Thousand Dollars ($5,000), to cover administrative expenses in connection with the transfer; no additional franchise fee shall be charged by Franchisor for a transfer. If transferee is a corporation formed by Franchisee for convenience of ownership, in which the Franchisee is the sole shareholder, or an existing Franchisee, no transfer fee shall be required.

14.04. Transfer on Death or Mental Incapacity. Upon the death or mental incapacity of Franchisee, the executor, administrator, or personal representative of such person shall transfer his interest to a third party approved by Franchisor within 12 months after death or mental incapacity. Such transfer shall be subject to the same conditions as any inter vivos transfer. However, in the case of transfer by devise or inheritance, if the heirs or beneficiaries are unable to meet the conditions in this Section, the personal representative shall have a reasonable time, but no more than eighteen months from Franchisee's death, to dispose of the interest in this Agreement and the business conducted pursuant hereto, which disposition shall be subject to all terms and conditions for assignments and transfers contained in this Agreement. If the interest is not disposed of within twelve or eighteen months, whichever is applicable, Franchisor may terminate this Agreement.

14.05. Right of First Refusal. Any party holding an interest in this Agreement, the Franchised Business or in Franchisee, and who desires to accept a bona fide offer to purchase such interest, shall notify Franchisor in writing within ten days of receipt of such offer, and shall provide information and documentation relating to the offer as Franchisor may require. Franchisor shall have the option, exercisable within thirty days after receipt of such written notification, to send written notice to the seller that Franchisor intends to purchase the seller's interest on the same terms and conditions offered by the third party. If Franchisor elects to purchase seller's interest, closing on such purchase must occur within sixty days from the date of notice of election to purchase by Franchisor. Any material change in the terms of any offer prior to closing shall constitute a new offer subject to the same rights of first refusal by Franchisor as in the case of an initial offer. Failure of Franchisor to exercise the option afforded by this Section shall not constitute a waiver of any other provisions of this Agreement, including all of the requirements of this Section XIV, with respect to a proposed transfer.

XV. TERMINATION

15.01. Franchisee shall be deemed to be in default under this Agreement, and all rights granted herein shall automatically terminate without notice, if Franchisee becomes insolvent or makes a general assignment for the benefit of creditors; if a petition in bankruptcy is filed by or against Franchisee; if Franchisee is adjudicated bankrupt or insolvent; if a receiver or custodian (permanent or temporary) of any of Franchisee's assets or property is appointed by any court of competent jurisdiction; if proceedings for a composition with creditors should be instituted by Franchisee or against Franchisee and not opposed by Franchisee; if a final judgment remains unsatisfied or of record for thirty days or longer (unless supersedeas bond is filed); if Franchisee is dissolved; if execution is levied against Franchisee's property or business; if suit to foreclose a lien or mortgage against the premises or equipment of any Franchised Unit is instituted against Franchisee and not dismissed within thirty days; or if real or personal property of any franchise unit developed hereunder shall be sold after levy thereon by any sheriff, marshal, or constable.

15.02. Franchisee shall be deemed to be in default and Franchisor may, at its option, terminate this Agreement and all rights granted hereunder without affording Franchisee any opportunity to cure the default upon the occurrence of any of the following events:

A. If Franchisee fails to open for business within one hundred eighty (180) days of execution of this Agreement.

B. If Franchisee ceases to operate the Franchised Unit or otherwise abandons the Franchised Unit, or loses the right to possession of the premises of the Franchised Unit, or otherwise forfeits the right to do business in the jurisdiction where the Franchised Unit is located; provided, however, that if, through no fault of Franchisee, the premises are damaged or destroyed by an event not within the control of Franchisee such that repairs or reconstruction cannot be completed within one hundred eighty days thereafter, then Franchisee shall have thirty days after such event in which to apply for Franchisor's approval to relocate and/or reconstruct the premises, which approval shall not be unreasonably withheld, but may be conditioned upon the payment of an agreed minimum royalty to Franchisor during the period in which the Franchised Unit is not in operation;

C. If Franchisee is convicted of or pleads guilty to a felony, a crime involving moral turpitude, or any other offense that Franchisor believes is likely to have an adverse effect on the System, the Marks, associated goodwill, or Franchisor's interest therein;

D. If a threat or danger to public health or safety results from construction, maintenance, or operation of the Franchised Unit;

E. If Franchisee, or any partner or shareholder of Franchisee purports to transfer any rights or obligations under this Agreement or any interest in Franchisee to any third party without Franchisor's prior written consent, contrary to the terms of Section XIV hereof;

F. If Franchisee fails to comply with the in-term covenants in Section XIII hereof or fails to obtain execution of the covenants required under Sections X or XIII;

G. If, contrary to the terms of Section VII hereof, Franchisee discloses or divulges the contents of the Manual or other confidential information provided by Franchisor;

H. If an approved transfer is not effected as required by this Agreement, following Franchisee's death or mental incapacity;

I. If Franchisee knowingly maintains false books or records, or submits any false reports to Franchisor;

J. If Franchisee, after or during a default commits the same default again, whether or not such default was cured after notice or if Franchisee defaults more than once in any twelve month period by failure to substantially comply with any requirements imposed by this Agreement, whether or not cured after notice.

K. If Franchisee refuses to permit Franchisor or its agents to enter upon the premises of Franchised Unit to conduct any periodic inspection.

L. If Franchisee uses any of Franchisor's Marks in any unauthorized manner.

M. Franchisor discovers that Franchisee made a material misrepresentation or omitted a material fact in the information that was furnished to Franchisor in connection with its decision to enter into this Agreement.

N. Franchisee knowingly falsifies any required report, makes any material misrepresentation in its dealings with, or fails to disclose any material facts to Franchisor.

15.03. Except as provided in Section 15, upon any default by Franchisee which is susceptible of being cured, Franchisor may terminate this Agreement only by giving written Notice of Termination stating the nature of such default to Franchisee at least ten days prior to the effective date of termination if the default is for failure to pay royalties, Contributions (including any other financial obligations owed to Franchisor by Franchisee), and thirty days, prior to the effective date of termination for any other default. Franchisee may avoid termination by curing such default to Franchisor's satisfaction within the ten day or thirty day period, as applicable. If any such default is not cured within the specified time, this Agreement shall terminate without further notice to Franchisee effective immediately upon the expiration of the ten day or thirty day period, as applicable, or such longer period as applicable law may require. Any agreement between Franchisee and Franchisor relating to past due amounts accruing hereunder (an "Arrearage Agreement"), including, but not limited to any promissory note, payment plan or amendment to this agreement shall be deemed to be a material part of this agreement and shall be incorporated herein by reference. A default under any Arrearage Agreement shall be a material default of this Agreement, regardless of the reason Franchisee fails to pay the amount which is subject to such Arrearage Agreement.

15.04. Franchisee shall indemnify and hold Franchisor harmless for all costs, expenses and any losses incurred by Franchisor in enforcing the provisions hereof, or in upholding the propriety of any action or determination by Franchisor pursuant to this Agreement, or in defending any claims made by Franchisee against Franchisor, or arising in any manner from Franchisee's breach of or failure to perform any covenant or obligation hereunder, including, without limitation, reasonable litigation expenses and attorney's fees incurred by Franchisor in connection with any threatened or pending litigation relating to any part of this Agreement, unless Franchisee shall be found, after due legal proceedings, to have complied with all of the terms, provisions, conditions and covenants hereof.

15.05. In addition to the other provisions of this Section, if Franchisor reasonably determines that Franchisee will become unable to meet its obligations under this Agreement, Franchisor may provide written notice to that effect and demand assurances reasonably designated by Franchisor, which may include security or letters of credit for the payment of Franchisee's obligations. If Franchisee fails to provide such assurances demanded by Franchisor within 30 days after its receipt of written notice, this Agreement shall terminate without further notice to Franchisee effective immediately upon expiration of that time, unless Franchisor notifies Franchisee otherwise in writing.

XVI.   EFFECT OF TERMINATION OR EXPIRATION

16.01. Upon termination or expiration of this Agreement, all rights granted herein shall forthwith terminate, and:

A. Franchisee shall immediately cease to operate the Franchised Unit as a Pete's "A" Pizza, and shall not thereafter, directly or indirectly, represent to the public that the unit is a Pete's "A" Pizza;

B. Franchisee shall immediately and permanently cease to use, by advertising or in any manner whatsoever, any menus, recipes, confidential food for formulae, equipment, methods, procedures, and the techniques associated with the System, Marks, and Franchisor's other trade names, trademarks and service marks associated with the System. In particular, and without limitation, Franchisee shall cease to use all signs, furniture, fixtures, equipment, advertising materials, stationery, forms, packaging, containers and any other articles which display the Marks;

C. Upon termination or expiration of this Agreement or upon cessation of the Franchised Business at the location specified, whether or not Franchisee continues to operate any business at such location, and whether or not Franchisee owns or leases the location, Franchisee shall make such modifications or alterations to the Franchised Unit premises immediately upon termination or expiration of this Agreement or cessation of operation of the Franchised Business as may be necessary to prevent the operation of any businesses thereon by Franchisee or others in derogation of this Agreement and shall make such specified additional changes thereto as Franchisor may reasonably request for that purpose. The modifications and alterations shall include, but are not limited to, removal of all trade dress, Marks and other indicia of the System;

D. Franchisee shall immediately pay all sums owing to Franchisor and its subsidiaries and affiliates. In the event of termination for any default by Franchisee, such sums shall include all damages, costs and expenses, including reasonable attorneys' fees, incurred by Franchisor as a result of the default; and

E. Franchisee shall immediately turn over to Franchisor the Manual, all other manuals, records, files, instructions, correspondence and any and all other materials relating to the operation of the Franchised Business and all copies thereof (all of which are Franchisor's property) and retain no copy or record of any of the foregoing, with the exception of a copy of this Agreement, correspondence between the parties, and any other documents which Franchisee reasonably needs for compliance with any provision of law.

16.02. Franchisor shall have the right (but not the duty) to be exercised by notice of intent to do so within thirty days after termination or expiration of this Agreement, to purchase improvements, equipment, advertising and promotional materials, ingredients, products, materials, supplies, paper goods and any items bearing Franchisor's Marks at current fair market value. If the parties cannot agree on a fair market value within a reasonable time, an independent appraiser shall be designated by Franchisor, and his determination of fair market value shall be binding. If Franchisor elects to exercise any option to purchase herein provided, it shall have the right to set-off all amounts due from Franchisee under this Agreement and the cost of the appraisal, if any, against any payment therefor.

16.03. If the premises are leased to Franchisee, Franchisee shall, upon termination of this Agreement and upon request by Franchisor, immediately assign, set over and transfer unto Franchisor, said lease and the premises, including improvements. Any such lease entered into by Franchisee shall contain a clause specifying the landlord's consent to assign such lease to Franchisor or its assignee in the event this Agreement is terminated.

16.04. Franchisee shall pay all damages, costs, and expenses, including reasonable attorneys' fees, incurred by Franchisor in seeking recovery of damages caused by any action of Franchisee in violation of, or in obtaining injunctive relief for enforcement of, any portion of this Agreement. Franchisee acknowledges that any failure to comply with the provisions of this Agreement shall result in irreparable injury to Franchisor.

16.05. All provisions of this Agreement which, by their terms or intent, are designed to survive the expiration or termination of this Agreement, shall so survive the expiration and/or termination of this Agreement.

XVII. TAXES, PERMITS, AND INDEBTEDNESS

17.01. Franchisee shall promptly pay when due all taxes, accounts and other indebtedness of every kind incurred by Franchisee in the conduct of the Franchised Business under this Agreement. Notwithstanding the foregoing,

Franchisee shall not be deemed in default of this Section if Franchisee asserts any legal challenge to the validity of any such taxes, accounts and/or other indebtedness and either (i) deposits all such amounts in an escrow account or (ii) provides such evidence as may be requested by Franchisor to establish that Franchisee is financially capable of paying such amount in the event the challenge is denied after due legal or administrative hearings.

17.02. Franchisee, in the conduct of the Franchised Business, shall comply with all applicable laws and regulations, and shall timely obtain any and all permits, certificates, or licenses necessary for the full and proper conduct of the businesses operated under this Agreement, including, without limitation, licenses to do business, trade name registrations, sales tax permits and fire clearances.

XVIII.   INDEPENDENT CONTRACTOR AND INDEMNIFICATION

18.01. This Agreement does not constitute Franchisee an agent, legal representative, joint venturer, partner, employee or servant of Franchisor for any purpose. Franchisee shall be an independent contractor and is in no way authorized to make any contract, agreement, warranty, or representation on behalf of Franchisor. The parties further agree that this Agreement does not create any fiduciary relationship between them.

18.02. Franchisee shall take such action as Franchisor deems reasonably necessary for Franchisee to hold itself out to the public as an independent contractor operating pursuant to a franchise, including, without limitation, exhibiting a notice of that fact at the Franchised Business in form and substance satisfactory to Franchisor.

18.03 Franchisee shall defend, indemnify and hold harmless Franchisor, its parent, subsidiaries and affiliates, and their respective officers, directors, employees, agents, successors and assigns from all claims, demands, losses, damages, liabilities, cost and expenses (including attorney's fees and expense of litigation) resulting from, or alleged to have resulted from, or in connection with Franchisee's operation of the Franchised Business, including, but not limited to, any claim or actions based on or arising out of any injuries, including death to persons or damages to or destruction of property, sustained or alleged to have been sustained in connection with or to have arisen out of or incidental to the Franchised Business and/or the performance of this contract by Franchisee, its agents, employees, and/or its subcontractors, their agents and employees, or anyone for whose acts they may be liable, regardless of whether or not such claim, demand, damage, loss, liability, cost or expense is caused in whole or in part by the negligence of Franchisor, Franchisor's representative, or the employees, agents, invitees, or licensees thereof.

18.04 Franchisor shall advise Franchisee if Franchisor receives notice that a claim has been or may be filed with respect to a matter covered by this Agreement, and shall immediately assume defense thereof at Franchisee's sole expense. Franchisor will have the right, through counsel, to control any matter to the extent it could directly or indirectly affect Franchisor and/or its parent, subsidiaries or affiliates or their officers, directors, employees, agents, successors or assigns. If Franchisee fails to assume such defense, Franchisor may defend, settle, and litigate such action in the manner it deems appropriate and Franchisee shall, immediately upon demand, pay all costs (including attorney's fees and cost of litigation) incurred by Franchisor in affecting such defense, in addition to any sum which Franchisor may pay by reason of any settlement or judgment.

18.05. Franchisor's right to indemnity shall exist notwithstanding that joint or several liability may be imposed upon Franchisor by statute, ordinance, regulation or court.

18.06. Franchisee agrees to pay Franchisor all expenses including attorney's fees and court costs, incurred by Franchisor, its parent, subsidiaries, affiliates, and their successors and assigns to remedy any defaults of or enforce any rights under this Agreement, effect termination of this Agreement or collect any amounts due under this Agreement.

XIX. APPROVALS AND WAIVERS

19.01. Whenever this Agreement requires the prior approval of Franchisor, Franchisee shall make a timely written request to Franchisor therefor, and such approval or consent shall be in writing.

19.02. Franchisor makes no warranties or guarantees upon which Franchisee may rely, and assumes no liability or obligation to Franchisee or any third party to which Franchisor would not otherwise be subject, by providing any waiver, approval, advice, consent, or suggestions to Franchisee in connection with this Agreement, or by reason of any neglect, delay, or denial of any request therefor.

19.03. No failure of Franchisor to exercise any power reserved in this Agreement, or to insist upon compliance with any obligation or condition in this Agreement, and no custom or practice of the parties at variance with the terms hereof, shall constitute a waiver of Franchisor's right to demand exact compliance with this Agreement. Waiver by Franchisor of any particular default shall not affect Franchisor's right in respect to any subsequent default of the same or a different nature, nor shall any delay, forbearance, or omission of Franchisor to exercise any power or rights arising out of any breach or default by Franchisee impair Franchisor's rights, nor shall such constitute a waiver by Franchisor of any rights, hereunder or right to declare any subsequent breach or default. Subsequent acceptance by Franchisor of any payments due to it shall not be deemed to be a waiver by Franchisor of any preceding breach by Franchisee of any terms, covenants, or conditions of this Agreement.

XX. NOTICES

Any notices required or permitted under this Agreement shall be in writing and shall be personally delivered, sent by registered mail, or by other means which will provide evidence of the date received to the respective parties at the following addresses unless and until a different address has been designated by written notice to the other party:

Notices to Franchisor:
Notices to Franchisee:

All written notices and reports permitted or required to be delivered by the provisions of this Agreement shall be addressed to the party to be notified at its most current principal business address of which the notifying party has been notified and shall be deemed so delivered at the time delivered by hand; one business day after sending by telegraph, facsimile, electronic mail or comparable electronic system with electronic confirmation of receipt; or if sent by registered or certified mail or by other means which affords the sender evidence of delivery, on the date and time of receipt or attempted delivery if delivery has been refused or rendered impossible by the party being notified.

XXI. SEVERABILITY AND CONSTRUCTION

21.01. Except as expressly provided to the contrary herein, each section, paragraph, part, term, and/or provision of this Agreement shall be considered severable; and if, for any reason, any section, part, term, and/or provision herein is determined to be invalid and contrary to, or in conflict with, any existing or future law or regulation by a court or agency having valid jurisdiction, such shall not impair the operation, or have any other effect upon, such other portions, sections, parts, terms, and/or provisions of this Agreement as may remain otherwise intelligible, and the latter shall continue to be given full force and effect to bind the parties hereto; and said invalid portions, sections, parts, terms, and/or provisions shall be deemed not to be part of this Agreement.

21.02. Except as has been expressly provided to the contrary herein, nothing in this Agreement is intended, nor shall be deemed, to confer upon any person or legal entity other than Franchisee, Franchisor, Franchisor's officer, directors, and employees, and Franchisee's permitted and Franchisor's respective successors and assigns, any rights or remedies under or by reason of this Agreement.

21.03. All captions in the Agreement are intended for the convenience of the parties, and none shall be deemed to affect the meaning or construction of any provision hereof.

21.04. All references herein to the masculine, neuter or singular shall be construed to include the masculine, feminine, neuter or plural, as applicable, and all promises, acknowledgments, covenants, agreements and obligations herein by Franchisee shall be deemed jointly and severally undertaken by all the parties hereto on behalf of Franchisee.

XXII. ENTIRE AGREEMENT: SURVIVAL

22.01. This Agreement, the documents referred to herein and exhibits hereto, constitute the entire and complete agreement between Franchisor and Franchisee concerning the subject matter hereof and supersede any prior agreements. Except for those permitted to be made unilaterally by Franchisor hereunder, no amendment, change, modification or variance of this Agreement shall be binding on either party unless in writing and executed by Franchisor and Franchisee. Representations by either party, whether oral, in writing, electronic or otherwise, that are not set forth in this Agreement shall not be binding upon the party alleged to have made such representations and shall be of no force or effect.

I have read this Section and agree that I have not been induced by and am not relying upon any representation not contained in this Agreement.
_____, Franchisee

22.02. Notwithstanding anything herein to the contrary, upon the termination of this Agreement for any reason whatsoever or upon the expiration of the Term hereof, any provisions of this Agreement which, by their nature, extend beyond the expiration or termination of this Agreement, shall survive termination or expiration and be fully binding and enforceable as though such termination or expiration had not occurred.

XXIII.   ACKNOWLEDGMENTS

23.01. Franchisee acknowledges that Franchisee has conducted an independent investigation of the franchise and recognizes that the business venture contemplated by this Agreement involves business risks and Franchisee's success will be largely dependent upon the ability of the Franchisee as an independent business entity.

_____ FRANCHISOR DISCLAIMS THE MAKING OF, AND FRANCHISEE ACKNOWLEDGES THAT FRANCHISEE HAS NOT RECEIVED, ANY WARRANTY OR GUARANTY, EXPRESSED OR IMPLIED, AS TO POTENTIAL VOLUME, PROFITS OR SUCCESS OF THE BUSINESS CONTEMPLATED BY THIS AGREEMENT.

_____ 23.02. FRANCHISEE ACKNOWLEDGES THAT FRANCHISEE HAS RECEIVED A COMPLETED COPY OF THIS AGREEMENT, THE EXHIBITS, AND AGREEMENTS RELATING THERETO, IF ANY, AT LEAST FIVE (5) BUSINESS DAYS PRIOR TO THE DATE ON WHICH THIS AGREEMENT WAS EXECUTED.

_____ FRANCHISEE ACKNOWLEDGES RECEIPT OF THE DISCLOSURE FRANCHISE DOCUMENT REQUIRED BY THE TRADE REGULATION RULE OF THE FEDERAL TRADE COMMISSION ENTITLED "DISCLOSURE REQUIREMENTS AND PROHIBITIONS CONCERNING FRANCHISING AND BUSINESS OPPORTUNITY VENTURES" AT LEAST TEN (10) BUSINESS DAYS PRIOR TO THE DATE ON WHICH THIS AGREEMENT WAS EXECUTED.

_____ 23.03. FRANCHISEE HAS READ AND UNDERSTOOD THIS AGREEMENT, EXHIBITS, AND AGREEMENTS RELATING THERETO, IF ANY, AND FRANCHISOR HAS ACCORDED FRANCHISEE AMPLE TIME AND OPPORTUNITY AND ENCOURAGED FRANCHISEE TO CONSULT WITH ADVISORS OF FRANCHISEE'S OWN CHOOSING

ABOUT THE POTENTIAL BENEFITS AND RISKS OF ENTERING INTO THIS AGREEMENT.

_____ 23.04. FRANCHISEE UNDERSTANDS THAT IT MAY INCUR OTHER EXPENSES AND/OR OBLIGATIONS AS PART OF INVESTMENT IN THE FRANCHISED BUSINESS WHICH THE TERMS OF THIS AGREEMENT MAY NOT ADDRESS, AND WHICH INCLUDE WITHOUT LIMITATION: OPENING ADVERTISING, EQUIPMENT, FIXTURES, OTHER FIXED ASSETS, CONSTRUCTION, LEASEHOLD IMPROVEMENTS AND DECORATING COSTS AS WELL AS WORKING CAPITAL.

XXIV. APPLICABLE LAW: VENUE

24.01. Applicable Law. This Agreement takes effect upon its acceptance and execution by Franchisor and shall be interpreted and construed under the laws of the State of Illinois which laws shall prevail in the event of any conflict of law (without regard to, and without giving effect to, the application of Illinois choice of law or conflict of law rules) except to the extent governed by the U.S. Trademark Act of 1946, 15 U.S.C. 1051, et seq. (the "Lanham Act") as amended; provided, however, that if the covenants in this Agreement would not be enforceable under the laws of Illinois, and the Franchised Unit is located outside of Illinois, then such covenants shall be interpreted and construed under the laws of the state in which the Franchised Unit is located. Nothing in this Section is intended by the parties to subject this Agreement to any franchise or similar law, rule, or regulation of the State of Illinois to which this Agreement would not otherwise be subject.

24.02. The parties agree that any action brought by Franchisee against Franchisor in any court, whether federal or state, shall be brought within such state and in the judicial district in which Franchisor has its principal place of business. Any action brought by Franchisor against Franchisee in any court, whether federal or state, may be brought within the state and in the judicial district in which Franchisor has its principal place of business at the time suit is filed, or in the jurisdiction where Franchisee resides or does business or where the Franchised Unit is or was located or where the claim arose. Franchisee hereby consents to personal jurisdiction and venue in the state and judicial district in which Franchisor has its principal place of business.

24.03. No right or remedy herein conferred upon or reserved to Franchisor is exclusive of any other right or remedy herein, or by law or equity provided or permitted; but each shall be cumulative of any other right or remedy provided in this Agreement

24.04. Nothing herein contained shall bar Franchisor's right to obtain injunctive relief against threatened conduct that will cause it loss or damages, under the usual equity rules, including the applicable rules for obtaining restraining orders and preliminary injunctions.

24.05. Any and all claims and actions arising out of or relating to this Agreement (including, but not limited to, the offer and sale of this franchise), the relationship of Franchisee and Franchisor, or Franchisee's operation of the

Franchised Unit, brought by Franchisee shall be commenced within eighteen (18) months from the occurrence of the facts giving rise to such claim or action, or such claim or action shall be barred.

24.06. Franchisor and Franchisee hereby waive to the fullest extent permitted by law any right to or claim of any consequential, punitive, or exemplary damages against the other, and agree that in the event of a dispute between them each shall be limited to the recovery of any actual damages sustained by it.

IN WITNESS WHEREOF, the parties hereto, intending to be legally bound hereby, have duly executed, sealed, and delivered this Agreement in triplicate on the day and year first above-written.

Glossary

Acceleration Clause: Causes payments to become immediately due upon the happening of stated event

Acceptance: Compliance or agreement by one party with the terms of another's offer so that a contract forms

Accord and Satisfaction: Agreement to accept and give payment or performance, different from that originally required by contract

Active Voice: The subject of the sentence acts

Adhesion Contract: A take-it-or-leave-it contract in which one party has all of the bargaining power

Adjudicated Incompetent: Court has declared person incompetent

Administrative Agencies: One of five (5) sources of legal authority; administers a particular law or program

Administrator: One who carries on the business of an estate; see Executor

Adversarial: Argues a position

Affirm: Appellate or higher court's decision to support or uphold the decision of the lower court

Affirmative Defense: Part of an answer to a complaint in which defendant attempts to limit or excuse liability, based on facts outside those claimed by plaintiff

Agency Coupled with an Interest: Agent has a financial stake in the transaction

Agent: One who is authorized to act for or in place of another; representative

Allowances: Contract total price includes "estimates" for components; if actual price of components differs from allowances, total contract price changes

Alternative Dispute Resolution (ADR): To settle a dispute other than by litigation, including arbitration and mediation

Analogize: To compare cases and find them similar

Annotated Statute: Statute with references to articles, cases, and other materials that explain and interpret the law

Ante-nuptial: Agreement in anticipation of marriage; typically involves a promise to convey property when marriage occurs or concerns division of property in the event of a divorce; see Pre-nuptial

Anticipatory Breach: Belief that other party will not perform

Apparent Authority: Principal's dealings with third parties have given third parties reason to believe that an agent has authority

Appellant: Party bringing an appeal; lost in the lower court

Appellee: The party that won in the lower court

Arbitration: A neutral hears both positions and imposes a decision

Arms-Length Transaction: Relationship where parties have equal power to negotiate terms

Assignee: One to whom rights are transferred by another

Assignment: Transfer of interest in property or some right (contractual entitlement) to another

Assignor: One who transfers rights to another

Assurance: A pledge or guarantee that gives confidence or security

Attachment: Creation of an enforceable security interest

Attorney for the Child: Attorney whose role is to advocate the child's position

Auction Without Reserve: A seller agrees to sell to the highest bidder and cannot revoke the offer to sell, even if bids are disappointingly low

Avoid: Make a contract void; see Disaffirm

Bailee: Person, other than owner, who is in possession of goods under an arrangement called a bailment

Bargained-for: Each party is induced to enter contract by consideration offered by other party

Bargaining Power: Ability to influence

Basic Assumption of Fact: An assumption essential to the value of a transaction

Battle-of-the-Forms Rule: UCC rule, overrides mirror image rule when merchants use forms

Bilateral: Contract in which both parties make promises

Bill of Lading: Documentation of the receipt of goods for shipment, issued by a party in the business of transporting goods

Binding Arbitration: Parties give up the right to challenge arbitration result in court

Blue Law: Prohibits certain transactions on Sundays

Blue-Penciling: Court edits parts of a contract

Boilerplate: Standard terms included in most contracts

Brief: Short case summary

Bulk Sale: Sale of major part of inventory, not in ordinary course of business

Capacity: Ability, as determined by age and mental competence, to enter into a contract

CALR: Computer-assisted legal research system

Case at Hand: The case under consideration

Case at Law: A case requesting damages (money)

Case Brief: Short summary of facts, issues, holding, and reasoning of a judicial decision

Case in Equity: Courts can issue orders based on fairness; see Equitable Remedy

Case Law: Judicial decisions

Chancery: A chancery court can order acts performed

Chattel: Moveable items, also called Personal Property

Citation: Address at which authority is found in law books or on line

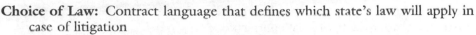

Choice of Law: Contract language that defines which state's law will apply in case of litigation

Cite: Verb form of citation (i.e., to cite)

Civil Law: Type of law pursued by an individual or group of people, a business, or a governmental body acting in a private capacity; result may be damages or court order

Click-Wrap Agreement: Agreement used in connection with software licenses; often found on the Internet as part of the installation process of software packages; usually requires user to manifest assent by clicking an "ok" button on a dialog box or pop-up window

Code: Legislation; also called statute

Codify: To enter a statute into a topical system

Cognitive Test: Mental incompetence determined by inability to understand the nature and consequences of a transaction

Collateral: Assets pledged by a borrower to secure a loan or other credit, and subject to seizure in the event of default

Collateral Promise: Promise to guarantee the debt of another, made without benefit to the party making the promise

Commercial: Between or pertaining to businesses

Commercial Impracticability: A party may be excused from contract obligations if an unforeseen circumstance makes performance impracticable

Common Law: Law from judicial decisions; governs contract disputes involving real property, intangible property, and services; also called precedent

Compensatory Damages: Damages intended to put non-breaching parties in the position they would have occupied if the contract had been fully performed

Concurring Opinion: Written by a judge who agrees with majority decision but for different reasons

Condition Precedent: Event that must occur before the contemplated transaction is completed

Condition Subsequent: Event that may "undo" an executed contract

Confession of Judgment: A clause that permits immediate entry of judgment without notice or an opportunity to present defenses

Conflict of Interest: Ethical issue: legal professional's loyalties divided

Connector: Symbol describing relationship between CALR search terms

Consequential Damages: Losses that do not flow directly and immediately from an injurious act

Consideration: Something promised, given, refrained from, or done that has the effect of making an agreement a legally enforceable contract

Consignment: An arrangement under which goods are placed for sale, but title does not transfer to the seller

Constitution: One of five sources of legal authority

Construction (rules of): Rules that are applied to resolve contract disputes and to determine parties' intentions

Consumer: Party to the contract who is not engaged in business, but has entered the contract for personal or family reasons

Consumer Goods: Items used primarily for personal, family, or household purposes

Consumer Loan: Loan for personal or family purposes

Contract: Set of legally enforceable promises

Contracts Under Seal: Formal contracts

Contrary to Public Policy: Not good for society

Co-signer: One who participates jointly in borrowing

Cost-Plus Contract: A way of sharing risk

Costs: Examples include filing fees, fees for service of process and similar charges incurred in litigation

Counter-offer: Offeree responds to an offer with an offer

Course of Dealing: What has been done by the parties in the past

Court-Annexed ADR: Use of the court system's own mediators or arbitrators before going to trial

Covenant Not to Compete: Provision under which party agrees to refrain from engaging in specified business activities ("non-compete")

Cover: Buyer obtains substitute goods

Creditor Beneficiary: A third-party beneficiary, to whom a contract party is indebted, and who is intended to benefit from the performance of a contract

Criminal Law: Category of law prosecuted by a governmental body involving a matter of concern to society as a whole

Criminal Plea Agreement: An agreement in which a prosecutor and a defendant arrange to settle a criminal case against the defendant.

Cure: Seller delivers conforming goods before contract deadline, after buyer rejects non-conforming goods

Damages: Award of money; also called Legal Remedy

Decision of the Court: Majority decision, governs outcome of the case

Default: Fail to meet obligations

Defined Term: Short-hand way of referring to a person, place, thing, or event that might otherwise require a lengthy description

Delegation: Pass contractual obligations to another

Disaffirm: Make a contract void; see Avoid

Discharge: Release

Discovery: Pre-trial investigation of facts by questioning, inspection, etc.

Dissenting Opinion: Opinion written by a judge who disagrees with the majority; not law but provides interesting facts and opinions about case

Distinguish: To compare cases and find them to be different

Donee: Person receiving a gift

Donee Beneficiary: A third-party beneficiary, intended to benefit from contract performance, as a gift

Donor: Person making a gift

Durable Power of Attorney: Creates an agency relationship that remains in effect during the grantor's incompetency

Duress: A wrongful threat, intended to induce action by the other party

Easement: Limited right to use real property

E-Discovery: Electronic recovery of e-mail, and documents from computers, servers, and hand-held PDAs

Election of Remedies: Injured party's choice between remedies available for a single actionable occurrence

Emancipation: Minor is no longer under care/control of an adult

Equal Dignity Rule: Requirement that agency contract be written, if contract to be established by agent must be written

Equitable: Based on fairness and individual circumstances

Equitable Remedy: Award that is non-monetary and involves court orders; see Case in Equity and Chancery

Err: To make an error

Escrow: Account held for the benefit of others, into which parties typically deposit documents, instructions, and funds for a transfer of property

Estate: The entity for managing finances of a deceased person, or an incompetent

Estop: To bar assertion of a claim or right that contradicts what has been said or done before

Exclusive Dealing: Contract under which parties agree to deal only with each other with respect to particular needs

Executor: One who carries on the business of an estate; see Administrator

Exculpatory Clause: Provision that attempts to excuse a party from liability for that party's torts

Executed: Contract in which all obligations have been fulfilled

Executive Action: One of five sources of legal authority; including orders signed by the President or governor

Executory: Contract in which obligations have not been fulfilled

Expectation Damages: Damages intended to put non-breaching parties in the position they would have occupied if the contract had been fully performed; Compensatory Damages

Express: Contract with significant terms stated orally or in writing

Express Authority: Authority given by words or conduct

Express Ratification: To state or write intent to honor a contract or, if the contract has been executed, to acknowledge the contract

Factual Issues: Trial courts use testimony and evidence to decide facts, (i.e., what happened)

Fee Recovery: An award of attorney's fees; also called Fee Reversal

Fee Reversal: An award of attorney's fees; also called Fee Recovery

Fiduciary Relationship: Relationship in which one person is under a duty to act for the benefit of the other on matters within the scope of the relationship

Firm Offer: UCC rule, no consideration required to hold offer open between merchants

Force Majeure: Contract provision excusing performance for an event such as "act of God," fire, labor dispute, accident, or transportation difficulty

Foreclose: Take property to satisfy debt

Formal: A contract required to be in a particular form

Franchise: Contract granting the right to operate under a brand name

Fraud: False statement of material fact, made with intent to deceive, on which another reasonably relies, to his detriment

Fraud in the Execution: Fraud relates to the nature of the agreement

Fraud in the Inducement: Fraud relates to the party's motivation in entering the contract

Frustration of Purpose: Contact has no remaining value for party due to an unanticipated event

Fungible: Interchangeable

Gift: Completed transfer of property without consideration

Good Faith: UCC definition: as applied to a merchant, means honesty in fact and the observance of reasonable commercial standards of fair dealing in the trade

Good Faith Buyer in the Course of Ordinary Business: A buyer who acts honestly, gives value, and has no notice of other claims

Goods: Also called personal property or chattel; moveable, tangible items

Gratuitous: Done without compensation; a gift

Guarantor: Agrees to be responsible for another's debt or performance under a contract if the other fails to pay or perform; see Surety

Guardian: Individual with legal responsibility for the minor

Guardian ad litem: Court-appointed person to advocate best interests of a child or incompetent during litigation

Headnotes: Summaries of individual points made in the case

Hold Harmless Clause: One party agrees to compensate other for losses arising from contract; see Indemnification Clause

Holding: Answer to the legal issue in a judicial decision

Identified: Goods designated as the particular goods being sold

Illusory: An illusion; stated consideration does not really obligate the party

Implied: Contract formed without express statement of terms, by words and actions

Implied Authority: Authority not expressed in writing or spoken words; arises from circumstances

Implied Ratification: Intent to honor contract or acknowledgment of contract can be inferred from behavior or words

In Pari Delicto: The parties are equally at fault

Incentive Consideration: Consideration changes to motivate faster or better performance

Incidental Beneficiary: A third-party beneficiary, not intended to benefit from contract, does not acquire rights under contract

Incidental Damages: Losses reasonably associated with or related to actual damages; indirect damages

Incorporation by Reference: A reference to an outside document, making that document part of a contract

Independent Contractor: One hired to undertake a specific project using his own methods (not an employee)

Indemnification Clause: One party agrees to compensate the other for losses arising from the contract; see Hold Harmless Clause

Injunction: Court order requiring or prohibiting specific actions

Infant: A minor

Informal: Contract for which no particular form is required

Insecure Party: Party has good-faith belief that performance by other party is unlikely

Insolvency: Unable to pay debts

Instruments: Formal written documents

Insurable Interest: Legitimate financial interest in a person

Intangible Property: Has no physical existence, such as debt

Integrated Agreement: Agreement that is intended to be final and complete

Intellectual Property: Includes patents, trademarks, copyrights, trade secrets

Intent to Deceive: Knowledge of falsity

Interoffice Memo: Also called objective memo, analyzes fact situation with citations to sources of law

Intoxicated: Under the influence of alcohol or drugs

Inventory: Goods held for sale or lease

Joint and Several Liability: Co-obligors can be sued together or any one can be liable for the entire obligation

Judicial Decisions: One of five sources of legal authority; also called common law or precedent

Jump Cite: The exact page number on which a fact or quote appears in a case

Jurisdiction: Area within which judicial authority may be exercised

Justifiable Reliance: Reliance on assertion is reasonable

Laches: Injured party delays in seeking remedy in a way that is unfair to the other party

LAPs: Lawyers Assistance Programs

Legal Issues: Determining appropriate consequences of the facts or whether a trial court handled a case properly

Legal Remedy: Award of money; also called Damages

Legalese: Overly formal, often archaic language sometimes used in legal documents

Legality: An element of an enforceable contract

Legislation: One of five sources of legal authority; also called code or statute; enacted by an elected body (e.g., Congress)

Letter of Credit: An irrevocable promise by a buyer's bank to pay the seller when conditions are met

Liable: To be found responsible

Lien: An encumbrance against property, typically to secure payment of a debt

Limitations Period: Time limit on bringing lawsuit, based on statute of limitations

Liquidated Damages: Damages agreed to in advance of breach, in the contract itself

Liquidated Debt: Debt that is not in dispute

Mailbox Rule: Common law rule, acceptance occurs when dispatched by appropriate means

Manifestation of Mutual Assent: Appearance that an agreement has been reached

Major Breach: Substantial breach of contract, usually excusing other party from further performance; see Material Breach

Majority: The age of adult status (typically 18)

Majority Decision: That which governs the outcome of cases; also called decision of the court

Malum per se: Inherently bad

Malum prohitum: Not inherently bad; less serious

Material Breach: Substantial breach of contract usually excusing other party from further performance; see Major Breach

Mediation: Neutral helps parties understand each others' positions and may suggest solutions, but agreement ultimately comes from the parties

Merchants: Deal in goods of the kind involved in transaction or, by their occupations, hold themselves out as having knowledge or skills relating to the goods or practice

Merger Clause: Contract provision stating that the document is the complete and final statement of agreement

Minor: A person who has not reached adult status, typically the day before his/her 18th birthday

Mirror Image Rule: Acceptance must be identical to offer

Misrepresentation: False statement made without intent to deceive, upon which a party justifiably relies to his detriment

Mitigate: Limit or reduce damages

Modify: Appellate or higher court's decision to change the decision of the lower court

Mortgage: Security interest in real estate

Municipal Law: Local law (as opposed to federal or state law)

Mutual Mistakes: All parties are mistaken about a basic assumption

Necessities: Things indispensable to life; reasonably needed for subsistence, health, comfort, and education, considering the person's age, station in life, and medical condition

Needs Contract: Contract under which buyer agrees to purchase all of buyer's needs from seller (see exclusive dealing); court may impose requirement of reasonable performance

Negotiable Instruments: A promise or order to pay, such as a check; can be passed along like cash

Neutral: A third party in ADR, mediator or arbitrator

Nominal: Minimal

Nominal Damages: Minimal amount of damages awarded, even if no financial loss resulted from the breach or if the loss cannot be proven with reasonable certainty

Non-Adjudicated Incompetent: Incompetence has not been determined by court

Notary Public: Person authorized by state to administer oaths, certify documents, attest to the authenticity of signatures, and perform other official acts

Notice of Claims Provision: Contract language requiring one party to give the other party written notice a specified time before filing suit

Novation: New contract, involving new parties; cancels earlier contract

Objective Impossibility: Impossibility in an objective sense; not personal

Objective Memo: Also called interoffice memo, analyzes fact situation with citations to legal authority

Objective Standard: Used to determine whether parties had "meeting of the minds," looks to what a reasonable person would believe, based on circumstances

Offer: An indication of current willingness to enter into a contract, communicated by the person making the offer

Offeree: Party receiving an offer

Offeror: Party making an offer

Open Terms: Also called "gap-filling" provisions; under the UCC a contract may form despite failure to specify certain terms

Operation of Law: Events, including death, insanity, destruction of subject matter, and illegality, may terminate an offer

Option: An offer, supported by consideration, may not be revoked at will

Output Contract: Contract under which buyer agrees to purchase all that seller produces; court may impose requirement of reasonable performance

Parallel Litigation: Single dispute results in cases in more than one state or in both state and federal courts

Parol Evidence Rule: A writing, intended by the parties to be a final embodiment of their agreement, cannot be modified by evidence that adds to, varies, or contradicts the writing

Partially Disclosed Principal: Existence of agency is known, identity of principal is not known

Party to be Charged: Party attempting to avoid contract liability

Passive Voice: Subject is acted upon

Perfect: To register or record an instrument so that the public is on notice of its terms

Perfect Performance: No deviations from contract; see Strict Performance

Perfect Tender Rule: Buyer has reasonable time to reject goods that fail, in any respect, to conform to the contract

Personal Property: Also called chattel or goods; tangible, moveable items

Power of Attorney: Document creating an agency

Precedent: Judicial decisions; also called common law; past decisions used to justify current decisions

Pre-nuptial: Agreement in anticipation of marriage; typically involves a promise to convey property when marriage occurs or concerns division of property in the event of a divorce; see Ante-nuptial

Present Worth Doctrine: The value, in "today's money" of payments to be made in the future

Primary Authority: One of the five sources of law

Principal: Party for whom agent acts

Privity: Being a party to the contract

Procedural History: The history of the court decisions that have moved the case to its current position

Promissory Estoppel: Theory under which a promise can be enforced, despite lack of consideration, because of reliance on that promise and knowledge of that reliance

Puffing: "Sales talk"

Punitive Damages: Damages unrelated to loss, intended to punish

Purchase Money Security Interest: Lien against property to secure a loan used to acquire that property

Pyramid Scheme: Multi-level arrangement in which money is made by recruiting new people

Quasi-Contract: Theory for avoiding unjust enrichment in situations in which a contract did not actually form

Qui Tam: Lawsuit in which a whistleblower can obtain reward for exposing misconduct involving government contracts.

Ratification: Acceptance of acts by agent after they occur

Ratify: To acknowledge or validate a contract after its execution

Real Estate: Also called real property or realty, consists of land and buildings

Reasoning: Summary of the court's explanation of its decision

Recission: Mutual agreement to cancel

Recitals: Short statements that provide background or explain the reasons for the contract; not technically part of a contract

Record: To record a document is to file it with the official charged with keeping documents such as deeds and judgments

Redline: Feature in word processing software that enables changes in a document to be tracked

Reformation: Rewriting contact; also called Blue-Penciling

Regulations: Established by administrative agencies

Rejection: Offeree terminates offer

Reliance Damages: Damages awarded for losses incurred by plaintiff in reliance on the contract; puts party in position that would have been occupied if the contract had not been made

Remand: Appellate or higher court's decision to send the case back to the lower court

Replevin: Recovery of property from one who is wrongfully in possession

Reporters: Print volumes that contain judicial decisions

Repudiation: A party's words or actions indicating intention not to perform the contract

Rescind: To terminate a contract before all of its terms are completely performed

Restatement: Secondary authority; a compilation of the "best" of the common law of contracts

Restitution: Return of, restoration of, or compensation for

Reverse: Appellate or higher court's decision to invalidate the decision of the lower court.

Revocation: Offeror terminates offer

Root Expander: Symbol used to pick up word variations in a CALR search

Sale-or-Return: Seller delivers goods to buyer who resells or returns them to seller; buyer takes title until sale or return

Satisfaction Clause: Contract provision requiring performance to the satisfaction of a specified individual

Search Query: Terms and connectors or natural language used in CALR search

Secondary Authority: Material such as text books and articles that help locate (finding tools) and understand primary law; form books, handbooks, encyclopedias, digests, etc.; not actual law

Securities: Evidence of investment in a common scheme

Security Interests: Interest in personal property to secure performance of an obligation; evidence of indebtedness

Self-Proving Document: Complies with formalities and can serve as testimony in court

Severability Clause: Contract provision that in the event that one part of the contract is found to be invalid, the rest of the contract shall remain in effect

Severable: Remainder of agreement can be enforced without unenforceable provision contained in the agreement

Sham Consideration: Stated consideration did not really occur

Silence as Fraud: A party has a duty to disclose and knowingly conceals the truth

Slander: False statements that hurt the reputation of another

Special Damages: Losses that do not flow directly and immediately from an injurious act, but are indirect; see Consequential Damages

Specific Performance: Court order requiring a party to perform contract obligations

Springing Power of Attorney: Comes into effect at a later date

Statute: Legislation; also called code

Statute of Frauds: Dictates types of contracts that must be written

Statutory Construction: See Statutory Interpretation

Statutory Interpretation: Interpretation of statute's terms; also called Statutory Construction

Strict Performance: No deviations from contract expectations; see Perfect Performance

Strict Liability: Liability regardless of fault

Subjective Standard: Imposed or influenced by individual position or bias

Subsequent Agreement: A separate, later agreement that changes or modifies the original agreement

Substantial Performance: Only minor deviations from contact specification; acceptable in most service contracts

Sunday Statute: Prohibits certain transactions on Sundays; see Blue Law

Surety: Liable for the payment of another's debt or the performance of another's obligation; see Guarantor

Synopsis: Summary of case, often provided in publishers' enhancements

Tender: To make available

Tender Performance: Party's indication that he is ready, willing, and able to perform

Third-Party Beneficiary: Not a party to a contract, but benefits from contract

Time Is of the Essence: Any performance delay constitutes breach

Timeline: A schedule of the times at which certain events took place

Title: Ownership

Topic: Generally, statutes are organized by topic; breaking the code into Titles, Acts, Chapters, or Sections

Tortious: Constituting a tort

Torts: Law applicable to injuries to people or property

Trade Usage: Industry standards for permissible deviations from specifications

Trial Court: Court in which most cases start, generally concerned with deciding issues of fact

UCC Financing Statement: Evidence that property is security for debt, typically filed with the Secretary of State

UCC Search: Activity conducted to find security interests in personal property that have been recorded under UCC Article 9

Unconscionable: A contract that is so unreasonable that it is "shocking"

Undisclosed Principal: Existence of agency relationship not known to third party

Undue Influence: A dominant party takes advantage of that position in entering a contract with party under domination

Unenforceable: A contract, otherwise valid, that cannot be enforced in court

Uniform Commercial Code (UCC): A uniform law, enacted as statutory law in all 50 states, in an attempt to harmonize the law of sales and other commercial transactions Code

Unilateral: Contract formed when one party acts in response to other party's promise

Unilateral Mistake: Where only one party is mistaken about a basic assumption

Unique Property: An item that is not readily available from other sources

Unliquidated Debt: Debt, the amount of which is in dispute; settlement of an unliquidated debt can constitute consideration

Usurious Contract: Charges an illegal rate of interest on a loan

Void: An agreement with no legal effect

Voidable: One party has power to invalidate contract

Volitional Test: Mental incompetence shown by inability to act reasonably with respect to a transaction

Waived: Claims have been abandoned

Waiver: Intentional relinquishment of right, claim, or privilege

Wildcard: Symbol used to pick up word variations in a CALR search

INDEX